DR. RAMMANOHAR LOHIA

His Life & Philosophy

DR. RAMMANOHAR LOHIA

His Life & Philosophy

Indumati Kelkar

ANAMIKA PUBLISHERS & DISTRIBUTORS (P) LTD.
4697/3, 21A, Ansari Road, Daryaganj,
New Delhi 110002
Phone: 23281655, 23270239

First Published 1996, 1997

by

Shripod Kelkar

editor: Lohia Sahita Akshar Bhandar,

Sadashiv Peth, Pune

Reprint 2009

ISBN 978-81-7975-286-9

PRINTED IN INDIA

Published for Samajwadi Sahitya Sansthan, Delhi 110091 by
Anamika Publishers & Distributors (P) Ltd.
4697/3, 21A, Ansari Road, Daryaganj, New Delhi 110002.
Typset by Aadil Printographics, Delhi 110092 and
Printed at Nagri Printers, Delhi.

CONTENTS

PROLOGUE

"The people will pay due attention to my views and thoughts only after my death". said Dr. Rammanohar Lohia in his public speech at Arjun Sagar on the 25th September 1962. His prophecy was based on a strong self-confidence. It revealed State reality. During practically his last phase of life Lohia had realised it. The common people had arrived at the conclusion that after Gandhiji, Lohia was the only eminent person who would unreservedly give justice to the feelings of anguish of the poor, deprived and depressed.

A biography of Lohia is synonymous with the history of the struggle of Indian socialism. History is progenitor and exponent of future events. If the perception of the past, of certain individuals and groups is similar, their analyses of the extant order and apprehension of the reasons of pleasure and sorrow are also similar. They have similar dreams about the order of future society. It is but natural that their ways and means of pulling down the structure of the stagnant worn out social order have mutual resemblance. The persons and groups cherishing similar ideas and dreams, especially the backward classes and women, will amply benefit by a critical in-depth study of Dr. Lohia's thoughts and deeds. Lohia's concepts, dynamic action, imprisonments suffered by him, all aimed at social justice. The clarity of his conceptions, vision of the future and well balanced views impart momentum and inspiration to the struggle against injustice.

Lohia was very eager to pursuade Jayprakash to plunge again in the thick of revolutionary politics. When Jayprakash joined the struggle for restoration of fundamental rights in 1974, Lohia's young associates gladly accepted his mentorship. So it is only befitting that Jayprakash Narayan has written the preface for this biography. There are vast multitudes of people who are ideologically influenced by Lohia & Jayprakash. They are expected to come forward increasingly to carry on the mission of Jayprakash and Lohia for establishing a new social order based on equality.

Poona

Indumati Kelkar

BLESSINGS

It gives me great pleasure to write a foreword for Smt. Indumati Kelkar's book on Dr. Rammanohar Lohia. It is a revised and enlarged edition of the original biography written by her and published earlier in Marathi and Hindi. Apart from being a reputed author, Smt. Kelkar has been an activist in the socialist movement. She was closely associated with Dr. Lohia, and she has tried to faithfully depict his life and work in this book.

Rammanohar was very much misunderstood by his contemporaries. Perhaps his ideas were too original to be understood fully while his straightforwardness was unpleasant to many. He tried to shape Indian politics according to his light. But, unfortunately he died just when he seemed to be succeeding. Lohia was very close to me ideologically, although we had drifted apart politically. This is why all those who were inspired by his ideas were later easily drawn to my movement for total revolution.

I hope this book will be widely read, and the readers who did not have the opportunity to meet Lohia, will have in it the glimpses of a highly original mind and a turbulently eventful life.

Jayprakash Narayan

Patna, 8th, August, 1978

FOREWORD

I read with great care and consideration this beautiful life of Rammanohar Lohia by Smt. Indumati Kelkar. The first and foremost reason for this is that I think it an honour to count Dr. Lohia as a personal friend. It was in 1933-34, he had just come home from Germany and visited the late Shri. Jamanalal Bajaj. We were travelling together on a journey, and Dr. Lohia was in constant conversation with our friend Shri Gopalrao Kale. The passing of time has not however lessened my great esteem for him and his friendship. We may not appreciate each and every action of a friend. And so far as opinions are concerned, change is their unavoidable characteristic, almost a religion. In my very first meeting with him, I could divine that Lohia was a person with a razor sharp intellect. Whatever may be the question or issue, his thinking and way of dealing with it were different from those of others and always his own. This is what we call originality.

Among prominent people in the political field in our country, I have no doubt that Lohia's name would be in the first rank. His personality is pungent and always attracts attention. His way of thinking and conduct arouse varied and very often contradictory emotions, and his personality in one sense could be described as extremely provocative. At times he even behaved as if he was inviting a person to fight with him. In short, one cannot neglect or disregard him. Whatever the field he enters he never fails to impress people as a highly awakened alive and aware human being, who possesses unique originality. His intense nature gives a rare sharpness to his language and expression and his irony is pungent and incisive. His speciality is to express the truth he experiences in as blunt a manner as possible. To demonstrate this, he adopts three symbols—

Jail, hoe and vote.

In the heat of expressing his thought, Lohia does not contemptuously distort or mangle the words he uses, as some do, but at times he might use them with such acidity that they might break friendships and make him suffer from the acute agony of losing friends. It is rather strange that a person like Lohia, who is essentially friendly by nature, besides being faithful and honest, should not be able to divine so simple a thing. That is why his plain speaking does not merely stop at outspokenness but takes the form of volubility or even scurrility. Emotional fervour takes the form of sharpness of words. The result is that even with all his honesty, introspection and friendly nature, he has to suffer from the agony of losing some of his friends. He realizes this and once, while speaking before the working committee of his own party, he said frankly: "My language should not come in the way of the proposition I am trying to place before you for consideration"

In one of his depositions in a court of law, Lohia once mentioned three eminent Satyagrahis: Socretes, Thoreau and Gandhiji. In the context we are discussing, one cannot but remember Socretes, who once said to the people of Athens, "You are like a lazy and drooping horse, rolling at ease. I have turned myself into a gadfly and come to awaken you from your torpor". Socrates was the only genuine Satyagrahi. It could not be his intention to hurt people and wound them permanently. His aim was to prompt them to action by his wordy blows and make them awake and aware. The words he used were sometimes so harsh and cruel that people were agonized and this at times turned their attention away from the principles of social good that Socrates was advocating. Again, what is dear and desirable to a person is not necessarily an untruth. Lohia has once been reported to have said to Einstein that during this century, there have been only three great men: Gandhi, Bernard Shaw and Einstein himself. About this, Shaw wrote an epilogue preface to Saint Joan (1924) in which he analysed the attitude of such heroic souls who, for the propagation of truth, endured harassment or even death. According to Shaw, if these brave martyrs of Truth were artists they would not have provoked such severe indignation in the minds of people. Lohia has plenty of artistry in his nature and his is also a 'risky', a connoisseur. Those who have seen him how while watching a painting or an artistic piece of sculpture, he can completely identify himself with the beautiful object. If he applies his mind to it, his speech too could be capable of taking on an artistic garb. If love of truth expresses itself in such artistry, it gives birth to a sense of fulfillment which pervades the entire universe.

Lohia has time and again declared very distinctly that he does not want a competitive type of revolution, which is rooted in hatred and filled with jealousy. What he wants is an indignant type born out of compassion, which would be capable of counteraction. From the traditional objects of worship in the Hindu pantheon, Lohia has chosen three deities: Rama, Krishna and Shiva. Of these there is an astonishing grandeur in Shiva's form, despite the fact that destruction is his mission. However, when he wills it, Shiva's indignation is transformed into a boon, which blesses the entire universe and bestows on it goodness and prosperity. Lohia must have been moved by this auspicious aspect of *Krodha* or Indignation which transforms itself into one impelling principle of revolution. Lohia's compassion for the downtrodden, the meek and the poor is unbounded. That is why he suggests with earnest insistence that sixty percent of the seats of power should be reserved for aboriginals, untouchables, and women, irrespective of merit. The term *'Krodha'* he has used is the spontaneous and acute sensation that arises in the mind of a compassionate person at the sight of the sufferings of the deprived and the downtrodden. If this *Krodha* is born out of compassion it will be moderately expressed befitting the nature of Rama. Again it is natural for a compassionate person to be agitated at the sight of injustice. To remain calm when there is molestation around you is not being peaceful. To maintain the balance between anger *(Krodha)* and compassion *(Karuna)* is like balancing on the edge of a sword. After undergoing two months of illegal jail sentence, Lohia admitted that he was scorched with anger and his mental balance between anger and compassion was disturbed.

In spite of this, Lohia does not want the Communist revolution. His complaint is that socialism can also assume the garb of hatred and not of anger and compassion. For the Socialists, Henry Ford and Joseph Stalin are both equally irrelevant and therefore Lohia has declared his resolve to end both communism and also the accumulation of wealth. Lohia declared earnestly that in non-violent revolution, non-violence is as important as revolution. If the question is posed whether it should be the vote or the *ballot,* Lohia poses the counter-question: *Satyagraha* or the bullet? What he means thereby is: When we oppose, there should be a proper balance between anger and compassion, otherwise there would be chaos.

Lohia's personality is enriched by five principles: human sympathy, unconquerable ability to oppose, faith in people, irrespective of national boundaries and ceaseless ability to resist. To add to these, he also has rescuable genius or *Pratibha,* coupled with debating skill. All these qualities combine to give him an appearance of a statue forged out of seven metals. So far as genius and originality are concerned, Lohia could be ranked with M.N. Roy, Vinoba Bhave and Jayprakash Narayan. No comparison is implied here nor am I writing as a reviewer or a critic. My role is that of an ordinary connoisseur. Names of great men cited above are given merely as an illustration. As a critique of post Marxist revolutionary technique and sociology, M.N. Roy's contribution is admirable. His new Humanism and novel revolutionary technique have cast a spell on many an intellectual. Vinoba Bhave has carried out unusual experiments in the technique of non-violent revolution. Jayprakash's critique of the Socialist revolution contains a logically developed form of Sarvodaya. According to Lohia, our age has produced only two thinkers: Gandhi and Atomic Power. Lohia declares his faith in Gandhiji's greatness, but immediately he says that he is no Gandhian nor is he an opponent of Gandhism, Marx himself was no Marxist and Gandhi too, if it comes to that, was no Gandhian. Lohia is Lohia and therefore he is important. When he placed before his fellow socialists the Panchmarhi thesis, it was Jayprakash who described this discernment or vision as a great *Vichar-Yajna* (Thought sacrifice) and again on another occasion called it a classic creation of original thoughts. Lohia's personality cannot be contained in any organisation, institution or cult. To be a world citizen and establish a world government arc not merely his dreams—they are a part of his practical desire. That World Socialists should accept a world mind and world view, is a demand he has made. For the revolutionary technique which he desires, he has evolved a novel system of historic investigation. For the entire human organisation he has planned a demonstrable conclusion or a theorem. He has put together from time to time mutual codes of conduct between the whites and the nonwhites in one single thoughtful formula. He has an astonishing command over English. His books and his articles in *Mankind,* I found extremely edifying and agreeable. I am no expert in languages but as compared to his English, his Hindi writing did not appear to me so rich or tasteful.

When an American gentleman asked Lohia about the influences on his life, his reply was: "There two persons who have influenced me. All that I would say about Nehru's nature is that he was very kind hearted and compassionate man. The other person who influenced me was Gandhi. To me, Lohia himself once said that in this country there are only a person and a half. The whole man was Gandhi and the half or fifty per cent was Nehru.

If we speak of freedom from all techniques, Lohia is the only person who fits in with this description. The phrase "Free from all techniques" has two meanings and both these are applicable to Lohia. A person who is an expert in all the techniques is one of the meaning of the phrase. Another connotation of this word is "One who is an expert in the field which 'immediately concerns him". This has a limited connotation. Both these apply to Lohia.

If it came to relying on any authority, Lohia would rely on his own That is why he said once. "The Praja Socialist Party need not make a distinction between welfare of a party and the welfare of the nation. However seriously he might have given this advice, he would not have hesitated to snap all ties with the party and start acting as if he loved himself alone. Many a time, he has given a ripping exposition of the faults of his fellow partymen. In the Travancore- Cochin State, when Pattam Thanu Pillai ordered firing, Lohia showed a kind of moral courage which has never been emulated even by the greatest of Gandhians. Not only did he condemn the shooting order given by his partymen in the severest of words but asked for their resignations. Acharya Kripalani, at this sublime moment, praised him, saying that in translating Gandhian theories into practice, Lohia took the Gandhian doctrine steps ahead, which even the greatest of the great Gandhians had never done. Why Rajaji and Lohia undertook the programme of founding the party is a puzzle to the common man, who is unawakened and has a limited intellectual capacity. Lohia, however, appears intent on, founding a World Parliament. Thus to be a World Citizen seems to be his ideal. He would also go so far as to launch a non-violent Satyagraha movement against his own party with a view to giving a concrete shape to the World Parliament.

That is why the idea of building small houses would not be to his liking.

A common friend, who is intimate with both Lohia and me always tells me, "Look, in the whole of our country, there are only two persons, who have normal heads over their shoulders. The first is myself and the second is Lohia. who has uninterrupted splendour of ideas, astonishing originality and eccentricity or self confidence without exception. Boundaries between these pairs are very thin, according to a well-known verse. Lohia too, very often suspected that many of his colleagues did not have a steady head over their shoulders, The friends also had precisely the same suspicion about Lohia! However, we have no right to act as judges in this controversy among the great. Joking apart, though some of the problems Lohia deals with might appear to be inconsistent and strange to the people, they contain much that is thoughtful and well worth consideration. In fact, there is the famous saying of philosopher that one who attains greatness is very often misunderstood. This is also applicable to Lohia to a certain extent. Morly, in writing about Voltaire, has once said that with a mild and sweet argument you can change the hearts of just a few persons. To move a whole crowd of men, you have to resort to extremes. That is why, when trying to arouse people, Lohia uses a type of language which might be objected to by a mature citizen. This gives more and more room for misunderstanding.

From 1933 to 1941, I used to meet Lohia often and since he visited Jamanalal and Gandhiji frequently almost on each of these occasions, we had the honour of playing host to him. During these visits, I could experience his selfless love and his openness without any strings attached. For a long time I had been eager to know his life and character. This wish has been more than fulfilled by this Biography written by Indumati Kelkar. In this volume, she gives a very detailed account of Lohia's life and achievements. In writing this life, she has become completely one with him and has written this life with a close devotion of purpose, born out of faith in him.

This book, therefore, has attained the sweetness of hymn. Hymns show the inferiority of other deities to the hero of the hymn with the result that the peculiarity of the hymn. viz. to sing the praises of the hero becomes a defeat. Those who differed from the hero and opposed him tend to become villainish. The purpose of this is not to censure the hero but to give prominence of the portrayal of his character.

Whenever Lohia acted like a hero, he is described in a very touching manner by the author. Indutai's style has a great naturalness and a vigorous flow. I have no knowledge of idioms and my knowledge of languages is also very moderate but I feel that certain words and phrases in this book are used a little loosely. The book however is so readable that its sweetness is not at all marred by these occasional lapses. That is why I could read it with such eagerness. I am very much thankful to Smt. Indutai for introducing me to a friend's life and his manly progress by completely identifying herself with him.

Dada Dharmadhikari

प्रिय इन्दू,

करीम नगर
2/12/69

तुमको बताते बताते मैं थक गया। तुमसे जरूरी काम है। अगर तुमसे हो सके, बम्बई आना और मैं वहां रहूं। यशोदा से कहना चुनाव जरूर लड़े। हारने से क्या होता है अभी उसकी उमर है एक दो बार हारे। फिर तो जीतेगी ही। लोकतंत्री राजनीति में चुनाव लड़े बिना उपाय नहीं।

श्री पाद की तबियत ठीक रखना।

तुम्हारा
राममनोहर

A letter writter to Smt. Indumati Kelkar

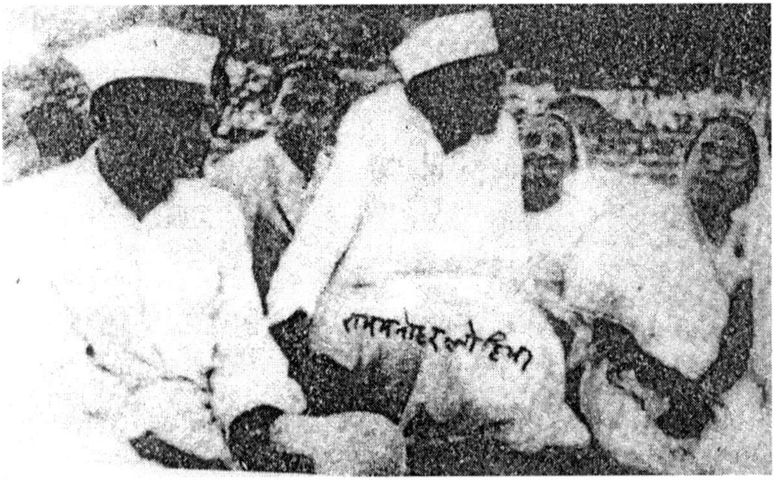

Dr. Lohia with Jaiprakash Narayan and Prabhavati

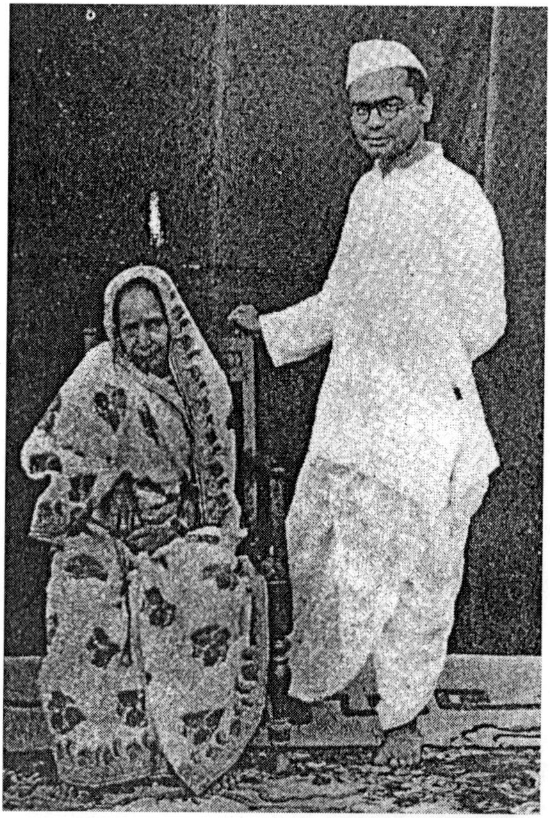

With his beloved 'Chachi'

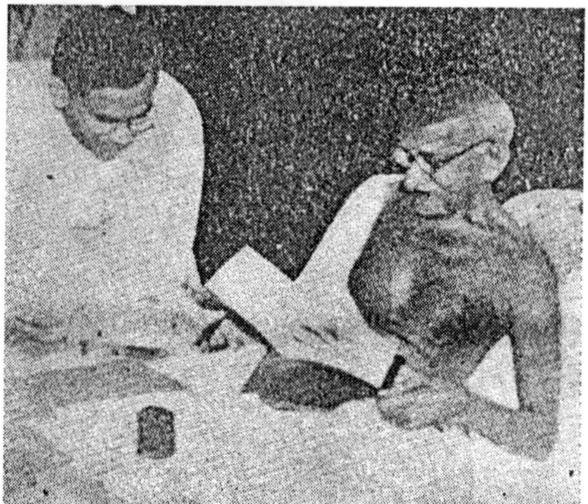

And with revered 'Bapu'

Dr. Lohia with Rama Mitra

Participating in Goa Freedom Movement

A thinker . . .

. . . And an Advocate of equality

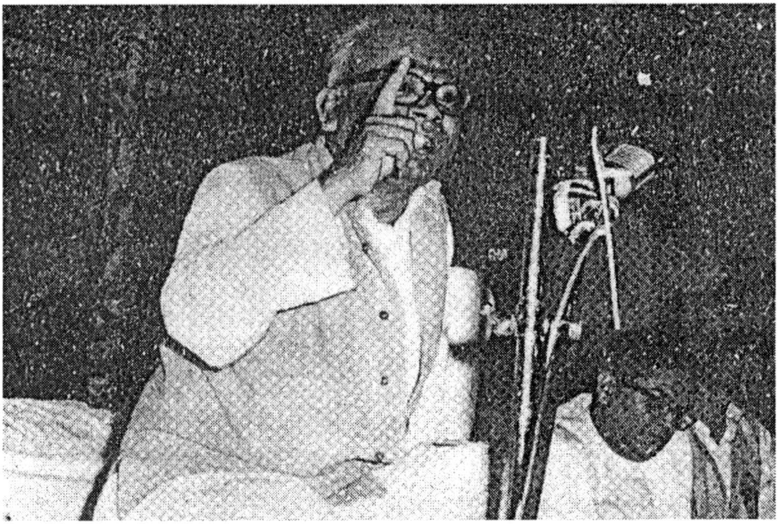

1. WORLD CITIZEN

Rammanohar Lohia's personality is very fascinating and inspiring as a theme for a biography. It simultaneously reveals his self in multiple forms as an unparalleled, inspired, persistent crusader, as an inborn sharp-witted and intelligent philosopher, as a political leader, as a large-hearted citizen and as an instinctive rebel.

Lohia has never written even a line of poetry. Yet he was a man endowed with the sensitive mind of poet. The grand imagination and soaring flight of his poetic mind are revealed in a number of his thoughts and actions. He remained a persistent crusader and never got entangled in routine rituals. Instead, his ever-blooming imagination looked out for fresh intellectual inspiration. He linked action with thought and tried to bring ultimate truth and ideals into the realm of day-to-day life. Thereby he captured the minds of people and became their powerful leader. Although he was a leader of just one country, he had a firm faith in the unity of the whole of mankind, and was proud of being called a 'child of mother earth'. He spent his entire life in ever new experiments and non-stop investigations in the field of thought.

It is well-nigh impossible to understand his greatness by a mere perusal of his books and articles. In fact, for such an understanding, it is necessary to have a thorough study of his life, achievements, twenty-two incarcerations, the fundamental questions raised by him and the revolutionary movements launched by him. Every incident in his life, from the beginning to the end, every, thought every action, roused the intellect of people and stirred them to action.

The world is not short of great men, nor is India, yet Lohia's intellectual contribution must be considered as a unique gift to the world. He instilled confidence in the neglected, backward, black people in the world and created grandeur in their lives. He told them that the wheels of history were continuously moving and the day of emancipation of the exploited was not far off. Every instant of his life was devoted to secure for the common, unprivileged man, the life of a human being. It was his dream to mould a new man who would establish a new world, in which the two worlds of haves and have-nots would coalesce into one. A world parliament would be established on the basis of adult franchise. He carried out several experiments in his life to achieve this objective. Each thought and each action of his were directed towards building up this new world order.

Lohia desired that the ancient ideal of *'the truth, the good and the beautiful'* and the modern one of *'socialism, independence and non-violence'* should exchange their places. In fact, he had a clear vision about total revolution and was struggling hard for launching an all-out offensive against the old society to bring about that revolution. He attacked on all fronts; viz. economic, social, political and cultural. He went on striking against all the then-prevailing false dualities which obstructed the march towards total revolution. He propounded, that, the false dualities like the spiritual and the material, the good and the beautiful, the good and the agreeable, the individual and the environment, the body and the soul, political and social etc., made the human intellect waver and human life complex. On one hand it is improper to accept the principle of duality. On the other, it is equally wrong to accept pantheism. In the scientific age of today, the problem of hunger or intellect can be solved neither by dualism nor by pantheism. Furthermore he felt that, "the possibility of continuing equilibrium in view of the dynamic and demonism of the material also to be denied". According to Lohia the way to create a new world order was to attain an approximation and amalgamation between the two.

Throughout his life, Lohia struggled to attain such a balance and approximation. He was a staunch nationalist, however, he was not tied down by geographical and national boundaries, while thinking about Universalism. He had a proper perspective of both the motherland and the mother earth. He held that one should be free to travel the entire world without a passport, and must have the freedom to live and die anywhere. Accordingly, he once travelled to Burma without a passport. It was believed that socialism grew out of the capitalism of the west. It was also believed that nationalism and true socialism were antagonistic. Lohia was a socialist. Yet he could not see any contradiction between nationalism, socialism and large-minded internationalism. He identified himself with the land, culture and soul of India, yet he thought about suppresse people in the entire world. In his article entitled 'Rama, Krishna, Shiva' he prays to Mother India to bless him with the outlook of universalism thus: "*O mother, kindly bless us with the unbouded intellect of Shiva; the exuberant heart of Krishna and the extraordinary ability of Ram...* "Lohia's biography is a story of his thoughts and deeds with which he tried to realise his ideals.

Lohia had quite a fresh and new look at the thoughts of both Marx & Gandhiji. He considered the traditions of both as incomplete. If the tradition of a sage like Marx swerves away from its path, it ends in cruelty and if the tradition of a saint like Gandhiji becomes corrupted, it results in narrow-mindedness and heresy. Hence he tried to approximate between the tradition of a sage and of a saint. While exploring, he made the following significant observation: "Neither capitalism nor communism can end the poverty or belligerence in this world. Both give rise to unlimited production, revolutionary technology and an insatiable desire for a pleasurable and spiralling standard of living. Communism is the latest weapon of Europe against Asia. For 300 years, Europe has been the prince among continents, and liberalism, Christianity or capitalism, have admittedly served Europe's imperial purposes. For the white man, this has led to frustration and for the black, it has led to a mania about modernism which he can never attain in his life. The rich society of the white man has not only assumed control over material wealth, but has remained engrossed in its anxiety to maintain it. On the other hand a handful of middle class men has come up among the black people aping the white man. The result is an increase in disparity".

While discussing the duality of Gandhism, Lohia says, "Gandhiji rejected materialism by resorting to asceticism. This gave rise to false dualities. Gandhism assumed the form of ritualism". Gandhiji gave the philosophy of satyagraha, decentralization and the rationale of the means and ends. Lohia coordinated them into the ideology of socialism. Lohia picked up the threads of Gandhism and tried to weave them into a homogeneous fabric of socialism. He tried to give the revolutionary ideas of Gandhiji a scientific form. Thus he can be considered as an heir to the progressive aspect of Gandhism. In the post-independence era, he handed over to the common people the weapon of satyagraha which had been lying unused and rusted. According to Lohia, elections held once in five years and the parliamentary system, are inadequate from the point of view of the welfare of the backward people. The alternative before the poor, black, people is neither choice between constitutionalism and armed insurrection, nor between vote and bullet. To Lohia, politics was not a subject to be discussed only in the parliament but to be faced in the streets.

While commenting on 'ends and means' and the Gandhian principle of 'one step is enough for me', Lohia put forward his thesis of immediacy and tried to execute his idea about decentralization and four pillar administration. He condemned the outlook of those people who resorted to falsehood today for realizing the truth later, accepted dictatorship for establishing democracy at a later time, and sacrificed national independence for achieving world unity in future. He combined satyagraha and immediacy to forge socialism. He supplemented his revolutionary ideas about political and social reconstruction with universalism and humanism. He tried to approximate between the sage and the saint.

Lohia's life was profoundly influenced by Gandhiji. These two great men had certain things in common. Lohia considered the range of Gandhiji's thoughts as boundless; with no length, breadth nor depth. He believed that Gandhiji's mind was as delicate as a lily in the heart, but firm as a citadel in action and always true and nothing but true, in his word. In 1939 itself, Lohia described Gandhiji as a 'little finger guiding history'. He did not agree with some of Gandhiji's views viz.; his ideas of trusteeship as an alternative to class struggle and class antagonism, his view on religion, his acceptance of the traditional division of Hindu society based on four castes, his faith in God, his views on the relationship between man and woman, and his fetish of purity of the body. Even after admitting the greatness of Gandhiji, Lohia did not absolve him of the sin of partition. Gandhiji did not die fighting the partition. Between partition and his death there is a period of less than six months, but these six months were crucial to the history of the country.

However certain things are common to Gandhiji and Lohia

viz.: a profound compassion for mankind, basic all-round consideration for human life, and the indignation necessary for fighting injustice. Both considered the oppressed man as the centre of all thoughts and actions, and their thoughts revolved round that centre.

Lohia was shocked to see Gandhian ideology being abandoned by his disciples after his death. He felt disturbed. Gandhiji's disciples, who were then in the government, daily resorted to firing, setting aside Gandhiji's principle of non-violence. They started concentration of power and wealth in secretariats, factories and big cities. They began wallowing in corruption, graft, pomp, extravagance and nepotism. On the other hand, Gandhiji's hermetical disciples took up only one aspect of Gandhiji viz.; compassion and cooperated with the Gandhians in the government. Lohia considered himself, and others like him, as an outcaste Gandhian. He believed that a new force could arise in the country only if these Gandhians did something with the cooperation of the people.

When Lohia came down heavily on the licentiousness of the post-independence period, all the people involved in such activities stood up against his revolutionary policy. They joined hands against his attempts to bring about the expected post-independence revolution. Lohia fought against them resolutely. He tried with all his might to unite all revolutionary and militant forces, but had to pursue a lone path. His opposition to the prevalent ways, preference for basic values instead of shallow superficialities, and his indignation towards treachery and inaction, created a number of obstacles in his way of building up a powerful front of revolutionary forces.

All through his life he had to fulfill the difficult task of swimming against the current. It is true that give and take is inevitable while organizing the people, but Lohia generally refused to do so. Things have deteriorated further since the Gandhian days. One must accept that the call for freedom invoked a stronger response than the call of equality. Consequently, the degeneration that set in on the eve of the end of the Gandhian era, could not be resisted successfully. In the hands of the self-styled heirs of Gandhiji, man became a monster. So making any real breakthrough was out of the question.

Lohia felt most intensely for the dignity and pride of mankind.

He resolved not to sit in a man-driven rickshaw, He held that the most lowly deserves the highest remuneration. He could never accept the fact that manual labour was held in low esteem in comparison to intellectual work. He considered the exorbitantly costly game of cricket as a game of feudals and slaves. With a keen insight of discernation of what was Indian and what was foreign, he considered Selenkas, Gazni, Hoons, Babar etc. as aliens, and Kanishka, Sher Shah, Rana Sanga, Bahadurshah, and Razia Sultan as Indians.

His editorial talent came to light when, at the age of twenty-five, he edited the *'Orient"* and the *'Congress Socialist"*. The editing of the Bengali weekly *'Krishak'* by a Hindi youth like him, was undoubtedly an adventure. Journals like *'Jana'* and *'Mankind'* bear testimony to his great editorial skill.

Twenty years of Congress rule has degenerated the entire politics in the country. Bad tendencies like compromising with evil, indulging in unprincipled politics opportunism, and harboring a lust for power (and its trappings) shot up in the post-Gandhi period. Lohia tried to destroy them by launching several ideological attacks.

Gandhiji demanded from his followers a devotion to ideology, but only upto a point. Gandhiji got some work done from each man with whom he came into contact, according to his ability. But Lohia expected from his followers complete devotion to his ideology. He tried to reform them. He insisted on maintenance of unity between word and deed. In the event of non-fulfillment by a worker, of a socialist action expected by him, Lohia resorted to non-co-operation and, at times, even boycott. Throughout his life he struggled hard to see that his party remained pure and acted according to its principles. Consequently, some selfish and shallow politicians and even some of his close friends deserted him.

Lohia's ideology has the sharpness of a sword's edge. His soul was that of a rebel. He had a powerful will and strong determination to resist injustice resolutely. He despised jail. But he believed that "as long as tyrants roam the earth, prisons will be filled with those who hate them". Due to having a natural attraction for everlasting (stable) values, he never took interest in the occasional temporary and superficial problems which did not have even a remote relation with such values. His gaze was ever focussed in looking out for something beyond the horizon. Being able to see far ahead into the distant future, many years away, he could discern any problem in its true as well as distorted form. Similarly he would be alert about the duality of a problem by correctly sensing its natural form and its subsequent distortion. By comprehending impending developments he used to give a warning from time to time about the natural and distorted forms of the basic question.

He uninterruptedly tried to strengthen the tottering feet, bewildered intellect, shallow mind, and the inactive hand of the socialist movement. He called for a balanced personality and said "Friends, enjoy boundless freedom of thought, but limit action within bounds as an ideal for the political man".

Lohia's bravery and patience are manifest not only in his political work at Geneva, Lahore, Nepal, Goa, Mississipi, etc., but also in the courageous way in which he broke the bonds of emotions like greed, temptation, despair etc. He felt more hurt by the treachery and disloyalty of his friends than by the physical torture inflicted by the British. Although he was always ready to fight his enemies, he felt very despondent when it came to crossing swords with friends. Inspite of his being successful in keeping himself clear from jealousies, quarrels, competition and the craving of high posts, he was often treated by his friends as an enemy. Jayprakash once said, "Your aloofness itself is responsible for this. We quarrel amongst ourselves, but later on make up. You generally don't quarrel, but if at all you do, the quarrel that you resort to is the last one".

His colleagues often betrayed him. There was sometimes a dirty exhibition of jealousy too. Lohia had several bitter experiences in the political life when even his friends treated him with spite. On such occasions, his mind would be very upset. In order that he should not have to face such occasions, he scrupulously avoided holding any executive post in the party. To this he made only two exceptions. Due to various reasons like pressure of friends, fear of party split and desire of carrying out party policy conscientiously, he reluctantly became General Secretary of P.S.P. in 1953 and thereafter, the Chairman of the Socialist party in 1956.

Having been required to face various such occasions, the initial emotionalism in Lohia must have atrophied. When crises arose at the Betul session of P.S.P. in 1913, Lohia said: "I believe in the law of divorce where men and women are concerned, but in politics

I am somewhat conservative. I have from time to time been a member of Kripalaniji's family. Over the last fifteen years, Jayprakash and I both faced bullets together. Beyond saying, that I have had no brother of my own, Ashok (Mehta) and I have in the past talked till early hours of the morning. We all belong to a family that cannot wreck".

However these friendly feelings of Lohia evoked no response. The ties of the friendship broken at Betul were never to be revived again. Lohia is dubbed as the breaker of the socialist movement. But it was he who always tried to maintain unity in the socialist movement. Prominent leaders like Achyutrao Patwardhan, Aruna Asaf Ali, Jayprakash Narayan, Ashok Mehta, J.B. Kripalani etc., left the Socialist party, but Lohia never deserted the socialist movement, nor did he betray it.

However, Lohia was always a target of abuse both in the party and outside. He had become the victim of intense ridicule, condemnation and malicious propaganda. He himself once said, "I am sometimes surprised why such baseless charges are continuously made against only one man". To this he himself gave the answer: "The custodian of India's intelligentsia is Nehru. Had I compromised with him, such abuse would have not been hurled at me. It is due to my powerful attack on the ruling class and the age old, firmly entrenched social traditions, that I have become the target of the anger of powerful static forces in the country".

Almost all the Indian and some prominent foreign newspapers, as well as all the publicity media of the ruling class, had come together for several years just to condemn Lohia. Their boycott of Lohia was severe. However, Lohia's life was so full of struggle and action, that even his critics had to take note of his sacrifice, thoughts and acts.

The policy of the ruling class was to ignore his basic thoughts. Very often, Lohia's statements and utterances were published by the newspapers in twisted forms. It was impossible for Lohia to refute every piece of false news through the press and offer a clarification. Lohia himself considered it as contrary to his notion of self-respect. Further, if at all he issued a clarification of a false news, the newspapers published it not in its true but distorted form. As mischievous propaganda and derogatory news appeared in the press, even his friends would ask clarifications from him. This annoyed him. Once he said: "I become downcast when even my friends ask such explanations. I feel extremely sorry that my friends add insult to injury. I feel that during the last few years my aptitude to create enemies has increased and the ability to maintain friendship has declined. I don't know whether this is only the result of a defect in my nature or the outcome of revolutionary politics of which I have become an unfortunate symbol".

Lohia has often been condemned by his colleagues as a dictator, but the tragedy is that Lohia himself had often become a victim of dictatorial tendencies. No other leader in the socialist movement had ever tried as hard as Lohia to preserve intra-party democracy. He believed that democracy can be preserved in the country only by protecting intra-party democracy. He also felt that a democratic party would muster enough strength to fight out clear and obvious injustice, only if it remains alert about vague and unrevealed injustice. Lohia struggled hard to clean the vision in a hopelessly Orwellian scenario in which injustice is considered as justice, thoughtlessness as thoughtfulness, a bad deed as a good deed, and falsehood as truth.

It is true that Lohia showed ascetic attitude towards the static symbols of power like the chair or the post. But he never showed a dislike for power as such. To him, power was an instrument of revolution. He said: "I have been fired with the desire to do something good in life and a will to power. This will is the centre of every political act, as it should be. Sometimes I am also tempted by power". At the time when Jayprakash Narayan —a leader of a party himself, stood up against the party system, Lohia tried to rouse in the party a "will to power", the greatest test for any political party. He said: "The will to power must indeed be a chaste and vigorous will, as far away from perversity as it should be from weakness. A healthy will does not make use of lies, deceit and violence. Only a frustrated will indulges in perverse conduct and is consumed by its own despair. The will to power of the new party will be faced with the danger a like of perversity as of weakness. To strive cleanly to capture power on the morrow, is the high trust but an equally sacred obligation is not to give up to weakness or to give in to perversity, should power not come for a decade or more".

1942 marks his rise to all-India leadership. In fact, this leadership steadily sought him out as it were. Even as an all India leader, he led a very simple life in respect of food and clothing.

Once, when it was suggested to him that he should have a room cooler, he said, "For heaven's sake, not in my own room. These luxuries are not for me". Since he had faith in non-violence he remained a pure vegetarian by conviction. His dress consisted of dhoti and Khadi kurta. He was very fond of visiting the coffee-house. But on realizing that his followers were imitating him and indulging in gossip in the coffee-house he himself put a curb on this hobby of his. He had a habit of working late, till about 3 or 4 o'clock at night and consequently also getting up very late in the morning. However, he gave up this habit by regulating his daily routine for the convenience of others during the last 10-12 years of his life. A chain-smoker in his youth, Lohia managed to quit smoking later. Due to frequent jail terms and constant travel, high blood pressure and heart trouble made a home in his body. His eyes were weak to begin with, and eventually he developed a trachoma. In fact, various diseases attacked him, but Lohia continued travelling all over the country in defiance of those diseases. At the time of fourth general election, he again roused the whole country. He knew each and every corner of the country well. Millions of people had listened to the philosophy of Dr. Lohia as propounded by him. That ideology had touched their hearts and that's why the ruling class and the handfull of white-collar middle and upper-middle class people could not tarnish his image in common people, inspite of their efforts to do so.

Lohia was a real lover of art. He not only loved arts like cinema, drama, music, dancing and painting, but had a good understanding of them. He has expressed his views on various topics like ancient Indian literature, architecture, universe and sculpture. Those, who visited any cultural centre in India with him, were lucky indeed. Whenever he came across a historical or cultural monument, his mind would get engrossed in its past history. He became sad on seeing the battlefield of Plassey. His mind flew back to the past to visualize the patriotism of Siraj-ud-daula—Mirmadam, betrayal by Mir Jafar—Jagatsingh, and the callousness of the people. He felt sad that this was the place where our country first became a slave. He held his hand on the soil from the land of the Gouds, and touched the trees. People wondered as he gazed at the monuments at Konarak, Khajuraho, Mahabalipuram, Kailas, Ellora, etc. for days on end. But endowed with a third eye, he experienced a strange kind of grief. It was this grief which inspired him to write, spurred him to action, and urged him to speak out. He was a worshiper of nature's beauty. As he revealed the mysteries of the sculptures while sipping tea or coffee, he held his listeners spell-bound. His poetic heart and fiery mind are revealed in his various articles 'Krishna', 'Ram-Krishna-Shiva', 'Dilli', 'Vashishtha-Valmiki', 'Sculpture' etc. His sense of beauty could see the grandeur of moonlight from his confinement in Lahore jail. He used to say: "The great promoter of beauty is the moon-light, the fuller the better. It was not for nothing that prospective brides in ancient India and probably elsewhere showed themselves for the first time under the soft light of full moon. The moon bathes everything in beauty, but it is unable to impart the cleanliness of the dawn. I cannot to this day recall without a heart throb the clean majesty of the line under a dawn that threads softly and very slowly". His poetic heart was revealed still further when he wrote of Rama and Krishna. He considered Rama of 'Treta' as a God of north-south unity and Krishna of 'Dwapar' age as the God of east-west unity. He says, "Rama symbolizes a man eternally trying to become a God, and Krishna, a God eternally trying to become a man. Sharayu and Ganga are rivers of duty, while Yamuna and Chambal are rivers of sentiments".

Lohia's oratory, as described by one woman, poured out sentences which pierced like arrows. Indeed his speech was sharp. His oratory was neither theatrical nor bombastic. His logical speeches at once appealed to one and touched one's heart. Besides being enlightening, they had sweetness and musical rhythm. His style was powerful and pithy and conveyed maximum meaning with minimum words. He avoided use of high flying jargon like learned scholars. He coined new simple words easy enough to be understood by common man. He himself characterized his literary style as an embodiment of hereditary miserliness. Besides it was indeed unusually sharp. While speaking in Maharashtra at the time of '*Samyukta* (united) *Maharashtra* movement, he said "Bombay belongs to Maharashtra but not to Maharashtrians". His oratory in English was sweet. However, due to his anti-English policy he had stopped using English in his public life in his later years. He had an art of coining new words and phrases.

The intellect and inspiration of Lohia commanded respect not only in India but even abroad. Once, when a Japanese socialist leader complained to Dr. Schumacher, the German Socialist party leader that socialist ideology had become static, Dr. Schumacher asked him to read Lohia's book 'Fragments of the world mind'. Lohia accepted many challenges for 35-40 years of his political life. He struggled to bring about a total revolution with the trident of jail, shovel, and ballot-box. He chalked out various programms prompted by his deep compassion for the common down-trodden people and his indignation over the injustice done to them. His programmes include 'March ahead', 'End poverty', 'Land army, food army', 'Free water to 26 crore acres of cultivable land' etc. He led various movements: 'Abolition of land-tax on non-profitable farms', 'Wage Fixation', 'Caste Abolition', 'Drive out English', 'Save the Himalayas', Form an Indo-Pak federation', 'Save the country from Congress rule', etc. He formulated substantive theories like 'Third power', 'Clean rivers', 'Four-pillar state', 'Balance between constructive and agitational activities', etc.

Lohia once remarked: "In London I was once chided by a waitress for not taking sufficient care of my coat and warned of what my wife would say and do to me. To my lament that nobody ever wanted to be my wife, the waitress quickly answered, 'Ye, never asked any!', which I found pretty and good. I once said that God and woman are probably the only two purposes of life. I never met God and woman is elusive". In fact the number of women who got attracted towards Lohia is none too small. Like the sorrows of the exploited, he understood the woes of women too. He had a special consideration for the women. He started a movement for 'Man-Woman equality'. This was not only one of the seven revolutions propounded by him, but the one which assumed the place right at the top among them, since he believed that sex equality was a pre-requisite for ushering in the remaining revolutions. He had high respect for women. He did not like Indians aping the westerners in respect of showing ostentatious regard for women. According to him, such Indians were doing injustice to our women folk, since their regard for women remained restricted to educated, high class women only.

While Gandhiji threw the entire social field open to women, Lohia secured for them a distinct status of importance. To him, woman was not a lifeless doll or an object of enjoyment. Somehow, he didn't marry in his young age and later on lost faith in the institution of marriage. This was revealed when he participated in the debate on Svetlana in the parliament. He considered a wife and children as hurdles in the path of political and social workers. It does not mean, however, that no women ever came into his life. Hence some people's view, that due to being unmarried his life remained unfulfilled and that told upon his nature, is entirely baseless. In any case, it is true that Lohia did not marry. He considered all women beautiful. He felt that soul of a woman was an afflicted soul, just like that of other exploited people. He was then the only leader who gave expression to the woes of women and suggested means for their emancipation.

He was all alone with no wife, no children, no money, nothing whatsoever. But he had established relationship with the wide humanity. Once, while cautioning a woman about her health, he said; "You have got a family and children. So you must take care of your health. Mine is a different case. Who is there to shed tears when I am no more?" Lohia is no more. But the stream of revolution that emerged from his life is flowing. Is it going to grow wider and wider, or wither away at the source itself? The task of ensuring a continuous flow has now fallen on those who agree with Lohia's views. Traditionally, the philosophy of a great man is put to an end to by his disciples and followers.

Why is defection on such a large scale, seen in the history of the socialist movement in India? It is necessary to think about the total failure of the socialist movement. At the Betul convention of the P.S.P. in 1953, Lohia clearly said: "Much ridicule has been poured on me for refusing to accept organizational responsibility. Let me state here very definitely, that I have neither the taste nor the talent for the organisational responsibility. But that does not mean, that although I do not have the talent, I should not express my taste for policy making".

Lohia always avoided being an office-bearer in the party. This weakened the efforts to maintain unison between the theory and the practice of the socialist movement. Practice ran counter to theory and there was always a tug-of-war between the two. Later, in the editorial of the December 1966 issue of *'Jana'* magazine, Lohia wrote: "I admit one mistake. Till I was 45 and thereafter I fully believed in exalted life, but had no faith in an organisation. To me people appeared better than what they really were. I felt that inner urge would make men adventurous, intelligent and thoughtful. However, for about 10 years now, I have been thinking that men are dry broken blades of grass, unless they are bound together by the chain of an organisation. I am now too old to show this in practice, nor is the present time suitable for it.'"

How far are these self-assertations of Lohia realistic? Is it really difficult to organize people without compromising with evil? The atmosphere in the country is far more polluted than in Gandhian days due to licentiousness of the Congress, moreover, a call for equality is not as catching as the call of Independence. Nobody has been able to hold up the degeneration that has set in after the Gandhian period. Not only that, but it is surging up and flowing unabated. Lohia tried to check it with all his might. He insisted that practice must accord with the theory. As a result, holding on to unity in the socialist movement became an ordeal. As stated by Lohia, an unfavorable time persisted. But according to Lohia, the failure of the socialist movement was, in some measure, due to wrong ideas about organisation. There appears to be a misconception about an expert party organiser, that, such a leader is one who;

(i) tries to win praise from all by being not outspoken,
(ii) is a multi-tongue speaker, speaking according to the situation,
(iii) pushes ahead even by compromising with bad elements, and,
(iv) never wishes himself to bound with policy and principles, nor expects others to be bound likewise.

But to build up a revolutionary organisation, the standards required are different. A multitude of people cannot hold a torrent of degeneration. Just a group of people will not bring about a social revolution. In fact, Lohia had some basic ideas about organizations and leaders. He used to say: "The symbol of socialism and democracy is neither a revered leader nor a collective leader, but a restrained leader bound by policy and principles". Lohia himself adhered to these limitations and would not allow others to transgress them.

Lohia possessed a special power to influence and drew into the politics of socialism anyone whom he came across. He used to develop confidence in others by rousing their latent power of intellect and action, and would set them to work. As regards organisation, he had faith in youth. But he wanted them not to follow the current elderly leaders, lest they should imbibe all their faults and make it impossible to create a new social order. In due course, leaders develop in themselves a feeling that they are indispensable. To prevent this, Lohia suggested and pressed for a convention that no office-bearer should hold office for more than two years. In order to ensure that the parliamentary wing does not dominate the organisation, he had long ago put forth his view that these two leaderships should be different. He insisted that the party should accept his ideas in order to maintain it's youthful vigor and make the socialist movement militant and pure.

Lohia stood up against opportunist and unprincipled leadership. He felt that the sequence of ideas embodied in well-known Buddhist quotation *'I bow to Buddha, I bow to the Sangham. I bow to the Dhamam'* was wrong. In stead he put the sequence as follows: Buddha, Dhamam, Sangham i.e., principles, organisation, leadership.

There was a simultaneous presence of dynamism and consistency in Lohia's life. He could understand: "Every moment is no doubt a passing link to the great flux, but it is also an eternity in itself. The current age of man has laid great stress on achievements and little on being. Forgetful of the material and the spiritual which would never have been done... The moment as flux is material, while moment as eternity is spiritual....man must live for the future but he must also live in present".

He appears to have accepted life in its fully organized form. He described truth as it appeared to him: "Truth is either whole or not at all. All truth is discovered from the aspect or the angle which the seeker or the knower adopts. Error may lie in not taking up the proper angle". He chose the path of satyagraha. He used to say that continuous civil disobedience implied continuous defeat and continuous defeat involved continuous efforts. Lohia had extremely high regard for human dignity and values. He described concrete forms of abstract non-violence and raised up a storm on question of firings. Lohia thought of 'Indian' socialism in the context of India. He discarded the traditional way of thinking. He expressed that here the talk of class war is inadequate. In the peculiar situation in India it is the caste system which is coming in the way of establishing socialism. Here socialism is impossible unless there is the struggle for the abolition of casteism. He pointed out that communists cannot establish socialism here without taking into consideration the realities of the Indian society. Once while talking about how the caste system in India makes a man helpless and slave, Lohia raised the following question: "During the ceremony when Draupadi was to select a husband of her choice, why did Karna not challenge the propriety of her linking the highness or lowness of his caste family with her choice of husband, instead of merely saying: *"To be born in a high class family is a matter of destiny, but to show manliness is upto me".*

Like the caste system, Lohia considered English, too, a great obstacle in the path of total revolution. While attacking the tendency of Indians to imitate the earlier rulers, Lohia once stated: "Indians are traditional slaves. Due to their desire of aping the rulers a handful of people have taken support of English dress and English language for holding power in their hands".

Lohia used to feel excited over the indifference, servility and lifelessness of Indian people. Lohia followed various paths in order that the slaves should break the tradition of feeling happy in slavery. The ruling class in India had carefully preserved for thousands of years two instruments of exploiting the common people, viz.; caste system and language. Characterizing the caste system as the creation of God, the upper class thrust mental slavery on the lower classes. The upper class related conduct *(Karma)* with virtue and vice, through earlier births and rebirths and secured unquestioned acceptance of the observance of the caste system by the lower castes. Thus they enslaved women, low castes, and religious minorities. To end this, Lohia suggested reservation of 60% of the government posts for the depressed classes irrespective of merit. He put up the equation:

"Socialism = equality + prosperity"

He believed that, in India, socialism could not be established by resorting to class war alone, but by combining it with caste war as well. That was the keynote of his 'caste policy'. He favoured grant of special facilities to the backward people. He considered the principle of equal opportunities as a big hoax and an unequal race.

Lohia firmly believed that economic inequality and casteism were twin demons. A fight with one entailed a fight with the other also. Lohia made the caste system and language inseparable parts of his total revolution. Lohia didn't believe in caste system, theory of religion and the four-tier Hindu society. Religion is God himself. However, people did not forget his caste. They invariably used it as an instrument against him. Even in parliament, Indira Gandhi's flatterers hurled at him dirty abuses and called him 'son of a Marwari usurer'. Being born in a Marwari merchant family, he had to face certain handicaps, with no gains whatsoever. He said: "Right from Manipur to Kerala, they all take advantage of my Marwari lineage, when my stand is unassailable or my view unrelishable. As regards money, I have none. My community also has not given me a single paisa. Once a Marwari friend of mine, while refusing to give me any money expressed, "Congress had some consideration for us, but you are out to strip us of everything".

A few months before his death, Lohia said: "In a sense I hold a unique place in Indian politics. My popularity has been continuously waning for the last two or three decades. Yet there is none in the country today who excels me in popularity. Even then I do not think too highly of my position or power. I hold no post nor wield any power. With the loss of power, popularity declines and leadership is also not sustained. After all, my strength lies in my morality. I am a man of morals and not of coordinated miscellaneous culture. A man of miscellaneous culture would become a 'king'. In virtue of such ideas, Lohia could not hold on to any post long. Once the well-known cartoon journal *'Shankar's Weekly'* presented a cartoon about the imaginary assumption of power by Lohia with the caption: "Dr. Rammanohar Lohia was sworn as Prime Minister this morning. However he sent his resignation to the President in the evening, due, not to his incapacity to hold power, nor to his shirking of responsibility, but due to the fear that his colleagues might become corrupt and opportunist and that would be too much for him to bear".

He would never tolerate contradiction between words and deeds. That is why all through his life he remained the leader of the opposition only. He believed that power made a man corrupt and a selfless man, a selfish one. His natural desire was that socialists should put under control their lust for power by means of self discipline. It was his cherished desire that socialists should become, not slaves, but masters of power. He could tolerate a split based on principle and programme. However to him intellectual clarity was all the more important, as against unprincipled unity. Regarding power he had developed some sort of apathy, due, perhaps, to the behaviour of Nehru. In 1946 itself, Lohia was disillusioned about Nehru, when Nehru himself admitted that Congressmen were committing all possible crimes. The result was that Nehru started compromising with evil. Out of greed for power, he disregarded Gandhiji. The result was increasing selfishness, lust, greed for power, luxury, corruption etc. Before independence, Lohia regarded Nehru as his leader and had love for him. Nehru too, paid great attention to him during the four months when he was Nehru's guest at Allahabad. Nehru, as a host, personally looked after even small conveniences of Lohia viz.; whether his towel was clean, whether the mosquito curtain was being properly hung, whether the fan was in order, etc. Nehru did this with warmth and affection. However, the main reason for Lohia's attraction towards Nehru was his role as a valiant leader during the independence struggle.

Frustration in ideology is more painful than frustration in love, or sudden loss of wealth due to misfortune. Lohia had great expectations about Nehru. Hence his frustration also was great. He says: "This was a man whom I loved once. But now I don't love him at all. I have no personal grudge against him. However 50 lakh well placed people are blindly imitating him. This has completely ruined the country. Hence it has become imperative to criticize Nehru".

Many people believed that Lohia hated Nehru's lineage, however this belief was not true. Once Lohia suggested the name of Nehru's sister, Vijayalaxmi Pandit, as an opposition candidate for the post of the President of India. In January 1957, when Indira Gandhi in her speech at Allahabad, alleged that P.S.P. was getting foreign money, Lohia admired her courage. She made the same allegation against the communist party also. Later on Nehru snubbed Indira Gandhi, saying that he did not like such utterances. Lohia had no hatred for Nehru's lineage, nor for Nehru as a person. Clarifying his position on this point, Lohia said: "If people think that a certain organisation is dangerous, it is their duty to attack it at its very roots, and expose the man at its top. I have not done anything beyond this".

Personal devotion and personal hatred lead one to wrong thinking. Criticism of a person for some political or social actions is not a criticism of that person. Similarly regard for a person, due to his political action is not personal devotion. Lohia was always a target of varied criticism. Sometime his opponents would say that Lohia was going to settle abroad. Another time they would say that Lohia was going to retire from politics. At last Lohia got fed up and said: "As long as I am alive I shall continue to work for socialism. So also I shall remain in politics so long as my heart is sound. I left Congress on my own accord; and P.S.P. expelled me. Indian politics has become awfully dirty and terribly treacherous. But I have not become dirty enough to run away from the filthy arena of politics". With full confidence he used to say: "People will listen to me, perhaps, only after I am dead, listen they must, some day".

Lohia's burning revolutionism was too powerful for Congress MP's to bear in silence. Flatterers of Indira started the campaign of vilification against Lohia. They called him such bad name as "the son of a pig, the man sustained on Nehru's crumbs" etc. They charged him with a fraud of 10 to 20 lakh Rupees. When he took up the cause of striking policemen in March 1967, the then Defence Minister, Yashwantrao Chavan, got enraged. He had to answer to Lohia's questions. So he laid out a crooked conspiracy. With mean mentality, he narrated the story of a French soldier who had a habit of pointing out the mistakes of others. To take revenge on him, his Commander gave him the order 'Quick march!'. When he reached the other end of the ground, beyond which there was deep valley, he requested the Commander for an order to return. However, the Commander said coolly "Sorry, now the only order is 'good bye'". Citing this example, Yashwantrao said with meanness, "To Lohia's words and deeds, I have got only one answer; Good bye Lohia!"

That was poisonous. Though an atheist, Lohia loved the God Neelkantha or Shiva, a mythological entity. Like Neelkantha Shiva, he swallowed the poison. Jesus Christ, Socrates, Lincoln, Kennedy, and Gandhi were fortunate to become martyrs. However the living martyrdom of those suffering agony during life is more difficult. A band of living martyrs alone can change the destiny of the country. Such poison Lohia had gulped down several times with a smile. It was Gandhiji, who really understood Lohia. In fact, Gandhiji had always been his saviour, whether Lohia was under arrest in Goa or Nepal. Even when Lohia was being harassed in Lahore jail, Gandhiji took up the matter with the Viceroy. Perhaps, during his last days, Gandhiji must have felt that his choice of Nehru as the leader of the nation had been wrong. Anyway, Gandhiji had been disappointed with his so called disciples.

About the Lohia-Jayprakash relationship also, some people showed their mean mentality. The preface written by Shri N.G. Gorey to the biography of Jaiprakash, written by Shri Rajhans, may be cited as an example. In that preface, Shri Gorey wrote that the relation between Jayprakash and Lohia had not been cordial. In fact, Jayprakash could never speak about Lohia without tears in his eyes. Even during the last 4 or 5 years, Jayprakash often said: "My relationship with Lohia was a singular 'you'. People could never understand the essence of our friendship. There were differences between us, no doubt. Certain differences were relating to Nehru, even then, our mind was one. Lohia was a wonderful genius". Inspite of repeated failures, Lohia tried again and again to bring Jayprakash back into politics. Lohia always used to say to his socialist friends: "You people will never understand what is Jaiprakash". It is futile to argue about the relationships between ordinary people. However, it is worthwhile looking into the intentions and emotions of public men who are instrumental in shaping the destiny of the nation and inspiring the people. Very often one finds petty people circling around celebrities. They indulge in backbiting and spread hatred. Even to this day, there are some people harboring hatred for Lohia in their hearts although it is now almost 20 years since his death.

About a month before his death, Lohia met Jayprakash on 13th September 1967. Newspapers hailed this meeting as historic. There was a free exchange of views between them. Perhaps Lohia had then sensed that for him the countdown had begun. He said to Jaiprakash, "My last desire is that you should enter politics for the sake of the people". Thereafter at a public meeting at Patna he said: "Even his last days Jayprakash will kindle the plane of revolution and the entire country will stand behind him".

What reply Jayprakash gave to Lohia was not known. But his answer in the form of action later on, is now too well-known. He waged a war against the dictatorship of Indira Gandhi. While giving a clarion call for total 'revolution', he said, "There is absolutely no difference between Lohia's 'seven revolutions' and my total revolution'". Had the Lohia-Jaipakash unity come about during Lohia's life, the face of the country's politics would have changed entirely. In his last days Lohia became disappointed. Like Gandhiji, he too had the misfortune of seeing his followers become opportunists and corrupt. It is said that revolution devours its own offspring. Even Jayprakash had to say in the end: "But who listens to me? Mine is only a feeble voice". And yet if only Jayprakash and Lohia had come together 10 to 15 years earlier, history might have been different, since these personalities were complimentary. However, it is now meaningless to think about what is impossible.

It is a subject for thought and anxiety, as to why Lohia's followers deteriorated much faster than Gandhiji's. The key-note of Lohia's 'Will to power', was to capture power, but he was ever-ready to relinquish it. He used to say: "The seat of power at Delhi is a throne of thorns and will continue to be so, unless the one who occupies it is prepared to burn it down along with himself. This means that one must be alert and have strict self-discipline, must stick to doctrines and programmes, and have no compromise with evil. Once the rot sets in, it ruins individuals and organisations. Once self-control is lost, man is over-powered by immorality and opportunism".

Knowing the truth Lohia said: "Shiva the God of destruction, reigns supreme in this country. Time speeds up the process of decay. The stages of childhood, youth and adulthood, appear in turn only to disappear in course of time. When a party starts growing it feels elated even with a minor gain, even if its real position in the world is ridiculous. The decay begins and in the due course time disintegrates party. Selfishness goes on increasing with no holds barred. The degree of selfishness must never be allowed to exceed that of selflessness, but in reality it does exceed. Hence the best man is he who aims at long-range selfishness. Short-range selfishness is some times extremely dirty". Perhaps Lohia had realised that after his death his followers and disciples would stall the pace of the revolution.

Lohia drew attention to a terrible tradition: in Indian life there is an extensive and unnatural slavish mentality. "The meaning of practical skill must soon be understood in this country. Who is more practical? a Mansingh or a Pratap? Among contemporaries, Mansingh is praised and Pratap is considered obstinate. After death however, it is Pratap who is worshipped, while Mansingh is condemned. So long as the country does not learn to appreciate Pratap in his life time, it can not acquire the strength of determined will and resolution which makes a nation great. This outlook is the result of our repeated defeats by foreign aggressors for eight centuries. Most of the Indians worship Pratap, but themselves behave like Mansingh. This is true mostly of Hindu or Muslim religious organisations, which are in some respects progressive, but try to strike a deal with the party in power. It is only after this filthy outlook is washed off the Indian mind, that the country can be strong enough to get over the sorrowful experiences of the last eight centuries. The tradition of worshiping the flatterers of Delhi rulers and reviling the selfless, self-sacrificing patriots, must come to an end.

Lohia was faced with a critical question. The rotten and corrupt Congress government, which had brought disgrace to the nation has to be brought down. However, he had not yet been able to make up his mind as to whether the weapon of non-Congressism could be used for that purpose. He knew that such a weapon forged out of mutually opposing political outlooks, would be no better than the Congress and would, therefore, increase the greed for power. Lohia reminded the people of the story, 'Devil's legs', which is popular among the children all over. The story is like this: one leg of the devil was bent forward and the other backward. To those who looked at him it appeared that the devil was running helter skelter and dancing all around with overflowing joy, while in fact he was steady at one place. Lohia also laid bare two more aspects of non-congressism, viz., channeling and strengthening the awakening among the people and executing a full-fledged, time-bound, revolutionary programme..

Lohia said: "Due to contradictory thoughts and conflicting outlook non-congress governments will not be able to make much headway in any direction whatsoever. However, it will atleast remove from the people's mind the belief that the Congress government at the centre can never be removed from the power. 20-25 crore voters would feel a sort of mental relief and may feel inspired to use their intellect in a better manner".

Lohia held that if a non-Congress government turns out to be bad, it also should be thrown out. Just as to cook a chapati well, it is necessary to turn it on the griddle, so also to attain a good government, it will he necessary to turn out a bad government and bring in another, and repeat the process till a good government is placed in power. A housewife removes the garbage accumulated in the house daily. Similarly inequality daily goes on pilling up in the lives of unfortunate people, and has to be cleared out everyday.

However, after Lohia, non-Congressism degenerated into party Politics of 'Samyukta Vidhayak Dal'. Lohiaites lost interest in consolidating the revolutionary urge, implementing the solid, timebound programme and cleansing daily the filth. Political power assumed paramount importance. After Lohia, the faith in equality disappeared altogether. Wheels of politics started turning fast. Lohia's followers could not keep the situation under control and also could not take proper decisions. As an example, after the death of Lohia, the most important event was the election of Giri as the President in 1969. This was the turning point in the politics of the country. It heralded the advent of goondaism, dictatorship and the cunning of Indira Gandhi. Almost all the leaders of S.S.P. were swept away by the current. This was due, perhaps, to the desire for power. Some people did oppose this tendency no doubt, but theirs was a voice feeble and unorganized. Since nothing had been done for mobilising the revolutionary urge of the people and to build up a powerful struggle, the net achievement of non-Congressism was nil.

With the nationalisation of banks, the feet of a section of the S.S.P. leadership began tottering. Some members became completely softened. They had no capacity left in them to understand Indira's guiles. In 1967 itself, Lohia had prophesied that the Indira government would try to lead the country astray or deceive the people by exploding an atom bomb in one form or the other. That prophecy came true. Bangla Desh had become a live issue. Lohia had raised the voice against the discriminatory and repressive policy pursued by Pakistan in 1950 itself. Having supported Mujib, S.S.P. was fighting for the recognition of Bangla Desh as an independent country. The S.S.P. insisted that India should help the Liberation Army of Bangla Desh by taking military action. However, Indira Gandhi took 9-10 months before ordering the military to march into Pakistan, by which time rivers of blood had already flowed in East Pakistan (now Bangla Desh) which was devastated by the Pakistan army. Immediately after the liberation of Bangla Desh, Indira Gandhi announced general elections, to reap the fruit of the victory over Pakistan. Some of Lohia's followers forgot their previous policy and joined the Congress bandwagon in praise of Indira.

In the 1971 elections, the opposition parties were routed completely. The opposition within the Congress had been finished off, and the Prime Minister, Indira Gandhi, speedily marched towards 'democratic' dictatorship. Flatterers, 'yes-men' and backbiters made headway in the administration. All feeling of security began to disappear. On 22nd June 1975, the Prime Minister declared a state of emergency and arrested all the leaders of the opposition. All freedoms, viz.; freedom of justice, freedom of press, freedom of thoughts etc., were suppressed. Inspite of all this, it became impossible for Indira Gandhi to keep the situation under control. She herself had, so to say, become a prisoner in the cage created by her. To get out of that situation, she was forced to hold general elections once again. The elections were held in 1977 and the sinking house of the Congress sank under the weight of its sins. On 23rd March 1977, on the 67th birth anniversary of Lohia, the Janata Government came into power. Lohia's cherished dream of routing the Congress at the centre had come true. In fact, however, there was no strength left in them. Official Lohiaites could not show any courage, inspiration or loyalty essential for carrying on a struggle for the implementation of the points mentioned in the election manifesto of the Janata Party inside the party as well as outside. Thus Lohia met the same fate as Gandhiji.

The age of Gandhiji was the age of sacrifice, that of Nehru and Indira Gandhi, the age of luxury, power and money, and that of Lohia, the age of duty. The need of today is the co-ordination of Gandhiji's sacrifice and Lohia's duty. Lucky were those who participated in the struggles launched by the two really great leaders-Gandhiji & Lohia. The endless journey of both is still on. The two great men have a message for the people of India: "Don't be afraid. Follow my path. This path is strewn with thorns and entails suffering. However, tread along with courage and you will build up a new world of justice, equality and prosperity, whereby poverty and war will be banished for ever".

Will the people of the country of Gandhi and Lohia unite and do something? Hope is eternal. As Bhavabhooti, a learned, ancient, Indian Sanskrit poet said, *"Time is unlimited and the world is vast"*.

2. SON OF SHARAYU AND AYODHYA

Rammanohar's ancestors hailed from Mirzapur in Uttar Pradesh. His great grandfather, Mansukhram, was an affluent merchant dealing in cloth and hardware. For generations the family had dealt in hardware. Due to this, perhaps, it derived the surname *'Lohia'* meaning one who deals in iron. Mansukhram had his shop in Mirzapur and his house at a village on the other bank of the Ganga. The Brahmin zamindar of the village had taken a loan from Mansukhram, pledging the village as security. He was, however, unable to repay the loan during Mansukhram's life time. The village had to be auctioned to recover the amount. The Brahmin felt utterly disgraced. He committed suicide. The incident shocked the Lohias. They felt that they were responsible for the Brahmin's death and were haunted by the feeling that they had become the object of the wrath of the Brahmin's ghost. Mansukhram's two sons died untimely deaths, one of them at a young age. Seized with the fear of the curse of untimely death, Mansukhram's two surviving sons, Shivnarayan and Bishnudayal, quit Mirzapur some time between 1870 and 1875 and settled at Akbarpur near Ayodhya. The two brothers lived together. Shivnarayan had four sons; Ganeshnarayan, Shankar, Babulal and Hiralal, while Bishnudayal had three; Purushottam, Gillu and Kashiprasad.

Situated on the bank of the Tamasa, Akbarpur was a big centre for handloom industry in U.P. The Lohias had their house and clothshop at Shahzapur on the other bank of the river. Subsequently, the two brothers separated. Bishnudayal's family became successful in business and came to be ranked among the affluent. Bishnudayal's sons bought landed property near Ratanpur. They had a large farm too. They opened a school at Ratanpur. The Lohia brothers started Congress activities at Akbarpur and took keen interest in the development of the handloom industry as part of national activities.

Shivnarayan's family could not acquire wealth. It was well off, but comparatively poor. All the members of the family were strong and stout Shivnarayan was a lover of the Indian athletics like *Dandpatta* and *Dandbaithaks.* He had the physique of a gymnast. Shivnarayan's sons inherited his physical fitness. After the Lohias migrated to Akbarpur, Ganeshnarayan, died in 1902. Babulal, though in sound health, died when he was only 30 or 32. Hiralal escaped the 'wrath' of the Brahmin's ghost. Shankar's widow lived at Mirzapur. Bishnudayal's eldest son, Purushottam, had 24 sons. Of them, Motilal alone survived. He lived in Calcutta. His other son, Kashiprasad died in 1910. His only son, Murlidhar, lived at Varanasi. Death claimed Kashilal's second son, Ramkumar, who had settled down in Calcutta, in 1940.

On March 23, 1910, Hiralal had a son Rammanohar. Rammanohar's mother, Chandri, was from Mithila on the bank of Sharayu. She was the youngest daughter of the Jhunjhunwala family who hailed from Chanpatia in Bihar. Of Shivnarayan's branch of the Lohias, Rammanohar was the only child to survive. Another noteworthy feature was that no girl was born in the family. Chandri was short in physique. Rammanohar resembled his mother. As the children in the family did not survive, Chandri was said to have "sold" Rammanohar either to a Bhangi or a Muslim for a half paisa in a desperate bid to "save" him. Rammanohar survived, but lost his mother when he was only about 2 years old. Ganeshnarayan's widow had adopted her younger brother-in-law Hiralal as her son. The responsibility of bringing up Rammanohar devolved on his grandmother. Hiralal was young when Rammanohar's mother Chandri died. But he did not remarry, afraid that a step-mother might ill-treat his son. Rammanohar regarded his grandmother as his mother. Only when he grew a bit, did he begin to wonder how his father and he could have a common mother.

Rammanohar's grandmother was virtually the grandmother of all the people residing in the locality. Lohia received lots of love and affection from her. Women in the neighbourhood also showered affection on the lad whom fate had denied a mother's love and care. The mother of his neighbour, Mevalal, Sarjoo Devi were very much fond of Rammanohar. Sarjoo belonged to the barber community and served the Lohia family. As long as she was alive, Sarjoo attended on Chandri. Sarjoo's son Ramnandan, senior to Rammanohar by ten years, was his childhood playmate. He used to take Rammanohar to the Tamasa for a bath once a week. They spent a long time, swimming and playing games. Rammanohar was a very mischievous boy. Often he used to hit Ramanandan and push him into river water. But they were deeply attached to each other. Dadi used to feed both of them. Rammanohar was her pet.

Rammanohar joined the Tandon Pathshala in the neighbourhood, and later, the Vishveshwarnath High School. The high school was near the railway station on the other bank of the river. Ramnandan used to escort Rammanohar to the school and back. Occasionally, Hiralal too escorted him to the school. Both in the class, as also on the playground, Rammanohar proved his extraordinary talents. Almost always, he stood first in the annual examinations. He also learnt to play the flute.

Rammanohar lost his grandmother too when he was barely ten. Now Hiralal had to assume the role of both father and mother. As a father, Hiralal was a hard task master, but he was quite unorthodox. He did not believe in old, out-dated customs and usages. He did not get his son's ear lobes pierced, as was the custom. Despite his rough exterior, he was very soft and kind hearted. A great admirer of India's cultural heritage, he taught Rammanohar Sanskrit to enable him to understand and respect India's an ancient history and culture. Hiralal lost all interest in household affairs after the death of his adopted mother. He stayed on at Akbarpur somehow for two years thereafter. He then left for Bombay and started his business there. He used to visit Akbarpur occasionally. Later he turned to politics and started taking interest in Congress activities.

Ever since his childhood, Rammanohar derived great pleasure in helping the poor, the sick, the physically handicapped and particularly people belonging to the weaker sections of the society. As all his childhood playmates were drawn from backward communities like barbers, he developed a broad outlook and a feeling of brotherhood transcending all the barriers of caste and community. As he grew up, this tendency became his second nature. Rammanohar was a student of the Marwadi Vidyalaya in Bombay. Many of his contemporaries there remember him as a brilliant but mischievous student. He was known for his eloquence and especially for his proficiency in English. The Principal of the Vidyalaya, Shri Jakti remembered him as a brilliant student.

1st August 1920, is an historic day in the annals of India's struggle for freedom. During the monsoon, the climate in Bombay is always depressing. It was particularly so on that day. As the news of the death of Lokmanya Tilak spread, a pall of gloom descended over the city. All roads led to Sardar Griha, where the "Father of Indian unrest" had breathed his last. There was an unending stream of men, women and children towards the hotel since early morning. Students of the Marwadi Vidyalaya organised a hartal that day. Rammanohar was their leader. They all went to Sardar Griha for the Lokmanya's last darshan.

The rise of Mahatma Gandhi on India's political scene synchronized with the death of Lokmanya Tilak. Gandhiji fired the nation with the intense feeling of patriotism and discontent against the alien British rule. A wave of nationalism swept and convulsed the entire country. Not only men and women, but children too also were drawn into the struggle. The people took the programme of boycotting foreign goods. Women ceased wearing foreign sarees and bangles and gave up use of imported sugar. Tiny tots organized *Prabhat Pheris,* parading through streets and bylanes, shouting slogans and singing songs preaching, the boycott of foreign goods.

Gandhiji called upon government servants to quit their jobs. Pleaders, doctors and teachers were asked to give up their professions and join the freedom movement. Responding to the call, Rammanohar gave up his studies for a year and participated in the movement. The young freedom fighter once cut out the overhead wire of a tram car.

It was during this period that Rammanohar had the first glimpse of Gandhiji. Hiralal took young Rammanohar along with him to see the Mahatma. Rammanohar felt attracted towards him at the very first sight. The young Lohia, who never touched any body else's feet outside his family, touched the feet of Gandhiji and in turn, the Mahatma patted him on his back.

Rammanohar passed the matriculation exam in 1925. He

stood first in his class. With this ended his career as a student in Bombay. The next phase began with his joining the Kashi Vishwa Vidyalaya at Varanasi. There too, he became popular among students and professors because of his brilliance, eloquence and above all, his charming personality. He had a very strong memory. Whatever he heard in the class room would suffice him. It was his habit to go to the root of every subject and problem. He launched a campaign against distortions and falsehood contained in a book called *'The Rise of Christian Power'*, which was prescribed for studies in history. He contended that the incident of the 'Black Hole of Calcutta', described in the book, was a cock and bull story. He pointed out that the Englishmen who were supposed to have died in the 'Black Hole' in fact never came to India. Besides, the place could have never accommodated 140 persons. Shivaji, the great Maratha hero, was called a plunderer in that book. Quoting Kafi Khan, a contemporary of Aurangzeb, Rammanohar pointed out that Shivaji was a strict disciplinarian and would not tolerate any disrespect to women or to a place of worship.

Lohia demanded that all books written by Englishmen ought to be revised and re-written. But who would hear a mere 16-year-old boy like Rammanohar Lohia? The very basis of the educational system was wrong. The doubts raised and queries made by Lohia used to embarrass and harass his professors. Some of them tried to silence him by asking: "Did you read this in a newspaper?" His reply to such caustic questions from the professors was: "Newspapers publish news and not views".

At Varanasi too, he was the youngest student in the class. Dressed in Khaddar clothes and wearing gold-rimmed glasses, he was known among the students as the only son from the wealthy family. He had an inimitable knack of collecting around him an ever-increasing circle of friends. He was fond of discussing political and other subjects of public interest. The originality of his ideas and his logical arguments enlivened the discussions. He convinced all those who came in contact with him about the economic practicality of Khaddar. According to his contemporaries at the university, atleast one professor and a large number of students took to Khaddar influenced by Lohia's arguments.

His method of study was also unique. He would ask one of his classmates around him to read the text book and he would listen lying on a cot. This would be enough preparation for him to pass examination. There used to be something new, something original, reflecting his vast general knowledge, in his answers which impressed examiners *'Julius Caesar'* was one of the prescribed books for study. One of the most common questions asked used to be "Who is the hero of the play?" Lohia had an original answer. According to him, Claudius was the hero and not Caesar nor Brutus, as was generally taught. The arguments advanced by Lohia in support to this unusual reply were so impressive that they pleased the examiner exceedingly. As his reading was extensive and not confined to text books, he used to shine in the class room with his depth of knowledge and brilliance of his intellect. He never adopted the familiar technique for answering question papers. That inevitably resulted in a disparity in the intellectual brilliance witnessed in the classroom and his performance in the examination.

In 1926, Lohia went to Gauhati to attend the session of the Congress. Party as a visitor. This was his first encounter with the national organisation. Punjab Congressmen included his name in the list of delegates from their province and sent his name to the president for inclusion among speakers on the resolution. But the speech did not come off, either because there was a large number of speakers or Lohia felt diffident.

In the vacation, he had gone to Allahabad to meet his friends. They all went to see the fort there. Lohia asked the British sentry at the gate some information about the Ashoka pillar. None of the friends however, could understand the reply given by the sentry. It provoked Lohia to remark: "If we cannot understand English after so many years of study, it will for ever remain a foreign language in India. It will never become our language". After passing the intermediate examination in 1927, he went to Calcutta for further studies. Here he joined the Vidya Sagar College. In his class at the college, Lohia was the junior most, and here, too, the professors were fond of him. There used to be frequent exchanges between him and the professor of English, one Shri-Bannerji. Once, when he went late to the class, the professor asked him the reason for not being punctual. He replied: "I have been following your example". On another occasion, there was a heated argument between the two, when the professor passed some adverse remarks about Nehru.

Lohia lived at Marwadi Chhatravas. His relations with the inmates of the Chhatravas were very cordial. But he used to be somewhat aloof from them. An introvert and a voracious reader, he was almost lost in the world of his own. He was always absorbed in reading, often far into the night, books on economics, politics and English literature. As at Varanasi, he became famous for his eloquence at this college too. Once, a rival in the elocution competition made himself scarce just on reading Lohia's name listed among the competitors displayed on the notice board.

In 1928, the Simon commission visited India to study the question of political reforms. The people of India boycotted it, and slogans of "Simon Go Back" rent the air. Tension was mounting in the country. Lohia used to participate in the activities of the All India Students organisation. Nehru presided over the Bengal conference of the organisation which was held in Calcutta towards the end of 1928. Netaji Subhashchandra Bose was the president of the subjects committee of the conference and Lohia a member. Nehru and Lohia were attracted towards each other when they met at the conference. The meeting resulted in increasing Lohia's love and regard for Nehru, while Nehru liked Lohia for his sharp intellect, eloquence and idealism. Somehow the meeting did not produce a similar feelings between Subhas Babu and Lohia.

Next year, he passed B.A. examination with honours in English. However, he belied the expectation that he would top the list of successful candidates and stood second. For a student like Lohia who took keen interest in politics, it was impossible to concentrate all his attention on his studies in those hectic days.

Though Lohia's personality was not fully developed at the end of his student life, those individuals and forces which in his later life influenced him greatly, had left their deep stamp on his way of thinking and actions.

3. IN BERLIN

After he had done his B.A., Rammanohar wrote to a friend: "Babuji (father) desires that I should go abroad for higher studies. If 1 do not do so, I have decided to go straight to Gandhiji".

Hiralal was not so wealthy as to finance his son's education abroad. Rammanohar obtained scholarships from a couple of trusts and left for U.K. About his experience in the U.K. he wrote a friend: "Here Indians are treated like dogs. I do not wish to stay here even for a day". On the eve of his departure from India in 1929, he had expressed his aversion to pursuing higher studies in U.K. Not that he could not make friends in that country. But he did not feel at home there.

He had developed friendship with a youth called Gerard and his parents. Rammanohar once asked Gerard's mother: "Who is the most popular Indian here?" "Cricketer Ranji", she replied. "Who ranks second?" he asked her again. Her reply was: "The Aga Khan". He then asked: "Who is the most maligned Indian here?" When Gerard told his mother what Rammanohar had at the back of his mind in asking the question, the woman remarked: "You naughty boy, you want me to name Gandhi; is it?"

One day, Rammanohar had gone to the library and was searching for a book. The feeling of being at sea in the strange land, which had enslaved, his country was, perhaps, visible in the expression on his face. A person, who had been watching him, asked: "Can I do something for you?"

Rammanohar explained to him the dilemma he faced. He told him that though he had come to U.K. for higher studies, he did not feel like continuing them in that country and sought his advice. The gentleman said: "If you have come here in the hope of learning something new or original, your studies will be of no use. Go to Berlin instead". He left the library, thanking the gentleman for the advice. He decided to go to Berlin.

When Rammanohar left for Berlin, he did not know German. On his way he picked up some German words and phrases of common use in daily life. At the Humboldt University, there, a student had to choose his professor and examiner. Rammanohar chose the class of Prof. Werner Sobart, who was then the foremost economist of Germany. At his first meeting with Prof. Sobart, he replied in English to the questions the professor asked him. The professor smiled and said in German: "I do not know English". Rammanohar felt somewhat ashamed. "I shall meet you after three months" he told Prof. Sobart and left.

Germany was then in a ferment. Her economy was in doldrums, as a result of the First World War. The economic depression of 1929 had worsened the situation further. The country appeared intoxicated with the feeling of ultra nationalism. The Weimar Republic was unable to cope with the situation, and Hitler had risen on the German political scene. With evergrowing unemployment, factional fights and fierce controversies, tension was continuously rising in the country.

The situation in India was also tense. Gandhiji had set out on the historic Dandi March on the 12th of March. After having covered 250 miles on foot, he defied the Salt Act on the sea shore on 6th April. This sparked off a nationwide conflagration. Satyagraha started at a number of places all over the country. Satyagrahis went in *jathas* (batches) to places having salt pans to break the Act. The police resorted to the wanton lathicharge, when a batch of 51 selected volunteers offered Satyagraha at Dharasana on May 21, 1930, under the leadership of Sarojini Naidu. The police beat each of the Satyagrahis till he bled and then pushed him out of the place. A representative of the international news agency serving 1300 newspapers, said about the incident in his eye-witness account: "I have visited as many as 22 countries during the last 18 years and covered movements, riots and rebellions. But nowhere else did I witness a gruesome incident as the one at Dharasana. It became so impossible for me to see the plight of the Satyagrahis that I had to close my eyes".

Hiralal was among the Satyagrahis at Dharasana. He wrote to Rammanohar, giving a graphic account of the inhuman behaviour of the police at Dharsana. A session of League of Nations was in progress in Geneva then. India was represented by the Maharaja of Bikaner. Acting as a stooge of the British imperialists, the Maharaja was obviously expected to shower praise on the British for the 'peace' in India. Lohia strongly felt it was necessary to tell the world that India was afire and there was nos peace in the country.

Rammanohar decided to stage a demonstration within the meeting hall of the League. Lohia went to Geneva with a friend and with this purpose in mind. With great difficulty he obtained two tickets of admission to the visitors gallery from some Indians who worked in the League secretariat. The two friends took up their positions in the gallery. As the Maharaja rose and began to speak, Rammanohar gave two piercing whistles from his seat. The unexpected incident startled the gathering. The president looked up in surprise. He ordered the guard to remove the visitors who had booed and insulted the Maharaja by their unseemly behaviour. The guard approached Rammanohar and addressed him in French. Rammanohar replied back in Hindi. The guard tried his English and Rammanohar again responded back in Hindi. The guard and officials later discovered that Rammanohar knew not only English and French but German too.

Rammanohar was not going to give up his attempt so soon. The next morning, he wrote an open letter to M. Titulescu, the Rumanian delegate who presided over the session. He described in the letter incidents which had occurred in India, like the hanging of Bhagat Singh and the Dharasana, atrocities. A Geneva newspaper, the *'Humanite'*, published the letter. Rammanohar bought a number of copies of the paper, stood before the gate of the League building and distributed them among the delegates. In the letter, he had challenged the Maharaja's credentials to represent India and argued that he was not entitled to speak on behalf of the country.

Once, while in Berlin, Rammanohar went out for a drive with his friend. He was driving his car with a speed of 70 to 80 miles an hour. The car collided with a goods truck. The truck owner, a poor peasant, was driving the vehicle, laden with vegetables, on the wrong side of the road. It did not have head lights either. His mother who was on the truck, was thrown off the vehicle as a result of the collision. She was, however, injured only slightly. The peasant flew into rage and began to abuse Rammanohar. He told Rammanohar : "Wait here till I return with the police. I will break your head, if you try to leave the spot".

Rammanohar replied : "Bring the police within half an hour, I shall await your return". It did not occur to the simple peasant that it was possible for a person to run away, even if he had promised that he would await his return and that once he had fled the spot, it would not be possible for him to break the person's head. The peasant did not return for a long time. Rammanohar's friends pressed him to leave the place. But he declined to do so. "I had given him my word. How can I prove false to it?" he asked.

The peasant returned after some time, but without the police. He began to abuse the police. He said that they intervened in even a private matter which was none of their business. But they would not be available, when one needed them. Rammanohar told the peasant that he appreciated his criticism of the police and added that the administration and the police functioned in the same manner everywhere in the world over. In no time, the two became friends.

Berlin students took keen interest in politics. Rammanohar could not keep himself aloof from it. He was the secretary of the Central Europe Indian Association, founded by Indian students. It conducted a powerful campaign against British imperialism and advocated the cause of India's freedom. The communist sponsored League Against Imperialism was also in the field. The association organised a conference at Berlin about the time the Gandhi- Irwin pact was signed. The League also joined the conference. The anti-Gandhi and anti-Congress policy of the communists had by then become known. The communists charged Gandhiji with having betrayed the cause of Indian freedom by signing the pact and brought before the conference a resolution denouncing Gandhiji.

Rammanohar strongly opposed the resolution. He pointed out to the delegates the fact that under the pact, the people of India had secured the right to manufacture salt. He contended that the pact had demonstrated that not only the Congress but the British also had been defeated. He told the communists that to oppose the force with force was "as foolish as trying to cross the Niagara in a boat". Ultimately, the communist-sponsored resolution was defeated.

Rammanohar and other anti-communist students later held

a separate meeting. The meeting passed a resolution, urging the Congress to conduct the business of its Karachi session in a manner that would further the objective of complete independence. As the resolution had been drafted in English, there was a lot of debate at the meeting on whether to use the word "request" or "demand". Rammanohar felt that the issue would have been settled within a couple of minutes, had the resolution been drafted in Hindi. The association soon became the centre which had the twin object of propagating socialism and fervent nationalism. At about the same time, a socialist centre was in the process of development in India also.

Rammanohar took a keen interest in Germany's political life. He used to attend all meetings held in Berlin, including those addressed by Hitler. As Rammanohar was an anti-imperialist, communists showed special regard for him. He was always present at the meetings held under the auspices of the Social Democratic Party. One day when he went to attend the meeting organized by the SDP, and to be addressed by a socialist leader from some other country, the hall was packed to capacity. Rammanohar tried to enter the hall. But a party worker told him that no accommodation was available in the hall and regretted that he could not, therefore, be admitted. That might have happened because of the party worker's regard for courtesy or for rules. But the fact remained that Lohia could not attend the meeting.

The Nazis and Communists, on the other hand, were more anxious to gain friends and so more accommodative than the Social Democrats. When Lohia was about to leave the place of a communist meeting, because the meeting hall was full and he could not enter, a communist who knew him approached Rammanohar, talked to him and conducted him to a seat in the hall. His experience of a meeting addressed by Hitler was also unique. He had found it impossible to enter the over-crowded hall, though he had an admission ticket with him. The police, too, could not help him in the matter. But the president of the party had espied him. He came out of the hall and greeted Rammanohar with a salute in the Nazi style. "He is our foreign representative", he remarked and took Lohia inside the hall.

Nazi friends tried to persuade Rammanohar to propagate their party's ideology. He told them categorically that none outside Germany would accept their philosophy based on the *'Herrenvolk'* concept. It did not have even an iota of universality of equality. "You regard the people of your Nordic stock as the purest in the world. Next in order come the Anglo-Saxons, the French, the Latin like Italians and Spaniards, and then the Chinese and the Japanese", he pointed out, "while Indians and the other peoples with 'mixed blood' are regarded by you as those belonging to an inferior race. Under these circumstances no patriotic Indian will accept the Nazi creed".

Rammanohar obtained his doctorate in Economics early in 1932. He had written his thesis on "The Salt Tax and Satyagraha" in German. In Germany, the professors who guide the students are also the examiners. Prof. Schumacher told him towards the end of 1931: "You should not live in this country much longer". The professor had sensed the impending victory of Hitler.

At Berlin University, an examination meant a discussion between the professor and the student on serious topics. Even wrong answers, given by students did not displease the professors.

Prof. Schumacher was his first examiner. Rammanohar reached the examination place ten minutes late. When the professor asked him the reason why he was late, Rammanohar replied: "Have you not yourself called in your book the Chinese peasant industrious and the Indian counterpart lazy?". The reply seemed to have pleased the professor, but he said: "Being an Indo-German, you must become efficient".

The examination was conducted in a cordial and informal atmosphere. Towards the end of the examination, the professor asked: "What is your country's currency?" The British Government had given up the gold standard early in 1932. But Rammanohar did not remember it, and replied: "Gold standard". He paused for a while and began to recapitulate the history of the development of Indian currency. When he came to events of 1931, he abruptly stopped and said: "I am wrong. Why did you not stop me?" The professor replied: "Why should I stop you. I wanted to give you the opportunity to think over the matter. I was sure, you will ultimately give the correct answer".

After an hour-long discussion on gold mines, the professor asked "What is the difference between gold mines in Africa and those in the U.S.A.?" Rammanohar did not know the answer. But he had seen Charli Chaplin's picture, "Gold Rush". He remembered it and replied: "Operation of the mines in U.S A. is based on the village industries in California, while those in South Africa are mechanically operated". The examiner asked him : "Can you name an industrialist?" The question stumped Rammanohar. The scanty knowledge he had derived from films was of no avail and he could not reply.

The professor wrote out the result sheet, put it in an envelope and handed it over to Rammanohar. He went with the envelope to Prof. Ludwig Vernard. After he had handed the envelope to him, the Professor asked him : "How did the examination go?" "How should I know?" said Rammanohar "Why do you say so? Didn't you have a result sheet with you?", the professor asked him. "Am I so uncivilized as to open the envelope and see the result?" replied Lohia. The reply favourably impressed the professor.

Prof. Vernard's examination over, he went to Prof. Oncken with the envelope, containing the result sheet handed over to him by Prof. Ludwick Vernard. He reached there on time, though it was snowing heavily. The professor asked him why he had come, when it was snowing so heavily. Prof. Oncken had written a book dealing with the British foreign policy during the preceding 120 years and the question of social security in India. He asked Rammanohar whether he had read the book. Rammanohar replied that he had. Many subjects cropped up during the discussion that followed. Among them there was 1857 rebellion.

The professor asked him: "To what extent events outside India had influenced the 1857 uprising?" Rammanohar could not reply the question. The professor told him that some Indian soldiers had fought in the Crimean War and said: "If ever you develop interest in History, write on the extent to which foreign events had influenced the rebellion".

Prof. Desnaur was the last examiner. The professor of philosophy asked him: "Are you Hindu or Muslim" Rammanohar's usual reply to such a question used to be that he had nothing to do with any such sectarian faith. But on that occasion, he replied that he was a Hindu. Prof. Desnaur then asked him the meaning of word, "Mahatma". Rammanohar explained the term and said that there could be and there had been a Mahatma among the Muslims too. The professor was impressed by the answers. At the end of the examination, he told Rammanohar: "That is all right. You may go now. We shall talk on the subject some other time".

Rammanohar returned to India in 1933 after obtaining his

doctorate. His thoughts had matured somewhat by the time he left Germany. Gandhiji had begun to exercise a profound influence on him. But he had not become the devotee of the Mahatma. Though he regarded non-violent resistance to evil and injustice as Gandhiji's greatest gift to humanity, he did not agree with the economic aspects of his philosophy. He was attracted towards India's cultural history because of his study of Sanskrit. He did not believe in the Marxist interpretation of history. That was why he was attracted towards socialism as a new form of civilisation. He believed that it would be possible to usher in a new civilisation devoid of social, economic and political inequality and exploitation through socialism alone.

When Rammanohar left Germany, he took with him a large number of books. But all his luggage was confiscated before he reached India's shores. He landed at Madras with no belongings except the clothes he wore. He wanted to go to Calcutta, but he had no money to pay the railway fare. He was never much ruffled by situation like this. He worked out a plan. As soon as he disembarked from the ship, Rammanohar went straight to the *"Hindu"* office. He offered the editor an article on European developments, which he wrote on the spot in the office of the paper. It was accepted and he was paid Rs. 25. He had earned enough money to reach Calcutta.

4. PLUNGE INTO POLITICS

The political climate in India was depressing when Lohia arrived in Calcutta. Gandhiji had been arrested immediately after his return from the Round Table Conference. The then Viceroy, Lord Willingdon, had vowed to crush the Congress movement within six weeks. Nehru had also been arrested, while Khan Abdul Gaffar Khan had been interned in Burma.

Hiralalji was in Calcutta. He had given up his business and devoted all his time to Congress work. Lohia's uncle, Ramkumar, also lived in Calcutta. Hiralalji used to have his food almost every day with his brother. It was at Ramkumar's residence that after his return from Germany that Lohia had his first meeting with his father. Everybody was of the view that Lohia should start earning his livelihood. But he returned to India with the decision to plunge into politics. However the political climate somewhat dampened the enthusiasm with which he had returned to the motherland.

After spending some time in Calcutta, Lohia went to Varanasi to see a friend. Lohia had then become a chain smoker. As the financial condition of his friend was bad, it was not possible for Lohia to borrow cigarettes from him. The situation impelled him to give up smoking. During his stay at Varanasi, Lohia spoke at the teacher's College on "Education in freedom". He made several efforts to obtain employment. On hearing that there was a vacancy for the post of the Professor of Economics at the Kashi Vishwa Vidyalaya, he went to see Pandit Madanmohan Malviya, the founder of the institution, but before could meet him, another person had already been appointed to the post. He happened to meet Rameshwardas Birla, who offered Lohia the job of his private secretary. Lohia declined but agreed to accompany him in his travels with the expectation that he would gain experience from it. He, however, gave up the job after some time.

Jamnalal Bajaj invited Lohia to live with him. Jamnalal regarded Lohia as his third son. Lohia once went with him to see Gandhiji. Jamnalal told the Mahatma: "This boy wants to enter politics". Gandhiji asked Lohia : "Are you well off?"

Recalling this first meeting with the Mahatma, later, Lohia said that if anyone else had asked him such a question at the very first meeting, he would have felt awkward about it. "But as it came from Gandhiji", he said, "I had not a slightest awareness of any thing wrong in it". Jamnalal assured Gandhiji that he need not worry on that topic. It appeared as if the whole load was off his mind, "then it is all right; we shall meet again", was all that he said and the whole matter was dismissed.

Lohia returned to Calcutta, after a few days' stay with Jamnalalji. Life in Calcutta which was now full of difficulties and strife, made him take things more seriously, and think more rationally. Lohia's strifeful life in Calcutta had its impact on his political thinking. He felt that it was through intensifying the struggle, and not by undertaking parliamentary activities, that the Congress could be strengthened. Gandhiji was also opposed to the Congress contesting elections to legislatures.

The proceedings of A.I.C.C. meeting, held in Patna in May 1934, revealed that a section of Congressmen favoured making the Congress more revolutionary in character by laying greater emphasis on its agitational activities, while another wanted the organisation to fight elections to legislature. The meeting decided in favour of the Congress resorting to the parliamentary activities. Gandhiji wanted that the Congressmen with the "Parliamentary mentality" should be provided with the opportunity to pursue their activities. He severed his connections with the Congress and placed his construction programme before the people.

There were many in the national movement who believed in socialism. Some of the socialists in the Congress were together in the Nasik central prison. Some were connected with the Kashi Vidyapeeth, while another group tried to establish centers of socialist workers abroad, such as the one at Berlin. It had become imperative to unite these forces into a single organisation.

Socialists from all over the country met in the conference at Anjumane-Islamia Hall at Patna on 17th May 1934, and decided to establish a Socialist party. Acharya Narendra Dev presided over this first socialist conference. Lohia was among the members of the committee set up by the conference to draw up the constitution and programme for the new party. The resolution moved at the conference sought to outline the objective of the party merely as the establishment of a socialist society. Lohia moved an amendment to the resolution, seeking to incorporate attainment of complete independence as one of the party's objectives. Acharya Narendra Deva supported Lohia. But others, including M.R. Masani, Purushottam Trikumdas, and Sampoornanand opposed the amendment. Their contention was attainment of independence was implied in the object of establishing the socialist society. They also argued that the government might outlaw the party, if attainment of complete independence was included in its aims and objects. If this was not defined as one of its objects, the party would be able to function when the Congress is declared an unlawful organisation, they added.

In order to evade the issue, Jayprakash Narayan said: "Let us take the decision on the subject at the next meeting". Lohia's amendment was lost. The next day, the A.I.C.C. passed the resolution, in favour of the Congress contesting elections to the legislatures, in the teeth of the socialists opposition. Congressmen entered the Central Legislative Assembly in due course and the ban on the Congress was also lifted by the government. The foundation conference of the Congress Socialist Party was held on October 21 and 22 at Readymoney Terrace in Bombay. 150 delegates from all over the country attended the conference. Lohia was elected to the party's National Executive. The conference decided to start a journal, the *'Congress Socialist'*, to serve as the party's mouthpiece, with Lohia as editor. The journal soon earned people's acclaim. The thought provoking articles it published helped promote clarity of thought and sharpening of intellect. In one of the issues, Lohia wrote an article criticising the activities of Gandhiji's All India Village Industries Association, started as an effort to overcome the frustration that had come as the result of the failure of the 1932-33 movement. Lohia suggested in his article that India's freedom could not be won by such piece-meal, minor activities of the association. They might, by the most favourable reckoning, be able to give 'some more vitamins' to the people, but would never be able to set them up on their own feet in order to combat the British Empire. He pointed out that the task of ending foreign rule in India was so colossal that activities like husking and hand-pounding of rice were not commensurate to that end.

Lohia sent a copy of the journal to Gandhiji with a request that he might express his ideas on the subject. That was perhaps the only occasion when the Mahatma was really angry with Lohia. He got a post card from Gandhiji in reply. Gandhiji wrote: "You must never expect me to write because I find that you have not the slightest patience with your opponent's viewpoint". Lohia wrote back to say that he was probably careless in the use of his phrases. But he could have tried to get at his meaning and could very well have written a reply to it. Swiftly a sweet reply came from Gandhiji.

Lohia's life in Calcutta was full of hardships. He did not have even a place to live. He used to stay occasionally at the office of the trade union centre where there was no bathroom or a kitchen. Two tables joined together served as his bed at night. Sometimes the used to live at the Marvadi Chahhtravas also. He later shifted to a friend's place on Mirzapur street. He devoted all his time to editing the *'Congress Socialist'* and organising party activities. Lohia and his friends were always in difficulties because of paucity of funds. There used to be meetings every day, but they did not have money even to go to these meetings.

An affluent friend once tried to persuade Lohia to change. He praised Lohia and advised him to give up the life of hardships. The friend urged him to take some gainful vocation and presented him Rs. 200. Both Lohia and the friend with whom he stayed, first bought a dhoti, a shirt and a pair of chappals each. Lohia bought a Gandhi cap too. He spent Rs. 70 on books. They then dined in a hotel, bought a tin of cigarettes, and moved along the Hooghly harbour studying the conditions of the dock workers till daybreak. When they returned home they had only Rs. 30 left. A woman's voice in the next room, woke Lohia at about 10 a.m the next day. She was a revolutionary's wife and had come to seek financial assistance. The friend gave her Rs. 5. Lohia went out and made his friend pay her all the money with them.

One day Hiralalji and Rammanohar had been to a wedding. The topic of Rammanohar's marriage naturally cropped up during the conversation there. The father of the prospective bride approached Hiralalji with the proposal. As the two were engaged with their talk, Rammanohar took off his glasses and said: "Look,

I am almost blind. Why do you want to marry your daughter to a blind man like me?" After returning home from the wedding reception, Hiralalji remarked: "What a reply you gave to the gentleman!"

The decision of the Congress to enter the legislatures had disappointed Lohia. The national leadership of the Congress Socialist Party was under the influence of Marxism, which also he did not like. The party leadership was trying to forge a united front of all Marxists in the country. Lohia was opposed to the proposal.

Ever since its foundation in 1924, the Communist Party of India had opposed the national movement and Gandhiji's leadership. Communists had called the Congress Socialist party a party of "Social Fascists" as soon as it had been launched. The CPI had been blindly toeing the Comintern line. In opposing the national movement and Gandhiji's leadership, it was faithfully following the policy outlined by the Comintern of the Soviet Union. However, the Comintern reversed the policy of its seventh Congress and directed its affiliates the world over to form united fronts. The CPI dutifully revised its stance. It began to support the national movement and also decided to accept Gandhiji's leadership to a certain extent. It suddenly started showing fraternal feelings towards the socialists. Jayprakash Narayan, who had a soft corner for the communists, fell for the bait. The doors of the Congress Socialist Party were thrown open to the communists, at the party's convention at Meerut in 1936, by its leadership without even bothering to understand the reasons for the change in the communist strategy.

Jayprakash had succeeded in enlisting Acharya Narendra Dev's support for his policy of forging a united front with the communists. The communists took full advantage of the opportunity. They had kept their separate organisation and trade unions intact. They captured vantage positions in the CSP and began to disrupt it from within. Still the party leadership continued to chase the mirage of a united front. Lohia, Achyutrao Patwardhan, Masani and Ashoka Mehta criticized the policy and said that it would prove suicidal for the party. Each one of them opposed the policy for different reason of his own. Lohia was opposed to the Marxist dogma. All the four leaders resigned from the national executive of the party on the issue.

The same year the notorious purges started in the USSR. A number of prominent leaders of the communist party, the government and eminent men from different spheres of life were denounced as traitors, tried, convicted, and sentenced to death or sent to concentration camps on trumped up charges. These trials created doubts and suspicions about communism and Soviet Russia in the minds not only of socialists but also of Marxists all over the world.

Serious differences arose in the CSP too on the policy to be pursued towards the communists. At its convention held at Lahore in 1938, the communists even tried to capture the party, proposing their own panel for election to the national executive. The attempt however failed. A majority of the members of the new executive were in favour of expelling the communists from the party. Lohia was among them. But Jayprakash was not still prepared to do so. However the situation changed radically after the outbreak of the second World War. In this situation allowing communists to remain in its fold would have been suicidal for the party. At long last, the decision to expel them from the party was taken at the time of the Ramgarh session of the Congress. But the experiment of the united front with the CPI proved very costly for the socialists. The communists had seized vantage positions in several State units of the party particularly in the south, like in Kerala and Andhra and disrupted its organisation, thereby inciting entire units to defect to the communist party. It resulted in weakening the party in south India. The Socialists have not yet been able to build up a strong party organisation in that part of the country till today.

5. THE RISING STAR

Jawaharlal Nehru presided over the annual session of the Indian National Congress held at Lucknow in 1936. It passed the resolution, moved by him from the chair, deciding to set up a foreign department at the office of the All India Congress Committee at Allahabad. Hailing Lohia as "a new star that has arisen on India's political firmament", Nehru urged him to join the new department as its secretary. Lohia was immersed in his activities and was reluctant to give up the freedom, zest and joy of his own political life at Calcutta. But Acharya Narendra Dev ultimately persuaded him to accept the assignment. The Congress did not have a foreign policy of its own till then though it had begun to take increasing interest in world affairs and pass resolutions on international events from time to time, particularly since 1920. But, a well-defined foreign policy was yet to emerge. This was also true for other organisations and groups in the country, except the socialists and Communists. The Communist Party of India, founded in 1924, was a blind devotee of the October Revolution. Though the Socialist party generally supported the Russian Revolution, it was not its uncritical supporter and the party did not blindly toe the Soviet line. Ever since his return to India, from his visit to the countries in Europe including Soviet Russia, Nehru had begun to emphasise the need for the national movement to have an approach of its own to world affairs.

Two distinct trends had influenced the national movement's approach to world affairs. One of them stood for the policy based on opposition to Fascism and imperialism and support to democracy and world peace through collective security. It implied preservation of the *status quo* through the maintenance of balance of power. The socialist movement in U.K. was it's source of inspiration and Nehru its principle protagonist.

Mahatma Gandhi represented the other trend. He ardently believed in the principle: "One step enough for me". He was not, therefore, in favour of adopting any line of action in world affairs till India had attained freedom. His was a humanitarian approach. He had condemned the Japanese aggression against China, and the rape of Ethiopia by Italy, from the humanitarian angle. A believer in the brotherhood of man, Gandhiji was convinced about the failure of the present civilisation. He was influenced in his approach to international affairs by a noble aspiration to create a new world order. Lohia gave it a concrete form, outlining a foreign policy based on the elimination of imperialism, opposition to all wars, freedom and equality of all nations and peoples, and a world parliament. He also succeeded in securing Gandhiji's support to it.

There was thus a latent contradiction in the foreign policy of the Congress, which was, in fact, the blend of two trends. But the basic difference between the two trends did not come out into the open immediately, as they had anti-imperialism as a common factor. Perhaps, Lohia, too, did not, for some time, realize the contradiction inherent in the two approaches. He, therefore, felt that he would be able to run the department on the lines he had in view and accepted the responsibility of conducting it. But within about two years, differences over the character of the national movement, enhanced by differences on the approach to world affairs, emerged, and his position became untenable and he had to quit the department.

The object of the foreign department was not to formulate a foreign policy for the Congress. The aim was to establish contacts with labour organisations and other organisations in other countries, free as well as under foreign domination, and disseminate correct information regarding India's struggle for freedom, with a view to enlisting their sympathy and support for the national struggle.

Lohia's achievement in the direction was remarkable. Within eight months after the department was opened, he had established contacts with such organisations and movements in 12 different countries and attracted their attention to India's freedom movement. The report he presented to the annual session of the

Congress held at Faizpur the next year, reflected the success of his performance.

After outlaying the fundamentals of nationalist India's foreign policy. Lohia said in his report that the function of the department must be to "tear India away from her mooring in so far as world politics is concerned".

"The U.K. foreign policy", he said "aimed solely at serving British interests. Relations of India with other countries were a reflection of the British foreign policy. India must put an end to this". "True", he stated, "we cannot have accredited ambassadorial corps to represent our country, nor can we adjust our trade relations and tariff policies so as to reflect our foreign policy. We cannot yet put an end to the use of the Indian soldiers and police in the distant parts of the British Empire. We can, however, declare the considered will of the nation that the British Indian and our armed forces have no support or sanction of Indian opinion. More than that, we can outline, in broad contours, the new system of the foreign policy that will actuate free India and even motivate our struggle for freedom". He also stressed the necessity of establishing contacts with political and social leaders in other countries.

Nehru was reflected president of the Congress and he continued the setup and personnel of the Foreign Department. His work as the Secretary of the Department, earned for Lohia, the reputation of a brilliant intellectual and erudite spokesman of nationalist India's foreign policy. The result of his work were soon evident. A letter received from a newspaper from Palestine on 7th April 1937, said: "We are following with much interest what is going on in India. I must admit, however, that very little news of value reaches us through the press. Hence the newsletter which we received from you is really very valuable. It has already appeared in the Arabian press and will also appear in Syria and Baghdad".

A letter from British Guiana, after describing the conditions there, said: "Out of 136,000 Indians, who form over 40 percent of the entire population of this colony, over 53,000 are employed as labourers in the sugar estates. These are weak and disorganised and live in perpetual fear of unemployment. The Guiana East India Association has long been demanding the appointment of a Resident Agent-General from India, to the British Guiana Government. The Agent, they think, would mediate between the plantation owners and labour to the advantage of the latter".

The dark clouds of war began to gather on the horizon. The League of Nations was on its last legs. Japan had occupied the large part of China. The Fascist, General Franco, had rebelled against the Republic of Spain. The British policy was to see that neither Fascism nor Communism, gained in strength and to ensure that *status quo* was maintained somehow, so that Britain's imperial interests were not jeopardized. The Foreign Department took two significant steps. Tearing away India from British foreign policy, the Congress called upon the people of India to express their support to the countries fighting for freedom and democracy. This had a tremendous impact on the people. The Congress sent a medical mission to China. It condemned Italy's aggression against Ethiopia. The Foreign Department asked the people to observe Ethiopia Day all over the country to denounce the aggression and express sympathy for Ethiopians. To highlight India's dissociation from British policy, it decided to collect funds in aid of a Ethiopian freedom fighters.

The Congress declared that Indians "are no longer subject to the policies of Mr. Anthony Eden or the British Government. We have foreign relations of our own". The Department published a booklet, written by Lohia, explaining nationalist India's foreign policy. In the booklet *'On the Struggle for Civil Liberties'*, he emphasised the fact that the world conflict was not a confrontation between democracy and totalitarianism. In support of his contention, Lohia cited the example of the French Republic. He pointed out that all men were supposed to be equal before law, but in actual practice, courts in France discriminated between men. The fundamental principles of the French revolution were not only not implemented, but were also trampled upon. On the U.S., he wrote that the country was fast becoming the heaven of the affluent and people's democratic rights were being violated. The police were suppressing striking workers and forcing them, at bayonet point, to manufacture bombers. Severe restrictions had been imposed in the U.S. colonies on the people's right to peaceful organisation and even on the urge for freedom. In the U.K. too, civil liberties were being denied. While in the U.S., the danger to civil liberties stemmed from the law, the administration was endangering them in the U.K., he added.

The so-called democracies were in fact pursuing policies designs to serve colonialism. Lohia exposed this reactionary character of "democracies" through an interview to the Associated Press on the deceitful nature of the British policy towards the Fascist rebellion against Republic of Spain. "The British Government's policies", he said, are professedly guided by the principle of non- intervention. That is deceit. The British Government intervened in the Spanish affairs on the day it sponsored an international ban on the right of the Spanish Government to buy arms. Right under the nose of the British controlled non-intervention committee, Fascist powers sent battalions of soldiers, planes and tanks to Spanish territory. Non-intervention is surely not the guiding principle the British foreign policy. The British foreign policy can have only one guiding principle and that is the safeguarding of their empire and maintenance of the capitalist order. It has been demonstrated that British policy towards the Spanish affairs is not one of non-intervention actually it is of the intervention in favour of the Fascists".

Lohia wrote a number of other booklets and pamphlets for Foreign Department including those on the foreign policy of the Indian National Congress, Indians in foreign lands and India and China. Besides, he issued a weekly bulletin. In the bulletin he used to comment on current affairs and outline India's approach to the world events. In some issues, he said that the capacity of the League of Nations to act exhausted at the time of the Spanish civil war and its task was entrusted to the non-intervention committee in the U.K. "London", he said, "was general regarded as a broker between Fascism and Communism. It was not, infact, a conflict between democracy and dictatorship. On the one hand, London desired that the strength of Fascism should not grow; on the other, actions were aimed against socialism too". Criticizing the reactionary character of the British Labour Party's policies he said that the slogan for the so called peace actually undetermined democratic forces in the world. The labour policy was not calculated to promote world peace, a prophesy which came true when the second World War broke out.

He also condemned the developments in Soviet Russia, the purges and trials. Lohia said that these developments were unfortunate as far as future of the Soviet Russia in particular, and the world in general, was concerned. Workers the world over had a soft corner for the Soviet Union. They regarded her as the vanguard of the world peace and looked upon her as a land where experiments in establishing a new civilisation were being conducted. He was afraid that there developments would weaken their faith in her and create a climate 'of doubt and suspicion about the country. He added that the developments had also revealed the fact that the dictatorship of a faction ruled at the country. However despite these purges, trials and killings, Soviet Russia could not be said to have abandoned the basic principles of nationalisation and to that extent, she still constituted a challenge to the capitalist world. But they have no doubt given a severe jolt to the believers in the new civilisation.

The manner in which Lohia functioned, as the secretary of the Foreign Department, also revealed the independence of Lohia's personality. During the regime of the Congress Ministry, formed under the Government of India Act of 1935, industrial workers faced police firing, at Kanpur, Uttar Pradesh. Lohia condemned the firing in one of his weekly bulletins. Pandit G.B. Pant, who headed the ministry, lodged a protest against it with Nehru. Nehru told Lohia that he should not have done so. He urged that such condemnation, contained in the bulletin of the Department, which was meant for circulation in other countries also, might undermine the prestige of the Congress. Lohia countered Nehru's contention in strong terms. That silenced Nehru and the matter was dropped.

As war appeared imminent, there developed the tendency in a section of the Congress leadership, in favour of supporting the so-called democracies, like the U.K. and France, in the event of world war breaking out. The Congress was saved from such an eventuality as a result of Gandhiji's strong opposition to this trend. Lohia had begun to campaign against the tendency from the very beginning. He said: "It is no doubt our duty to support nations like China and Spain which are fighting for freedom. But we should not get ourselves involved in the conflict between big imperialist powers like the U.K. and Germany".

A meeting, held at Allahabad in observance of the Anti-war Day under the auspices of the Congress Socialist party, passed a resolution on the subject, moved by Lohia. It said: "Preparations for the next war, which will be in the interest of imperialism, are definitely against the interest of the poor masses...the people of India will not participate in this war. If war breaks out, they will utilise the opportunity to further their own struggle for freedom".

The socialists strongly opposed the entry of the Congress in provincial autonomy in 1937. The opposition culminated in the resignations of Acharya Narendra Dev, Jayprakash Narayan and Achyut Patwardhan from the Congress working committee. The socialists also organized a protest day on 1st April 1937, against the decision of the Congress to accept office. According to Lohia, the opposition of the socialists to acceptance of power by Congress was based on, among other things, the fear that the Congress, while working in collaboration with the British officials, might fall prey to the the policy of compromise with the British.

The entry of the Congress in power gave an opportunity to the socialists to pressurise the Congress ministers to fulfil their commitments the Indian peasantry given in the Congress election manifesto of 1937. As Acharya Narendra Dev put it in his address to the All Indian Kisan Sabha conference in March, 1939. "At the time of elections a spirit of independence ran through the peasant masses which forced the incorporation of the immediate demands of the peasants in the election manifesto. . ". The Kisan Sabha demanded the implementation of the promises to Kisans and launched a vigorous campaign of agitation for agrarian reform.

The socialists believed that the dire poverty of the Indian peasantry cannot be ended without the revolutionary changes in the economic structure of the society and that an all out economic struggle for this was necessary. This again must be linked up with the national struggle for freedom so as to reinforce it with social content. The emphasis of the socialists on peasant struggles gave birth to an interesting debate between Gandhiji and Lohia. Lohia wanted an extension of Satyagraha programme to economic and social struggles. Lohia enquired of Gandhiji, "Is it not possible to universalise the principle of Satyagraha to make it the bedrock of the other programmes?... The people today do not regard your constructive programme and the ministerial action as wholly adequate. They are experimenting with such programme as those of peasant action".

To this Gandhiji responded by saying, "I have never suggested that there can not be any departure or addition to my programme. But I cannot bless or encourage a new programme that makes no appeal to me". "Take the peasant action... I regret to have to say that in most cases the peasants were in the state of perpetual excitement and made to entertain hopes which can never be fulfilled without a violent conflict".

The new independence pledge was framed by Gandhiji in the year 1940 to be taken on 26th January—The Independence Day. This pledge demanded of the Congressmen to declare complete faith in Charkha and other constructive activities as the means of Swaraj. This gave rise to serious debate among the leaders of the Congress Socialist Party and Gandhiji. The dialogue between Lohia and Gandhiji in this respect is most instructive Lohia asked Gandhi: "Does independence pledge necessitate belief in a social order for free India, which will be based exclusively on the Charkha and the present constructive programme? I personally feel that it does not. The pledge is inclusive of Charkha and village-craft, but it is not exclusive of other industries and economic activities. It is undoubtedly necessary that any one who takes the pledge must be ready to express his positive faith in the principle of decentralised economy".

Gandhiji in reply stated: "The Charkha will include everything that will promote the well-being of the villagers. I do visualise electricity, ship building, iron works, machine making and the like, side by side with village industries. But the order of dependence will be reversed. Hitherto industrialisation has been so planned as to destroy the villages and their handicrafts".

In passing, Lohia's faith like Gandhiji in decentralised industry can be instructively contrasted with the position of Nehru in this respect. Nehru, in his speech at the session of the Indian Economic Conference in 1940, had stated that village industries were essential and should be developed in the coordination of big industries.

An annual convention of the Congress Socialist Party was held at Lahore in April, 1938. It passed a resolution on the international situation. While moving the resolution, Lohia said that the Congress should draw up a definite policy and programme to avail of the situation. Lohia was elected to the National Executive of the party at the convention. By now the Congress had laid down a new rule that a member of the Congress Socialist Party's executive could not hold office of secretary of any department of the A.I.C.C. It was obviously intended to get rid of Lohia who had become inconvenient to those controlling the Congress. Lohia resigned from the secretaryship of the Foreign Department in August 1938.

The beginning of the year 1939 saw fast, dramatic changes

in the international situation. They had their impact on India's national movement. The Congress President Netaji Subhas Chandra Bose, was of the view that the Congress should avail of the situation created by war to intensify the freedom struggle. The Congress Socialist Party and Lohia were of the same view. Gandhiji was, on the other hand, of the opinion that the Congress should hold its patience. This led to clash between the rightists and the leftists, or the moderates and the extremists, in the Congress.

According to Lohia, the clash was artificial and unreal. Subhash Babu decided to contest the election again. Maulana Azad and Dr. Pattabhi Sitaramayya were the other candidates in the field. The Maulana withdrew from the contest, leaving Subhash Babu and Dr. Pattabhi in the arena. The election campaign took a unhealthy and acrimonious turn. There was spate of statements and counter statements attacking each other. Dr. Pattabhi had Gandhiji's blessings, while Subhash Babu became the leader of those opposed to the Mahatma. Writing on the controversy, Lohia said that the conflict between the so-called right and left would cause a split in the freedom movement. He referred to Subhash Babu's allegation that the rightist faction in the Congress was trying to arrive at an understanding with the British Government on the issue of the formation of Indian federation and said that Subhash Babu's suspicion was baseless. He stated that none desired to arrive at such a settlement with the British Government. Gandhiji especially, did not at all have such a desire.

Subhash Bose won the election by 213 votes. Lohia abstained from voting in the election as he believed that both the candidates were equally good or bad. The rest of the socialists voted for Subhash Babu. But for the socialists votes, he would have been defeated. At the subject committee of the Congress session at Tripuri on 9th March 1939, Pandit Pant moved a resolution, reaffirming the organization's faith in the leadership of Gandhiji and his policy and programme.

Expressing its confidence in Gandhiji's ability to lead the national struggle and the Congress, the committee asked the president, through the resolution, to nominate the working committee in consultation with the Mahatma. M.S. Aney, Subhash Chandra Bose and others opposed the resolution. According to them, it smacked of dictatorship and personality cult. Subhash Babu's victory in the Congress Presidential election created for the socialists a situation with an uncertain future. It led to a chain of events in Congress politics which perplexed and puzzled them. They had landed themselves in a difficult situation of their own creation by supporting a person on whose future policy they had no control. As a result, the socialists found themselves caught in an embarrassing position of serving two masters simultaneously.

Speaking on the resolution Jayprakash Narayan said: "True, we voted for Subhash Babu. But from the very beginning, we were averse to get ourselves involved in the clash between the right and the left. We voted for Subhash Babu because we felt that he was a better candidate than Dr. Pattabhi. We approached Subhash Babu, but the view he expressed on the question of resolving the differences did not satisfy us. We saw the leaders of the right, but they too did not satisfy us. It is impossible to restore unity unless the working committee is constituted according to Gandhiji's wishes. We have, therefore, decided to remain neutral".

The posture of neutrality, after having voted for Subhash Babu, only added to the confusion. Lohia's stand on the issue was different. He was of the view that, once having accepted Gandhiji's general approach and direction, there was no point in opposing it on irrelevant grounds. Lohia also spoke on the resolution. He said that the resolution constituted an answer to all those who had predicted that there would be a split in the Congress. The organisation was passing through critical times. The Congress might have to fight British imperialism even that year itself. That was why restoration of complete unity in their ranks had become the need of the hour. Gandhiji had said that Subhash Babu's election was his defeat. The resolution respectfully assured Gandhiji that it was not so.

Lohia elaborated his views on the subject in an article, published under the caption, "Basic Unity of the Congress". He wrote: "The terms 'right' and 'left' indicate a contrary line of march. If you were to go 'right' and I were to go 'left', our backs would at once be turned against each other. Even if we attempted sometimes to look back, we would increasingly see less of each other, until either sees nothing". He said that right and left are relative terms. According to the moderates, the Congress was a leftist organisation, but there were sections in the Congress, some of which could be regarded as leftists and some rightists. These terms could be useful for revamping a party and for propaganda as long as there was mutual understanding. Lohia believed that the Congress was the symbol of national unity. It did not rely on the constitutional methods alone. It resorted to peaceful movements also. It believed in social justice too. It was the four point basic approach of the Congress that activised the people. In this context, the terms, left and right, were unscientific and unreal, he said, and added that only right course was to work for a joint struggle, a joint programme and a joint leadership.

But the conflict was not resolved. At the A.I.C.C. meeting at Calcutta, held on 29th April 1939, Subhash Babu expressed his inability to form his working committee with Gandhiji's approval and resigned. The committee later passed a resolution, expelled him from the organisation for having defied the Congress resolution. Rajendra Prasad was elected Congress President in his place. Subhash Babu founded the Forward Bloc Party.

Writing on the developments, Lohia said that he split in the congress was detrimental to the national movement. While launching the Forward Bloc, Subhash Babu had said that the split would strengthen the Congress instead of weakening it. The split could have been regarded as unavoidable, Lohia said, if the differences between the two sections had been of a fundamental nature, or if one of them had become counter-revolutionary and the other being numerically weaker, had to face expulsion. But this unnecessary split might harm the Congress, he added.

The Munich Pact, signed on 30th September 1938, had made war inevitable. As India was not the master of its destiny, the creation of war psychosis was injurious to her national interest. In an article, published on 29th March 1939, Lohia said that the war was playing "hide and seek with us". He remarked that the Indians were being lulled into a false sense of security and the people had become complacent.

"On four occasions during the past year", he said in the article, "we were on the verge of a world war, but never got into it. In March, when Germany annexed Austria; when the lightening thrust into Czechoslovakia did not take place due to any fore-knowledge; in July, when Russia and Japan fought over a little hill; and in September, when Germany finally annexed Sudetan land. Out of these crises, the war-making forces emerged triumphant and their striking arm grew stronger than before. But we grew fond of our complacency".

He said that it would be unwise on the part of India to be caught unaware by the outbreak of the war. India must be prepared to resist, through non- violent means, any attempt at being drafted into the war. He outlined a four point programme for the purpose. It was; (1) opposition to recruitment of Indians to the armed forces; (2) organizing a similar movement in the princely States; (3) organising labour so that it would refuse to transship war materials for the British during the war; and (4) refusal to pay war tax and subscribe to war loans. Mahatma Gandhi had already declared that India would have nothing to do with such a war. He had also warned the British Government that if it forcibly involved the country into the war, the attempt would be resisted.

Criticizing 'pseudo moralists' and 'pseudo realists' for their posture, Lohia said that India's co-operation with the British would debase the country. Indian soldiers would be used in Africa and Malaya to serve and protect the interests of the British Empire, he pointed out, and added that those who aspire to usher in a new world order should not allow their faith to be sullied by such 'pseudo-realistic' politics.

To the 'pseudo radicals' who disfavoured any opposition to the British engaged in the war with the Fascist powers, Lohia said that their contention betrayed their failure to probe deep into the real source of danger to world freedom and peace. It had also been shown that they had panicked into searching for palliatives in place of real remedy. At any point of time, British imperialism was as much a monster evil as Hitler and Japan. It was British imperialism that had given birth to Fascism. Afraid that it was endangered by its own brood, British imperialism wanted to kill its own litter. India must, therefore, resist both Fascism and war. Free India could help protect world democracy, he declared.

In an article published on June 1, 1938, Lohia urged Gandhiji to start Satyagraha immediately. After analyzing the world situation, he suggested a four-point plan for the world peace. The points were: (1) all people will be free. Those newly acquiring freedom will determine their constitution through a constituent assembly, elected on the basis of adult franchise; (2) all races are equal and there will be no racial privileges in any part of the world. There will be no bar to anyone in settling anywhere he likes; (3) all credits and investments of one country in another will be scrapped or submitted to international tribunals for an impartial review, they will then be owned not by individual but by the State; and (4) there will be total disarmament.

Gandhiji endorsed this plan but did not comment on the suggestion to launch a Satyagraha campaign immediately. The Mahatma said it was impossible to decide on the Satyagraha campaign as the people lacked discipline and had not imbibed the spirit of non-violence.

Nehru was of the view that it would be wrong to launch a struggle against the British Government, when it was fighting in defence of democracy. Lohia was opposed to this approach. He submitted a plan for a struggle against British Government. He said that there was a strong desire among the people to fight the British Government and listed four reasons which had strengthened the desire. They were: (1) the progressive increase in the strength of the force of nationalism; (2) urge for freedom; (3) a sense of Britain's weakness during the war; and (4) a vague dislike for war and slaughter, reinforced because of our non-violent method.

Besides, he held that "the difference in the extent of justice between the two groups in the next war will not be so great as to justify our intervention on either side. In fact, if imperialism and fascism would fight each other, it will be a fight between two partners who have fallen out. The object, which is to resist British imperialism, which is already making extensive war preparations in India and will attempt to drag us into war, can be effectively realised by non-violent action. The necessary mass strength and capacity to suffer will be available and can be further improved".

He suggested that for this purpose, a programme with items like the settings up of anti-war committees, publication of a weekly, opposition to recruitment to the armed forces, preventing the supply of war materials to the Government, forging national unity and organising a boycott of foreign goods.

Lohia was arrested on May, 24, 1939, at Calcutta after he had delivered a speech on "The Congress and our present duty" under the auspices of the South Calcutta Congress Committee. The arrest was effected in connection with the speech he had delivered earlier at the Calcutta University on "India and the next war". He was released on bail and later tried before the Chief Presidency Magistrate of Calcutta, Shri Ranjit Gupta.

Lohia conducted his own defence. He was acquitted on 14th August. While acquitting him, the Magistrate praised Lohia for his knowledge of Law, and said that if he became a lawyer he would attain great success.

A meeting of the A.I.C.C. was held at Bombay on 24th June 1939. Lohia had come to know earlier that the Congress President, Nehru had sent a telegram to the World Peace Congress, in Paris, to the effect that India would cooperate with the British in the war, if the country was granted freedom. Lohia disliked this. Through a question, which was preceded by a letter, he compelled Nehru to make a statement, in which it was said that there was no reference of military cooperation with the British in the telegram.

At the meeting, a resolution on the passive resistance and civil disobedience by Indians in South Africa came up for consideration. Lohia found that the resolution had referred to Indians in South Africa as "British Indians" and called upon the community in that country to carry out civil disobedience. He moved two amendments to the resolution, one that Indians had better be called simply, "Indians", and second that the effort at civil disobedience in South Africa had better be a kind of a united front of all the oppressed communities in that country—Indians, Negroes, Arabs and even the poor whites.

Speaking on the amendments, Lohia condemned the British policy of segregation of non-Europeans in that country. The only course open to Indians and other oppressed communities was to join together and present a united front against the Government's racial policy. Nehru remarked to Lohia that "He spoke so fast that it was difficult to follow his speech". Lohia remarked "How will you follow it, if you collect a group and gossip, when others are speaking?" Overhearing the conversation, Mrs. Sarojini Naidu turned to Lohia and said: "Why do you quarrel with Nehru? He really wants to help you". Lohia asked "what help?" Nehru said that the amendments were all right, but they were not happily worded. Lohia replied that he was prepared to accept any modification in them, provided their spirit was retained. Both of them then made some verbal modifications in the amendments and the resolution as amended was passed by the meeting.

Lohia was happy that his amendments had been accepted and wandered about, until there was a hurried search after him. He found that Mahadev Desai had come with a message from Gandhiji and there was flutter, flury and excitement. The members of the working committee were seated on the dies. Everyone of them was trying to call Lohia towards himself. When he settled down with Nehru, he came to know that Gandhiji was opposed on his amendments and that he would have the A.I.C.C. pass his resolution as it was, or none at all. When Mahadev Desai and Sardar Patel tried to persuade him to take another view of things Lohia said: "It is only four hours between now and when we passed the resolution. What sudden development has taken place in the meantime?" He thought a while, looked at Mahadev Bhai and said: "Your reasoning does not convince me, but the fact remains that neither the A.I.C.C. nor any person like me is in the position to conduct civil disobedience in South Africa. That movement has to be conducted by Gandhiji and, therefore, if he is unable to accept my viewpoint, I have naturally to choose between that which takes place, although of a inferior variety, and none at all". He therefore consented simply to the withdrawal of the amendments.

The resolution was placed before the meeting again and passed in its original form. However, his amendments, seeking to delete the word "British" before the words, "Indian community in South Africa", contained in the resolution, was accepted. As he was leaving the meeting, Subhash Bose came along and asked if he had realized who the power was, Mahatma Gandhiji or the Congress. Lohia replied that he had been realising it at all along and acting accordingly. Gandhiji's moral strength was indeed greater than the strength of the Congress. Some time later Gandhiji wrote an article in the" *Harijan",* an affectionate criticism about Lohia's inexperience. Gandhiji invited Lohia to meet him. He told Lohia that he was not opposed in principle to his idea of all the oppressed people forging a united front to end the established order of things.

Though Lohia had to withdraw his amendments, the idea underlying them, of all the oppressed communities in South Africa offering a joint resistance to injustice and indignity, actually materialized after 13 years. The Satyagraha campaign launched by all the communities in that country against the unjust and oppressive laws of the South African Government in 1952, resulted in the imprisonment of more than 1000 Indians, Negroes, Arabs and even poor whites.

Those were the days when Mahatma Gandhi represented Lohia's "dream", Nehru "his desire" and Subhash Bose his "deed". About this Lohia said after few years: "The dream shall never beckon, and although it had its blemishes in detail, its glory, shall, I hope, brighten with time. The desire has soured and the deed was not completed. The fact, that the deed, the desire, and the dream, could not travel in harmony, not only among themselves, but also in respect of the effects that they produced on the people, shall be a source of pain to us, who have lived under their influence, and of sadness to the historian".

6. STORMY PETREL

Hitler invaded Poland on 1st September, and Britain declared war against Germany on the 3rd September 1939. In India, Gandhiji met the Viceroy on 9th September. After the meeting, Gandhiji wrote: "Having made my position vis-a-vis the Congress clear, I told His Excellency that my own sympathies were with England and France, on purely humanitarian grounds. I told him that I could not contemplate without being stirred to the very depth, the destruction of London which had hitherto been regarded impregnable. And as I was picturing before him the House of the Parliament and the Westminster Abbey and their possible destruction, I broke down".

In broadcasting the news of the meeting, the All India Radio edited Gandhiji's statement. The parts of the statement that were broadcast made Lohia angry. This was one of the rare occasions when he was really angry with the Mahatma When he read the statement in full in the newspapers the next day, his anger subsided somewhat. Nevertheless, he felt Gandhiji had expressed certain sentiments which seem to convey a preferential attitude towards England in the war. He did not, however, think that Gandhiji had agreed to compromise with the British on the issue of India's freedom. On the contrary, he was sure that he must have expressed those sentiments out of pure humanitarism. He wrote to Gandhiji that although he was angry with the statement that was broadcast over AIR, the statement in full, which appeared in the newspapers the next day, somewhat removed the doubt from his mind.

It was perfectly clear to him, he wrote, that when Gandhiji talked about destruction of Westminster Abbey, he was trying to embrace whole mankind and all its architectural achievements and the historical glories; and because he could not do so concretely, he had selected Westminster .Abbey as a representative of all such symbols that existed all over the world. He took it that he would also break down in tears quite in the same fashion, if the museum of Munich were destroyed. Gandhiji wrote out another statement for the *"Harijan"* to say that it was so. When Lohia later met Gandhiji, the Mahatma told him that he should write to him at once whenever he felt that Gandhiji had missed any national or world issue in relation to the war. That gave him perfect freedom to write to Gandhiji whenever he felt like on any occasion.

On 15th September 1939, the Congress Working Committee invited the British Government to declare its war aims and warned that only a free India would associate itself with other free nations in the war efforts. In October, the Viceroy declared that it was the ultimate object of the British Government to grant dominion status to India.

Other leaders like Dr. B.R. Ambedkar and V.D. Savarkar offered unconditional support to the British Government in the conducting the war and started a campaign for recruitment of the army. The A.I.C.C. meet at Wardha on 9th October 1939. The resolution on the war situation placed before the meeting stated that the committee could not take a final decision on its attitude towards the war as it desired to give an opportunity to the British Government to revise its policy.

On behalf of the SP, Jayprakash moved an amendment to the resolution to the effect that the Congress would, not only not be able to accept any piecemeal advance towards Indian freedom, but would also refuse to entertain the settlement of the issue of freedom which pledged in advance the country's support in the war. Supporting the amendment, Lohia said that the question of offering help to British would arise only after India got her freedom and the misconception that India would get her freedom automatically, if she supported Britain, had to be removed. Declaring that "only the Congress had the right to be consulted on the war situation".

This was a reference to the meetings that the members of the Congress High Command, including Sardar Patel, had with the Viceroy in the first week of October. The statements made by the Viceroy and the Secretary of State for India, subsequently, made it clear that the terms laid down by the Congress leaders for a settlement were not acceptable to the British Government. As a result, the Congress Parliamentary Board had to issue a directive to the Congress Ministries in the Provinces to resign by 21st October. Accordingly they resigned and Governor's rule was imposed in those provinces.

Subhash Babu had convened a conference against imperialism at Nagpur two days prior to the AICC meeting at Wardha. Socialists had a bitter experience of the earlier attempts at consolidation of the Left. They, therefore, regarded that attempt as childish. Criticizing the conference, Lohia said: "The future does not take care of those who do not take care of the present". He appealed to Subhash Babu not to hold the conference and to maintain unity in the Congress.

Lohia wrote an article, captioned, "To help with arms", on the horrors wrought by arms used in war. He said "in the early stages of the Sino-Japanese war, Japanese fliers in American planes bombed Chinese cities and the Chinese brought them down with German bullets. The Republic of Spain killed a fair number of German soldiers sent by Hitler to fight for France. But how would German soldiers like to know that some of them were killed with guns and bullets manufactured in their own country? It suited Germany's barter trade economy to buy tobacco from Greece in exchange of munitions and it suited Greece to sell these to Spanish Republic. Even now a large number of patriotic soldiers serving their country loyally on the battlefield are being killed with weapons manufactured in their own country and on a very large scale. We must not forget that Czechoslovak and Polish armies were to a very large extent furnished by British factories and banks, and these arms are today in German hands. Presumably, Britain and France too have fair quantities of munitions manufactured in Germany. All killing is more or less a savagery, but this is heinous. The nation kills its own nationals? Are you not sick?"

"Armament manufacturers, we are told, do not recognize any frontier limitations, and sell their wares to whoever has the money to buy them. Are we to believe that money is dearer to them than their own nationals? Soviet Russia has all along condemned imperialism, aggression, and wars of conquest, and yet Italian planes continued to receive Soviet fuel as long as they rained death over defenceless Ethiopia. Germany too was receiving Soviet war material. And yet Russian weapons were being used to kill those who, in morality and idealism, ought to be Russia's friends.... This has a lesson for the countries that had not taken the road of armies and weapons. Czechoslovakia fell with out striking a blow and Poland was laid low by the conqueror within 15 days. It was amazing even that there were good and intelligent people in India singing praises of arms, They are crazy. To hell with arms.'

Lohia presided over the Sultanpur District Political Conference held at Dostpur on 11th May 1940. In the course of his address, he said that the imposing edifice of the British Empire, built on the exploitation and domination of other countries, had begun to topple. Nothing could save it. Ten provinces in the country, he said, were under Governor's autocratic rule. 'No-tax Satyagraha' must be launched to fight it, and so people must be prepared for all kinds of suffering.

The Uttar Pradesh Congress Committee met at Lucknow on the 18th and 19th May. Acharya Narendra Dev moved an amendment to the political resolution placed before the meeting, The amendment said that a freedom should be granted to India and other countries, The force thus released might bring the war to a speedy end and assure reconstruction of the world on the basis of the freedom of the people and peace among them.

Supporting the amendment, Lohia said that recent events had shown that neither was Germany as weak as some people thought, nor was Britain as strong as was made out by some. The turn of events had moved some leaders to say that they should prepare the people for their defence and arm themselves for the purpose, but that was not the way to look at the problem, he pointed out. He felt that to meet a power as well armed as Germany, several years of preparation and organisation would be necessary. To think of preparing ourselves for defense at this stage was ridiculous, he remarked, He said that what was needed was consolidation of the world forces for freedom of all people. That was the only way to fight Nazism. They must reorganize themselves on these lines and thus release forces which assure all peoples of the world, including Czechs, Germans, Poles and others of freedom, both economic and political.

Lohia was arrested in the compound of the AICC office on 7th June 1940, under the Defense of India Act in connection with his speech at Dostpur. He was taken to Sultanpur and kept at the police station the be night. He was forcibly handcuffed and made to walk to the court, a distance of three miles, to stand the trial. He was sentenced to two years' imprisonment on 1st July 1940.

A correspondent wrote to Gandhiji: "You must know that arrests are being made under the Defence of India Act. Now your favourite Lohia is taken up. I suppose, you will see no reason for civil disobedience; or, may be, you think that these arrests are legitimate". Gandhiji published the letter in *"Harijan"* and wrote: "Dr. Lohia is no more my favourite than any other Congressman. True, he has come nearer to me than he was. Every arrest evokes my mental protest. But I am not in the habit of reducing all my thoughts to writing. I believe our thoughts, too, produce effects, though not known to the world. I felt that any public protest by me would be ineffective. All things are illegitimate in war. All repression is bad from my stand point. But I have as yet no effective remedy against war. As I suffer war, I suffer these acts of war markers".

In his statement before the court, Lohia said that all their actions must be non-violent, because non-violence was not only the practical need, but also, the moral necessity. "Those who rely on weapons", he said, "do not rely on their hearts. They turn into slaves of their weapons. They have no strength left in themselves. I am opponent of the cult of the lathi, and its modern equivalent, the aeroplane. There is an inner contradiction between this cult and the enduring human life, a contradiction which is daily becoming more fierce". Towards the end of the statement, Lohia said: "Let me, in conclusion, state that I have no ill will towards any people. I have lived among the German people and liked their thoroughness of inquiry, their scientific bent of mind and their efficiency of action. I am unhappy that today they have to carry on their shoulders a system which results in war and conquest. I have no intimate knowledge of British people. I dare say that they have their virtues. I do not want the destruction of Britain. The British had done evil to us, but I do not want to do evil to them. Again, I am unhappy that the British people had to carry on their shoulders today a system which enslaved the people of the world".

While convicting Lohia, the magistrate said: "The accused is a highly intelligent and learned gentleman, perhaps with a doctorate degree of some European university, a man of high principles and morals whose honesty of purpose nobody can doubt.

He does not mind suffering for his conviction and does not care much for his sentence or its duration. We certainly do not punish him for holding certain political view about the present Government". The magistrate added: "For the claim of the Government that it is democratic and run on public opinion entitles the public to criticize it according to its light by constitutional means; but we must protect such a government from embarrassment in relation with the masses who are bound to be disaffected by a speech like the one the accused had delivered in Dostpur and particularly when the British Government and empire is in grip with the most unscrupulous enemy. I, therefore consider that his detention in jail until the end of the war is very desirable". The Magistrate sentenced Lohia to two years' rigorous imprisonment.

Commenting on Lohia's trial and conviction in the *"Harijan"* Gandhiji referred to his statement before the court. He said that all the points made by Lohia in the statement were sound but he had to resist the temptation of publishing the statement in full. Gandhiji published those parts which he felt were of lasting importance. Gandhiji also published the magistrate's judgement and wrote, "Then why has he been rewarded with rigorous imprisonment? The duration of the term I understand. He must be kept away from the supposed mischief. I wonder whether the fact of imprisonment will not aggravate the mischief. Of this the court must be the judge. But the people will remember that love of one's country and outspokenness are crime in a country where the state is not responsible to the people. Dr. Lohia's and other Congressmen's imprisonments are so many hammer-strokes that must weaken the chain that binds India. The Government is inviting the Congress to start civil disobedience and deliver the last blow, it would fain have reserved for a better day, better for the British. It is a pity".

Lohia was taken to the Bareilly prison from the Sultanpur jail on August 12. The indignities and hardships imposed on him pained Babu Purushottamdas Tandon. Tandonji remarked to newspapermen that in this respect, the British were cousins of the Germans. Prisoners were marked by the prison authorities, with ink stamped on their hands, before granting them an interview with their relatives. In protest against this humiliating system, Lohia declined to see anyone.

Speaking at the AICC meeting held at Bombay on 15th

September 1940, Gandhiji said: "I cannot sit still when I see Rammanohar Lohia and Jayprakash Narayan, than whom I do not know braver or straighter men, in jail. They had not preached violence, but simply carried out behests of the Ramgarh resolution".

With the bombing of Pearl Harbour, by the Japanese on 7th September 1941, the war took a new turn. Within three months, Japan invaded and occupied strategically important countries in Asia. The fall of Singapore, till then regarded an impregnable fortress, dealt a moral blow to the prestige of the British Navy. Over-running Malaya, Indonesia, Philippines and Burma in a blitzkrieg, Japanese armies reached India's frontiers.

Japan's victories thrilled the people of Asia. The simmering discontent, and hatred against the white rulers burst into the open and Asians began to glorify the Japanese. These developments had their impact on the people of India too, who were already angry with the British government for having dragged India into a war to which they were opposed.

This forced the British Government to review the situation afresh. Neither the British Army nor the British Navy was strong enough to defend India any longer. Besides, its allies the U.S. and China, began to pressurize the British Government to reach an understanding with the Congress. The British Government had no option left but to change its posture to some extent. National leaders, including Nehru, Achyutrao Patwardhan and Acharya Narendra Dev were released from jail.

Generalissimo and Madame Chang Kai Shek, who were among Asia's most prominent leaders then, visited India in February 1942. The purpose of their visit was to intervene in India's favour. The British Government was naturally cool towards their visit to the country. The Congress, however, accorded them a rousing reception. The Government turned down their request to visit Wardha to visit Gandhiji. They in turn rejected the Government's suggestion that they should invite the Mahatma to meet them at some other place in India. The Generalissimo said: "In the first place, I am his guest. It would be improper on the part of the guest to invite the host. Secondly, I am younger than Gandhiji. Propriety demands, therefore, that I should go to meet him where he lives".

But the Viceroy, Lord Linlithgow, said that India was infested with Japanese agents and spies. He could not, therefore permit the Changs to go to Wardha. Gandhiji ultimately met them in Calcutta during their visit to that city. Lohia wanted to suggest that the Generalissimo, as a representative of non-whites, to arrive at a settlement with Japan. He, therefore, requested Nehru to arrange a meeting with the Chinese leader. He also pressed Nehru to speak the Generalissimo on the subject. Infatuated as he was with the white nations, Nehru ignored Lohia's suggestion.

The British Government issued a statement on 29th March 1942, outlining its policy towards India, and sent Sir Stafford Cripps to negotiate a settlement with Indian leaders. The Cripps proposal contained a vague promise of granting dominion status to India after the cessation of hostilities. The proposals had several dangerous features, including a provision granting the option to any State not to join the Indian Union. Close on his heels came. America's Johnson. Cripps resented Johnson's interference in the course of negotiations. Some of the Congress leaders, either because they were aging or frustrated, were inclined to accept an unprincipled settlement based on the Cripps proposals. They had adopted the posture in the name of helping Britain and their allies in fighting Fascism.

The Congress Working Committee used to meet at the place of Sir Stafford's residence in Delhi for a fortnight. Gandhiji had already called the proposals as a "post-dated cheque". It was a mystery why Britain's war cabinet had sent Cripps to India with such proposals. Britain was anxious to relieve the pressure from China and U.S. Cripps and Nehru were intimate friends. These and other factors, perhaps, led to the despatch of Cripps mission to India. The talks finally broke down on the 10th April. Cripps began immediately to harp on religious differences and bitterly criticized India. Lohia tried to unravel the mystery in his booklet, *"Mystery of Strafford Cripps"*.

After having rejected the proposals, it had become necessary for the Congress to plan for a struggle. Against this background, Lohia outlined a plan of a broad-based struggle of the people of India and other nations under foreign domination. He appealed to the Britain and the U.S. to convert the war into one for the freedom of all the enslaved nations in the world.

He exposed the real nature of Britain's war policy in an article which was published in the *"Harijan"* on 19th April 1942. In the article Lohia said that it was made out by Britain that Japan struck treacherously and her onslaught was so sudden that the British Government in Asia was taken unaware and the swift series of the Japanese victories inevitable followed.

The real reasons for the Japanese victories, he said, was Britain's complacence and arrogance. The Governor of Malaya had pooh-poohed the idea of Japenese attack on the country. The soil of Malaya was too soft to bear the weight of the 5 and 10 tonne tanks, the Governor had stated. The Japanese actually marched into Malaya with their heavy tanks, Lohia pointed out.

Lohia said that the might of an army would be of no avail, if it was not backed by an organised civilian population. The people of Asia did not sympathize or support Britain. The British themselves were responsible for that attitude amongst Asians. "Have not motor cars been commandeered from Indian owners from Burma, ostensibly for war effort, but actually for the evacuation of the Europeans?" he asked, and said: "An Indian refugee has come back to this country with the pathetic story of how, when he was trekking, he glimpsed his car with the British evacuees inside. Indians and Burmese have no inducement to fight the battles of Britain against Japan. Indians are a humbled and humiliated race; let us not run away from that fact. And Japan is an Asiatic power. Had I been trained merely in European ethics and not been impressed by Mahatma Gandhi and what I consider as the nobler side of my history, I would have hailed Tojo. As it is, I regard Tojo as wicked as Hitler and Churchill, for, if his wretched slaughter were to end in the victory of one or the other, my hopes of better world would be dashed".

"It is perhaps too late for British to save India and presumably too early for India to save Britain. But what we can do, Indians and Britons alike, is to attempt to save the whole world. That is not so absurd as it sounds. Formulate a genuine basis for the free and peaceful world and ask every power to accept it. And should some powers prove too greedy and arrogant, it might then be a different power war for Asiatics". Gandhiji wrote a note at the end of the article, in which he said, "I do hope that this will receive the attention it deserves from all concerned".

Lohia had been urging Gandhiji to launch Satyagraha from the beginning of the war, Gandhiji's moral sympathies initialy were with the British. But there was now a change in his approach to the issue. In an article in the *"Harijan"*, addressed to foreign troops stationed in India, he wrote that he felt as if the rise of Nazism was meant to punish the British for having enslaved and exploited the people of Asia and Africa. He ended the article with the advice to the British to withdraw from India.

Newspapermen interviewed Gandhiji in Bombay on 24th May 1942. Their questions related to his "Quit India" demand and his concept of non violent non-cooperation. They asked: "To whom amongst the belligerent powers should India extend her sympathy and support?" Gandhiji replied that in the beginning, he had sympathised with the British, but his mind now told him that he should not extend to British even his moral support.

The Congress Working Committee met in Allahabad in May 1942. Gandhiji did not attend the meeting. He, however, sent with Miraben a draft of the "Quit India" resolution. Nehru was still in favour of supporting Britain and her allies in the war. He talked of raising guerrilla forces in India in support of the allies. At the meeting he naturally indulged in vague generalities. This made Lohia suspect that Nehru was trying to commit Congress to the support the British in the war.

At the meeting of the Uttar Pradesh Congress Committee, held on 20th & 21st July, a member sent a note to Nehru, who was in the chair, asking him whether Congressmen could take war contracts. Nehru said, in reply, that a friend from Delhi had declined to supply war materials to British and described this action as foolish. He stated that the British would not find it difficult to secure the necessary materials, even if Congressmen refused to accept contracts for their supply. Then why should Congressmen suffer a monetary loss by refusing such contracts, he asked. This reply from Nehru stunned the gathering. Lohia told Nehru that he was asking the people to be dishonest. Nehru then advised his secretary to seek Gandhiji's advice on the subject.

At the Almora district political conference, held subsequently, in the course of his presidential address, Lohia called Nehru a "quick-change artist", and warned him that if he did not mend his ways, the people, particularly the youth, would listen to just one man, though he himself had been till then listening to two-Gandhiji and Nehru.

Lohia was emphatic that the Congress should launch Satyagraha immediately. He met Gandhiji at Wardha and assured that his party would participate in such campaign whole-heartedly.

The two discussed the political situation. In a war, it is possible for a country to demand that a certain city or a group of cities be recognized as open even by the enemy. When a city is declared open, the country is not able to garrison that city or use it as a theatre for the production of weapons. Also, the enemy will not destroy that city or bomb it. He suggested to Gandhiji that he might ask British government to declare all cities of India as open. To commend the suggestion to Gandhiji, he tried all the knowledge of the history and geography at his command. He even cited *Ashwatthama* and *Kurukshetra* in support of his plea. He said that even in ancient times, warring armies used to leave out big cities. Gandhiji finally said: "There seems to be some kink in your argument".

Lohia was not aware of the "kink", except his desire that India should have a full final combat with the British Empire. That was the idea at the back of his mind. In fact, the suggestion was but a partial manifestation of that desire. The Mahatma had discerned it. He said: "I can see what you are driving at. You want to fight the British, don't you?" Lohia replied: "That is what I want". Then Gandhiji said: "Why don't you say so? All right, let us go ahead with it. But then, we can't just have a fight by asking for it. Let us see what things happen".

Lohia had a three day debate with Gandhiji on the subject. On the third day, Gandhiji called Lohia to him and said: "You may laugh at my inner voice". The call had come. He said he had been pondering over the idea and the previous night he woke up at two in the morning and wrote out a letter to the Viceroy. He showed him the letter. The letter was clear. In the letter, he called Lohia a socialist with a pronounced leaning towards non-violence and had then gone on to say that he had approached Gandhiji to get Indian cities declared open. Lohia told Gandhiji that the letter was perfectly all right; but asked him whether, in some slight way, he could indicate that he also approved the idea. Gandhiji said he could not. Lohia said: "Why should the Viceroy react to my idea?" But if Gandhiji accepted it even partially, the Viceroy would think twice before replying to it. Gandhiji said, and rightly so, that he was wrong. The mere fact that Gandhiji wrote the letter embodying the idea would indicate to Lord Linlithgow that the reply had to be given after serious consideration. This reply satisfied Lohia. But another person present there said: "Look, Bapu, you are only handing him over to the British police by writing the letter". And that was the end of it. The letter was not sent because that was the conclusive argument with Gandhiji. Lohia tried his very best to tell him he need not fear on that score; that the British would arrest him anyway; and whether he got arrested now, as a consequence of that letter, or two or three months afterwards, would not really matter. But no argument could persuade Gandhiji and he did not send that letter.

During that period, Lohia also wanted Gandhiji to approach the Governments of different countries with the scheme of setting up the foundations on which the new world could be built. The four bases Lohia had outlined were: (1) cancellation of all the past investments by one country in another; (2) unobstructed passage and the right of the settlement to everybody all over the world; (3) political freedom of all peoples and nations of the world and constituent assemblies and (4) some kind of world citizenship.

Gandhiji did not write such a letter probably because he felt that it would be an unpractical step. But he did endorse the suggestion in the *"Harijan"* and endorsed it completely after reproducing the scheme in full. This was followed by publication of articles advocating a policy of neutrality towards the war. When the two met again on 29th July, Gandhiji remarked to Lohia: "Wait for ten days".

The much-awaited day dawned on 8th August 1942. On that historic day, the AICC met at the Gowalia Tank Maidan in Bombay, just a few yards' distance from the hall where the Indian National Congress was born in 1885, to plan the final combat with British imperialism. Gandhiji called upon the British to "Quit India" and his writings in the *"Harijan"* in the preceding weeks had thrilled the people. An unprecedented wave of enthusiasm swept the country from end to end and the people appeared poised to strike the final blow against the imperialist power that had held the nation in its thralldom, They were only awaiting the signal from the Mahatma. The mounting tension reached its climax when the "Quit India" resolution was placed before the meeting.

Speaking on the resolution, Lohia said that India's attitude towards Britain had undergone a revolutionary change during the last few weeks. The course of events showed that the British power was not that invincible which it was hitherto supposed to be. Consequently, subject people had shed their fear of Britain.

Discontent against the way Britain was handling the Indian problem was growing daily. Lashing out at the communists, Dr. Lohia asked "How come, these people, who had been demanding immediate revolution earlier, are now opposing the proposed struggle?"

The adoption of the resolution by the AICC marked the beginning of a new phase in India's political history as also in the life of Rammanohar Lohia.

7. THE 1942 UPRISING

The British government was already poised, with all its might, to crush the national movement It was only waiting for the AICC formally to pass the "Quit India" resolution. The resolution was passed late in the evening on 8th August and Gandhiji and other Congress leaders were arrested in the early morning of 9th August In a simultaneous swoop, thousands of men and women, who had taken prominent part in the national, trade union and peasant movements, were rounded up all over the country.

The people accepted the challenge thrown by the arrogant British imperialists. They rose spontaneously against the alien Government, inspired by Gandhiji's stirring call to "Do or Die". Smarting under the humiliation and defeat suffered by them in the different theatres of war, the imperialists launched a ferocious attack on the unarmed freedom fighters, as if to avenge the ignominy of their reverses in the war. The British police and army unleashed a reign of terror in the country. No amount of bullets, lathi blows and other atrocities perpetrated by the police and the army could, however, deter the people. They resisted the attack in any and every manner they could. Innumerable men and women, boys and girls wrote in their own blood, a glorious saga of bravery and courage.

For over two decades, the people had learnt, under Gandhiji's leadership, to resist peacefully all injustice and oppression, unmindful of the sufferings and sacrifices such resistance entailed. With their leaders, and small, whisked away to prisons, they were anxious for guidance and needed a radical and effective plan of action to force the British to quit India. They were not interested in the hair-splitting discussions on the ethics of violence and non-violence.

Lohia, with his socialist party colleagues, stepped into the breach and kept the flag of revolution flying. This was the moment Lohia was long awaiting. With all his ability and resourcefulness, he set about the task of channelising the people's wrath against the British for an organised uprising.

Jayprakash Narayan, Lohia, Achyntrao Patwardhan and Aruna Asaf Ali constituted the "underground" centre that organised and guided long "Quit India" movement. They set up a network, manned by patriots eager to sacrifice their all at the altar of freedom, and drew up a comprehensive programme which provided an opportunity to the people from all walks of life to contribute their mite to the struggle.

There was a tacit allocation of work among the socialist leaders. Achyutrao Patwardhan undertook the task of setting up the necessary organisation, Aruna Asaf Ali became the source of inspiration to the freedom fighters, while Lohia strengthened their morale and steeled their determination to continue the fight, undaunted by odds, howsoever heavy, through his underground radio speeches & articles in bulletins.

Through a series of booklets and bulletins, Lohia provided content and direction to the popular uprising which convulsed the country. The programme aimed at paralysing the administration through destruction of communications, seizure or destruction of administrative offices and other centres of alien power, and blowing up of trains laden with arms and ammunition. Lohia and Patwardhan repeatedly emphasised the need of scrupulously avoiding loss of life, while carrying out the programme.

In conducting the underground resistance movement, Lohia did not think in terms only of India's liberation. He approached the task with a broader perspective. He had the dream that free India emerging from the fire of revolution, should serve as a beacon light for the entire world. In all the booklets and bulletins, Lohia emphasised this aspect of the struggle. "Though an enslaved country" he said, "India has been the subject of world history during the last 150 years. Free India must not remain merely a subject of world history; it must become its creator".

Lohia led the underground movement from 9th August 1942 to 20th May 1944, successfully eluding the police intelligence (CID) of the British Government. The story of his life and activities during the underground period is an inspiring one. It can be the subject matter of a separate book. Besides, details about many of the events are still unknown. Some underground radio stations were being run independently by groups of freedom fighters. Lohia established contacts with them and co-ordinated their functioning. The underground Congress Radio spread the gospel of revolution in the country for 94 days from 13th August to 14th November, 1942. Most of the speeches broadcast over the radio were Lohia's. Through his broadcasts, he launched a blistering attack on the British for their obstinacy in hanging on to the Empire and for their reign of terror in India. The speeches cast a spell on the people, including students, industrial workers and even the police and the other Government employees. Through these broadcasts he also tried to arose the sympathy of other countries for the cause of India's freedom. When the police ultimately raided the building where the radio station was housed, Lohia managed to escape with a few friends. Those who could not do so, were arrested. The police subjected them to third degree method in a bid to extract from them information regarding Lohia's whereabouts. Their association with Lohia and the inspiration they had drawn from him had made them strong in spirit and the police could not succeed in extracting any information whatsoever from them.

One day, when Lohia, Aruna Asaf Ali and Achyutrao Patwardhan were engaged in a discussion in a flat on the top floor of a building, they saw the police suddenly crowding the balcony. Out of curiosity; Lohia came out, only to find that the police were raiding the flat on the ground floor of the building. Luckily the police intelligence made a search of that flat only, seized a cyclostyle machine and went away. Had they come to the top floor, they would have been able to arrest the triumvirate in one swoop. The topic of their discussion, incidently, was how to escape arrest if the police raided the building, where they lived incognito.

Lohia conducted his invigorating propaganda over the Congress Radio from Calcutta too. This helped to intensify the struggle in that city.

It was during the underground period that a high ranking officer of the Indian Air Force, Mazumdar, better known in army circle as Jumbo, met Lohia and his colleagues at a secret place. He told them that the Air Force personnel should have risen in support of the revolution on 9th August, but some how, that had not happened. He, however, assured them that if there was a fresh uprising, the men of the Air Force would cooperate with the revolutionaries.

But that was of no use any longer. There were unmistakable signs that the uprising had begun to fizzle out. The leaders decided to make a fresh attempt to rouse the people. But most of the other prominent leaders had been traced and rounded up. Indian communists played a treacherous role. For the convenience of their foreign master, they had converted overnight the "imperialist war" into a "people's war", and went to the extent of supplying to the police secret information about the places where the leaders of the movement had been staying incognito. This perverse behaviour of the communists appalled Lohia. That impelled him to reassess the doctrine of Marxism in order to recover its truth and demolish its untruth. The result of this inquiry was the thesis he wrote, while underground, on all the four aspects of the doctrine—economics, politics, history and philosophy. However Lohia could write only on economic aspect, before he was arrested. The thesis was subsequently published under the title, "Economics After Marx".

Lohia used to move about, most of the time, immaculately dressed in the western style. When he was living with a family in Calcutta, a neighbour began to pester the hostess with inquiries about the stranger. She told them that he was the brother of her mother-in-law, who had lost all his money in speculation. "The poor fellow remains indoor for all the time to avoid meeting acquaintances", she used to add and somehow silence them. The 'underground publication, *'Do or Die'*, was also started at his instance during the period. In his writing, he outlined the socio-economic structure free India should have. Centralised economy had made man a slave of the machine. He, therefore, said that it would be wrong to view the spinning wheel, the Charakha as crude vestige of the medieval age. It could be converted into the symbol of the future economy by improving upon it. A power operated spinning wheel could help end centralisation of the economy eliminating textile mills which had made man their slave.

A camp was being run in Nepal at that time to train underground workers in the use of firearms. Once Lohia went to Nepal to visit the camp. Jayprakash Narayan was already there. The Government of Nepal arrested Lohia, Jayprakash Narayan and three others under instructions from the British. A contingent of the British army, despatched for bringing these political prisoners to India, was on its way to Nepal. The news provoked the members of the "Azad Dasta"—freedom fighters trained in guerilla warfare at the camp. They planned to arrange for the escape of their leaders from government custody. The Nepal government had lodged them at Hanuman Nagar in a hilly area, 70 miles from the camp. The guerilla group reached the place at night. The members of the group fired in the air and set fire to the nearby huts. The sentries, taken unaware, began to look in all directions to find out what the matter was, The guerillas opened fire again. As they had already cut the telephone wires, it was not possible for the sentries to contact Kathmandu. The guerillas were small in number, but the police lost their nerve and became terror-stricken, as the attack was unexpected and sudden. To add to their confusion, the guerillas killed the lights. Lohia and Jayprakash were asleep. Lohia's sleep was so sound, not unusual in his case, that all these noises and trouble did not disturb him. However, the noise woke up Jaiprakash, who slipped out from the place, availing of the confusion, forgetting to wake up Lohia. Lohia woke up and began to search for his glasses when the guerillas entered the room. In the darkness, they wondered there was anybody at all in the room. Lohia's movements made them aware of that somebody was there. They thought that it was a policeman searching for his weapon. One of them, therefore, pointed the

barrel of his gun against Lohia's chest. Lohia immediately asked: "Who is there?" Recognising his voice, the guerilla dragged Lohia out of the room without allowing him to pick up his glasses or cigarette tin.

Lohia and Jayprakash were anxious about each other's safety till they met again 24 hours after their escape from the Nepal government's custody. Their dress and movements aroused suspicion among the people of the villages through which the party passed. Members of the group used to remove the suspicion by telling the people some cock and bull stories. When Lohia expressed his disapproval of their action in opening fire at Hanuman Nagar, members of the guerrilla replied they did so only to scare the police, Lohia ultimately reached Calcutta safely.

The British Government had announced a big prize for any one who could supply information leading to Lohia's arrest. It had made desperate efforts to trace him, but all of them ended in failure. However luck smiled on them in Bombay on 19th May 1944. That day, it appeared as if police had thrown a cordon round the entire city. They camped in the city for two days and raided eleven buildings. A secret service man at last got a clue on the second day, 19th May, and the police surrounded the building on Babulnath Road, where Lohia was staying. The people had crowded the balconies of the buildings in the neighbourhood to witness the police operation. Lohia was then holding a discussion with a group of friends in a flat on the third floor of the building. The police started searching each and every flat on all the floors of the building. Lohia remained calm and quiet, made no efforts to escape and was arrested. Later describing his state of mind when the police raided the building, he said: "I had turned to stone, This is probably the defense, that my peculiar system devised, against the interval between the beginning of a tense situation, and its eruption into the first cognisable act".

Thus ended Lohia's underground life. His arrest also marked the beginning of a phase of his life which was full of inhuman suffering and torture. He was kept in a Bombay jail for one month and then transferred to the Lahore Fort. In addition to the old third degree methods, new ones were tried on the prisoners lodged in the Fort, to extract information from them. The Punjab government later disowned all responsibility of the tortures to which Lohia was subjected at the Lahore Fort, and said that the centre was responsible for them. The British Under-Secretary of State for India, in turn, passed the blame on to the Punjab government. The government of India was, in fact, responsible for the treatment meted out to Lohia and Punjab government had merely carried out the behest of the Centre. The British Under-Secretary, Arthur Henderson, dismissed the charges made by Lohia as baseless. But at the same time, the government suppressed the communication from Lohia in which he had described the tortures to which he had been subjected. The people never knew the charges Lohia had made in the matter.

Lohia was granted permission to file his *habeas corpus* petition in December, 1944. In January 1945, he filed an addendum to the petition. His petition was heard in camera and the government took good care that nothing appeared in newspaper about the hearing. The court asked Lohia some questions with a view to scrutinising the contents of his petition. However, the government got the hearing postponed, while Lohia's examination was in progress, on the plea that he was to be transferred to a prison in another province. Ultimately, in dismissing the petition, the court held that the government had not detained Lohia with the sole object of harassing him. He appealed against the decision to the Federal Court, but the appeal was dismissed.

When Lohia was brought to the Lahore Fort, he did not know for a few days where he was. "I do not quite recall", he said later, "the whole complex of emotions that went through me during the first days at the Lahore Fort. I did not know where I was, but knew perfectly well what was in store for me. I can, however remember a certain thread of curiosity that ran through; all the fear, helplessness, anger and despair that must have passed through me and also of a certain stodginess which sometimes comes over me in such situations". But Lohia was aware of the fact that one could not forever stay in such a stodgy situation, particularly in prison. Nor does a prisoner have as much opportunity to act as a free man does. He cannot read, write or engage in discussions. He is alone and feels that the world outside does not think anymore about him, or does it have any information about him.

The police who tortured Lohia were adept at the task. They knew that man cannot stand tension and torture for long. The process of torture was started gradually with a view to probing the weakness of his mind and peculiarities of his nature. At the beginning of the process, they started taking Lohia from his cell to the prison office at any time of day and night made him sit on a chair and went on repeating one and the same sentence continuously. They denied him sleep. He was not allowed to lie down in bed, and was also forced to sit in a chair. If ever he was found to close his eyes, they would pull the chair attached to the hand cuffs or hold and shake his head. "The periods of forced sleeplessness" he said, "grew three days and five in the second and the third month of my torture. By that time, I had lost the will for a physical fight, if ever I had any".

"I was mad only twice during those four months of torture" he said "once, when the policeman in charge started abusing national leaders and my friends filthily. That made my blood boil, but I kept quiet until he started playing with Gandhiji's name. I asked him to shut up with all the force could muster. That gesture was pretty useless inside the Fort, where I had no friend. I suppose that one does not reason out such matters and that an element of rare irrationally which helps a person to get out of his skin".

"The other occasion transpired on the fourth or the fifth day of the longest single stretch of my forced sleeplessness. It was around four in the morning. My head felt as though it was smouldering in a burnt up fire of hot ashes. The policeman would beat the table with some metal object and make sudden or continuous loud sounds. Each one of these sounds went to the heart; some times like a hammer stroke and sometimes like the small point of a knife. I closed my eyes. The policeman fumed and shouted. I still kept my eyes closed. He sprang up from his chair and made as though he would assault me. The officer was at that time alone with me; he had sent away the other constable. I asked him simply not to engage in a physical fight, for that would not be good for him".

"Normally, there would be a team of several policemen, more often only two to keep watch over me. They would change their duty as though in a shift. Every four hours or so, the policemen would change, for they had to replenish their tired body and mind".

"The officer shrank back. He shouted for help with a shriek of a maniac. Four or five policemen came running to the room as also the armed sentry, who always stood in front of my cell or the office room. They lifted me up from the chair and stood me up against the wall. The officer tried again to come near me in a posture of assault. I told him he was 'the Coward of the Fort'. I learnt later from some policemen that this phrase rang throughout the Fort, for this officer was harsh also to his men. I closed my eyes again. The officer had dragged me in circles on the rough matting on the floor. This must have gone on for over an hour. My palms and elbows were slightly bruised. But no other forms of assault took place. I was then led to a bath, after which the torture continued".

"My police officers" Lohia went on, "particularly the highest of them, knew how to intersperse my ugly despair with flattery and cagelings. Some of them even touched my feet or bowed in reverence. It was a most peculiar experience to be so cruelty treated on some days and on others the seeming worship. This sometimes brought me near to relenting. But on such occasions, I had a dreaded picture before me. It was as though I had been imperceptibly and in stages brought near to drinking gutter water. I told them that I would not refuse to tell them of my own acts, but that they could not expect me to give them incriminating information about others".

"The chief officer who had been put on to me had also been put on to Bhagat Singh, who had avenged with violence many a wrong done to India and was later hanged by the British. Bhagat Singh, so this officer said, had spoken. I asked him as to how old Bhagat Singh was at that time. He was a younger man. What may be forgiven or atleast understood in case of a younger man is more difficult to forgive or understand in an older man". The longest stretch of forced sleeplessness lasted ten days and nights. At the end of it, blood came out of Lohia's nose. He seemed to have acquired a fairly high fever. During this period, he was not supplied with tooth paste, brush or powder to clean his teeth. This torture made Lohia's teeth unhealthy and his heart weak permanently. Talking about the thoughts which came to his mind while he underwent the tortures, Lohia said that every-Indian had heard of Yoga and its variant, Hatha Yoga. As a child he had heard his father recite the first two Sanskrit Mantras of Patanjali's Yoga Sutra: *'Yoga is the control of the will.'* "I some times thought", he stated, "that I was practicing Hatha Yoga under compulsion", and added; "no pain is unbearable. Man is frightened by the idea of pain in future, and not by the actual pain".

From prison Lohia wrote a letter to Prof. Harold Laski, who was then the chairman of the central executive of the British Labour Party, in which he graphically described the reign of terror unleashed by the British in India, and the bloodshed, the torture to which the political prisoners were subjected in the Lahore Fort and the Bengal famine.

He told Mr. Laski: "By its plea that everybody still in prison is a socialist and an advocate of violence, the socialists are deliberately enabling the British fascist in this country to work out their lawless ire against the Indian socialist. The British fascist government in India is torturing socialists why does not a single member of your labour party in the parliament this, question or expose the lie?"

Lohia added: "I have little desire for release. The British government is welcome to keep me in prison as long as it lasts in this country. But the fact remains that there was not one man in your parliamentary party who could tell the Under Secretary with facts that he was lying, that he had not so far, nor shall he ever, put me up of trial. Lohia wrote to the Viceroy, Lord Linglithgow, and Mr. Hallet also. He had applied to the federal court seeking his transfer to Agra jail from the Lahore Fort. He was ultimately transferred to the Agra Prison towards the end of 1944.

Underground life and activities did not suit the very nature of Lohia. He had been an ardent believer in the Gandhian concept of loud thinking and functioning in the open. Underground work necessitated maintenance of secrecy about one's movements and activities. At times, departure from truth became unavoidable, strict adherence to non-violence also became possible under certain circumstances. All this must have imposed a severe strain on Lohia, besides the physical hardships he had to undergo during the period.

8. WOUND OF PARTITION

The war ended, inflicting untold suffering on both the victorious and the vanquished alike. Cities and towns were destroyed and countries devastated. It virtually resulted in uprooting humanity. Britain no longer remained a first rate power as it was before.

Mahatma Gandhi was released in May 1944, while members of the Congress Working Committee were released in January 1945. By the end of the year, all political prisoners, except those charged with the offences like dacoity and murder, were set free. Of the national leaders, only Jayprakash Narayan and Lohia remained in prison.

Meanwhile, in the elections held in the U.K. after the end of the war, the British Labour Party was returned to power. In March, the Labour Government ministers, Lord Patrick Lawrence, Sir Stafford Cripps and Mr. Alexander, came to India to hold negotiations with Indian leaders to find a solution to the problem of India's freedom. On their arrival in India, the members of the Cabinet mission started their rounds of discussions with the leaders of different political parties and groups. They first held a discussion with Jayprakash Narayan and Lohia in the Agra jail itself. The two leaders were released in the evening of 11th April 1946, in Agra. The news of their impending release had spread in the town earlier and huge crowd had gathered in front of the jail to receive the leaders. Jayprakash Narayan and Lohia shook hands with the jail authorities before taking their leave. As the two emerged from the prison gate, slogans shouted by the people rent the air. Jayprakash was profusely garlanded. Lohia declined to accept the garlands. Both of them thanked the people for the reception, but said that they could not comment on the political situation in the country until they had met the leaders and acquainted themselves with the developments.

Lohia went to Calcutta immediately after his release. Hiralalji had died while Lohia was in the Agra jail. He had told Lohia when he came to see him in the prison earlier; "I do not think I shall be able to see you again". He died of heart failure in the bus, while he was on his way to the venue of a meeting in Calcutta. It had been suggested to Lohia that he should secure parole in order to be able to perform the funeral rites. But Lohia had declined to do so. Hiralalji was a staunch Congressman. He had given up his business to be able to devote all his time to Congress activities. He was very generous and genial person. Everybody coming in contact with him loved and respected him. He had earned the regard and respect of his 400 co-prisoners in the Calcutta residency jail because of his genial nature. He had deep faith in Bhagwad Geeta. Calcutta, particularly, Bada Bazar, was the field of his activities. He was interested in constructive activities and always refused to accept any office in the Congress organisation. He had set up a Charkha Samiti. He used to call the Charka "The Swadesh Gun".

Besides Congress work, he used to take active interest in other activities too and was associated with the number of the organizations including the Hindi Natya Parishad. He was very outspoken and courageous. He always used to be in the vanguard of a procession, marching with a tricolour and would never relax his grip on the flag staff, despite any amount of lathi blows received from the police. Hiralalji courted imprisonment during the civil disobedience movement in 1930-32 and 1940-41. He undertook the *'Pada Yatra'* (march on foot) from Calcutta to Delhi, unmindful of the scorching summer heat, in response to the call of *"Chalo Delhi"* during the initial Satyagraha campaign in 1941. He had also participated in the underground movement in 1942. If any socialist youth tried to argue with him, he would tell him; "If you are socialist, I am the father of a socialist". His entire life was an example of Karma Yoga and Anasakti Yoga. He was a great lover of books, particularly books on religious subjects, and had a collection of more than 600 books. A library, Hiralal Lohia Pustakalaya, was opened subsequently at Kashipur, at the hands of Aruna Asaf Ali, to perpetuate his memory. The Lohia Sevagram was started at Dacca in 1949 as a memorial to him. A school, a hospital and a gymnasium are still being run at the place.

Hiralalji's ardent desire was to spend the evening of his life at the holy place of Vindhyachal. After Rammanohar returned to India from Berlin after obtaining his doctorate, it was naturally Hiralalji's hope that his son should marry and settle down. But when Rammanohar told him of his decision to enter politics, he did not oppose. On the contrary, he tried to help his son in all possible ways. A mammoth crowd had gathered at Calcutta station to receive Lohia, orphaned by the death of such a loving father. As soon as the train steamed into the station, the gathering observed silence for two minutes as a mark of respect to Hiralalji's memory.

A few days after his release, the Congress Working Committee met in Delhi. Mrs. Asaf Ali, Achyutrao Patwardhan, Lohia and Jayprakash Narayan also gathered in Delhi to discuss the proposals brought by the British Cabinet Mission; "To help India to obtain her freedom as speedily and fully as possible". However, these proposals envisaged dividing the provinces in three groups, while conceding the demand for a constituent assembly to draw up free India's constitution. This served as an instrument for Jinnah and the Muslim League to obstruct the country's progress towards freedom.

Lohia was opposed to the proposals. Addressing the meeting of the college students in Calcutta on April 24, he said that the Cabinet mission had come to India because the British had ample evidence of the Indian people's indomitable urge for immediate freedom and strength. Lohia called upon the people not to bother very much about the success or failure of the Cabinet mission's talks; but consider the steps they should take in the event of the failure of the talks & develop such strength that they could carry on the freedom struggle as long as necessary. In this meeting he refused to speak in English. He also asked the students to boycott the English language and exhorted them to ask their teachers to teach them in their own language,

Lohia attended the meeting of the AICC which was held in Bombay in 1946. Nehru who was then the Congress president, invited Lohia and Jayprakash to meet him. Till then, whenever the socialist leaders had anything to discuss with Nehru, four of them Lohia, Jayprakash Narayan, Achyutrao Patwardhan and Aruna Asaf Ali, used to meet him together, so he did not feel it proper that only two of them should see Nehru this time:

At the meeting, Nehru urged that Lohia to become Congress

General Secretary. But the name of Jayprakash was being mentioned in this connection. This embarrassed both Nehru and Jaiprakash, Nehru told Lohia that he and other Congress leaders earnestly desired that he should become the General Secretary of the organisation. Lohia replied that he would accept the post on three conditions. They were; (1) No member of the Congress Working Committee should become a government minister, (2) some formula permitting benevolent criticism by the Congress party of its own Government should be evolved, and (3) the Congress President should keep out of the government.

Nehru and Lohia had three sessions, all the past midnight and one reaching upto three in the morning. While explaining his position in the matter, Lohia criticized Nehru's belief that he was indispensible, and said that he should choose between the offices of the Prime Minister and the Congress President. Lohia laid down the conditions because the air was then thick with rumours about the impending Congress—British agreement. The object was to reform the Congress organisation and improve the functioning of the Congress governments. However Nehru was not prepared to impose any restriction on his personal ambitions. The talks were ultimately wound up by Nehru with the remark: "These are all meaningless things". Thus, the first attempt made by Lohia, while Gandhiji was alive, to curb Congressmen's lust for power ended in failure.

By this time, serious change had taken place in Nehru's outlook. He had begun to loose faith in the people, in his colleagues and in the Congress, The Tribunal for internal election had stated that Congressmen violated every single section of the Indian Penal Code in their fight with each other. Referring to this, Nehru told to him how he had tried, after his release from detention, to reorganise the Congress Committee at Allahabad and within a bare three months the closest of his friends amongst city Congressmen stopped meeting him. Pessimism had gripped Nehru's mind and he had begun to feel that the only way to do good to the country was to obtain control over the administrative machinery.

The ban on the Congress Socialist Party was lifted in 1946. A salutary effect of the "The Quit India" movement was that it made the leadership of the party more united and homogeneous and earned prestige for the party in the country's political life. However, it has also made party workers complacement. Speaking at the meeting in Calcutta on the 9th August to observe the "Quit India" day, Lohia stressed the need to shed the feeling of complacency and strengthen the organisation. He said that the constituent assembly might prove to be another bluff of the British. "What is the way out if there is a deadlock in the Constituent Assembly?" he asked, and said; "freedom could be achieved only through mass action".

A three day convention of the Congress Socialist Party was held at Kanpur from 26th February 1947. Socialists from all over the country met there for the first time after an interval of 9 years. Presiding over the convention, Lohia said that he had no doubt that the British would quit India. But they would partition the country before doing so. People could maintain the unity of the country, only if they remain united. The pointed out that national unity did not mean merely territorial unity of the country. Real unity could be brought about by removing all distinctions of high and low, rich and poor, touchable and untouchable. The caste system was a great handicap in forging such unity and its total abolition was therefore, an urgent necessity. This could be achieved only through a complete change in the people's social and mental outlook, he pointed out. The conference decided to delete the word 'Congress' from its name. Explaining the decision, Lohia said that deleting the word did not mean that the bond between the Congress and the Socialist Party had been snapped. The bond had been only loosened. This enabled persons other than Congressmen also to join the Socialist party. "We wanted greater freedom in our functioning. It was also being contended that by using that particular word, we were utilizing the prestige of the Congress. We have every right to avail of it, but we have no desire to exploit it", he said.

Lohia added that the Congress organisation had become mere appendage of the Congress ministries. The main task before the party was to convert India's freedom into a people's Government, where no distinctions to class, creed, caste or colour would be allowed to exist. They would have to bring the industrial workers in the main stream of the national life, ridding them of all pro-British and pro-Russian influences. The slogan, "Workers of the world unite", was meaningless as long as there was disparity in the wages and production in different countries. The Indian communists did not know when the occasion to strike had come and were now indulging in destructive activities to regain their lost prestige, he remarked. He claimed that the party's policy outlined at the Faizpur convention was based on Marxist principles. The policy adopted at Kanpur reflected Lohia's thoughts which were free from any such dogma. He advocated the need of decentralized economy and stressed the necessary to work for social equality.

There were Hindu-Muslim riots in different parts of the country. The Muslim League boycotted the Constituent Assembly. Following this deadlock, the British Prime Minister, Mr. Attlee, announced in February 1947, that the British would withdraw from India in June 1947. He said that if there was nobody to whom power could be transferred at the Centre, they would hand it over to the different provincial governments and quit. Formation of Pakistan was implicit in that declaration. Lord Wavell was recalled to Britain, and was replaced by Lord Mountbatten as Viceroy. As soon as he arrived India, the new Viceroy started negotiations with the Congress Working Committee. During the talks, Congress leaders virtually accepted the Mountbatten plan including the proposal for the partition of India. There were indications earlier that Congress leaders were becoming progressively inclined towards accepting the proposal of partition of the country.

When Nehru visited Noakhali towards the end of 1946, he spoke, in the course of a conversation with Lohia, of the water, slime, bush, and tree that he found everywhere in East Bengal. He said that was not the India he or Lohia knew and wanted. Lohia felt Nehru was prepared to cut East Bengal away from the mainland of India. It was obvious that he had set his heart on the partition of India and was trying to discover reasons of geography in support of the proposal. Gandhiji had been so much opposed to the partition of the country that he had declared that it would be affected only over his dead body. But Congress leaders had already committed themselves on the issue.

It was against this background that the Congress Working Committee met in Delhi in June 1947. Prior to the meeting, Gandhiji had several talks with the socialists in the Congress, jointly and separately, on the subject, presumably to sound their reactions. He was trying to find out whether they could be sufficiently strong agency on which he could rely in order to combat both the British authority and his own Working Committee. He came to the conclusion that the leading elements of the Congress Working Committee had accepted the Mountbatten proposals and he was perhaps sensing and groping for other centres of strength in the country which could enable him to fight the partition proposals inspite of the desire of the Working Committee to accept them. But the socialists were a weak group in this respect. Gandhiji made his last attempt to oppose the partition at the meeting of the Working Committee. The meeting turned out to be very strange affair. Jayprakash and Lohia were invited to attend the meeting. Barring those two and Mahatma Gandhi and Khan Abdul Gaffar Khan, no one spoke a single word in opposition to the partition proposal.

Throughout the two days of the meeting Maulana Azad sat in a chair in a corner of the room, puffing away his endless cigarettes, and spoke not a word. Acharya Kripalani, the Congress President, was a pathic figure at the meeting. He sat drowsily and reclined. At some point in the debate, Gandhiji referred to the exhausted Congress President, and Lohia shook his arms in deep annoyance. Kripalini volunteered the information that he was suffering from a bad headache. Khan Abdul Gaffar Khan spoke a bare two sentences. He expressed his sorrow over the fact that his colleagues had accepted the scheme of partition. As a small mercy, he wanted them to find out if the proposed plebiscite in the North-west Frontier could include the alternative of independence along side the other two choices; accession to India or Pakistan. Jayprakash Narayan vehemently spoke against partition in a single stretch and was silent during rest of the meeting. Lohia opposition to the scheme was persistent, and vocal throughout.

As there was a great deal of temper at the meeting, Nehru and Sardar Patel were offensively aggressive to Gandhiji. Gandhiji turned to the two in mild complaint that they had not informed him of the scheme of partition before committing themselves to it. Before Gandhiji could make out his point fully, Nehru intervened with some passion to say that he had kept him fully informed. On Gandhiji's repeating that he did not know of the scheme of partition earlier. Nehru slightly altered his earlier observation. He said that Noakhali was so far away that, while he might not have described the details of the scheme, he had written broadly about partition to Gandhiji. It was clear that all that Nehru had done as writing to Gandhiji doling out hypothetical and insubstantial information.

That was definitely the hole and corner aspect of the business. Patel and Nehru had obviously decided between themselves that it would be best not to scare the Mahatma away before the deed was done.

Lohia had a sharp exchange with Nehru and Patel. The Sardar asked Lohia to forget all the talk about what would happen to India after the partition. He would talk to Jinnah in the language of *danda* (lathi). Lohia retorted that he had been listening to the Sardar's language of sword for years; now he would in future have to listen to the language of a danda. Sardar Patel then said: "We have fought for the freedom of India for your sake. After all, we want to leave a free India to you in order that you may be able to make something out of it". Lohia replied: "Thank you very much, but I say that if you have fought for the freedom of India as generals, so have we as soldiers".

In connection with the resolution on the Mountbatten proposals, it was suggested that negative mention might be made in it of the two nation theory. In the original draft Nehru drew out of his pocket, there was no mention of it. The two nation theory was just accepted by implication. That the picture of India that they had cherished in the past would ever remain in their dream was an idea that did not appear in the draft, it was added later. It was on Lohia's suggestion, backed up by Gandhiji, that the sentence was finally introduced. But when he made the suggestion and Gandhiji backed it up, Nehru said in anger that they were obsessed by the views of Jinnah and were arguing with him all the time. "What is the cause of calling the people who are flaying at each other's throat brothers?" he asked. Lohia replied that the Americans had their civil war; they killed 300 to 400 thousand persons, or may be more, on both sides; they did not cease to be brothers. Hindus and Muslims might have been, out of bestiality killing each other, but they did not, therefore, cease to be brothers. Gandhiji listened to all the conversation with interest. Sometimes, he backed certain suggestions, and sometimes smiled with approval. His heart was wholly against partition. Then came a great suggestion from Gandhiji. He said, "Now that you had committed yourself to it; you have accepted partition. I do not want you to go back on your word. But will you consider the suggestion I make? Write to the British Viceroy that this principle of partition has been accepted by the Congress Working Committee, but for working out this principle, there shall be no British authority and representatives of the Congress and those of the Muslim League would sit down in order to work out the principle and concrete details".

The suggestion was a grand tactical stroke. If it had been accepted, it would have saved the face of those who had already committed themselves to the principle of partition and would have meant completely a turn in the destiny of the country. Lohia did not know whether Gandhiji was a politician wanting to be a saint or a saint wanting to be a politician! The only response the Working Committee gave to this suggestion was silence. Dr. Khan Saheb, elder brother of Khan Abdul Gaffar Khan, was the only one to shout down the proposal as utterly impractical. He said with obvious impatience, "This will mean that we reject the scheme. The Muslim League will not agree to sit with the Congress to work out its details, if the British authority is not there". The Working Committee did not even discuss the proposal.

The amendment, suggested by Lohia to the resolution, said: "Geography and the mountains and the seas fashioned India as she is and no human agency can change that shape or come in the way of her final destiny. The picture of India we have learnt to cherish will remain in our minds and hearts and the false doctrine of two nations in India will be discredited and discarded by all". The resolution, as amended, was passed by the Working Committee.

The meeting of the national executive of the CSP, held in Delhi on the eve of the AICC meeting, to consider the Mountbatten scheme, decided that the members of the party should neither oppose the Working Committee's resolution nor make any amendments to it. The AICC meeting was held in Delhi on June, 14. Lohia explained the party's decision in the AICC meeting. Certain people ridiculed the stand taken by the party on the issue. The decision also incurred the displeasure of Nehru and Patel. They scoffed at it and asked", What sort of decision is that?" In a statement, Lohia said that he could understand if people indulging in sectarian politics decried the party's decision. But Nehru's criticism was not in consonance with the spirit of democracy. He said that the party did not want to meet, at the moment, any challenges except those posed by poverty and disruptive forces. There were a large number of people in all parties trying to meet unreal challenges. The socialist party would work for a strong progressive State and for the establishment of the Panchayati Raj.

However, the policy of the SP on the issue flowed from its feelings of helplessness. They could hope to oppose the partition only by relying on Gandhiji. But he too could not do anything about it, and the partition had become an accomplished fact. Ten years later, Lohia remarked: "I was a man of no consequence. So were millions of others like me. We could not have changed the course of history in an immediate sense, but we might have atleast registered our protest against it. It is a matter of great sorrow to me, today, that I did not protest and get thrown in jail, when this great land of ours was partitioned. It was really a decisive moment in the history of our country, as well as my life".

The position of the SP had become difficult and embarrasing. The reactionary and irresponsible regime of the Congress government added insult to the injury inflicted on the nation by the partition. The people took the socialists to be Congressmen, while the Congress government did not consider them to be the Congressmen but regarded them as socialists. The step-motherly treatment meted out to socialists by the Congress governments provoked Lohia to say: "We have been only endeavouring to reform and strengthen the Congress, but Congressmen do not want our services any more". The Socialist Party would have to take a decision in favour of breaking away from it and work as a party in opposition to the Government. Lohia did not favour leaving the Congress. He was confident that as long as Gandhiji was there, he would not allow the organisation lose its revolutionary character. He would ensure that justice was done to the socialists inside the Congress and would pursue the party's programme to fight injustice, inequality and exploitation. Besides, the climate created in the country by Hindu-Muslim riots also compelled the socialists to remain in the Congress at least for some duration.

Ram Naresh Vidyarthi had died a martyr in the "Quit India" struggle with five of his colleagues, at Chowlpur near Varanasi. When Lohia went to Chowlpur to lay the foundation of the memorial of them, he got involved in another affair. Some workers from Nepal saw him and acquainted him with their problem. They urged him to do something in the matter. Lohia advised them to see Nehru, who was the national leader, and Jayprakash Narayan as his home province of Bihar was immediate neighbour of Nepal. Lohia told them that they should see him only if they failed to receive from these two leaders guidance or help in the matter. The Nepali leaders followed the advice, met the leaders, but B.P. Koirala received no encouragement from the two. The Nepali leaders met Lohia again. "Do something first, and then I shall come", Lohia told them.

The meeting of the Nepalis was held at Calcutta in January 1947. Lohia advised them to establish an organisation to conduct their struggle. A decision was taken at the meeting to hold the conference to found the Nepal National Congress near Calcutta on 25th January. As the Bengal government promulgated a ban under section 144, the conference was converted into a meeting. Lohia, who was then at Belgaum, left for Calcutta to attend the meeting, but reached late. Representatives of the Nepal Congress met Lohia on 26th January and discussed the plans for the movement to be launched. In a statement, Lohia said: "Nepal is another secure island of British Imperialism where soldiers in lakhs have been traditionally recruited to put down their own brothers in Hindustan and to do other acts of service to the Empire"

Lifting the dark curtain that hung over Nepal, he said that the Nepal government did all that it could, to keep the people of that country in utter ignorance about the world outside. The British decided the Nepal's foreign policy. The Nepal National Congress must fight this. They must break down the barriers between the different sections of Nepalis, like Gurkhas, Nawars and Medites. The people of the country must obtain freedom of thought and speech. The people and the government of India must persuade the government of Nepal to set free the freedom fighters who had been rotting in jail for over seven years, he added.

The Nepal Congress had already launched its struggle in April 1947. Addressing the meeting of the organisation on 16th July, Lohia encouraged them to continue their fight. Criticising the "constitutional reforms" offered to the people by the Maharaja of Nepal, Lohia said that a mere change of personnel did not constitute a representative government. Lohia was scheduled to address a meeting on 25th April at Sukia Pokri near Darjeeling under the auspices of the Nepal Congress. As he was proceeding to this place in a car, the District Superintendent of Police stopped the car and served Lohia with an order prohibiting him from addressing the meeting. As he announced his decision to defy the order he was arrested. On his being let off after a couple of hours,

Lohia again proceeded towards Sukia Pokri and was arrested again, and again released after some time. In the end, Lohia could not go to Sukia Pokri.

9. LION OF AGUAD

Dr. Rammanohar Lohia went to Assolna in Goa in June 1946, to stay with his friend Dr. Menezes for some rest. He had heard from Dr. Menezes earlier, in 1935, the conditions in that Portuguese colony. Native Goans had no civil liberties whatsoever. They could not print hand bills or even wedding invitations, let alone publish newspapers or hold public meetings, without prior approval of the police. He had then remarked to Dr. Menezes: Goa is a part of India. We cannot allow Goa's movement for freedom and unity to be suppressed with such ferocity".

When Dr. Menezes had met Dr. Lohia in Bombay, while the socialist leader was spearheading the "Quit India" movement, he had expressed his desire to visit that part of India just to have a look at it. But Dr. Menezes was not prepared to run the risk of such a visit to Goa involved. During the war, Goa had been virtually turned into a British possession and the territory was replete with British secret agents. He had, therefore, persuaded Dr. Lohia to give up the idea.

This visit provided Dr. Lohia an opportunity to study the conditions in Goa, besides having a much needed rest. By then, Goans had heard about his leadership of the "Quit India" movement and his underground work and knew that he was a national hero. The news of his arrival in Goa spread, in no time, all over the territory and there was a stream of visitors for him. They were drawn from all walks of life—students, teachers, traders, government employees and even the police. After hearing from them about the conditions, he made up his mind to launch a direct action by defying the ban on civil liberties. He changed his headquarters and moved to Madgaon with Dr. Menezes on 15th

June. Some young men from Panaji met Lohia in Madgaon, and invited him to address a meeting organized by them at the capital. He accepted the invitation and went to Panaji. The meeting proved to be a great success. Lohia spoke for an hour. Informed of the goings on, the Governor was intrigued by the novelty of the spectacle of Goans holding a gathering without his prior approval and motored down to the meeting place thrice.

It was decided to launch a direct action on 18th June. Dr. Lohia and Dr. Menezes went to Madgaon the previous day. On their arrival there, a meeting of Goan activists was held to draw up the programme of the struggle. Some traders with vested interests tried to persuade the meeting to abandon the plan, while some wanted that direct action should be launched after six months so that the necessary preparations could be made before starting the movement. Purushottam Kakodkar replied that the meeting had been convened to finalise the details of the programme and not to consider whether or not the movement should be started. Lohia pointed out that before he arrived on the scene, Goans had so many years at their disposal to make whatever preparations they wanted to and declared: "We shall start the struggle now. Meantime, you may make your preparations and plunge into it after six months".

18th June became a red letter day in Goa's political history. The monsoon had burst over Goa and greenery had added to the scenic beauty of the territory. The season, which was generally the farmers sowing season, was also propitious to sow the seed of freedom struggle in the minds of the people. Goans groaning under the yoke of the ruthless totalitarian regime for well neigh four centuries, appeared to have become dull and docile. The Portuguese imperialism, with its medieval barbarism, was an anachronism in the twentieth century and provided a inhuman slavish influence on the population, which no outsider could imagine. The peace of the graveyard prevailed in the territory.

But the spark lit by Lohia revolutionised the scene overnight. The people of Goa rediscovered their self-respect and the fear that had gripped them for generations became a thing of past. They shed the servility which had almost become their second nature and stood erect, determined and defiant, to throw off the Fascist yoke. It convulsed Goa and the people began to trek to Madgaon in their thousands, from all over the territory, to participate in the public defiance of the Portuguese authority which had once struck terror in their heart. This sudden change in the people's psychology bewildered the rulers. Perplexed and puzzled, the popular uprising unnerved them.

As Lohia accompanied by Menezes reached the place of the meeting in a horse drawn carriage, Captain Miranda rushed to the vehicle and asked them not to alight from it, but to return to the hotel. Lohia pushed him aside, got down from the vehicle and proceeded to the maidan, where thousands had gathered to hear him. On seeing them approaching the maidan, three Goans came forth to garland him. The excited Captain took out his revolver and pointed it at the three persons. Holding the Captain's hand Lohia warned, "Don't be impatient. Don't you see the vast crowd? If you shed their blood, would there be peace?" and proceeded to the huge gathering. The dramatic incident thrilled the people who had gathered there. Never before had any one dared to challenge openly the authority of the mini dictators of Portugal. This, Satyagraha, an open resistance of tyranny and injustice, was the first ever in the whole history of the Portuguese rule in Goa. It left it's indelible impression on the people's mind and boosted their morale.

As soon as Lohia started to address the meeting, the Commissioner of Police arrested both Lohia and Menezes and whisked them away to the police station. No sooner had they been removed from the scene, than the copies of Lohia's speech were distributed among the people. He said in the speech that he had not come to Goa with any specific object in view. But the simple people of the territory had attracted him towards them. They were unhappy because they are denied even the elementary civil liberties, and were at a loss to know how to express their anger.

He said that he had no doubt that the Portuguese rule over the territory would end as soon as the British were forced to quit India. But the basic question in Goa was cultural in nature. The Portuguese had denationalised the people of Goa. They had made the territory a citadel of imperialism. To force the Portuguese to rescind the black laws, denying civil liberties, was the first step towards destroying that citadel of imperialism. Many Goans approached me and sought my help in the matter" he said and added, "I would not have kept quiet, even if none of them had seen me. Goa is an integral part of India. The people from all over India must help Goans in their struggle for freedom". Copies of the speech had been sent to the newspapers in India in advance. It was prominently featured by them all.

The news of Lohia's arrest spread in Goa far and a wide. The people out processions in the town, shouting slogans. Thousands of them went in a procession to the police station, braving a heavy downpour. A wanton lathi-charge made by the police proved of no avail. The people, who wanted a 'darshan' of their beloved leader, became menacing. Realizing the gravity of the situation, the police commandant urged Dr. Lohia to address the people and request them to return home. Lohia went out and addressed the crowd and the people dispersed. Lohia's satyagraha sparked off a conflagration in Goa. The people of the territory who appeared servile and spineless till then, woke up to rise and fight for their freedom with determination unmindful of the consequences. His arrest was followed by the spontaneous hartal all over the Goa, a demonstration unprecedented in Goa's history. No single shop was open—not even a tea shop. Processions and meetings became the order of the day. The Portuguese unleashed a reign of terror. But no amount of repression could deter the people. At Panaji, the people took out huge procession and staged a demonstration in front of the Governor's palace.

The place near the municipal building, where Lohia had addressed the meeting and was arrested, was named by the people as 'Lohia Maidan' and they began to hold meetings there everyday. A rumour spread that the people planned to storm the police station, where Lohia and Menezes had been lodged. The commandant was scared. He contacted Panaji for instructions. He was ordered to remove the two prisoners to Panaji. They were put into the motor van and taken to the capital. On the way to Panaji, the people shouted slogans on sighting the van. At Panaji, both leaders were lodged at a dusty hall with two unclad cots, covered with dirty linen. A guard was posted at the gate.

The next morning, on 19th June, a soldier came to them and showed them the way to wash. It was the washing place meant for the soldiers. Lohia refused to go there and asked for a better place. This was communicated by the soldier to the officer-in-charge. After consultations, they were allowed to use the place where officers attended to their toilet. The commandant told Lohia that the

Portuguese administration would be please to allow him to tour the territory, accompanied by the police officer. Lohia firmly turned down the offer.

The news that Lohia was being taken to the railway station of Colen at the Goa border, later the same day, spread in the capital. A huge crowd gathered at the station to give a hearty send-off to the leader. The police grew panicky and lathi-charged the crowd several times. A number of persons were arrested. The people of the Panaji observed a complete hartal in protest against the lathi-charge and arrests. Several processions including those of women and school children, were also taken out. A little girl in the women's procession, Shashi Bandodkar, was hit by the police on the face for having shouted, "Jai Hind", and began to bleed through the nose. Another girl. Ratan Kirtane, was also injured in the lathi-charge.

The tricolor was hoisted at the Lohia Maidan on 21st June. The police commandant announced that no prior permission from the police would be necessary any longer to hold public meetings. It would be enough if the organisers of such meetings gave prior information about their programme to the police station concerned. Kakodkar warned the people in the statement that this should not make them complacent and exhorted them to be prepared for sustained struggle.

Gandhiji alone whole-heatedly endorsed Lohia's action. Writing in the *"Harijan"*, on June 26, the Mahatma said: "It would appear from : newspapers that Dr. Lohia went to Goa at the invitation of Goans and was served with an order to refrain from making speeches. According to Dr. Lohia's statement, for a hundred years now, the people of Goa have been robbed of the right to hold meetings and form organisations. Naturally he defied the order. He has thereby rendered service to the cause of civil liberties and especially to the Goans. The little Portuguese settlement which merely exists on the sufferance of the British Government can ill-afford to ape its bad manners. In free India, Goa cannot be allowed to exist as a separate entity in opposition to the laws of the free state. The present Portuguese government will no longer be able to rely upon the protection of the British arms to isolate and keep under subjection the inhabitants of Goa against their will. I would venture to advice the Portuguese government of Goa to recognise the signs of the times and come to honorable terms with its inhabitants rather than rely on any treaty that might exist between them and the British government".

Gandhiji added, "To the inhabitants of Goa, I will say that they should shed the fear of the Portuguese government as the people of other parts of India have shed fear of the mighty British government and asserted their fundamental rights of civil liberties and all that it means. The differences of the religions among the inhabitants of Goa should be no bar to the common civil life. Religion is for each individual, himself or herself to live, it should never become a bone of contention or reason for quarrel between religious sects".

On his return to India, Lohia launched a vigorous campaign in the country in support of Goa's struggle for freedom. Addressing a meeting in Bombay on 29th June, he told the people that it was necessary to end Portuguese rule in Goa, not in the interest of the Goans alone, as the existence of this vestige of imperialism constituted a danger to India's freedom also. It was, therefore, necessary in the interest of India's security to help Goans to throw off the Portuguese yoke, he pointed out. A purse of Rs. 15,000— was presented to him at the meeting. At another meeting addressed by him on Chowpatty the next day, he reminded the Portuguese government of the three months warning sounded by him before leaving the territory.

The AICC met at the C.J. Hall in Bombay on 6th July. Nehru told the press conference on July 10, that the Congress had concentrated all its attention on the struggle for India's freedom. It had no time to bestow any attention on minor issues. Goa was a 'small pimple' on India's fair face. India would be able to crush it in no time with the help of a single finger after the country became free. There was no need to organise any movement in Goa. The Portuguese domination over Goa would disappear as soon as the British withdrew from India, he stated. While dismissing Goa's struggle for freedom with such contempt, Nehru did not fail to make the Kashmir problem a national issue in the same interview. He said, "The Kashmir issue has not remained a personal adventure any longer. The Congress Working Committee is now seized of the matter. It has been taken up by the Congress and States Peoples Conference. It is now a confrontation between the Government of India and the Kashmir Darbar.

In a rejoinder to this interview, Lohia said on July 19 that

Goa might well be a small pimple on India's face, but this pimple has made the country's face uglier than the pimple of Kashmir. The mind of the people of Goa was in a bondage far stronger than the restriction on the people of any other part of the country. He referred to the support lent by Gandhiji to Goa's struggle and remarked that it would be futile for the people to look to other leaders for leadership and guidance. Sardar Patel also declared that he did not have anything to do with the Goa movement. The people of Goa desired that the rightists leaders like Sardar Patel and Nehru should also support their struggle for freedom. The stance of these leaders on the issue had an adverse effect on them. Lohia did not receive the necessary support from his own party either. Jayprakash Narayan did not favour according priority to the Goa movement. The now defunct Marathi mouthpiece of the party, *'Usha',* said that the party had outgrown the infantile tendency of rushing about to deal with the situations, big or small, that cropped up, abandoning the main tasks already undertaken. The irony of the situation was that the very author of that article felt it necessary, in 1954, to plunge into the Goa struggle leaving aside all other tasks. But in 1946, Lohia had to go it alone as far as the Goa issue was concerned.

The Portuguese Governor-General of Goa wrote to Gandhiji to say that he too was a jurist like the Mahatma. However, he claimed a higher status for himself than Gandhiji as he was a judge too. He accused Gandhiji of having "unnecessarily" interfered in Goa's internal affairs. He declared that the civil liberty was not at all in jeopardy in the Portuguese settlement and said that the agitation in Goa was being conducted by some disgruntled people. He told the Mahatma that the Portuguese had come to Goa with the sole object of spreading the gospel of equality and brotherhood.

Replying to him in the *"Harijan"* dated 2nd August, Gandhiji said: "It was kind of you to write to me in reply to what I had written in the *"Harijan"* about Goa affairs. I suppose that you know that I had visited Mozambique, Delagoa and Inhambane. I did not notice, there, any government for philanthropic purposes. Indeed, I was astonished to see the distinction that the government made between Indians and the Portuguese and between South Africans and themselves. Nor does the history of the Portuguese settlement in India prove the claim set forth by you. Indeed, what I see and know of the condition of the things in Goa is hardly edifying. That the Indians in Goa have been speechless is proof not of the innocence or the philanthropic nature of the Portuguese government but of the rule of terror. You will forgive me for not subscribing to your statement that there is full liberty in Goa and that the agitation is confined only to a few malcontents. Every account received by me personally and received in the papers here in this part of India confirm the contrary view. I suppose, the report of the sentence by your Court Martial of eight years in Dr. Braganza's case and his contemplated exile to a far off settlement, is, by itself, a striking corroboration of the fact that civil liberty is a rare article in Goa. Why should a law-abiding citizen like Dr. Braganza be considered so dangerous as to be singled out for exile? Though the politics of Dr. Lohia probably differ from mine, he has commanded my admiration for his having gone to Goa and put his finger on its black spot. Inhabitants of Goa can afford to wait for independence until greater India has regained it. But no person or group can thus remain without civil liberty without losing self-respect. He has lit the torch which the inhabitants of Goa cannot, except at their peril, allow to be extinguished. Both you and the inhabitants of Goa should think thankful of the Doctor for lighting that torch. Therefore your description for him as a 'stranger' would excite laughter if it was not so tragic. Surely, the truth is that the Portuguese coming from Portugal as governors exploiting the so called weaker races of the earth are the real strangers". Gandhiji added: "I hope that you will revise your view on philanthropy, civil liberty and caste distinctions, withdraw all the African police, declare yourself whole heartedly for civil liberty and if possible even let the inhabitants of Goa frame their own government, and invite from greater India, more experienced Indians to assist the inhabitants and even you in framing such Government".

Lohia met Gandhiji in Bombay on 21st September and acquainted him with the progress of the freedom movement of Goa. He announced at a public meeting his decision to return to Goa to fulfill his earlier promise. On his way to the Portuguese settlement, Lohia undertook a tour of Poona, Sangli, Miraj and other places and reached Belgaum on 29th September. He was accompanied by Shanti Nayak, Secretary of the Poona City Congress Committee, Yogendra Singh and Ravi Pandit, an artist. Some people including B.S. Borkar, an eminent Goan poet, tried to dissuade Lohia from re-entering Goa. Lohia's firm reply to them was: "I must keep my word. I have to go".

When Lohia and his party arrived to Colem railway station, the Portuguese arrested him. He was first taken to Dicholim and then was taken secretly to Aguada fort. He was kept there from September 29 to the mid-night of October 8. He was subjected to torture and denied facilities usually given in civilised countries. He was later taken to the border and released.

Lohia's release was unexpected. His arrest had given a fresh impetus to the struggle in Goa. Processions, meetings and arrests had again became the order of the day in the settlement. His release in the circumstance was therefore, a miracle. Gandhiji had brought about the miracle. The interim government headed by Nehru, was then in power at Delhi. Gandhiji first tried to persuade Nehru to try for Lohia's release at the government level, but Nehru expressed his inability to do so. Gandhiji declared, "Dr. Lohia is not just an ordinary individual. Not just Lohia but the soul of India is in prison". Gandhiji then wrote to the Viceroy, Lord Wavell, to exert pressure on the Portuguese government to secure Lohia's release. Gandhiji repeated his plea to the Viceroy. It was either due to the Viceroy's intervention, or that of the Church, that Lohia was released. But for Gandhiji's efforts, the socialist leader would not have been released by the Portuguese.

On reaching Belgaum on November 9, Lohia said: "Aguad fort is no worse than the Lahore fort. The Portuguese sometimes treated me as a foreigner and some times in a different manner". As there was no ban on Indians entering Goa, any one had the right to go to the settlement. The inhabitants of Goa too used to enter freely what was then called British India. The Portuguese government announced through a statement that "it had prohibited Lohia to stay in Goa and released him "in the interest of law and order in the settlement" at the India-Goa border earlier on 18th June when he first entered the territory. His action was calculated to lead to breach of the peace and to incite the people of the territory to rebel against the Portuguese government. Even then, the government had treated him well it stated. Dr. Lohia has now re-entered Goa. We are now serving on him an order prohibiting his entry into the settlement for the period of five years", the bulletin announced.

On his arrival at Belgaum, Lohia wrote a letter to the Chief Judge of Goa High Court. "At the time of my arrest", he said in the letter, "I had not, as far as I knew, violated any Goan Law. I may have an intent of doing so, but that is irrelevant. The police officer at Colem walked into my compartment, asked me no questions and put me straight away under arrest. International law, as it stands today, probably empowers the Portuguese government to arrest and deport any one whom they consider an undesirable alien, but they are surely not empowered to hold him in prison unless he has actually violated some Law. The Portuguese government have in the past declared me as an alien and taken up their stand with regard to the provision in international law. They owe me an apology and damages for illegal imprisonment or else they must give up their attempt to misuse the International law in relation between Goa and the rest of Hindustan. Furthermore, between September 29 and October 2, they kept me in the cell, which has probably as much ventilation as just keeps man alive. They owe me an added apology and damages for the kind of the treatment. I continued to be held in solitary confinement, although under better conditions, and I was held incommunicable. These add to the illegality of my imprisonment".

Writing under the caption, "Dr. Lohia again", Gandhiji published the text of Lohia's letter in the *"Harijan"* and said: "Let me for one laugh at Dr. Lohia's presumption in asking for damages. If he had power behind him, the Goan authorities would quickly apologise and offer to pay damages. It is not an unusual thing for big power to ask for damages and obtain them for injury or insult done even to insignificant subjects. Dr. Lohia is not a little man. Well, India has a National government. I am sure they are as sensitive as any can be. I should not be surprised if they have lodged their protest and asked the Portuguese government to mend their manners. Any way, let the force of public opinion be behind the National government and the injured Dr. Rammanohar Lohia".

Lohia stressed the need to impose an economic boycott of the Portuguese government in Goa. Accordingly, import to and export from Goa of articles like fruit, butter and cattle came to stop. Scarcity of meat heat hit the non-vegetarians in Goa as a result of the boycott. Feeling the pinch, the Portuguese government promulgated an ordinance, requiring the people having the cattle, to retain one cattle head each with them and surrender the rest to the Government. That enraged the people. Seventy five persons enlisted themselves as volunteers to offer Satyagraha after Lohia had addressed a public meeting at Belgaum. It was decided that ten persons should offer Satyagraha in Goa at the interval of ten days. It was also decided that Lohia should not offer Satyagraha again till it became absolutely necessary.

Lohia undertook a tour of Sawantwadi, Kolhapur, Karwar, and other places along the Goa border, to enrol Satyagrahis and collect funds for the struggle. While he was engaged in this activity. Lohia received a telegram from Gandhiji inviting him to meet at Delhi. Gandhiji had left for Noakhali when Lohia reached Delhi. Lohia therefore returned to Belgaum and resumed his activities. While these activities were in full swing, the news was received that the United Nations had rejected Portugal's application for membership of the organisation on the ground that civil liberties were denied to the people in its colonies. The Goa National Congress met at Belgaum on 24th November. Some people, hostile to the movement attended the meeting and tried to buy it up. Lohia severely condemned the attempt. The Congress however split into two factions at this meeting.

At the beginning of December, Dr. DeMello, a surgeon of K.E.M. Hospital in Bombay, paid to Lohia Rs. 10,000 as his contribution to the Goa movement fund. Lohia handed over the money to the treasurer of the Goa Congress and left to Noakhali to meet Gandhiji. Gandhiji dissuaded Lohia from re-entering Goa. He told him that the movement in Goa must be conducted by the Goans themselves. Gandhiji said: "The Government of India is trying to settle the Goa issue at the governmental level. Your attempt at re-entering Goa is likely to create difficulties in its way. The Muslim League is anxious of bringing the government into difficulties. You should not, therefore, visit Goa again. In fact, this was Nehru's view. Nehru was then infatuated by immature, pseudo international politics. His effort to secure Goa's liberation through the intervention of the Pope or France was foredoomed to failure. It was not however possible for Lohia to speak these things out in the situation prevailing in India then. Even then, he placed the realities before the Goans, as clearly as possible. In the statement issued at this time Dr. Lohia said: "You are expecting me to enter Goa again. I would have normally done so, but I must wait. Mahatma Gandhi and our Foreign Minister, Pandit Jawaharlal Nehru, have wished that I should not enter Goa just yet. Pandit Nehru would take some time before diplomatic exchanges with

Lisbon are over. After that, and I trust that it shall not be more than two or three months, I shall be free to do as I please". In the meanwhile Lohia appealed to the Goa freedom fighters; "With awareness as your role of the creator of full democracy go speedily ahead in your task. Look not to Delhi nor to U.N. for your deliverance; your freedom lies in you. Five lakhs of full democrats can shake the Portuguese into submission".

Lohia addressed a largely attended meeting at the Jinnah Hall in Bombay in January 1947. Money was literally showered at Lohia on the meeting. Some women donated their jewellry to the fund. Rs.1,600, the proceeds of the performance of a Marathi play, "Kulwadhu"—were presented to him at Poona. The hero of the Quit India struggle in Maharashtra, Nana Patil, inaugurated a camp of 60 freedom fighters from Goa, at Khanapur near Belgaum on 1st January. Speaking at the camp, Lohia again emphasised the need for sustained action for Goa's liberation, but the people had by then come to know the attitude of Gandhi and Nehru towards the Goa movement.

After holding his patience for four months, Lohia began to prod the people to continue the agitation. It had, however become evident that the agitation had begun fizzling out. New recruits did not come forth to court imprisonment. Differences and dissensions cropped up in the organisation. Leaders of the movement, who were drawn from the upper strata, were avoiding jail under the pretext of looking after organisational work. Lohia reorganized the executive of the Goa Congress in a bid to provide representation of non-Brahmin masses. Yet the eleven member executive included 9 Brahmins. At the camp, Lohia tried for two days to persuade executive members to court imprisonment. However it became apparent at the camp, that the Goa struggle was destined to end in a tragedy. Replying to the question in the legislature on 10th February, Nehru said that the government could not say categorically that the people of Goa, Daman and Diu favour their territory's merger with the Indian Union. The government was however aware that they had expressed such a desire on one occasion, he added. This had an adverse effect on the situation. The Portuguese collected a large number of Goans at Panaji to demonstrate their loyalty to Portugal.

Nehru's diplomatic efforts to persuade the Portuguese to withdraw from Goa failed, as expected. The mass upsurge which

Lohia's Satyagraha sparked in Goa on 18th June 1946, had panicked the Portuguese government. Had the movement been sustained upto August 1947, the Portuguese would have quit Goa simultaneously with the withdrawal of the British from India. Sardar Patel wanted the Goa movement to continue, though he desired that it should be led by rightist Congressmen. After the Sardar's death, the Goa issue receded into the background. The Portuguese, whom the movement had rattled, regained self-confidence, when the policy of the Government of India on the issue became evident.

There is a common belief that history repeats itself. It proved true in the Goa struggle. As in 1946, Nehru betrayed the Goa liberation movement in 1955, too. He corrupted the movement in 1954 by providing it financial assistance and by trying to control its leadership. When Dr. Gaitonde suggested to Nehru in 1953 that the socialists should lead the movement, the Indian Prime Minister said that the suggestion was acceptable to him, provided the socialist was not 'cantankerous', which meant that he should be someone willing to toe Nehru's line. Earlier, some persons tried to persuade Lohia to intercede with the government of India on behalf of Goan freedom-fighters in 1948-49. Lohia firmly turned the request down. Peter Alvares sought Lohia's advice in 1954. Lohia told him that if they really desired to do anything for Goa's liberation, they should first storm Dadra-Nagar Haveli, which was Portugal's weak spot. But his advice was not heeded. Other people later did it, but then it was too late. He once said during this period: "The freedom-fighters and the people of Goa are a part of me and I am a part of them. But at the moment, their friend and guide is the man who sits on the throne of Delhi. I do not see any difference between Dr. Salazar and Pandit Nehru, except that Pandit Nehru is somewhat hampered by democratic traditions and precepts of India's freedom struggle and by Mahatma Gandhi".

The spark lit by Lohia in 1946 resulted in galvanising Goa's spirit where the people had appeared meek and submissive earlier. The people of Goa have not forgotten this historic contribution made by Lohia to Goa's liberation. Goan women have gratefully woven Lohia's achievement in their folk songs, while the famous poet, B.B. Borkar has eulogised Lohia's leadership of Goa's freedom struggle in his popular song on the liberation movement. In his message to the special number of *'Amcha Gomantak'*, published on

18th June 1947, Lohia said: "Goa was the first gate for Europe into Asia, in Goa we shall smash the supremacy of Europe over Asia".

Later, Lohia said on one occasion that five years ago, he took a keen interest in international affairs and specially in the issues of Nepal, Manipur, Kashmir and Goa. He no longer had that much interest in them. Bitter experience had taught him, he said, that it would not be possible to take such issues to a successful conclusion, until and unless, the affairs of Delhi were improved. That is why the persons outside the government must devote their major time and energy to this task, even if they took some interest in these issues.

Speaking at a public meeting in Bombay on 23rd October 1961, on the eve of the general election, Nehru, with an eye on impending general election, declared that the Government had decided to give up the means used till then for Goa's liberation and adopt "other methods" for the purpose. Lohia, disgusted with the tactics adopted by Nehru on the issue all along, reacted sharply to his Bombay statement. "I abhor war, because it corrupts the nation's soul. But stop indulging in the statements hinting at armed intervention for Goa's liberation once and for all and take the step without loss of time", he told the Prime Minister. The apostle of peace and non-violence, Jawaharlal Nehru, ordered the Indian Army to enter Goa on 19th December 1961, an action which prevailed worldwide debate.

Free Goans invited Lohia to a reception on 18th June 1963. Nehru Government's attempt to belittle the significance of 18th June 1946, in Goa's history also came to light on the occasion. Referring to it, Lohia said: "June 18, symbolises the people's strength, while December 19 symbolises armed might. This symbol of popular strength must not be allowed to be obliterated".

10. ORPHANED AGAIN

1946 was the blackest year in India's recent history. The Muslim League observed August 16 as "Direct Action Day", which sparked Hindu-Muslim riots in major cities and towns in north India. Communal frenzy gripped the people and men turned into beasts. There was an excruciating orgy of violence and killings. An Interim Government had been set up at the Centre on September 2, headed by Nehru. Five seats had been reserved for the Muslim League. The Congress nominated its own representatives for those posts too, as the League had declined to join the Government. The League revised its stand after two months and nominated its representatives. Mr. Jinnah, however, continued to talk in terms of boycotting the Constituent Assembly. Although there was a national Government in Delhi and Nehru was designated Prime Minister, Lohia could not forget the fact that the Viceroy at Delhi, the Governors at the provincial headquarters, and the Commander-in-Chief with the British Army, were the supreme power,

Lohia set out on a tour of Bengal and Assam on 16th August. He reached Chattagaon the next day. Though the climate was surcharged with the communal hatred, thousands of people had gathered at the railway station to accord him a warm reception. They included the workers of the Forward Bloc, the Revolutionary Socialist Party and Congressmen, besides the Socialist Party workers. He was taken in a procession to the party office. A few Muslim League workers tried to pick up a quarrel with the Socialist Party workers, but were driven back. He addressed the meeting of the party workers at the office for about three hours. He was later accorded a reception by the railway workers at the Railway Institute. He was scheduled to address a public meeting in a hall at Gandhi

Maidan. There was a vast gathering at the maidan and the people sat on the surrounding hillocks too. But they would not enter the hall, much as the party workers asked to do so.

The District Magistrate, Mr. K.A. Karim, went to the hall, accompanied with the League workers, 'tested' the microphone and went away. That served as a signal for the followers of the League who had come to the place with a plan to create trouble. As soon as Lohia rose to address the meeting, they began to throw stones at the dais; the microphone was smashed, its coils were snapped and the buntings and banners were torn to pieces and trampled upon. Then followed the attack by goondas on the people, who ran helter skelter in panic. The maidan was actually turned into a battlefield. A member of the audience did not move from his place, undaunted of the orgy of violence. He was hacked to death, all but three party workers fled the place. The three encircled Lohia to protect him while brickbats were being hurled by the goondas in his direction. He, however, sustained injuries on his hand and the chest. He somehow succeeded in avoiding any injury on his head. Some cries of *"Maro! Marol"* and *"Allahhu-Akbar"* rent the air. Some students cried; "We want Lohia's head". Lohia leaped forward and shouted "Here I am; come on". Though injured, Lohia insisted on addressing the meeting but soon there was a drizzle and the Maidan became deserted. Lohia was then escorted to the house of a respected and influential gentleman of the town.

Muslims constituted 80% of the population of Chattagaon. Lohia witnessed there how a majority community could perpetrate atrocities on members of the minority and persecute them. There was an orgy of assaults, stabbing, arson and looting in the town, but the police had made themselves scarce. The District Superintendent of Police was a Muslim. The Superintendent was an Englishman and the Additional Superintendent a Hindu. The two non-Muslim officers were forced to remain at the control room. The English Superintendent offered to shelter Lohia and other party workers in his own house. But Lohia did not wish to secure protection from an officer of the very power which he had been working to overthrow. A prize of Rs. 10,000 had been announced by Leaguers on Lohia's head. The house where Lohia stayed was heavily guarded by the party workers. At grave risk to their lives, party workers went round the town at night, picked up the wounded and took them to the general hospital. Lohia left Chattagaon on

18th August for the tour of Assam.

In an interview to the *'Daily Mail'*, London, on 11th September, Jinnah had stated that there was a danger of a civil war in India and reiterated his demand for his Pakistan. Denouncing the view expressed by the Muslim League leader in the interview Lohia said: "It is absurd to imagine that any section of the Indian people can, at the time of crisis, adopt a policy different from that accepted by the people as a whole and their own Government". The task of promoting Hindu-Muslim unity and restoring peace now faced Lohia, besides the issues of Goa and Nepal. Under his inspiration, party workers formed the "Gana Fouz", a volunteer organisation, and the relief and rehabilitation centre was also opened at Kashipur.

Addressing a meeting of party workers at Chandipur, in Noakhali, on 30th December 1946, Lohia said that Gandhiji's work in Noakhali had two aspects. One was to remove the distrust between Hindus and Muslims and the other, to give courage and confidence to those who stand for nationalism. He could not say how far the Mahatma had succeeded in removing the distrust between the two communities. "But he is certainly succeeding in increasing our strength. Let us now think what part we can play in his work", he added. "Two dramas are now being staged in the country" he said, "the drama at Shrirampur, which means accession of new strength, and the other of the Constituent Assembly. Patriots do not get excited about the news from Delhi. The British Empire in India will break up not so much in Delhi as on its frontiers around Shrirampur, Naga Hills, Nepal, Goa and thousands of other villages and districts".

Referring to the madness in Noakhali, Lohia pointed out that it had to be considered against the background of the socio-economic conditions prevailing there. He pointed that Hindus numbering less than a fifth of the population owned more than half the land of the area. The problem could not, however, be solved by replacing the Hindu landowners by Muslims. He felt that the solution lay in introducing some form of co-operative agriculture.

Dealing with the Hindu-Muslim problem, he said that it would betray lack of perspective to say "I am first an Indian and then a Hindu. These are two separate spheres altogether. There can, therefore, be no 'first' or 'second' in the matter". He told

Hindu workers of the party that they must remember that they were not a 'Hindu' minority, but a 'nationalist' minority. In the fight against communalism, they must act with the greatest vigour and courage and then they would win.

When he met Gandhiji at Calcutta, the Mahatma urged him to stay there to assist him in his mission. Lohia first resisted, as he felt that he was incapable of doing anything whatsoever with regard to the bloody riots between Hindus and Muslims there. He, however, remembered that Gandhiji had, immediately after his first arrest in Goa, issued a statement, supporting his action, even without asking Lohia as to what had been done and how it had been done. Gandhiji had told Lohia, when they met in Bombay later in September 1946 that he read about his arrest at about 10 o'clock in the morning and within two hours, he condemned the arrest and gave his support to the Goa movement. But he had added with a touch of regret or complaint: "Although you did not tell me what you planned to do, I tried to do my duty". Lohia replied to Gandhiji that before he went to Goa, he did not at all know what was to happen after he reached there, because he had not been to the territory with any purpose other than of meeting his friend, Dr. Menezes. As he himself did not have the faintest notion of what was to follow, he could not obviously tell Gandhiji about it before visiting Goa.

Lohia felt that the generous support given by Gandhiji to him on the issue of Goa and Nepal without delay or ado had put him under some kind of obligation. The background of Gandhiji's reasoning, he felt, might well have been that, once a man proved his liking for other, one assumed that his acts would be more good than evil. He had began to like Lohia, and therefore, assumed that the socialist leader's actions could only be good. As Lohia recalled all this, he was overwhelmed with the feeling of gratitude towards the Mahatma, and on the third or forth day, he succumbed and told Gandhiji: "All right, I will stay on".

Until Lohia had agreed to stay on in Calcutta, Gandhiji had not made the slightest mention of what he was to do. When he finally agreed, Lohia said, "In fact I do not want to ask you that question, but any how, what do you want me to do?" He should do whatever he thought best, he should just stay on in Calcutta replied Gandhiji and then he added, almost as an after thought: "I would like you to find your Muslim friends and visit them in their homes and renew your friendship with them".

It first appeared to be very simple, a very minor prescription. But that was not so. The city was split up into two embattled sections, one belonging to Muslims and another to Hindus. It was difficult for a Hindu to go into a Muslim mohalla. Actually for the whole long year, there were markets in the no-man's land between the two warring mohallas. Fantastic as it might seem, the people who slit upon each other's throat, seemed to be a very punctilious and honest with regard to trading of commodities, and in the no-man's land, exchange of goods took place very well. There was a specific time fixed for each group for this trade. A group would come to the no-man's land during the appointed time and leave its baskets of goods and commodities there. Then the other group would come, gather the baskets and leave the other goods for them to collect.

Lohia had a number of Muslim friends in Calcutta and tried to look them up. But whenever he sent some persons to their houses, he got the reply that the man had either left Calcutta or was not at home or that he would come along. But no one turned up. This went on until the fifth or sixth day when he got disgusted with himself. As required by Gandhiji Lohia had not met a single Muslim friend in his friend's house, so Lohia himself started out to find a Muslim friend and meet him. Lohia went out to meet his friends in the Muslim mohalla. As he crossed the no-man's land, a crowd of 200 to 300 anxious Hindus stood on the border of the no-man's land, waiting to find out what happened to him. As he walked into the Muslim mohalla, he felt an emotionally surcharged atmosphere. The faces of the Muslims that he came across looked angry and violent. He at once realised the meaning of the task, which had then appeared to him quite insignificant, that Gandhiji had assigned to him. Whenever he saw an angry face, Lohia smiled. If it was too angry a face, he sometimes asked where a particular person he wanted to visit was. That simple query from him would considerably relieve the tension. That normal human approach produced an equally normal reaction from the persons he met, and some of them were good enough to show him the way. A young boy took Lohia to his destination, a house which then served as a centre for the Muslim students in Calcutta.

He had two hours discussion with the students. Tension eased as the discussion proceeded. Those Muslim students too had regard for Lohia as a leader of Quit India movement and discussion soon assumed the unusual form of discussion between the leader and the group of students anywhere else in the country. Lohia mastered the situation in no time. Students put him blunt questions. They asked him if he agreed with Jayprakash Narayan's contention that Jinnah was a traitor or a 'Mir Jafer'. Lohia knew that it was a question surcharged with emotional fury, but he had to give them an honest answer. He said: "Yes although I had never used the word nor would like to" and gave explanations at which some of them were very angry. They said that if he also thought so, they too would regard him a traitor. Lohia replied: "That is precisely what I had come to find out about, and if you like you could take me for a traitor.

Then the young men tried to put forward a solution. They said that he should accept the idea of Pakistan; then they would fight the Birlas and the Ispaahanis together. All the students were Muslim Leaguers, with the exception of Lohia's friend, who was a socialist. As they rose to take a leave after tea, one of the students asked: "Why is it that our university professors or Congress leaders do not come to visit us as you have done, although we are beleaguered here?" Lohia replied: "Well, I do not know; in fact, I may not have come myself but for Gandhiji's idea". He then asked them if they realised what would happen to the professors or leaders, if they visited their students here. The students laughed and remarked: "Well you are leaving this place unharmed". The students accompanied Lohia as far as the end of no-man's land. The crowd of Hindus was still anxiously waiting at the other end. As he returned from his visit, Lohia marvelled at the efficacy of Gandhiji's prescription. He, however, remembered that this prescription had been tried earlier by his friend, Satin Mitra, and he had died in one such effort. Many more persons had died in the same fashion. But in the effort at removing the malaise with which the society was afflicted, such incidents were inevitable, he thought.

The situation in the country began to worsen. On hearing of the carnage in Bihar, Gandhiji rushed to that province, abandoning the mission in Calcutta. Then he began his one-man peace mission to all the places where communal frenzy had made the people insane. He rushed from one place to another, Bihar, Delhi and Calcutta. He had to go it alone. The apostle of peace was engaged in wiping the tears of the victims of the gruesome outbursts. When the news of the recurrence of communal riots there reached him, he hurried back to Calcutta and camped at the Sodepur Ashram. After the four day stay there, he shifted to Belia Ghat, accompanied by Suhrawardi and that became the centre of his 'Operation Peace'. Tram cars had gone off the road in some parts of the city. Gandhiji called Lohia and asked which party controlled the tramway workers' union. When Lohia told him that the Socialist Party controlled it, Gandhiji asked him to try and see that tram services in those areas were resumed. Lohia discussed Gandhiji's suggestion with Ashwin Kumar Gupta, secretary of the city unit of the party and volunteers of the Gana Fouz were posted near the driver and the conductor. A Muslim crowd stopped the tram car at one place. Volunteers shouted the slogan: "Hindu Muslim Bhai Bhai". Convinced about their sincerity, the crowd allowed the tram to proceed.

On 14th August 1947, a mammoth meeting was held at Shraddhanand Park; and celebrating the advent of freedom at midnight, the gathering converted itself into a procession. The all-night procession, led by Lohia, broke down all barriers. There was tumultuous rejoicing, when Hindus and Muslims started embracing each other. For a moment, all the accumulated bitterness and fanaticism of a year and more was gone and all the mohallas were open to each other. However, this climate lasted only till 31st August. That day, Hindu youths in Calcutta staged a demonstration against Gandhiji's peace mission. Men again turned into beasts and rioting and bloodshed restarted in the city. Gandhiji went on a fast and declared that he would continue it till the orgy lasted. A Muslim League Ministry was in power in Bengal and the goondas of the League had been employed to provoke and continue the riot. This added to the traditional Hindu-Muslim conflict a new dimension—that of confrontation between the Government and the people.

Lohia felt that Gandhiji might give up his fast earlier, if unlicensed weapons used in the rioting were surrendered to him. Some of these weapons had been left over from the "Quit India" rebellion. The users in some cases were same. He, therefore, set out to meet such people. He first met Jagmohan Bose. After considerable hesitation, he agreed, but told Lohia that to complete the mission, he will have to take him after dark to a friend, and Lohia would have to do some talking to convince him too. Jaggu drove Lohia fast in an automobile through many winding lanes obviously to ensure that the location of the place would not be known. Lohia was then taken to the upper storey in a building to a tall and heavy-faced man. The man shot a question at Lohia, asking why he had come to him. Lohia told him that he would very much like to know himself why he was there. The man said: "You want me to surrender all the weapons. Don't you know what the Muslims are doing?" Lohia replied: "Yes, I know it all". He asked Lohia, "Where would the Hindus get weapons, should they need them again". Lohia told that he was asking to surrender the weapons not their hands. "I do not know", he said, "where you were in 1942. We had not collected the weapons in advance. We collected them, when the need arose. The hands of persons and heart which move them decide the issue, for they can obtain weapons when they so choose or even fight without them". Jaggu was also confused. The man and Jaggu had some discussion and then the man gave Lohia a sten gun, some hand grenades and a few other firearms.

He went to Gandhiji's camp with those weapons at midnight. He thought that Gandhiji might be asleep. He asked the friend to quietly enter the room and leave the weapons there. But the Mahatma was awake. He was somewhat pleased. Lohia and his friend felt like relaxing and drove out it a place eight miles away. On the way, it struck the friend that the hand grenades were live. They hastened back, his friend entered Gandhiji's room again in order to put the grenades into a bucket of water. A peace committee was later formed at Calcutta and Gandhiji broke his fast on September 4.

Gandhiji subsequently left Calcutta for Delhi. Lohia also went to the capital to assist Gandhiji in his peace mission. On one occasion, somewhat peeved and despairing, he asked Gandhiji to let him go away, because he was not able to produce any results. Gandhiji looked at him and was silent for a while, and then asked him to drop him a postcard, wherever he succeeded in producing results, so that he could join him wherever he was.

Delhi was faced with the formidable problem of rehabilitation of refugees. One day, a young Muslim man wished to accompany Lohia on his rounds of the city in a car. He had a premonition of sad events to come. As the car reached the area of the Faizbazaar police station, a group of Muslim men, women and children, was running back and forth, with tear-streaked faces like haunted animals. A group of Hindu & Sikh rioters was chasing them. Lohia stopped his car. The Muslim youngster accompanying him came out of the car and stood before Lohia in order to protect him. Lohia forced him into the car and himself stood on its foot step. The group of rioters reached the car. Some of them recognized Lohia and with folded hands implored him to step aside, while some took courage & tried to drag Lohia away. They wanted the Muslim boy with Lohia. They repeatedly tried to rush to the boy. Lohia firmly stood on the foot step to save the boy from the rioters.

Lohia felt that if something had happened to the youth and if he had not tried to prevent it, his self-respect would have been damaged beyond repair. It would not have been impossible for the crowd to push Lohia aside and catch hold of the youth. But the real hooligans in the crowd were only a few and the rest were passive. Members of the crowd alleged that the youth had weapons with him and had concealed them under his clothes. They, therefore, asked Lohia to step aside and allow them to search the youth. The so called search could have led to any thing. A soldier fortunately arrived on the scene and handled the situation tactfully. He told the crowd that to search the youth was the task of the government and he would discharge it. The soldier asked Lohia to sit into the car and signaled the driver to drive them away.

During the campaign for restoration of amity and peace in the capital, Lohia asked Gandhiji one day if he would be willing to conduct a meeting of the representatives of Hindus, Muslims and Sikhs. The city unit of the Congress had appeared to him to be the natural auspices for such a meeting. When Gandhiji accepted the proposal Lohia asked the secretary of the Congress committee to issue invitations to the meeting. He agreed to do so. But for two weeks or more, nothing happened. In disgust, Lohia told Gandhiji that no good could come out of the Congress any more and that the best man must riot if he office red the party. Lohia asked whether Gandhiji desired he could have the meeting arranged under the auspices of the Socialist Party. Gandhiji told him that the agency did not matter, so long as the work was good and that he would go wherever Lohia wanted him to go. The threat of the Socialist Party taking lead over it worked and the city Congress Committee assured Lohia that it would call the meeting without delay.

Nevertheless, many difficulties were created in the way of holding the meeting. Some leading dailies gave advance publicity to the small gathering of representatives as though it were a public meeting. Lohia suspected that some men not in authority in the Congress Party wanted to foil the effort. He ran to Gandhiji a few hours before the gathering with the distressing tale of unwanted newspaper publicity. Gandhiji, always so understanding, told Lohia that all good work was obstructed in like manner.

A large crowd gathered at the place of the meeting. But after the correct position was explained to the people, all except the invites left the meeting. Microphone arrangements failed. Usually the microphone of All India Radio used to be there at every gathering addressed by Gandhiji; but strangely enough, that too failed on this occasion. What surprised Lohia most was that to pursue their selfish ends and their narrow interests, Gandhiji's disciples in Congress and government did not shrink from making their Master suffer. A piquant situation developed, as the gathering met in a neighbouring room because the Congress Working Committee was scheduled in Gandhiji's own room at the same time. While this meeting was in progress, members of the Congress Executive were regaled with soft drinks at Gandhiji's behest and asked to do their business without him. After making vain efforts to wheedle Gandhiji into their midst, they departed one after another, after having waited an hour or more. Before going away, Sardar Patel and Maulana Azad came to the meeting convened by Lohia, sat for an hour or so near Gandhiji, but did not speak a word. Nehru alone sat in the meeting right upto the end. He took a rear seat and did not speak. The meeting lasted three hours. It took no decision. That such a gathering took place in riot-torn Delhi was itself a great achievement. Gandhiji was delighted. He felt that in the existing situation promotion of communal harmony must get the top most priority. Before the date of the meeting Lohia had reminded Gandhiji that the Congress Working Committee was scheduled at the same time. Gandhiji probably wanted to play the imp to the Congress executive. It was perhaps the first time when the meeting of that body had to be adjourned in this manner. Lohia was naturally pleased at having been able to cock a snook at that pompous body.

When the meeting was over, Lohia and Nehru alone were left in the room and they walked towards each other. Nehru remarked that Lohia was learning to be crafty. He must have seen the anger on Lohia's face but disregarding his vehement question as to what he meant, he put his arm around him in a gesture of affection and offered to take up Lohia in his car wherever he wanted to go. Lohia escorted him upto the door and then bowed himself away.

Lohia was invited to serve on the Foodgrains Policy Committee appointed by the government, under Gandhiji's pressure. He agreed to join the committee, whose other members included, G.B. Birla, Purushottam. Thakurdas and Dr. V.K.R.V. Rao. There were differences in the socialist party over the question of controls. Lohia was against control on foodgrains". The committee met at Delhi on the 3rd & 6th November. At the very first meeting of the committee, Lohia called for Gandhiji's articles on food control. Lohia had met Gandhiji before the meeting and Gandhiji's article against controls appeared in the "*Harijan*". Lohia appended a note of dissent to the report of the committee. In the note, he had recommended a six-point programme. The points were: (1) increase in food production; (2) ban on import of food grains; (3) lifting of controls; (4) formation of foodgrains co-operatives; (5) regulation of prices; & (6) equitable distribution of available stocks of food grains. The programme, although based on Gandhiji's idea, was of course ignored.

During the stay at the capital, Lohia once rang up Nehru and complained that the government was not taking effective steps to curb Hindu-Muslim riots. After taking up some trivial matters, Nehru invited Lohia for lunch. Lohia replied that he would do so, if the Prime Minister sent him a car to reach him, which Nehru did. After lunch, Nehru asked Lohia about his future programme. Lohia replied that he wanted to leave Delhi. But when he met Gandhiji later, the Mahatma prevailed upon him to stay at Delhi. When Nehru still found Lohia with Gandhiji in the evening, he asked Lohia: "Were you not to leave Delhi?" Lohia replied: "Ask Gandhiji".

Lohia resumed his work for Hindu-Muslim unity at Delhi. A peace meeting was held at Gol Market as part of the campaign. After this meeting, Lohia suggested three alternative courses to end the country's partition. They were: (1) Muslims should fight the Pakistan Government and the Muslim League; (2) the leaders of Pakistan should express their willingness to reunite Pakistan with India, assuming that the two nation theory was a wrong conception; & (3) Muslims should join in the war against Pakistan, if the country attacked India.

Lohia told the audience that if Muslims joined such campaign for unity, their action would touch the hearts of the Hindus. That would mark the beginning of the new liberal politics in India. That would be neither a Hindu or Muslim polities but the politics of India as a whole.

One day, when Lohia went to see Gandhiji a curious episode took place. Sardar Patel was coming out of Gandhiji's room. The Sardar stopped and asked Lohia when he proposed to finish them off. Lohia jokingly replied: "Our strength is not adequate for that purpose. We are therefore, at present utilising it so that others worse than you might not substitute you". Gandhiji had overheard this conversation. As Lohia entered Gandhiji's room, the Mahatma asked him whether he planned to finish the Congress leaders in office at the centre in the manner in which Aung San and other Burmese leaders had been assassinated. This question from Gandhiji shocked and dismayed Lohia. He failed to understand why the Mahatma should have asked such a question. Lohia said that the idea was thoroughly stupid. He pointed out to Gandhiji that even in the days 1942-43, he had made a distinction between dislocation of communication, sabotage or destruction of material on the one hand and destruction of personnel on the other, and had insisted that in pursuing their programme, any harm or injury to the personnel, even if they were British, must be scrupulously avoided. He said: "Bapuji, now we are independent. How could I entertain such an idea about our own government? I consider the Congress government inefficient, corrupt and stupid and I would like to remove it at the earliest possible moment but in a democratic manner".

Gandhiji then explained to Lohia how that question arose. The Nagpur secret police had reported to the government that Lohia had recommended an underground movement and the wholesale assassination of the government leaders as was done in Burma. Disclosing this Gandhiji laughed and asked Lohia to write to the Union Home Minister, saying that he had no such plans of assassinating the members of the Central Cabinet. Lohia replied: "I certainly will not write such letter, because I would consider it a thoroughly insulting thing to do. Why should I write him such a letter? He stays in his home and I stay in mine. And if he had got his report, he had better ask me if it is true". "I can see that it is not at all necessary for you to write to the Home Minister, but you can write to me, can't you?" Gandhiji asked. Finally, Lohia wrote a letter to Gandhiji, saying that the report was malicious, but of course, he considered the Congress Government inefficient, corrupt and stupid and he would like to remove it at the earliest possible moment in a democratic fashion. Gandhiji tried to obtain the copy of the report, but it was never made available to him.

While Lohia was working for restoration of communal harmony at Delhi, a morning daily carried a report of the discovery of three hundred and three rifles in a Muslim area. The report enraged Lohia for it was one of his work areas. Only one rifle has been discovered from a Muslim home; it was 303 rifles. The news of finding one rifle with the specific marking had been falsified into that of 303 guns. Anybody would have been enraged, much more so whose job it was to smoothen tensions bulge and strains of Hindu-Muslims relationship. Lohia rushed to Gandhiji with the newspaper, just as he was, without even taking a bath. Flashing the report to him, he asked the Mahatma why he had made people like him working pointlessly for Hindu-Muslim unity, when a single report of that kind emanated from the Department of Information and Broadcasting could run the entire work that he had patiently done for several days or weeks.

Lohia thought that he had made a complete argument. Gandhiji remained completely unruffled and gave an unpredictable turn to the argument. He asked Lohia if he could not take over the department. When Lohia laughed over the suggestion Gandhiji accused him of running away from office. He perhaps had in mind the earlier occasion when he had tried, probably more than Nehru, to make him the Congress General Secretary. Lohia turned serious at once. He told Gandhiji that he should make this offer to him only when he had come to the conclusion, that the Congress leaders were not the best in the country. Gandhiji then tried to make fun of his wish; and asked if he wanted him to declare that he was better than Nehru. Lohia told Gandhiji as such in banter as with conviction, that he saw nothing wrong in such a declaration and that he would like to know what reasons he had against it. There was silence.

Amongst persons who were present during the conversation,

were some from the Prime Minister's household. Gandhiji obviously did not want to carry the argument further in their presence. He detained Lohia with one story after another much to the annoyance of the people around him until it was the time for him to go to bed. Then he beckoned Lohia to follow him to his bedroom. The Mahatma asked him: "When did you find me saying that Nehru and Patel are the best men in the country?" Lohia said with vehemence: "You have said so a hundred times". Gandhiji remarked: "Your intelligence which was earlier precise and capable for concentrated attention, appears to be deteriorating", and added that he had never called those men the best in the land, he had only said there were none better than them. The peerless subtlety of the logician gripped Lohia and made him wonder whether it was the argument of a lawyer or a saint? Who knows whether the path of the truth was not as sharp as the razor's or a lawyer's edge, he thought.

In the morning he had another talk with Gandhiji, a fairly long one. Gandhiji asked him to see him again in the evening, for he had something very important to talk to him. So he went over in the evening after Gandhiji had finished his prayer and the part off his walk. Gandhiji asked everybody else to leave. They resumed the walk with Gandhiji's hand on Lohia's shoulders. Gandhiji started a conversation on a subject Lohia had least expected; the way of Lohia's life. Gandhiji had known Lohia for 13 years and had developed great affection for him. Never before he had talked to him about Lohia's personal life. Lohia was, therefore, surprised when the Mahatma began to talk to him about his smoking habits and his drinking tea and coffee. He said Lohia smoked too much and that he drank too much coffee and tea and went off on a long dissertation on how ruinous it was to his health. He went on to give a prescription from China and Japan for gradually overcoming the habit. Gandhiji said that as a socialist, he must give up cigarettes to identify himself with the people and become their spokesman. He asked Lohia on what ground he could possibly justify smoking cigarettes. Smoking in India, debarred him from completing the process of identification with, and the spokesmanship of, his countrymen—the hungry and poverty-striken masses.

Lohia had very few such embarrassing moments in his life. Gandhiji's hand was on his shoulder, so he could neither move away from him, nor escape from replying his question. Lohia kept quiet, but that did not deter Gandhiji, he asked; "What do you think?" Lohia did not reply. Gandhiji however, was a great soul in the true sense of the term. He would not be perturbed by Lohia's silence. But it was difficult for Lohia to defy Gandhiji by not responding to his query. After all, here was a man who was telling Lohia the meaning of being a true spokesman of the people. Gandhiji once again asked Lohia, "Won't you say anything?" Still Lohia was silent. Gandhiji paused awhile and asked "Do you want me to stop and not to say anymore?" "Certainly not! you must continue" said Lohia, breaking his silence.

Gandhiji continued the dialogue and asked; "Do you think that I am concerned only with your public life?" Lohia replied; "I do not make a distinction between public and private life, and even if I do it for some time, it is not always a watertight compartment. I consider it ridiculous to practice in private life, the things that we condemn in public, and to that extent I won't make any distinction between the private and the public. And even if, I follow this distinction with certain other persons, I won't apply it to you in any case! You are free to ask me anything under the sun". The talk continued for about forty minutes or so, but remained inconclusive as Lohia was not responding to the questions raised by Gandhiji. Lohia however told Gandhiji that although he was not in a position at that time to answer all the queries posed by Gandhiji, he would definitely answer them soon. Lohia found Gandhiji's point rather unconvincing. "Will it really be possible" thought Lohia, "to identify oneself with the people in such a way and be their representative in the true sense of the term? It may or may not be!" Lohia was thus unable to make up his mind on these issues. He was in bewilderment, and in this state of mind he thought of giving up smoking. When he told Gandhiji about this, the latter simply smiled.

Gandhiji no doubt recognised Lohia's worth, and made no secret about it. "You are brave, but there may be braver people than you. You are intelligent, but so are lawyers. But you have a unique quality, rarely found in others, and that quality is *Sheel* or character".

Having been disillusioned by his own progeny, Gandhiji treated Lohia almost like his youngest or a grandson, and showered all his love on him. As Lohia was pondering these issues, a thought struck him. He thought that when a great individual like Gandhiji appeals to someone to do certain things, the latter is carried away by the influence of the great leader and behaves accordingly, even if he is not convinced by the logic of the argument. This could be one way, thought Lohia, to reconstruct Society. Lohia however, also wondered why our deeds are more the outcome of our faith than of our reason. It is faith that makes us move. Inner change is brought about more by faith than by reason. Lohia thought that the same must have happened to him in the matter of giving up smoking.

In January 1948, the Socialist party had launched a mill workers strike in Bombay. A trade union leader came to Lohia with a proposal to meet Gandhiji in Delhi. Lohia met Gandhiji in Delhi on the 29th January, and briefed him about the Bombay strike. Gandhiji said, "We will certainly talk about the strike, but that is not the important issue. We must decide something about the relation of your party and the Congress. Do come tommorow, we will discuss in detail". The words kept ringing in Lohia's ears, but what a nightmare the morrow was to bring! As Lohia proceeded to meet Gandhiji, the next day, 30th January, he heard the shocking news! Gandhiji had been brutally assassinated! Lohia rushed to Birla Bhawan. Gandhiji's body was lying there in an overcrowded room.

During the funeral procession, Gandhiji's body was carried on a military truck, and the so called followers and disciples of Gandhiji were sitting near the body. Lohia was shattered by this sight. What a degeneration! What arrogance and shamelessness! It is customary among blacks to accompany a funeral procession bare headed and bare footed. Even Europeans take care to remove their headgear in the presence of a dead body, as a mark of respect. It is customary all over the world that people whether rich or poor should honour the dead in such a way. But alas!, not only was the dead body of the father of non-violence being carted by a military truck, but the successors of Gandhiji were taking part in his funeral with caps on their head and chappals on their feet! So long as Gandhiji was alive he was worshipped, but in his death he was being thus insulted. Lohia could no longer stand this sight. He was totally disgusted. As he cast his sight over the millions of people who had gathered to pay homage to their beloved leader, he could see the shadow of his sorrowful mind in the vast multitude. The people were weeping and crying, and Lohia too could no longer control his feelings.

Lohia accompanied Gandhiji's ashes which were being taken by a special fast train to Prayag. At every station, the grief stricken people had assembled to pay their homage. At one place, Lohia saw a poor farmer showering some flowers on the train, as a tribute to the departed leader. Lohia saw in him a true representative of the country. Although Lohia loathed public mourning, he could no longer control his feelings, and tears rolled down his cheeks, after seeing the farmer. The masses thus evoked a subdued grief in Lohia.

Everything was over! His only support was no more. Gandhiji was Lohia's favourite dream. The dream was now shattered. There was no place now for Lohia to frankly speak out his mind, and rest for awhile on someone else's shoulder. Lohia had lost his father, Hiralal, two years back, but then Gandhiji was alive. When Lohia had been to meet Gandhiji after the demise of Hiralal, Gandhiji asked him why he had not met him after his release from Lahore Fort jail, on his way to Calcutta. "True Hiralal was no more. But so what, I was here" said Gandhiji. Such was Lohia's relationship with Gandhiji. So long a Gandhiji was alive, Lohia never experienced any loneliness, but now he found himself devastated.

There was no one who could guide and inspire Lohia by his self discipline and character. Lohia now experienced a strange sense of freedom. All of a sudden he found himself liberated. Gandhiji; his moral sentinel, was no more. Till yesterday, Gandhiji's moral presence would preclude anything that was unrestrained. Now there was no need, Lohia felt, to unneccessarily I restrain oneself. Did Lohia feel embarrassed in Gandhiji's company? Never. On the contrary, he was most outspoken, and straight-forward when talking to him. There was no embarrassment, no hesitation, only peace and solace. It is difficult to say whether others, too, experienced the same kind of feelings for Gandhiji. Some would suffer from diffidence, while others would sense a form of inferiority complex in Gandhiji's company, but this was never so in the case of Lohia. Rather, he would open up his heart only, to Gandhiji. With others Lohia would, at times, probably behave in a modest and civilised fashion, but with Gandhiji he had no reason to be unnecessarily 'civilised' or 'courteous', he had the freedom to be blunt, at times even harsh and spicy tongued.

With the demise of Gandhiji, Lohia felt that the nation had

lost it's conscience keeper, who would guide, inspire, and supervise over persons like Nehru and Lohia. Lohia felt that every nation should have a conscience keeper, but was it possible? Great souls like Gandhiji appear only once in centuries. There should be at least someone like Gandhiji who would be loved and revered by all.

Whatever it might be, one can consider whether Lohia was right or wrong in his approach to such questions. It is always desirable that individuals should voluntarily subject themselves to self discipline and behave accordingly Lohia always thought that all the problems pertaining to character are invariably related to philosophy and hence essentially philosophical. Characters can hardly be built up merely by preaching morals. Preaching might perhaps help children, but what about grown ups? In Lohia's opinion, one cannot think of ethics without thinking about human nature since these are inseparably inter-related. Lohia thought that it one advises someone against the habit of smoking, then we must also explain how this habit hampers the whole life process. Mere pleading is futile, particularly for those who are constantly growing, in every sense of the term. 'Knowledge is Virtue', thus spoke Socrates, but is it also not true that the chaste behaviour of Gandhiji also contributes to the growth of knowledge? After all, Knowledge is religion, and that is the only truth. Anyone who thinks of human nature, ponders over the deeper meaning of life, and tries to understand the mystery of life, is invariably led to ponder over the issue of character building. Once, Lohia complained to Gandhiji about the latter's practice of observing fasts, because he felt that such practices weaken the nation. In Lohia's opinion the practice of fasting is necessarily an individualistic action devoid of collective action and heroism. It enhances only the prestige of the fasting individual and undermines the role of collectivity. Gandhiji laughed and said: "Tell me, how do I become insincere because of the insincerity of the people of the world?" Gandhiji once asked Lohia, "Do you believe in God?" Lohia replied in the negative. Gandhiji remarked, "Then you may not be a good Satyagrahi". Was it that Gandhjji was not sure whether Lohia would be an ideal practitioner of Satyagraha?, however, Gandhiji recognised that every one has his own way.

Lohia's mind was thus full of Gandhiji's memories. He was however, very agitated and restless. He was agonised to see the way Gandhiji, the preacher of non-violence, had embraced death. What an irony of fate! Where was this country heading? Did it signify the beginning of the moral degeneration of the country? After all, what could be the destiny of the nation where the symbols of truth, honesty, and faith are being destroyed? With these thoughts, Lohia became more and more restless. He started smoking again as if he wanted to take revenge of his agonised state of mind. Lohia's taking to smoking again after his moral mentor's death was in a way both an expression of his child—like revenge upon Gandhiji leaving him alone in the world, and possibly a feeling of freedom from Gandhiji's moral control on his personal behaviour.

Fighting for the cause of non-violence, decentralisation, anti-English campaign, and anti-exploitation agitations, Lohia, in a way, proved himself to be a faithful follower of Gandhiji. Eventually he once again gave up the habit of smoking, and thus became emotionally one with Gandhiji. This was indeed a unique relationship between the Guru and the disciple. In 1939, at the time of the second World War, Gandhiji had categorically told Lohia, "There are so many problems and issues on which I am reflecting. If you find some fault with my arguments or in my articles, feel free to criticise me!" Rare are such Gurus who seek happiness in being criticised by their disciples, and rare also are such disciples who interrogate the Guru and keep him reflecting!

11. EXIT FROM CONGRESS, ENTRY INTO JAIL

The assassination of Mahatma Gandhi stunned and shocked the country. That the Mahatma fell to the bullet of the communal assassin in the capital of the nation when Gandhiji's own lieutenants, Nehru and Patel, were in power at the centre, was a matter of shame for the people. Madanlal had made an unsuccessful attempt on Gandhiji's life ten days prior to the assassination. The news that there was a danger to Gandhiji's life was already in circulation in Delhi. Why the Intelligence department of the government of India could not nip Godse's conspiracy in the bud, was a mystery which baffled everybody. In any other country like the UK, such an incident would have resulted in the immediate resignation of the Government.

Lohia declared that the ultimate responsibility for Gandhiji's murder lay with the Central cabinet and demanded its immediate resignation. A few days after the murder, Kamala Devi and Jayprakash Narayan went to Lohia and wanted him to put his signature on a joint statement which, inter alia, had accused Sardar Patel of having neglected his duty as Home Minister because he had taken over too many portfolios. Lohia objected to that part of the statement and wanted to have it generalised into an accusation against all such ministers, including the Prime Minister, who had taken over more than one portfolio. The three argued a little, with some heat, but the two of them had to go away without Lohia's signature. They returned to him next day with a change he had desired. The statement, as modified, was later released for publication at the press conference. Newsmen asked Jayprakash

Narayan whom they had in mind when they referred to the ministers holding more than one portfolio. Jayprakash Narayan replied that the reference was to Sardar Patel. Newspaper men must have already come to know something about what was going on in the Socialist Party circles, because one of them asked Lohia at one stage of the press conference whether he was in agreement with what Jayprakash Narayan had said. "I had, until then, not learnt how to combine democracy with intelligence, loyalty to comrades with unrepressed expressions of beliefs and opinion, so that I let this somewhat important occasion to slip through my fingers"; Lohia remarked subsequently.

The co-existence of the ruling Nehru-Patel faction and the Socialist Party in the Congress became progressively difficult after Gandhiji's murder. The ruling faction had been trying to ban the co-existence of the parties within the Congress since 1946. Gandhiji had sensed the situation developing inside the Congress. He had, therefore, suggested that the Congress, should either be dissolved or converted into Lok Sevak Sangh or its leadership should be entrusted to the Socialists. But who cared to heed Gandhiji's advice! Towards the fag end of his life, Gandhiji's close associates had disregarded his wishes and had continuously insulted him. With Gandhiji's death, whatever hopes the Socialists had on the subject of co-existence disappeared. The party ultimately decided to part company with the Congress at its national convention held at Nasik in March 1948.

The resolution passed by the convention about the problem of princely states said that those States were as much responsible for Gandhiji's assassination as communal organisations. The existence of as many as 650 princely States in independent India constituted a danger to the country's newly won freedom and progress. As the Mountbatten scheme had allowed the princes to opt for freedom, if they chose, they had been endeavouring to consolidate their position. Speaking on the resolution, Lohia said that, in the past, the princely States were the centres of the reactionary forces and had been the props of the alien power. After the advent of freedom, they had become citadels of the communal organisation like the Rashtriya Swayam Sevak Sangh and the Hindu Mahasabha. A few months before, they had planned an ambitious bid to capture Delhi through their organisations and with the cooperation of the vested interests, he pointed out.

Socialists spear-headed the movements against the princely States in Madhya Bharat, Madhya Pradesh, Rajasthan, Orissa, Hyderabad and Maharashtra. Lohia lent his powerful support to the struggle of the people of those States. The people had been facing bravely the savage repression unleashed by the medieval, autocratic rulers. Reactionary organisations like the Jat Sabha and the Rajput Sabha were also active in those States. India then represented an incongruous picture of the feudal regimes existing side by side with the sovereign, democratic setup in the rest of the country. Lohia demanded that real people's Government must be established in the princely states.

The government of India subsequently formed States like Saurashtra, Madhya Bharat and Pepsu, by merging the formal princely states like Indore, Gwalior, Rewa, Bhavnagar, Nawanagar and Patiala with the neighbouring areas. It no doubt reflected a correct policy. But the government appointed Maharajas as Rajpramukhs there, instead of holding elections and establishing popular governments. Privy purses, and privileges entailing an expenditure of crores of rupees, were granted to the prices. Besides, they were allowed to retain enormous personal properties too.

The resolution on the princely States placed a six-point programme before the people and the government to solve the problem. The National Executive of the party, at its meeting held at Mahabaleshwar subsequently appointed a sub-committee, headed by Lohia, to define the party's policy on the issue. The sub-committee directed the party workers to quit the Praja Parishads working in different States and to organise popular agitation for establishment of a democratic set-up in each of the States. The sub-committee demanded that separate provinces should be formed either by merging all princely States together or by integrating them with the neighbouring provinces and asked party men work for realisation of this objective. The Party launched a movement for the merger of all the princely states in Rajasthan into a single province.

The problem of Hyderabad State had become complicated with the Nizam's intention of declaring it an independent State. The situation in the state was grave. The Razakars were on the rampage and the Nizam was trying to give the issue a communal twist. The Socialist Party demanded that the government should take immediate action to solve the problem. In the statement,

Lohia said that the Nizam had become "a source of danger to Muslims of Hyderabad and all over South India, for against retaliatory fury, the Nizam would not be able to protect those whom he is goading today".

"Hyderabad" he stated, "is an active source of disorder. This rule must be tamed and destroyed in time". At the meetings he addressed all, over India, he made the people pledge solemnly that they would ensure that there would be no breach of peace, if and when the Government of India took police action against the Nizam. The Vindhya Pradesh ministry installed by the Centre had proved inefficient and corrupt. The real power was vested in the Commissioner. No election had been held there even two years after the formation of the Vindhya Pradesh. Though the Socialist Party and the Kisan Panchayat had been agitating to press the people's demand for elections, the Congress party and the administration had been functioning hand in glove, trying to suppress people's movement. To add insult to injury, moves were afoot to split Vindhya Pradesh and merge the area with the neighbouring Rajasthan, Madhya Pradesh and Uttar Pradesh. In all this, the people of Vindhya Pradesh were kept completely in the dark. Towards the end of 1949, the Rewa Municipality accorded Lohia a civic reception, when he visited the place. Speaking in reply to the reception, he said that the election was the only solution to the problem.

The people of Rewa took out a huge procession on 2nd January 1950, to voice popular opposition to the scheme to scrap the Pradesh and to demand immediate elections. There was complete hartal in the town and the big crowd gathered near the motor stand. The police resorted to wanton firing, resulting in the death of two persons and causing injuries to 22. In the police firing, some head of the cattle also were killed. A ban on meetings and processions was imposed in the town under section 144, and a reign of terror was unleashed to crush the movement, as it had been organised by the Socialist Party. The administration cut telegram and telephone wires and isolated Vindhya Pradesh completely from the rest of the country. Lohia, Jayprakash Narayan and Ashok Mehta issued statements condemning the acts of repression and asked the people all over India to observe January 15 as Vindhya Pradesh Day. Lohia himself reached Rewa on January 8. More than 5,000 persons had gathered at the railway station to accord him a rousing reception on his arrival there. He visited the place where the police had resorted to firings and lathi charges and met the injured at the hospital. Among them was boy of tender age, who told the socialist leader with tears in his eyes that he was unable even to drink water, as a result of injuries he had sustained. He also met family members of the persons killed in the firings. Among them was the widow of Ganga Prasad. He asked her whether she was prepared to go to Sewagram or any other place for training which would make her self-reliant.

In the view of the excesses committed by the police, the Madhya Pradesh government had to recall its officers who had been to Vindhya Pradesh on deputation. The Divisional Commissioner of Rewa met Lohia. Lohia demanded facilities to visit the prison to meet the persons arrested by the police and asked that the loud speaker, seized by the custodian of law and order, should be returned to the party, as he wanted to address the public meeting. The authorities expressed the hope that Lohia's meeting would help restore peace in the town. Shopkeepers had kept their establishments closed since January 2, despite the authorities' threat to revoke the licenses of those who would not reopen them. They agreed to reopen them in response to appeal from Lohia, who had pointed out to them that the closure of the shops had imposed severe hardship on the people, because they are unable to buy food grains and other necessities. Normalcy was restored at Rewa. He was scheduled to address the public meeting the same night. But for reasons best known to themselves the authorities suddenly arrested Lohia and released him at the Rewa-Mirzapur border. Tension mounted again at Rewa.

Commenting on the developments in Vindhya Pradesh, Lohia said: "The issue in Vindhya Pradesh is democracy versus autocracy. Five crore people of erstwhile princely States have been denied the right to vote for the last two years. To expel a person from one province to another is nothing but a mockery of the unity of the nation and of the Constitution. If the government had the courage, it would have imprisoned me. The government's action is reprehensible, as it undermines unity of India". The Government officials ruling Vindhya Pradesh had been appointed by the Centre. They were even called Ministers. Lohia demanded a judicial inquiry into the firings at Rewa.

It was during this period that Lohia's thoughts on the foreign policy the Socialist Party should adopt as a separate entity after it had quit the Congress, had began to crystallise. Lohia had been advocating the concept of the third camp in the international sphere, ever since the outbreak of the Second World War. India had voiced its opposition to the war as well. He developed this concept, while moving the resolution on foreign policy at party's national convention at Nasik. He said that the world was divided into two blocs led by the U.S. and the U.S.S.R. who were preparing for another world conflagration. He said that in international affairs, the Government of India had been alternately serving as a broker of the two super powers, and stressed the need to form the third camp. The world opinion expressed at the forum of the UN, on the Kashmir issue against India, had brought into bold relief, the failure of the India's foreign policy. He urged that the people should take keen interest in the international affairs and discuss the country's foreign policy. They should not regard the subject "out of bounds" for them. He said that the fresh air of public opinion must blow in the External Affairs Ministry, penetrating its closed doors and windows.

They were now being told that the government had committed a mistake in referring the Kashmir issue to the U.N. and that it had been done on the advice of someone else. But the fact remained that the Pakistan had a number of friends in the world, while India had almost none. The people must ask the Government why India had been left without any friends. In fact, the country's foreign policy must be based on well-defined principles of a permanent nature. The government had maintained intact the bureaucracy set up by the British Government, as also the style of functioning. They were also told that the policy of the government was not to align with either of the two blocs. But in the actual practice, it was negative in nature and inaction had become its hall-mark, he said.

Lohia added that the Government had not remained vigilant on the issues like the problem of Palestine and the right to veto granted to the big powers. Likewise, it has made no efforts to secure the U.N.'s membership for countries like Nepal, Ceylon, Thailand, Indonesia and Japan, and so Asia remained content with just five votes in the forty member body (as it was then).

Unfortunately it was not clear whether all the other leaders of the party subscribed to Lohia's theory of the third camp. In the report presented by him to the Nasik convention, Jayprakash Narayan had severely criticised the U.S.S.R., but refrained from criticising the U.S, in the same forthright manner. Lohia was the head of the party's foreign affairs department. He sent his report for submission to the party's convention held at Madras in 1950 but he himself did not attend that session. There were a reason for it.

The Korean war had broken out a short time prior to the Madras convention. At the meeting of the foreign affairs department in Bombay, Jayprakash Narayan and Ashok Mehta appeared inclined to support South Korea and endorse the U.S. action. Lohia's concept of the third camp clashed with the stance of these leaders of supporting South Korea and with the concept of collective security. Lohia, therefore, decided not to attend the convention. He also made it clear that he would not join the national executive, if the convention adopted a resolution, endorsing the U.S. action in Korea. He did not, however, give the expression of his views on the issue in the public. The Madras convention passed a resolution supporting South Korea. Acharya Narendra Dev was elected the chairman of the party for the next year. The Acharya told Lohia that he should regard the resolution rescinded and invited him to join the national executive. He also added that Lohia would continue to head the party's foreign affairs committee and would have the freedom to propagate his concept of neutrality and equidistance. Lohia agreed to join the executive, in response to the chairman's invitation.

In his report, Lohia referred to the functioning of international socialist organisations like Comisco and said that they had turned into "Post offices and nothing more". On the other hand, "international communism, whether as Commintern or Comminform, is a tool of coercion used by one country on all else. Must internationalism be either a post office or a prison house? International socialism must strive to become a world parliament of socialist parties, neither the ineffective thing that it is now nor the tyranny that communism represents".

He said that neither the Atlantic bloc, led by U.S. nor the Soviet bloc provided a meaningful answer to the major three questions of "full stomach for all men", of "free quest of the mind" and of "preventing war". The Korean issue was apparently a simple case of aggression by North Korea against South Korea. But the

Soviet bloc was fighting the Korean war to gain admission for Red China into the U.N. and thus serve its national interest, while the U.S. was doing so to strengthen the French in Indo-China, Chiang Kai Shek in Formosa and Syghman Rhee in South Korea.

After referring to the freedom movement in Asia and Africa, he said that the policy of the independence of the two power blocs, unsupported by the positive action, become illegal and puerile. India's action on Korea's issue was pro-Atlantic and its policy towards Tibet was pro-Soviet. This absurdity arose out of the belief that even while the basis of non-alignment with power blocs stayed, each international dispute could and should be judged on merits. According to this belief, North Korea had committed aggression against South Korea and, therefore, United Nations' action against it had to be supported. The Government of India, however, supported, at the same time Red China's inclusion in the U.N. in the place of Kuomintang China, the declared motive of the move being the loosening of tension between the two blocs and giving the factual position in China a juridical status. One could understand the pursuit of one or the other objective, but the simultaneous pursuit of both led to an absurd situation. To those who judge North Korea, a member of the Soviet camp, as an aggressor, it hardly behoved to help the Soviet bloc reap the fruit of aggression in the shape of the additional adherent in the U.N. and even a permanent seat of its Security Council. "What precisely is gained by such a policy?" Lohia asked and replied: "Nothing at all, except the alternative strengthening and touting for the two blocs."

As was expected, Lohia's concept of third camp came in for severe criticism from adherents of the two power blocs. Stalin and the U.S.S.R. were bitterly opposed to it, while the Communists Party of India subjected Lohia to scathing criticism, employing choicest invectives. '*The New Times*' a Moscow journal devoted to the questions of the foreign policies of the Soviet blocs, commenting to his report on foreign policy, drew the conclusion that the third camp theory was aimed at supporting the policies of the Atlantic bloc, led by the U.S. It also alleged that Lohia had, in his report, called for support to the American intervention in Korea.

Lohia wrote a letter to the periodical, replying the criticism full of distortion and deliberate misrepresentation of the facts. "The third camp", he said, "is not to be built out of only the new neutral states of South and South-East Asia. The third camp has its potential in all five continents. I have always made it clear that the neutral third camp should function in two capacities; when acting on the governmental level, it is the third bloc of governments and when acting on the popular party and political level, it is the third force of people. Even as the third bloc, wherever that may mature, its reach does not confine itself to Asia but extends to European states like Sweden and Yugoslavia and several South American states. As a third force, however, its voice may some day become strong enough to reach the Russian people or some of their sections".

The editor did not publish the letter, but said that the third bloc, outlined by Lohia in his report, would profit only the U.S. and British imperialists. In propounding the theory, the journal said Lohia, "is only trying to transplant to Indian soil a weed that had its origin elsewhere. One of the first advocates of the 'third force' was the notorious Leon Blum. Then the British Labour Party took to waving the flag".

The New Times said that the policy did not envisage opposition to the "furious preparations far war" in which the Atlantic bloc was engaged and the colonial oppression of the people of Asia, seeking to shake off the age old imperialist yoke. According to Lohia the countries comprising the third force should look on dispassionately at the American aggression in Korea, while they should remain neutral, if the U.S. and the British imperialists attacked Red China or the Democratic Republic of Viet Nam. *The New Times* further said that in his speech at the Socialist Party's convention at Madras, Lohia endorsed American intervention in Korea. It would only enable the colonial powers to gobble up country after country. Lohia wrote to the editor of the journal again, pointing out that he had suggested the idea of the third camp as early as 1938. Leon Blum and the French and the British Socialists started propagating a somewhat similar idea almost eight years later. "I do not know why the Russian Communists are so keen in falsifying dates in spite .of repeated clarification", he remarked.

He said that when Leon Blum and the European Socialists began to propagate the idea, their setting and motivation were altogether different. They did not start on a clean slate and their prejudices and obligations were numerous. Being a direct and physical part of the clash between the two blocs, they could not adopt the policy of the third camp out of genuine neutrality. They knew that ultimately, they will have to take sides and, therefore, their objective was restricted to the easing the tension between the Americans and Russians and to maintaining West Europe's precarious independence from the U.S. Lohia asserted that in propounding the idea, the Indian socialists were both original and right. "This original and distinct character of the idea has given it a meaning far deeper and more significant than in the hands of the European socialists. It can be genuinely neutral and start on a clean slate and is not burdened by the falsities of capitalism or communism.

He pointed out that he moved no resolution at the Madras convention of the party, much less a resolution on Korea. He was not even present at the convention. Lohia added: "I do not know why the *New Times* should go on repeating this lie. I believe that the Socialist Party had made an error of interpretation at the Madras convention. It should not have supported, in any manner whatever, the U.N. action in Korea. The war in Korea, being directly a war between the Soviet camp and the Atlantic, a correct application of the third camp policy would mean an abstentionism attitude. I agree, however, that this was a fleeting error of the movement. Since the Madras convention, I have made it repeatedly clear that the policy of the third camp necessarily means an attitude of abstention from the Korean war. I should imagine that the Socialist Party adheres to this view".

He added: "The third camp would not abstain in all conflicts. On the contrary, its aim would be to draw larger regions into its own and keep itself away from the reaches of the two war-mongering camps. It would certainly fight when attacked by either the Atlantic or the Soviet camp. But the inevitable corollary would be that the third camp should keep away from all such conflicts when it is in no position to engender the forces of world progress and peace". "In spite of the polemics of the *New Times*", he said, "I offer to the Soviet camp, as I do the Atlantic camp, the assurance that the Socialist Party shall never do either of them any positive service, but guarantee them negative advantage that the territories of the third camp shall not be used against either".

The *New Times* neither published the letter nor replied to it. After the first general election, the Communist party of India started the canard that the Socialist Party, particularly Lohia, had received funds from the U.S. to fight the elections, in a bid to malign the party. A Professor of the Moscow University, Mr. Verga, had repeated the white lie in his book on colonialism. When his attention was drawn to it, Lohia wrote to the professor. He said in the letter: "I learnt some time back from an Indian newspaper that you have, in your book on colonialism and imperialism, accused me of having received American money. You had even mentioned the amount as 60,000 dollars and stated that this money was used during the last general elections in India. The American money comes from or through me has always been a lie, continues to be a lie, and as far as I foresee my future, shall always be a lie".

Lohia said: "I wish there were some means of having such libel across the seven seas examined by the committee of scholars or a court of law. Even then, I do not know if I would approach a court, for I have been brought before the court as an accused or a prisoner and have a distaste for appearing before it as a complainant. But you are a scholar. And in this case, your fault consists in relying on the dirty information and making a specific accusation against a named individual. You may continue to have such dirty information, perhaps, not about me, but about others. A scholar should avoid making statements, as far as possible, on such a basis. At the moment, I am concerned with my case. You should make amends. Of course, you ought to remove the offending passages from the next edition of your book. At the same time the international press and the Russian press must certainly have given the currency to this lie and, therefore, the truth must be equally and widely published". Lohia had also requested the professor to contribute to the '*Mankind*'. But in reply, the professor neither replied to any of the points made by Lohia in the letter, nor admitted the mistake; he only expressed his inability to contribute an article to the *Mankind*, as he was unwell.

Lohia propounded at the meeting of the party's National Council at Nagpur in December 1950, the policy, that should govern India's relations with the countries on both sides of the mighty Himalayas. In his thesis on "Himalayan Policy", he pointed out that around 80 million people inhabitating Himalayan countries were astir and their old stability had gone. Warring ideas and armies were competing for their souls and, should they lose their freedom or fall under the influence of other people, they as well as the world would lose and the Himalayas would cease to be the traditional sentry of India.

From Afghanistan to Burma over Tibet and Nepal spread these peoples who were tempting missionaries for the idea and the sword. Beyond were the Russian and the Chinese and somewhat uncertain peoples like those in Sinkiang. All these were bearers of the Soviet idea and sword. What yet remained to be decided was the fate of Afghanistan, Tibet, Nepal and Burma.

He likened China's invasion of Tibet to an "infanticide" and said that it had brought out into the open, trends and clashes already visible to the more discerning. There was no such things as an Asian mind. There was perhaps an Asian necessity. But three types of mind were trying to give expression to it and had given birth to three mutually incompatible Asias. *Status quo* Asia, Communist Asia and Socialist Asia. *Status quo* Asia had collided with Communist Asia in Tibet, but neither could express the needs of Asia or the Tibetan people. The Government of India witnessed as a disinterested onlooker the rape of Tibet by China. It was indifferent towards the country's northern border. This policy of indifference to the events to the Himalayan ranges constituted an invitation to either the Atlantic or the Soviet camp to fill the vacuum that would arise from this policy.

The government not only did not stand by the democratic movements of the people of Nepal, Bhutan and Sikkim, but also entered into a compromise with the rulers there, the rulers who represented forces of *status quo* and tyranny. The government of India spoke of China's suzerainty over Tibet in imperialist terms, forgetting Tibet's relations with India which had been closer than with China. He pointed that the Socialist Party had striven in the previous three years to act in terms of such a Himalayan policy. When India's patrimony is squandered by the men in charge of Delhi, the people of the country and their political parties must act with even greater force", he stated, and added that the Socialist Party must become a conscious instrument of a Himalayan policy, basing itself on socialism at home and the third camp abroad. "Socialists and freedom loving Asia must defeat the equally dangerous forces of the *status quo* and the Communist Asia and thus provide the genuine expression for the Asian necessity and the Asian mind", he asserted.

Lohia had warned the people and the Government of India

of the danger Red China posed to India as far back as January 1949. But the government paid no heed to it and remained complacent. He had repeatedly said that Kailas, Mansarovar and the east-flowing Bramhaputra constituted the real border of India. He suggested that as a work of respect to the language and the emotion of the people of the Himalayan region, the highest peak of the Himalayas should be called Sarga Matha and not Mount Everest. Likewise, he wanted NEFA-North East Frontier Agency, to be named URVASIAM-Uttar Purva Simantha Anchal, and its administration entrusted to the Union Home Ministry. He had also demanded that a democratic government, responsible to the people, should be set up in URVASIAM, Bhutan and Sikkim.

The consequences of the Government of India's wrong policy towards the Himalayan region became evident in 1954, when the fact that, the Government had concealed from the people that China had built a road ling Aksai-Chin with Tibet and done nothing about it, was exposed in Parliament. The slogan, "Hindi Chini Bhai Bhai" was there in the air then. By 1959, no vestige of the so called India-China friendship had remained. China's aggression on India in October 1962 shattered Nehru's dream-world to pieces.

China had no doubt humiliated India. But the government's action in accepting the Colombo Plan, gifting away 12,000 square miles of India's territory to China, in utter disregard of the solemn pledge, given in Parliament in November 1962, to drive the aggressor from Indian soil, constituted the greater humiliation of India than the one the country had suffered at China's hand. This made Lohia boil with rage. He gave a call to the people to hold "Save Himalayas" conference and attended many of them. Through these conferences, he demanded the restoration of the northern frontier as it stood on 15th August 1947, conscription, a firm foreign policy of equidistance with the two power blocs in general, and about the Himalayan region in particular, and rousing the people through a domestic policy based on national interests that would appeal to the people's patriotism. He also demanded recognition of Dalai Lama as the head of Tibet's emigre Government and appealed to the people to reject the Colombo scheme.

Lohia's approach to Nepal had all along been revolutionary in nature. In fact, he was the father of the Nepal Congress which had launched a struggle against the tyrannical Rana regime.

Hundreds of workers of the Nepal Congress had been imprisoned. A former president of the Nepal Congress, B.P. Koirala, had begun his fast unto death from May 1949. The Socialist Party held a meeting at Connaught Circus in Delhi on 25th May to express India's sympathy and support the struggle of the people of Nepal. After the meeting, a morcha was taken out to the Nepalese Embassy, led by Lohia, to present to the Ambassador a memorandum, outlining the Nepal Congress demands. The morcha was stopped by the police at a distance of 500 feet from the Embassy on the ground that a prohibitory order had been issued under Section 144 of IPC. The members of the morcha squatted there, shouting slogans. After about an hour, the Magistrate suddenly ordered the police to teargas the people. The tear gas used against the demonstrators was so strong that the meeting, held at the Constitution Club, distance of one mile from the scene of the outrage, had to be abandoned. All but 50 party workers dispersed, as they could not bear the gas. Those who continued to squat sustained burns. Some were injured in the lathi charge that preceded the use of tear gas too. As they refused to disperse, alongwith Lohia they were too arrested at 9 p.m.

This was Lohia's first arrest since the advent of freedom. "True, the, British ill-treated me in jail; but the 'honor' of using tear gas goes to the, government of free India", Lohia remarked later. The arrested persons included two boys and two girls. They were let off and the remaining 46 were released on bail. When the trial opened on June 2, the government counsel pleaded for the cancellation of the bail order, on the ground that they were likely to participate in another meeting to be held two days later. The Magistrate asked Lohia whether he proposed to address the meeting. Lohia replied: "Yours is a political question and the reply can only be 'yes'". The bail order was cancelled.

Aruna Asaf Ali addressed the meeting held on June 4. But none of the speakers were arrested. The Socialist Party observed June 20 as "Lohia Day" all over the country to condemn the suppression of civil liberty and the use of the Punjab Security Act. The trial lasted a month. In his statement before the court, Lohia said, that "the bogey of an emergency would be raised by the Government in order to suppress the discontent among the people". He stressed the need to set up a people's court, as in Sweden, where the people could challenge injustice perpetrated by the government and seek protection of their fundamental rights. Lohia said that it was also necessary to set up a committee "to clear the prevalent jungle of laws". He pointed out to the Court that the Punjab Security Act under which they had been arrested was an emergency legislation and it was unjust to use it against them at the instance of Delhi in normal conditions. Referring to the Gandhi-Irwin Pact, Lohia said that the right to offer satyagraha had been recognised under the Pact. He criticised the use of tear gas, as the demonstration had been perfectly peaceful and said that they could have been arrested even without the use of tear gas against them. They were sentenced to two months' imprisonment and a fine of Rs. 100 each. In default of paying the fine, the further term of six weeks of imprisonment was awarded to them. However, the Government ordered their release on July 6.

The Nepal Congress devoted the next year and the half for the preparation of the revolution. Lohia helped the Nepal Congressmen in all possible ways. The revolution in Nepal began in December 1950. Though Nepal Congressmen lacked resources, they succeeded in scoring victories over the Ranas. They had to withdraw from Birganj shortly after they had successfully occupied it but were victorious in capturing Bharatnagar and the Treasury, containing Rs. 32 lakhs, also came into their possession.

Nehru created a number of difficulties in the way of the revolutionaries. He prohibited the Nepal Congressmen from entering India, as soon as the revolution began. Soon Nehru came to possess a trump card, King Tribhuvan, who had been under the thumb of the Ranas all along, sought and secured asylum in Delhi. Nehru began to pressurise the leaders of the resolution to negotiate the settlement with the king. The success had gone to the Nepal Congress leaders' head. They ignored Lohia's warning. Then began talks between Nehru, Koirala and King Tribhuvan. In fact, the Nepal Congress had succeeded in establishing its rule over the large part of the country. Lohia had advised them to hold elections on the basis of the adult franchise and establish Panchayati Raj in the part which had come under their control. But they betrayed the revolution. Nehru brought about a compromise between the Congress and the King and Koirala became the Home Minister for some time. But the objective of establishing democracy could not be realized even a decade after the settlement, while the task of socio-economic revolution was arrested for good.

12. MARCH FORWARD

The Socialists quit the Congress after the Nasik convention in 1948 and began to function as a separate party. But the leadership suffered from a kind of split personality. As long as they were in the Congress, the socialists accepted nationalist leadership though they believed in socialism. Even after parting company with the parent organisation, their minds appeared to linger in the past. Though they were physically in the new party, not withstanding the fact that the convention had adopted unanimously the resolution, outlining the party's policy and programme, the old behaviour pattern continued.

The belief prevalent was that there were no ideological differences between Congressmen and socialists; the difference lay only in sincerity and honesty in the practice of the ideals, and in the pace of implementation of the programme aimed at realising them. Many of the prominent leaders of the party continued to have very close relations with Nehru and regarded him as their leader. They considered Nehru a leftist and Patel a rightist and praised and supported Nehru and his leadership. According to them, the socialist party was not an alternative to the Congress. To them, the function of the party was only to reform the Congress and not to replace it. Speaking at the National Council of the party at Mahabaleshwar in October 1948, Lohia warned the leadership that it would not be possible to inculcate in its rank and file a firm faith in its destiny and loyalty to its ideals, unless and until the party's policy was based on clear-cut and well-defined fundamental principles. In that context, he subjected. Nehru and his leadership to a scathing criticism. Naturally, the leaders with split personality did not like the criticism.

Lohia continued to spotlight this weakness of the party. During his tour of Rajasthan, he said in one of his speeches that it was wrong to believe that the difference between the Congress and the Socialist Party was only of sincerity and faith in the ideal. "The difference between the two did not relate merely to the pace of implementation of the programme. The difference lies in the very direction of the two parties".

In his report presented to the Party's convention held at Patna the next year, Jayprakash Narayan also admitted the existence of this ideological confusion in the party leadership and had referred to the conflicting views held by the leaders on the party's approach. But he, too, had not defined the basic differences between the Socialist Party, the Congress, as also the Communist Party. Some of the partymen were under the influence of Marxism, flowing from their uncritical acceptance of the doctrine. No effort was made at a critical analysis of Marxism, through research in the validity of several of its postulates, which had become necessary. As a result, some partymen were being attracted towards the Congress and some others to the Communist Party.

At the Patna convention, the party was converted into a mass party rather than one whose membership was restricted to its cadre only. It had become all the more necessary, therefore, to end its amorphous nature and to replace the abstract generalisation, which had become the hallmark of its thinking, by concrete, well defined fundamental principle of its policy and objectives and the line of action. Moving the policy resolution at the convention, Lohia said that Gandhiji once told him: "I am surprised at the total degeneracy of Congressmen, their lack of organisation, their lack of integrity, their lack of vision, and yet the people are always marching ahead. I some times wonder why. There is one word for it, and that is hunger for freedom".

Lohia said that he had asked Gandhiji how Congressmen had still been able to inspire the people. Gandhiji replied: "Neither the leaders nor the Congress organisation had worked the miracle. It is their own unsataliated hunger for freedom that has moved the people to fight for independence". "The people's hunger for freedom had now been satisfied, but that for equality and prosperity remained to be satisfied", Lohia said, adding: "As the hunger for freedom took some time to affect millions of our people, that for equality and prosperity may also take some time to move them.

We have to create among them the yearning for getting this hunger satisfied and have to awaken and organise them to fight for it".

The hunger for freedom had been emotional in nature. But the hunger for equality was both emotional and intellectual in character. It was necessary, therefore, to appeal both to the emotions and the intellect of the people while working for the creation of a socialist society. Broadly speaking, the general principles of all parties were always identical. Though the ultimate truth was the same, the ways to realise it differed. Direction alone gave the will a concrete shape and led to its realisation. Will without direction had no meaning, he pointed out.

Speaking after the adoption of the constitution, converting the SP into a mass party, he said the convention had provided the skeleton, while the policy resolution aimed at infusing life into it. Partymen had to undertake the task of covering the skeleton with the necessary flesh and blood, and outlined a programme including the formation of a four-pillar State, formation of a food army, the setting up of small scale industries, and resorting to Satyagraha to fight injustice and oppression, to bring the task to joyous fulfillment.

Explaining his conception of a small-unit machine, Lohia said that it would not be desirable for India to ape the programme of industrialisation on the models of the U.S. or the U.S.S.R. through mass production machines, based on a centralised economy. He pointed out that in Europe and America, they gave tools and machines worth 1,000 or 2,000 dollars, equivalent to between Rs. 5,000 and Rs. 10,000 to each man to produce wealth in agriculture or industry, while India had productive machines and tools worth only about Rs. 150 per man. There was abundant raw material in both rural and urban areas of India, but it could not be utilised for want of resources. India would have to adopt a new technology of a small machine and a small tool run by electric power or diesel oil. "I have a dream", he said, "of an Indian engaged in increasing production in industry and agriculture through a network of small-unit machines spread all over the country".

Explaining the proposal to raise a food army, he said that the people were continuously advised to increase food production. But the government had been spending crores of rupees on import of foodgrains every year. It could, instead, bring crores of acres of land under cultivation through a food army. The country has huge manpower resources, a food army could be used to increase land under cultivation, providing men in that army with clothes, housing facilities and supplying them necessary agricultural implements. It would also be possible to increase productivity of the land by supplying this army with modern agricultural implements at a later stage. The food army could help to solve the problem of unemployment and hunger in rural areas. It could generate a new climate of enthusiasm in the rural areas and lay the foundation of future collective rural life, based on the principle of cooperation.

In this speech Lohia outlined his own concept of a four pillar State, which would be distinct from the capitalist or communist State. Lohia said under the present State, there existed a vast gulf between the administration and other social organisations on the one hand, and the common man on the other. The common man never had the privilege to participate actively in the conduct of the country's affairs. All power was concentrated in the hand of a few, under all forms of government, whether monarchy, dictatorship, or a democratic government was set up to run the administration. To change this state of affairs, the administrative set-up must be divided into four sectors. It must rest on four pillars; the village, the district, the state, and the centre. Decentralisation, planning, agriculture, industries based on the small-unit machine, education and ownership of property, which would be nationalised, would be consistent with the integrity of such a nation. Local self-government bodies; the district, city and village panchayats would acquire the status of the organic units of the Republic under the scheme. The defence forces and railways would continue with the Centre, while the armed constabularies would remain under the control of the state. Recruitment and training of the police would be the responsibility of the State, but their control would be transferred to the district and village bodies. Production of iron and steel would be under the Centre's control. Likewise, the Centre would fix prices, but the share of the capital outlay and the cost of labour, should be mutually decided by the district and village bodies, as far as the activities transferred to them were concerned.

Lohia said that, to some, this scheme might appear impractical, in view of the extent of illiteracy among the people and the prevalence of the caste system, outmoded customs and superstitions. But this was the only way to galvanise the people, suffering from the age-old passivity and fatalism, and to free them from the stranglehold of the corrupt and centralised administration. The four-pillar structure must become the way of life. He was confident that this noble and lofty ideal would take shape in a not too distant future, and serve as a source of inspiration for the entire mankind. It would make the people conscious both of their rights and duties.

Lohia declared that neither Congressism, Nehruism, communism, nor capitalism, was capable of solving the problems confronting the world. Socialism alone could accomplish the task. He referred to the weakness of the socialist movement and said that inactivity had become the only activity in the country. Ventilation of the peoples grievances must be accompanied by the creation of a creative force. While the party's resolutions were usually constructive in nature, partymen's speeches were purely denunciatory. It was high time that this negative attitude was given up. The other weakness was the almost pathetic faith in ritualism, the traditional tendency prevalent ever since the days of the Shankaracharya, of identifying one's religious faith with the help of distinguishing marks stamped on the forehead, persists even now. Such a belief in mechanical rituals would lead to political immaturity and hypocrisy, he remarked. He believed that elections had an important place in a democracy. It was also true that the party's aim was to change the government as early as possible. But he regretted that partymen lacked the political understanding necessary to realise this aim. It was wrong to regard discontent amongst the people against the Congress as synonymous with their support for the Socialist party. If partymen laboured under such an illusion, it might impel them to seek shortcuts, involving opportunistic bargaining, and other tactics, with the sole object of winning elections.

He warned the party that if the socialists failed in making the people politically conscious and awake, it would be easier for those believing in a violent revolution to gain ground. These people talked in terms of a revolution in season and out of season, and lived in a dream-world of their own. Both the votaries of a violent revolution, and those who believed in elections only, had a negative approach, both of them were always in search for an easy shortcut and were equally lukewarm towards constructive and combative activities. He felt that these weakness led to factionalism. Sources of compassion appeared to have dried up. It was once thought, that would be possible to remove the weakness with the pursuit of philosophy of socialism alone. But it was soon found that it was easier for the elite to become socialist, but not so in the case of those belonging to the oppressed, weaker sections of society. Socialism took the form of hatred but not of anger and compassion.

Alluding to Indo-Pak relations, Lohia said that the Govt. of India's policy towards Pakistan alternated between attempts to unnecessarily appease the neighbour, and to offend that country, also without reason. India's policy towards Pakistan must be based on firm principles. He pointed out that the small nations at the United Nations instinctively inclined to favour a small nation in conflict between the big ones. It was, therefore, necessary to acquaint the world, particularly the Arab world, with the orgy of killings, violence and incendiarism, whenever it took place in that country. At the time India was partitioned, he said, "Hindus and Muslim were at the same time one nation and two nations. They were in a fluid state of communion as well as estrangement. Partition suddenly separated them into two states, but the corresponding task of national separation is not so simple nor easy. Division of states might be effected with suddenness, but the division of a people is troublesome and tardy. The people of India have separated into two states, but as a nation, they are still in a fluid state, neither one nor two, perhaps more one than two".

India was committed to hold a plebiscite in Kashmir. The Maharaja of Kashmir should have been removed long ago and a number of the Union Ministers should have been resident in the State. Land reforms should have been introduced immediately. But the government's indecision and vacillation led to a victory that was not complete. On his return from a tour of Kashmir in 1947, Lohia had spotlighted the real situation in that State. It was at this time that Jayprakash had stated that Kashmir should be partitioned to promote friendly relations with Pakistan. Lohia said that, what Jayprakash said were his personal views, and not those of the Socialist Party. The party regarded Kashmir as an integral part of India, he declared. To those who regarded the Kashmir policy as impractical, he reminded them of Gandhiji's views on the subject. Lohia had met Gandhiji on the eve of his departure for Kashmir immediately after Pakistan's aggression on the State. Gandhiji had said: "Some persons are afraid that if the Maharaja of Kashmir is removed, the rest of the princes in the country might rebel. It would be a good development, if it happens. If we win, we shall have a clean slate to begin our task, and if we lose, we shall be able to start afresh.

Referring to the manner in which the Kashmir issue was handled by the U.N., he said that the organisation had become a clearing house of international intrigue and a stage for maneuverings of the great powers. No issue was judged there, except against a background of alliances and possible military alliances. He pointed out that the U.N. was made up of many nations and all of them were not anti-Indian. But India's Minister for Foreign Affairs was practising the caste system in international affairs by recognising the distinction between the five Brahmin nations and the 56 untouchable ones. He said that India and Pakistan really were one nation, as far as history, languages, geography and economy were concerned. He had, therefore, opposed the artificial partition of the country into two States. He had suggested (1) the formation of a confederation of the two states through negotiations, (2) bringing about a socialist revolution in India and (3) repulsion of Pakistan aggression by a counter-aggression against it. Pakistan is a slave. India has the freedom to change her employer; she can choose to serve either the U.S.S.R. or the U.S., but Pakistan does not have this freedom, he remarked. "Opposition to Pakistan but a fair treatment to the Muslim minority in India" must be the guiding principle of India's policy towards that country, he added.

The events of 1965 vindicated Lohia's stand on the Indo-Pak issue. In 1953, Lohia had repeatedly asked the people of India to remember that, in any event, their supreme weapon against the two-nation theory of the founders of Pakistan, was the treatment they meted out to the minorities within the Indian Republic. Whatever else might happen, the integration of Muslim and Hindus within the Indian Republic, would make the effort of Pakistan to create two nations impossible. Suspicion begot suspicion and it was necessary to break the vicious circle. He also blamed Nehru as much as Sheikh Abdullah for the Kashmir tangle. It was Nehru who boosted the Sheikh and inflated his stature. He had told the Kashmir leader, Lohia recalled, that it would be impossible to accord to Kashmir a status similar to that of Bhutan and Nepal.

A huge Kisan morcha was organised at Lucknow on 24th November. On the previous day, Kisans converged on the capital of Uttar Pradesh in their thousands, from all parts of the State, to participate in the demonstration. Tents had been put up on the banks of the Gomati river for them to spend the night. Braving the biting cold of Lucknow, the half naked and poor kisans carried with them a blanket each and Sattu flour and parched gram. That was all the food ration they could afford. They included women with babes in their arms. By next morning, their number had swollen to a lakh. The emaciated kisans, both men and women, clad in tattered clothes, but with indomitable courage and determination, symbolised a new spirit of rebellion against injustice and oppression and their determination to fight it.

Lohia and Acharya Narendra Dev led the several mile long morcha. Though Jayprakash opposed the demonstration, all the newspapers held it as 'historic' even heralding the emergence of a new party with grass roots. Its slogans rent the air as the morcha wended its way to the Council Hall. Though the programme had been notified to him in advance, the Chief Minister of the State, G.B. Pant, did not remain in Lucknow. A copy of the memorandum, listing their demands, was pasted on the walls of the Secretariat. Addressing the demonstrators, Lohia said: "The food problem cannot be solved by growing food grains in the compounds of bungalows or displaying poster's. The only effective way to solve the problem is to organise the people and raise a food army".

The U.P. legislation for abolishing the Zamindari system was a half hearted measure. Under the legislation, tenants were entitled to become owners of the land only on payment of a price ten times the land revenue. A steep fall in the price of sugarcane had hit the cultivators hard. The government had resorted to coercive measures to procure foodgrains from the kisans. A strong wave of discontent and resentment against the situation swept the rural areas and the kisans were with seething with anger. The agitation, under Lohia's leadership, on the issue forced the government to give up procurement of foodgrains by coercive measures. The recovery of an amount ten times the land revenue from the tenants was also abandoned.

Repeated efforts had been made to set up a kisan organisation ever since 1936, but they were not successful. The Patna convention of the Socialist Party in 1949, formed the All India Kisan Panchayat with Lohia as its president. The first session of the All India Kisan Panchayat was held at Rewa on 20th February 1950. The awakening among the Kisans which had been increasing during the preceding two years and the formation of the strong organisation rattled the government. The Vindhya Pradesh government tried to place all kinds of obstructions in order to foil the plan to hold the session. It declined to provide facilities for water supply to the delegates and to run special buses for their transport. Lohia told the government that the kisans would accept the challenge; "The Kisan conference will be a success, despite your obstructionist tactics. They will foot out the 40-mile distance from the Satna station to the venue of the conference. They will live under the open sky, unmindful of the inconvenience, that want of water supply will cause them". Kisans made the conference a great success much to the discomfiture of the government.

It was Lohia's dream that the kisans spread over half a million villages in the country should become the harbingers of a new civilisation in the country. He was unhappy that, though they had become more conscious during the past few years, Kisans had not made any significant contribution to the ushering in of such a civilisation. He undertook an extensive tour of U.P., Bihar, Rajasthan, and Vindhya Pradesh to organise the peasants under the banner of the Panchayat. Thousands of kisans had earlier organised morchas at state capitals. The Rewa conference adopted a charter of demands aimed at ending poverty. The charter included the demand for ensuring parity in the price of agricultural commodities and those of manufactured articles. It demanded that the minimum size of a family holding should be 12.5 acres, while the ceiling on land holdings must be fixed at 30 acres. It wanted imposition of ceiling on monthly income to be fixed at Rs. 1,000. The charter likewise demanded prevention of ejection of tenants from their land and measures to fight famine and arrest a fall in agricultural prices.

The party had appointed, as far back as 1947, a committee consisting of Ram Nandan Mishra, Khurshed, A.D. Naoroji, with Lohia as chairman, to inquire into the conditions of kisans in Champaran. As Gandhiji desired that the Bihar government itself should institute such an inquiry, the work of this committee had been suspended. A short time prior to his assassination, Gandhiji had advised Lohia and Mishra to resume the inquiry following the failure of the Bihar government to undertake the task. The two toured the district for the purpose and submitted their report to the party. As the kisan organisation had taken root in the country, the party decided to organise a mammoth peasant demonstration at Delhi. Jayprakash opposed this move also. Lohia was the chairman of the committee appointed to organise the demonstration. He asked party units in the country to observe a "Constructive work week" between April 20 and 27 in 1951. Lohia said that Charakha was the sun around which the various items of Gandhiji's constructive work orbited. "The spade should be the sun for our constructive activities to orbit around", he remarked.

The week was observed all over the country with great enthusiasm. Lohia inaugurated the work of constructing a nullah for a land of 300 acres in Bulandshahar. Kisans of Pathredi village constructed a bund, named after Lohia, on the Paniyari. Lohia toured several states including Punjab, U.P. and Madhya Bharat, to accelerate the pace of the programme. Addressing a mammoth meeting on May 1, Lohia gave the slogan of a constant struggle and criticised Nehru's concept of planning which he likened to an attempt at erecting "a seven-story structure without a foundation".

The week culminated in a huge Kisan Morcha at Delhi on 3rd June. Thousands of kisans arrived in Delhi to participate in the demonstration. The members of the morcha went to Gandhiji's Samadhi at Raj Ghat, and took a solemn pledge to fight injustice through non-violence struggle and to engage in the task of reconstruction through constructive activities. The morcha then went to Rashtrapati Bhavan and presented to the President, Dr. Rajendra Prasad, a six point people's charter.

The kisans of Kagodu, a village in Sabar taluka of Shimoga district in Mysore, had launched a struggle against injustice. Seventy kisans had been ejected from their land forcibly, as a result of machinations of selfish vested interests and the zamindars of the village. The zamindars were recovering from them rent, at Rs. 30/- per acre, while they paid the government only Rs. 2/- per acre. The Zamindars used to smuggle foodgrains into the then Bombay State, for sale in the black market. The kisans refused to pay rent at such a high rate. All the land in the village belonged to a single zamindar family, and one of its members was a Congress leader. Kisans offered Satyagraha under the leadership of the Socialist Party. Lending his powerful support to the Satyagraha, Lohia said that it was possible that Kisans tilling the land for generations were being ejected illegally and the Zamindars might be just trespassers. It was surprising that the Mysore Government had not come forth to protect the trespassers.

All the members of the executive of the Mysore State Socialist Party were been arrested and 400 kisans had been thrown behind prison bars. Atrocities were being committed against the satyagraha. The state government was determined to suppress the struggle, while the kisans were equally determined to fight till they secured justice. Their demands were: (1) the land must be restored to the Kisans who were the legitimate owners, (2) a judicial committee should be appointed to settle the dispute and (3) all the Satyagrahis must be released. Provoked by the Mysore Government's anti-kisan policy, Lohia declared that he was proceeding to Kagodu, which had become the symbol of the Kisan's struggle against injustice, to express his solidarity with the Satyagrahis and to participate in the campaign. He said that he proposed to enter the village with such of the party colleagues as wished to support the struggle launched by the legitimate owners of the land.

Lohia was arrested at the rest house at Sagar railway station at midnight, taken to Bangalore and produced before a magistrate. The magistrate remanded him to custody till 20th June. Lohia asked the magistrate as to the charges against him. The magistrate replied that he could make a statement before the court. "This means that you are not the court. Then how are you remanding me to custody?" Lohia asked him. When the magistrate offered to release him on bail, on the production of surety, Lohia remarked: "As you have not told me the charges against me, the question of producing a surety does not arise".

The Socialist Party observed "Kagodu Day" all over the country to protest against Lohia's arrest. Socialists in London also staged a demonstration against the arrest of Lohia in front of the Indian High Commissioner's office. He was scheduled to leave India for Stockholm to attend an international conference and to visit Yugoslavia. The Foundation for World Government had also invited him to visit the U.S. Lohia's arrest had become the subject of comment in the U.S. Lohia filed a habeas corpus petition at the High Court against his arrest. After a few hearings of the petition, the government realised that the High Court's ruling would go against it. To avoid the resultant discomfiture, he was released on 21st June, while the hearing was still in progress.

13. AROUND THE WORLD

The world earlier looked up to International Socialism for restraining parochial nationalism. But the first world war erupted in 1914, well before socialist thought could emerge as a total, all enveloping, ideology, and as a result Socialist Internationalism breathed its last. In the wake of the world war, all Socialist parties decided to support the capitalist governments. Once again, nationalism prevailed over internationalism. Role of socialism was reduced to raising the standard of living of the workers in the state of each party. International loyalties remained only as a cosmetic touch. With the advent of anti-imperialist and anti-colonialist struggles in the countries of Asia and Africa, the internationalism of the western socialists proved to be hollow.

Indian socialism, too, had an inadequate ideological foundation. It was nothing but the sympathy for anti-colonialists and imitation of western socialists. Lohia argued that the communism and capitalism are two manifestations of the same European culture, and both equally irrelevant to the under-developed world. He propounded a new socialism and a new internationalism for the third world. He argued, that rather than choosing the lesser between the two evils, a third path and a third force must be forged. During the second world war, he successfully sought Gandhiji's blessing for his stand. His attempt was to win over the socialists to this line of thought, in the post-independence era. He visualised this third force to be the pioneer of the new world order, with moral stature to influence the two blocks which would be brought closer for eliminating war from the world scene. Towards this end, Lohia propounded many projects including the Himalayan policy, Asian Socialist Organisation, elimination of war indemnities etc. He put forth the idea of a U.N. reorganized on the basis of equality and elections to constitute a world parliament and government.

Lohia was deputed as the Indian delegate to the world government conference in Stockholm because of his views on world government. Lohia was in prison in connection with the Nepal-Day case. But, on 3rd July 1949, he was suddenly released and could leave for Stockholm from Lucknow on 24th August. The conference began during the first week on September. Lohia elucidated his ideas on the third force (based on the five-tier hierarchy of village, district, province, nation, and world), international peace, the need of the reconstruction of a new world, opposition to extreme concentration of power in advanced countries etc.

Lohia had a meeting with the Swedish Premier, Mr. Orlander. He visited Copenhagen and Germany at the invitation of the respective branches of the movement for world government. His tour included Hamburg, Hannover, and Bonn—the capital of West Germany. He met Dr. Kurt Schumacher, the leader of the German Socialist Party. Both were impressed with each other's personality. Dr. Schumacher shared his thoughts with Lohia saying: "European socialism is outdated now. Asian socialism is new. And hence, while somewhat immature, it is resonant and courageous. European socialism cannot build a new world. Asian socialists can yet do something". Lohia also went to Berlin as a state guest of the Berlin Socialist Municipal Government.

This was Lohia's first visit to Berlin after nearly eighteen years. The memories of his student days still lingered in his mind. Berlin, the capital of Hitler's third Reich just four years before, was under the dark shadow of the postwar period. War had taken a massive toll. The whole German population was uprooted, and Lohia could meet only three friends from old times. In Berlin, Lohia addressed the local social democrats. He drew attention to the failure of European socialists in developing a forum for international socialism. Referring to the ideological factions among socialists, Lohia said, "European socialism has bogged down in statistics and moderate politics, Asian socialists are idealistic and enthusiastic but lack stature. As a result just like Asian communism and capitalism, Asian socialism is still in search of an identity. That is why some times it tilts towards one and sometimes towards the other".

In a radio talk in Paris, Lohia said, "Pacifist feelings are on the decline today. Europeans increasingly feel that freedom and progress are not possible without war. To talk of the Gandhism in Europe is meaningless till liberty and prosperity are divorced from war. The masses don't see any alternative other than monstrosities of Communism and capitalism. Intellect has stagnated, while thought has been replaced by propaganda. People stick to an idea half a century old, and refuse to get out of the mental rut. There is no communication between the conceptual and the concrete. Here we face a challenge. Neither communism nor capitalism can solve the problems of today. There is an extreme disparity between productivity of countries. An hour's labour in U.S. is equivalent to the three hours of work in Britain and fifteen hours of slogging in Asia and Africa". In this speech Lohia also put forward his ideas like third world, five pillared world state etc.

After France, Lohia toured West Africa, South and East Asia and Israel. In Egypt, he met the farmers, the Moroccan freedom fighter, Shahazada Abdul Karim, and the Secretary General of Arab League, Azam Pasha. Lohia had made up his mind not to discuss Indian government and problems in this tour. He stuck to international affairs only. On his return, in his press conference in Bombay on 25th November 1949, Lohia said, "Third World War can be averted by nurturing the third force. Instead, our foreign policy is based on inaction. Asian and African people look up to India to lead the organisation of the third force. India cannot be effective without changing its economic set up. Nor can India hope to carry out reconstruction with the aid of Europe and U.S. During the war, the British raised the women's land army to cultivate four million acres of farmland. Here in India we could bring under cultivation fifteen million acres of land in three years with a land army of two million. Our scientists and engineers must revolutionize production through the development of technology of the small machine".

The first World Convention of Socialists was held in Frankfurt on 3rd July 1951. Lohia represented the Indian Socialist Party. The resolution about international affairs before the convention basically supported the Atlantic block. It said that "the Korean war has proved that joint action of peace loving nations can contain aggression and avert a worldwide conflagration. This convention holds the view that democrats should join hands with the U.N. to prevent war".

The resolution was tabled on the first day. Lohia arrived on the second day. He opposed the resolution. He said, "Let me now proceed to say that I am opposed to the resolution on peace which is now before the Congress. I should hate to get the impression that I feel in any way superior to anybody here. I am only too conscious of the many unsatisfactory aspects of the Indian position. But this resolution, in my view, is not at all distinguishable from anything that a bourgeois party, Liberal or Conservative, could say on the subject. There is not a specific socialists idea in it. Behind this resolution, it seems to me, lie two basic assumptions with which I should like to deal. The first is that of collective security, the second, the contrast between the Free World and the Fettered World. We do not accept the division of the world in the Soviet Section and the Atlantic bloc. We believe that there is a third world, which is not at all satisfied with things as they are today, and which refuses to join either of the two antagonistic camps. This third world stretches from Indonesia, Nepal, & India, to Egypt, and includes many populous countries of the Far and the Middle East. This does not mean to say that we adopt an attitude of neutrality, or refuse to meet aggression. We simply do not believe that the present collective security system is going to protect all parts of the world from aggression. It is, in fact, meant for the Atlantic world. Moreover, it imposes a tragic burden upon Europe. Why should a similar burden be laid on the shoulders of the other nations as well?"

In the Frankfurt convention, Lohia enunciated his famous definition of Communism.

Communism = Socialism – Democracy and Centralism and Civil war and Russia.

Describing the parallels between the communist and the capitalist world, Lohia appealed to the convention: "Two-third of the world lives in poverty today. We believe that the essential international problem lies in the difference between rich and the poor countries. The rich countries have achieved much, and they therefore want to preserve and defend what they have, whereas we on the other hand have both to create & preserve. But our dilemma is that we lack the basis for such creation; capital and skill. It is this difference between creation and preservation, that lies at the bottom. Hence the difference in our political attitudes on international problems. The desire to preserve causes fear, whereas the desire to create causes courage. The resolution on peace which we are discussing here is a proposal based upon the wish to preserve. It does not appeal to us who are concerned with the creation. It does not appeal to youth. It is often suggested that the Soviet World stands for bread and the Atlantic world for freedom. I believe this to be a false contra-position. Bread and freedom are very closely linked together. What happens in Madagascar or Algeria refutes such claims. If we have these facts before our minds we shall fight shy of such glib statements. Nevertheless, the socialist parties of the Western Europe may have no alternative but to belong to the Atlantic World. But the socialist parties elsewhere do not feel the same compulsion. They wish to remain outside the system of competing, big power, alliances. They may find allies for their viewpoint in Europe, for instance in Sweden, Switzerland and Yugoslavia, also possibly in western Germany. Burma provides a test case of the validity of our viewpoint. Burma did not give into communist aggression. She defended her independence and had been successful in so doing without belonging to either the Atlantic or the Soviet system. She relied upon the strength and determination of her own people. There is also a caste system in the international field and it must also disappear. There are five big powers which determine everything and the fifty or sixty five smaller powers occupy a very subordinate position. We must realise that the equality of all nations is one of the most fundamental socialist principles".

The freshness of Lohia's thoughts impressed everyone. The British Secretary General of the International Socialist Organisation told him: "I agree with seventy five percent of your views". But matters took an unusual turn. The enthusiasm about Lohia's thoughts faded away at the time of action. The resolution was passed without any change. It was established once again that European socialist parties are not only nationalist but are pro-Atlantic-bloc. Lohia went to Yugoslavia after the convention.

After Europe and the U.S., Lohia visited Japan, Hong Kong, Indonesia. Thailand, Malaya, and Ceylon, before returning home. In Japan, a joint communique was published by Lohia and Hiruwada of the Social Democratic Party. Third force, equality, social and land reforms, nationalization, development of the two thirds impoverished world, equal status for Japan, aid of know-how and machinery to Asian countries from a progressive and socialist Japan, joint organisation of the Asian Socialist convention, by the Indian and Japanese Socialist Parties and other subjects were broached in the communique. Yashiki Homino, a senior leader, wrote to Lohia later; "I am greatly indebted to your efforts, your thought about decentralisation and showed us the path to real freedom. In all fairness, you are an heir to Gandhi, who is enriching Gandhism further. In case of Japan's failure to accept the principle of decentralisation, it will lead to loss of identity and creation of the base imitation of Europe. Unless our value system is revolutionised, we shall never be able to stand up to the United States. Unfortunately, Japanese socialism today thrives on centralisation. One wonders whether the Japanese youth will appreciate your thought and guidance.

In Hong Kong, Lohia was served with an order against making any statement. Lohia of course refused to be cowed down. The *Tiger Standard* and *South China Morning* widely covered Lohia's visit. They stated: "Hong Kong, so often extolled as the Riviera of the Orient by admiring tourists, has received a brushing down from a visiting Indian politician Dr. Lohia. While congratulating us for living in one of the most beautiful spots in the world, Dr. Lohia includes Hong Kong in a world of dirt and disease which stretches from Tokyo to Cairo".

Questioned about Nehru's apparent friendliness for the Communist China, Lohia would not comment except to say that a feature of Nehru's foreign policy was too much excitement and too less accomplishment, it has not created any new force. Nehru was a servant of both the Soviet and the Atlantic Camps. The Indian leader, further observed; "I think that Burma is a very interesting country in Asia, and I think that Yugoslavia should establish closer relations with Burma. Only Yugoslavia and Burma gave me some joy in the course of this year. India too, has similar elements, and this can also be found in Egypt, in Iran and in Afghanistan. These countries are following the course of Socialism, and what I wish to stress, is that the men in these countries do not want to belong to either the one or the other camp. During my four-day sojourn in Yugoslavia, I have studied various aspects of life in this country. As regards decentralisation, which is one of the basic characteristics of this country, Yugoslavia is now exerting serious efforts to decentralise not only politically but also the economic administration. If human civilisation is to progress in the future, I think it can progress only on the basis of such decentralisation. But, I should like to add here, that in my opinion, small-scale industries, are more suitable for this decentralization than large-scale industries. Japan will begin to rearm itself now. The Indian Socialist Party will soon call an Asian Socialist conference and will extend an invitation to parties in Burma, Indonesia, Japan, Lebanon, Pakistan, Syria, Malaya, and perhaps China". Criticizing U.S. policy Lohia said, "My party had taken the stand that victors and vanquished are in the same situation as in early 1947. Mr. Truman is now taking the same line".

At the end of his world tour this was what Lohia had to say regarding to the countries he visited.

Germany:

> No knowing whether this old courtesan is trying to recapture it's former looks or possesses real beauty and eternal youth; the most thorough people on earth and yet unable to sunder the strings of European civilisation.

Yugoslavia:

> A communist country trying in a partial way to turn Socialist; brave people who want to secure peace by their readiness to lay down their lives for it, rather than buy temporary peace by paying the price of freedom.

U.S.A.:

> The land where all women are princesses and where the egalitarian's dream of treating a duchess like a skivvy and a skivvy like a duchess is near realized; the country generously anxious to give but far too sure of itself to want to take; the most virile people on earth about to illustrate all human history hitherto, that if beauty sours into profligacy, truth also turns into cruelty very faint. A very faint possibility that they might yet mingle hard with soft, truth with beauty.

Hawaii:

> Where one is kissed on arrival and kissed on departure. And

in between Madame Pele hisses a fair but venomous warning through a tiny blowhole, if one steps too close to the edge of the world's largest active volcano, Halemaumau.

Japan:

A face that is drawn and sad, due to helpless condition but ripples with merriment and action when in movement; a peerless discipline alone prevents its inner struggle; lacks a sense of harmony.

Hong Kong:

A beautiful tumour which Peking and Taipei both feed on, and the British juggler is able not to let slip it out of his fingers; where the evil side of the twin evils of conformism and coexistence is clearly visible.

Thailand:

The King of Asian opportunism; while Asian governments are in varying measure opportunists, the Thai government is the cleverest and the most successful; a large bit from India; a bit from China; and the third bit from elsewhere, have produced a witty and carefree people, whose contribution may yet be unique.

Singapore and Malaya:

The meeting place of the Indian and the Pacific oceans and of various races and people and therefore a place of pilgrimage. But the mind is not yet so free nor the heart so big, as to turn this pilgrimage into a living shrine of the physical and cultural approximation of humanity.

Indonesia:

Same as in India, wanting to change, but taking it easy, too damnably easy. Older than Europe and Arabia, Indonesia may yet play a large part in achieving the new human civilisation of activity and poise.

Ceylon:

A beautiful bit of Asia that was trying to be Europe, is now baffled and may someday try to be human. Because of difference in looks and manners, and for other reasons all humanity is far away from its ideal and the night is dark. Among other activities a strong willed programme for the physical and cultural approximation of various peoples is essential.

14. IN THE LAND OF JEFFERSON & THOREAU

Lohia landed at New York's Idlewild airport on 16th July 1951. A large number of newspapermen had gathered at the airport to meet him, as the people had been roused by the widely reported "March on Delhi" which he had led on 3rd June: American interest had been further whetted by his weak long imprisonment in Mysore in connection with the Kagodu episode, which had caused the delay in his arrival. The "march" and his arrest at Kagodu had received wide publicity in the U.S. newspapers. "Indian opposition leader arrested on the eve of his visit to the U.S". was the theme of the newspapers stories there.

The very first question the journalists asked him on his arrival at the airport was about the occasion of his imprisonment. He told them of the eviction of the tillers by landlords and the socialist attempt to resist it by a nonviolent struggle, which often, as in Mysore, meant imprisonment. "Spade-prison-vote; that is our way of action", he said and explained that the spade symbolised constructive activity, prison stood for peaceful struggle against injustice and the vote for political action. "What do you hope the Indian people would do in the forthcoming election?" a reporter asked him. His reply was: "I would like them to rid themselves of the wicked of Government they are suffering". This shocked Mr. J.J. Singh, president of the India League of America and the defender of the Nehru government in the country. He interrupted Lohia and asked: "But Rammanohar, isn't that off the record?" Singh, who had come to the airport to greet the Indian socialist leader was again visibly shocked by Lohia's reply to the question.

Lohia replied: "Not at all! this is entirely on the record". Turning to old acquaintances he said: "But I must explain to my friends. Two years ago, when I was in Europe, I would not say such things away from home. Now I do".

This change was not simply because things had gone from bad to worse in the two subsequent years, but because, on thinking over, he had decided that it was wrong to speak "diplomatically". He explained, "If there is any hope for world citizenship, we must start speaking honestly wherever we are. Before I left India, I told the press that I intended to speak frankly in America, of course, I assured them I would use my useful restraint".

He was asked how his foreign policy differed from Nehru's "neutralism". Lohia answered; "I consider the present government's policy not as neutral, but one of the alternate service to both camps. Anyway it has done nothing to create a new force in world affairs. The Socialist Party, first of all, seeks to develop a new camp of peaceful change, of democratic socialism in the two thirds of the world which belongs neither to the Atlantic nor to the Soviet camp. We would like to secure that belt which is neither Camp, especially from Egypt to Indonesia. I would include Yugoslavia also. The reporters asked Lohia the purpose of his visit to America. He said: "As a boy I was interested in the deeds of Lincoln and Jefferson, and I come from a community or caste noted for doing business, I was also interested in Rockefeller and Ford. From there, the way was easy to Sinclair and to your clares and Maxims. I have a fascination for American People and doubts about modern civilisation, of which America was the climax. I came to find which is uppermost, my fascination or my doubts. I come from the oldest, but not the wisest, country to the youngest and the most vital". When Lohia saw the airport parking lot filled with thousands of cars, he shook his head. "Are there that many cars in all of India? How can we be ever friends, India and America, with all this?" he asked.

After a few hours' talk with Robin Meyer, national secretary of the Socialist Party of the U.S., Lohia flew to Washington, D.C. in the evening. From the plane, he watched the galaxy of coloured lights, shining up from every small town; red and green traffic lights, movie captions, neon advertisements over the city. He wondered if all of India used as much electricity as was being used in that one city. "This a technicolour civilisation" he remarked.

The same evening, he flew 600 miles south to Nashville, Tennessee, to visit the Fisk university, the chief Negro school in the South. Fisk having conducted its annual Race Relations Institute, which Lohia was to address at its closing session. That was his first public engagement in the U.S., and his first audience in the country consisted of Negroes and white workers for racial equality from all over the 'States who had assembled to assess the year's progress and problems. He exhorted the Negroes to take keener interest in the African struggle for freedom. He spoke of a notion he held, that if the Negro had the political power during the last four hundred years, if the African continent had been free, or had been subjecting Europe, then the aesthetic and philosophical concepts would have been very different. It was frivolous and meaningless to ask whether Africans would use their freedom well. It was not only for the advance of two hundred million in Africa, but also for the advance of mankind as a whole, that they must pray for the success of African liberation. It was necessary to end inequality between nations in modern civilisation usher in a new civilisation, ensuring a good standard living for all.

He recalled that some eighteen years back when he was in Berlin, an American lady had asked him to call on her when he reached Paris. He and another Indian friend went to her apartment but the watchman would not let them, two coloured men, into the building. So they phoned her from a side walk cafe. She came down in tears and thought as if some damage had been done to Humanity. That incident made him think that was something good in America, that the American women were very good and fine. No European girl would have cried openly like this, she would be too 'civilised', but the American lady was still primitive enough to show her sympathy and cry for her conscience. That was the beginning of his fascination with the American people Mr. Lohia said. "It made no difference", he stated; "in Tripoli the lips were thick, in Paris, they were thin, in Berlin the skin was fair, in Nashville, it was dark but the inner heart was the same".

Lohia met Dr. Charles Johnson; the first Negro President of Fisk. Before he left, Lohia asked him: "Why not a little jail going? Resist some of this injustice directly and nonviolently and go to prison if required?" Dr. Johnson seemed sad as he stood in his parlour and said shaking his hands negatively, "No, we are not like India. We are such a minority here, just thirteen million".

Lohia was driven from Nashville to the Highlander Folk School at Montagle, in the hills of South Tennessee. This was the first leg of four day 800 mile automobile trip through the "Black Belt". On the way, they passed Andrew Jackson's home. Lohia's knowledge of U.S. history appeared to surpass that of most his guides. Occasionally Lohia used to react to individuals and events. "I think, I like Truman better than Roosevelt", he remarked to his guide. "Truman is one of the people and that is better than being a spokesman for the people. He uses crude language, he swears, he defends his daughter, but I like this rough vitality", he said. He reached Highlander late in the afternoon to find several dozens of farmers and coal miners, and that many more children, sitting on the grass awaiting the "Hindu visitor".

While discussing American plumbing, of which he approved, and India's lack of such things, Lohia was interrupted by a farmer, who said that he did not have such things either. Most of them had only a well, with no electric pumps, no sewage system, none of the modern conveniences. Lohia found there were two teachers for all eight grades of schools, and that, if the number of children fell below forty, there would be but one teacher. Lohia talked for a while, about the need for village people of the whole world to be united, and about his idea of four pillar state. The habit of overhead showers appealed to him, especially in comparison to the European invention—the tub bath, which, he felt, was obnoxious. But he was surprised to know that the peasants here had a bath only once a week.

Replying a question about communism, Lohia commented: "I consider communism as much evil as the status quo. But I would like to issue a warning. The American mind is obsessed with the bogey of communism. Whenever anything happens, the American ruling powers say it is a communist beast. Beast he may be, but he is not as big as that. Communism was also in China, but that is a long story, and you are partly responsible for that. However, communism is not winning in Burma, or in India. Look at the republic of Burma with insurrections on all sides, with communists or the forces of reaction in control of most of the land, still the Republic had succeeded and has recovered its ground. It did this on its own, primarily because it had the native force of democratic socialism.

The meeting over, a dozen or so young men, from a nearby

work camp, which was building an artificial lake for the community, asked Lohia if they could make use of their team in India. They said that they were prepared to do any work, and willingly undergo any hardships. That made Lohia visualise Indian and American socialist youths doing "Shramdan", shoulder to shoulder, in rural India. This was the response he met at almost every meeting. The picture of such teams, living in Indian villages, working vigorously under the direction of the village panchayat and alongside Indian socialist volunteers, delighted him. He said it might produce a small example of the combination of Western activity and Asian poise that he was seeking. Wherever he went in the U.S. during the tour, the people he met came under the spell of his personality. Women in particular would say "there is an honest man".

On 15th July, Lohia left for Alabama in the deep south, dominated by the white reactionaries; ardent champions of segregation. Every time the party stopped to eat, during the journey, friends accompanying him wondered whether Lohia would be taken for a Negro. Instead, there was always a friendly curiosity. An Indian student driving with the party, asked Lohia if, in Delhi, when he stood his grounds nonviolently under teatgasing by the police, he would have done the same thing had they threatened bullets instead of gas. "Would you not have decided that your life was more valuable for other issues, than for this one protest over civil liberties?" he asked, Lohia replied; "The world is not on our shoulders. We can only do what comes along, and do it as best as we can. Calculation like that is stopping much action in India".

At Marion junction, Alabama, Lohia told a farmer's gathering the story of Dr. S. Radhakrishnan's talk with Stalin, when he was India's ambassador to the U.S.S.R. Dr. Radhakrishnan told Stalin that he had found much to admire in Russia, much in communism which the world could use, but that he found one thing missing; a strange absence of 'soul'. "What is this soul?" asked Stalin. "That which you do not have" replied Radhakrishnan. "Now I do not know about the soul", Lohia added, "but I have found something missing, in Europe and America, too, something I noticed when I looked at people along the streets, and when I talk to them in their homes. There is a disease, a dissatisfaction, a restlessness". He told the audience of his ties to America—Jefferson, Lincoln, Thoreau, and then, American women. "They are princesses-which does not mean that Indian women are no goddesses who get their way, more than people think perhaps, but a country is very fine, which makes every woman a princess".

He said: "We seek a revolution of anger and sympathy, not one of hate and jealousy. One man, Mahatma Gandhi, has proved, the first man to do so, that this joining together of anger or class and sympathy, with all men and things, is not a poetic fancy but a practical possibility. Is Gandhi only a luxury in the modern world? Is Thoreau only meant for an idle hour, to read and revere but not to affect our daily lives? So far Gandhi and Thoreau have not entered the mainstream of life. In history, the Jeffersons have always been beaten by the Hamiltons. The time has come on the world's stage, for the Jeffersons to win".

There was kind of electric atmosphere during the talk, of rapt attention but no acquiescence, of warmth but no conversation. With the first question, sparks started flying. Someone asked him if he thought Truman was a Socialist, when Lohia expressed his liking for the President, but would not claim him as a socialist. The questioner added, "Well as far as I am concerned, you can take Truman back to India with you". Lohia replied that he would not like to take Truman away from America, but he would be glad to give Nehru to America, if he were wanted there. When challenged about treating the head of his government in this way he answered "My government? It is not my government. My country, my state, my people, yes, but not my governments and heads of governments. I am fighting to destroy it. In passing, let me say that I am very disrespectful to all governments and heads of governments and the like". Next, someone asked about caste. He repeated his hate of the caste system, and told how it represented the worst of humanity. "Although India has climbed the scales of civilisation, than which no other has gone higher, it has also plumbed the lowest depths", he said, and added; "Caste was an evil wherever it occurred, a disease of the mind, but the human mind was healthy too and would yet overcome the disease".

From there, Lohia was taken to the headquarters of Tennessee Valley Authority. A public relations man received the party, But something was wrong. The PR man had not looked up the "files" on Lohia and had not read what Washington had written about him. He proceeded to read and explain to Lohia, the American Declaration of Independence. An Indian student traveling with the party interrupted to point out to the official that Dr. Lohia was a scholar, economist a philosopher and he had some question to ask. But the official persisted in continuing his "lecture". After the party left the place, Lohia remarked, amidst laughter; "So now I have met an American bureaucrat too".

The party then went to visit the Morris Dam. When they discovered that the two rest rooms at the project had two signboards marked "colored" and "whites", they decided not to stop there, and flew back to Washington D.C. Present at the airport, to receive Lohia, were members of Congress, government officials, Arab socialists, American students, and officials from the Indian Embassy. This was a surprise, since the embassy had declined to cooperate in any way with the trip. Stringfellow Barr had informed Smt. Vijayalaxmi Pandit, the then Indian Ambassador, of the Foundation for World Government's invitation to Lohia and of his arrival time. Barr had asked if she would like to make appointments for Lohia at the State Department. The only answer was a phone call from the New York consulate, saying that it was customary for Indian nationals to pay a courtesy call to the embassy. After indications of the embassy's anxiety about the trip, some of the organisers of the tour had reminded Indian diplomatic friends that for most Americans, the arrival of an outright opposition leader would only strengthen hopes for Indian democracy. After all, the two party system was the American test for political democracy, and if any well known leader of the opposition party in the U.S. went to Delhi, the U.S. Ambassador would be at the airport to receive him.

At the reception arranged by Clovis Magsondy, an official of the embassy greeted Lohia. He said that the Ambassador had sent her greetings, and hoped he would see her. Lohia replied; "Convey my greetings to your Ambassador, and tell her that I would also like meet her. Also tell your Ambassador", he added, laughing; "that if she were just the charming woman that she is, I would go a thousand miles to see her, but since she is an Ambassador of India, please tell her, I said that she, and her employer should learn protocol".

To those who teased him a little about not being a Gandhian enough to pay his respects to the Ambassador at the Embassy, he only answered sadly: "Don't talk about being Gandhian, who knows what he would done with such a government?" Lohia addressed a meeting at Washington. He also met some trade union leaders and officials of the State Department. Here Lohia picked up a story. President Harry Truman one day decided that the world's religious forces should be marshalled against communism. He could find out the names of the prophets and the religions books of all other religions of the world, except Hinduism. Four hundred million Hindus—no official leader, no Bible, no creed! He was simply puzzled.

Lohia spoke at the Harvard university, the only university established and financed by the U.S. Government, and visited the Jefferson and Lincoln memorials. In the compact American home, Lohia liked the "hideaway bed" which served as a couch in the daytime, the "pressure cooker" which produced miracles in a few minutes, the refrigerator with its "fresh frozen" orange juice, and the shower, in which he stayed interminately. He claimed that the pressure cooker fitted the requirements of the small unit machine. At New York, he met Louis Fisher and Sidney Hertsberg in the morning, and Pearl Buck and Richard Walsh in Bucks county, Pennsylvania, in the evening. To find actual samples of the small unit machine, Lohia had several times been told to visit the museum of tools in Dolyestorm, Pennsylvania. When he visited the museum, it became clear to him that tools there did not represent the new technology he had in mind. Thereafter, Lohia carefully tried to specify that the small unit machine must be competitive. Therefore, must not be from the past century of steam, but must be inventions designed for the age of electricity, or even atomic and solar energy.

In the taxicab taking Lohia to meet Einstein, he casually asked the driver what he thought of Nehru, "Never heard of him" was the reply. When pressed he asked, "Is he one of those foreign ambassadors?" Lohia said that was just about right. But the driver knew about Gandhiji, that he fought the British with fasts, in a loin cloth, and that he was assassinated. During the journey, Lohia was told that only one-third of all Americans had heard about Secretary Acheson. "The people are right". Lohia believed, "These politicians they forget, but they remember Gandhi".

Dr. Einstein was seated on the porch of his small frame house, when Lohia arrived. For the next few hours, Lohia and Einstein carried on the rarest conversion of the trip. Best of all were the great, hearty, laughs which the two men shared as they surveyed the ironic states of mankind. For sometime they talked in German, but mainly they spoke in English for the benefit of others present. Einstein's curiosity required that Lohia talk Indian politics and outline the socialist programme. The programme of abolition of landlordism and the redivision of land, Einstein approved immediately. When Lohia answered a question about compensation for the landlords with the firm stand against it, proposing only a small rehabilitation aid, Einstein said, "Good, good!" When asked why had Nehru not done these things, Lohia replied that he did not know. Einstein laughed and remarked; "Some men write admirably but act miserably. When Nehru had a great rider, he was a wonderful race horse, but riderless?"

Einstein seemed to like the concept of the small machine, and strongly supported the idea of decentralisation of the authority. They briefly differed about Communist China which Lohia opposed as completely as he opposed Chiang's China of Status quo. Perhaps they would differ about Europe too, for one moment when Einstein seemed almost hurt when Lohia said: "You know I am not one of those who believe that the Europeans are more cultured than the American". "What?" Einstein asked, and Lohia reiterated that he believed America to be the natural fulfillment of the Europeans mind, and that Europeans are now jealous even of American plumbing, and pressure cookers: "It is only that America has more of what Europe wants". Einstein finally laughed; "I see you have an independent mind". "May I ask you a question, Mr. Einstein?" Lohia asked. "Not about politics, I have come here to learn from you, and on politics I suppose I might even have something to tell you, but in the higher field of human mind we need your help. In India I have said that our century has only three great men, Gandhiji, Bernard Shaw, and you. In Berlin, I said that our age produced only two thoughts; Mahatma Gandhi and atomic energy; one is gone and your invention is a source of death. How is the human mind to get out of this stagnation, this confinement and rigidity which are stifling it? Do you see a new integration which can be free thought for new voyages of discovery?" In this vein they surveyed the world for a while. When the two parted, Einstein said: "It is good to meet a man. One gets so lonely otherwise!"

That evening, Lohia met a number of men and women of the New York Liberal Circle, where Barr had invited them for a reception. The editor of the '*Saturday Review of Literature*', Mr. Norman Cousins, who had just returned from India, aroused

Lohia's ire. Cousins called on Lohia to request him to reconsider his position against joining the Atlantic in collective security arrangements, and reminded him that the Indian socialists had been wrong once before about Japan. When Lohia asked him what he meant, Cousins replied that he had been told that some socialist leaders were strongly pro Japanese during the War, and had even adopted some orphans of Hiroshima. Someone had spread the word that Lohia had written a pro Japanese article for Gandhiji's "*Harijan*". Lohia felt the very fact that the alleged article was published in Gandhiji's newspaper should have made anyone to pause. Further he remembered: "The whole point of the article was that if one were merely an Asian one might be happy to see even an evil Asian power drive out an alien imperialist, but since an Indian has 6000 years of human history behind him, he knows that no good comes from any kind of domination of one country or one continent over another". Lohia also wondered who was at work digging out-of-context remarks from remote places. "I think your liberals may be worse than your McCarthys", Lohia said and added, "they think that they are liberal yet they are willing to use the same kind of tactics. It is not the American reactionaries that worry me, but your liberals".

In New York, Lohia met the American capitalists—bankers and business executives. He visited the headquarters of the Urban League in Harlem. He spoke at the Bard College on "the Battle of Ideas". He said, "But there is another battle of ideas from the one you mean. Rigid hard doctrines assail us on all sides. One doctrine reduces us to instruments of future progress, set at some indefinite date. Another reduces us to instruments of the order as it is today. Thinking has become propagandist. We are in the grip of an intellectual disease amounting almost to death. Therefore, I ask you not to think of ideas as instruments, as weapons, but in their primary creative role".

In the course of his tour, he spoke to the whites in the south of racial discrimination. He tried to induce Negroes to take keen interest in the African liberation struggle and to defy discriminatory laws and court imprisonment; he explained to capitalists the concept of socialism based on decentralisation of the power and economy, and pointed out to liberals that there was nothing to choose between the capitalism of the west and Soviet communism. The next day he met Eleanor Roosevelt.

Scott Buchanan, Secretary of the Foundation for World Government, a philosopher, took Lohia to his farm. At supper, when Lohia commended the bread, Mrs. Buchanan told him the story of how a New England lady grew so sick of pasty, mass produced, store bread, that she started selling home baked, hand-kneaded bread, with all the wheat in it. So popular did this became that an industry sprang up based on hand-kneading and decentralised production. Now, to compete, the great corporations were advertising 'enriched' bread. "So, in one case at least, the truth has come out about the so called "efficiency" of mass production!" Lohia remarked.

He attended the Unitarian General Conference on World Order at Star Island, New Hampshire. Speaking at the meeting, Lohia advocated the need for the a revolution through sympathy and anger. He said that the choice did not lie between constitutionalism, on the one hand, and revolution, on the other. The choice lay between a revolution with peaceful means and a revolution with a revolver to the atom bomb. A member of the audience asked him whether Nehru was not well meaning. He replied: "I am not concerned with men's motives, but with the consequences of their actions". When the same question was repeatedly asked, he said; "Sometimes a refusal to look into a man's motives is an act of kindness, not cruelty".

During his walk along the edge of the island later in the moonlight, some of his American friends suggested that his anger at Nehru's failure was the other side of an underlying affection. Halfway in confirmation, Lohia said, "I have moved, as you put it, by one and a half men in my life". If Nehru stood only half as high as Gandhiji, that still left him tall. I can say this; he is a very sensitive man. You should have seen the pain he felt once when he could not meet his daughter at the airport on her return from a trip. Someone would have explained his absence immediately, but that second in which she would be looking for him, he could not stand to think of it. "You may not believe this, but today, for all my anger, if he really took up our programme and was ready to go ahead with it, I would be the first one in the party to support him and close the door on the past, he added. He flew more than 300 miles to San Francisco in order to speak in America's Town Meeting of the Air. More than five million Americans listened to him. George V. Denny. Jr., founder of Town Meeting, found Lohia's luncheon talk so lively that he asked Lohia to speak without a script "You mean, you want me to be vulgar?" Lohia laughed, and said, "Very well". That evening, in the San Francisco Auditorium, seven thousand citizens came to hear Lohia, Horace Cleveland of the E.C.A., and George Park, Korean Minister of Education discuss: "Can Asia be saved from communist imperialism?"

"Bread and freedom is something I can understand", Lohia began in his introductory talk, "but I get burned up when I hear people speak as to whether Asians want more bread or more freedom. One would think as if unless Asians bellies were full, they would have no taste for freedom or democracy. I reject this vicious doctrine altogether, which reduces freedom and democracy into a luxury if the full belly. Freedom and bread are inseparable, at least in Asia, and neither communism nor capitalism can supply these two to us. I would suggest that Asia can be saved from communism only if it is saved from capitalism and feudalism". He went on "I consider communism as great a threat, as capitalism and feudalism are. But I would like to point out again that, in the background of human civilisation, I consider Henry Ford and Joseph Stalin equally irrelevant because you have to go beyond both". This familiar theme of Lohia met with applause. When the E.C.A. officer talked somewhat paternalistically about aiding Asia, Lohia replied, to more applause: "Is the relationship between Asia and America that of one-way traffic or two-way traffic? If you think of it as a one way traffic—America pouring help into Asia—I would, remind you of what some senator or the other said; "we should not pour any more money into this Asian drain", I should like to point out that if money is poured by America into Asia, that is not in order to save Asia, but to save America herself. If war is to be prevented, the only way to do so is to permit and to enable the two-thirds of the world to create what they need because without that you cannot conserve what you have already created". When Mr. Cleveland ridiculed his opposition to the "erosive urge to an ever increasing standard of living", he said "there is such a thing as a decent standard of living, which will permit people to observe and fulfil standards of life, rather than become enslaved to furniture and carpets as a standard of living. I feel for the poor harassed housewife, who is all the time trying to keep her house spic and span, and clean the furniture, as if the furniture existed nor for her, but she for the furniture".

When Lohia returned to New York City, Garry Davis, World Citizen 1, came by to give Lohia a "World Citizen Identity card". Though Lohia's American tour had not been arranged by the American Socialist Party, Norman Thomas, veteran American socialist leader, had cooperated in arranging it in many ways. Thomas said that he only wished the American Socialist Party had been able to take over Lohia's trip in a grand way. Replying to the welcome speeches by Thomas and "Winkie" Barr at the community church, Lohia cited the welcomes he received in America, as examples of how the barriers of nationality do not exist everywhere and will be brushed aside. "Norman, Winkie,— they are my keen friends and comrades, far more than an Asian capitalist can ever be" Lohia remarked. Some of the Indian students and Republicans in the audience did not like Lohia's direct attack on Nehru's action and inactions. The next day he met Mr. Mathews, the *New York Times* editor and Max Schachtman, the revolutionary anti-Stalinist Trotskyite. "Why isn't your Gandhi cap dyed red?" Lohia was asked by someone who remembered the *New York Times*'s despatch of 3rd June, describing a 75,000 strong peasant march on Delhi, led by Lohia. The colorful caps reported to have been worn by the socialists seemed almost a symbol of Gandhian Socialism. "I just hate those red caps", Lohia said angrily: "It is a symbol of our fickleness. It could also lead to its own kind of corruption. Let our spade-used for an hour each day be our badge", he added. A warm reception met Lohia at the *New York Herald Tribune*, where the publisher, Mrs. Helen Reid, had arranged an editorial lunch. They talked a lot about India after the lunch. The Reids impressed Lohia very much.

He met Walter Reuther, American trade union leader, at Detroit on the 2nd August. The talk was very interesting. After addressing a meeting of Indian students at the University of Michigan at Ann Arbor, Lohia spent few hours with the Reuther brothers. After visiting Chicago, Lohia went to Milwaukee, Wisconsin, the only American city with a Socialist mayor. He found the socialists there believed that the prosperity in the U.S. caused the decline of the American Socialist Party.

Lohia reacted sharply against this defeatism. "It is a miserable admission to say that Socialism is only applicable when there is only poverty. If that were true, I would not be a Socialist. I hate poverty!" At Chicago, Lohia addressed two students meetings. From there he went to Madison. He stayed with Joan and Hart Domike. The previous year, the Domikes had set out for India but had returned home from Rome, because Joan's pregnancy intervened. When they had left for India, Lohia was high on their list of people to meet. "Why do Americans feel since the last twenty five years that they should have more children?" asked Lohia. The reply was: "It is in a way acceptance of life right now".

Jayprakash Narayan had studied at the University of Wisconsin. Lohia went to see J.P.'s teachers. To see a successful mid-western farm, Lohia went to visit Wilbur Rank's farm estate at Sun Prairie. Wilbur owned 2500 acres and had invested almost 10 lakh dollars in the farm. "You know", Rank told Lohia seriously, "I often wonder if I wouldn't be better off, if I had only 50 acres and ploughed it myself". Lohia eagerly asked him to explain. Rank explained that he always under pressure, always working, at paperwork mostly. He seemed to have no time to enjoy life—even to read a book. One machine breaking down at a crucial point, could stop everything and cost thousands of dollars. He thought he could be happier if he could get back to simple farming. Lohia explained the Indian socialist dream of a small unit technology and a decentralised society. Rank nodded with interest. Rank impressed Lohia a good deal. Next, he was received by Governor Kohler in the Wisconsin State Capital. From there Lohia went to North Dakot a, a farmers state to observe farmers and their life. Addressing staff members of the farmers union, Lohia asked them to scrutinize the large scale technology, to make use of it when good and discard it when it went beyond a certain point.

At Laramie, Wyoming, Dr. Tarakanath Das, the famous Indian revolutionary exiled by the British, met Lohia, He considered Nehru a traitor for having used the Congress to accept partition and therefore, did not return to free India. He told Lohia that he knew that the Socialists and Gandhiji opposed partition and had abstained from the fateful vote, but he blamed them both for not having taken the issue to the people and risked everything to prevent this tragedy. On returning to San Francisco, Lohia issued a statement on Kashmir, having read misleading reports in the U.S. newspapers.

On 9th August, Lohia spent the evening with the Schauffer family. Mrs. Kenny Schauffer was an ardent supporter of the World Government movement. She complained that many Americans have no swimming pools at their homes. Lohia retorted: "I seems there exist two classes here; one having a swimming pool and other without it. In summer at least there is a possibility of class-war in America". He met Earnesto Galarza, the farm labour union leader, who was suffering from pleurisy, at his house in San Jose in California. Galarza brought Lohia up-to-date on the disillusioning state of Mexican and south American revolutionaries, most of whom had gone sour. He described the smooth techniques U.S. corporations had developed to tempt and corrupt promising young reformers. At the Congress of Industrial Organisation's west coast summer school at Asilomar, he found that the organisers were scared of the word 'Socialism'. The C.I.O. staff wanted Lohia to be cautious and to stay "within the workers' comprehension". Lohia reacted to the suggestion strongly. He replied that he would not speak at all, but they assured him that they did not want that.

Referring to U.S. aid, Lohia said: "Whether or not you assist us, we are determined to defeat communism as well as capitalism." He turned to his theme of jail-going for Americans on the race question and recommended civil disobedience to Negroes and Whites. He mentioned Cicero and Norwalk. The people of Norwalk, Connecticut, had invited to their town the Negroes dispossessed in Cicero. "Norwalk is an expression of the American spirit which makes me proud as a world citizen", Lohia remarked.

On 17th August, Lohia addressed a crowded meeting at the Stanford University, his last public engagement of the tour. Replying to a question about India, he said: "If the 1952 elections should once again seat that wonderful liberal in power in India—who doesn't like "isms" just the way you don't like "isms"—then perhaps either by the end of 1952, or the beginning of 1953, we will be faced with a very bad agricultural situation, perhaps famine and such like, and in that condition, if the Socialist Party of India were able to undertake a mass but peaceful rebellion for the removal for these injustices, that would be the kind of thing that would save India, Asia, and the Socialist Party. If it does not, I don't know what will happen". A tall young man, a veteran, rose from his seat, impressed by Lohia's speech, and said: "I have witnessed American politicians with great interest for the past five years. I now have witnessed your speech as a politician. If the day ever comes when I hear an American politician give such a speech I will be very proud". Lohia was asked what America ought to do.

He said: "I would reply this as a world citizen; America should shed its fear of communism. Soviet Russia may have the stronger fist, but America has the longer arm".

The next day, he met Socialists of Berkeley. He told them that if he were an American socialist, he would go all out on an immediate issue of some kind of a public health programme, nonviolent resistance against racial discrimination and attempt to connect foreign policy with the problem of war and with economics, as a part of an effort for a world parliament. The night of August 19 started at an Italian restaurant, proceeded to a Chinese club, then to an American night club. Lohia liked the burlesque show at the night club.

After visiting some fruit and vegetable farms, Lohia visited the Central Valley Project, the largest irrigation project in America. He visited Hollywood too, but could not meet Greta Garbo, who was out of town. Lohia left for Japan on his way back to India after his six week tour of the U.S. During his tour, he gave about 20 public talks, one in a national radio forum with over five million listeners and had good conversations with leaders of thoughts, labour and politics. Throughout the tour, Lohia wore a Khadi dhoti, a shirt and a Gandhi cap. Many people who met him lamented the lack of such a vital creative person in American politics. Commenting on the tour, Lohia said: "My fascination for the American people has grown, but so have my doubts about modern civilisation increased". "When will we see you again", he was asked. When you have done something worthwhile in this great country", he replied.

15. FOREIGN POLICY: A NEW DIRECTION

The Socialist movement in Asia had been a prototype of the Marxist movement in Western Europe, with its aim, as that of communism, limited to the ending of capitalism. In fact, the movement of democratic socialism ought to have been as much opposed to totalitarian communism as to capitalism. It had, therefore, become necessary to reorient the philosophical basis of the Asian socialist movement. With this end in the view, the national executive in the Socialist Party, at its meeting in August, 1947, entrusted to Lohia and Kamaladevi Chattopadhyay the task of preparing the ground for building an international Socialist movement.

Lohia discussed the subject with socialist leaders from countries in Asia at personal meetings and through correspondence. Nehru had convened at Delhi, in 1949, a conference on Indonesia's freedom. Lohia availed of the opportunity to discuss with the Indonesian representatives. His efforts to persuade Asian socialists to meet in conference bore fruit in 1952. Socialists from Indonesia, Burma and India, met at Rangoon from March 25 to 29 that year and laid the foundation of the Asian Socialist Conference. The right and left socialist parties of Japan had sent their representatives to attend the meeting as observers. Addressing the preparatory committee of the conference, Lohia outlined the task facing socialists in Asia. He said that from Rome to Honolulu, was one world, while from Tokyo to Cairo and beyond, was another. "All Asia is prostrate with the common disease of poverty and it is aggravated in that Asians know so little of one another", he said, and added: "All Asia must first understand and sympathise with itself and then if possible, evolve a common policy". He also referred to the weaknesses of Asia. "A major weakness of Asia, he said", is the existence of the politics of religion, caste, race, or language. Everyone is familiar with this weakness. It is not confined to India alone. It extends all over Asia. Even such a country as Indonesia, which only recently won freedom, is a victim to politics of religion. West Asia is continually being weakened because of religious politics.

Another weakness of Asia, he said, was the lack of integrated thinking and of discernment. "Asian statesmen talk socialism and act capitalism. Their phrases are radical and their acts conservative. The third major weakness of Asian politics is the disease of the big man who is really a small man. The big man is very clever at making phrases or actions as though on the stage, but his achievements in internal as well as external affairs are nil". Lohia stated that with the exception of Japan, all over Asia a new middle class of politicians and bureaucrats had emerged with very expensive European tastes and habits. After the advent of the freedom, this had created all kinds of difficulties and complications. This class is Asia's fourth weakness. "Finally the last great weakness of Asia is politics of assassination and terror" he added. "The big forces operating today in Asia, and throughout the world, are the capitalists and the feudal forces, the communist and the socialist forces. Asia has a fourth force in religious and racial politics. In addition to these forces, there is large number of men and women who have begun to feel that all politics is empty and meaningless. In Asia scepticism is born out of indignation, bitterness, and resentment, out of the feeling that some people who were deeply trusted have betrayed and played foul, and also out of a belief that men and women, no matter what political parties they belong to, are inclined to betray because of their personal self interest. All Asia is faced with a variety of tensions that may lead, or may have already led, to war. An all—Asian foreign policy must be formulated with regard to each of these tensions—of abstentions, confederated approaches, neutralisation, expulsion of imperialists interest and mutual assistance pacts–to suit the various types of Asian disorders. This is a peace policy as well as freedom policy and may be tested on the most recent tensions represented by Japan and its peace treaty".

"A peace policy in Asia", he said, "would have to be, at the same time, a freedom policy as well as a renovation policy. In that context, Lohia referred to the issue of formulating a peace and freedom policy for Japan. Japan, like Germany and Austria, belongs to that group of danger spots in the world, which comprises of nations defeated in the last war. A meaningful policy for this group must base itself on certain postulates: (1) complete freedom and sovereignty of the peoples concerned; (2) recognition of their neutrality by the Atlantic as well as the Soviet camps, and consequently, their armed forces to be kept at the reasonable minimum; (3) the nonrecognition of their neutrality by either camp to result in their right to keep armed forces at whatever level they like; (4) in the event of their neutrality being violated after recognition, such violator to be treated as the enemy of the world, and a corresponding resistance by the armed forces of the world to follow".

"Slavery and poverty represent the basic disorder of Asia, Africa, South, South America, in fact, of two-thirds of the world. The crisis of the foreign policy is a part reflection of the crisis in modern civilisation. Feudal, capitalist and imperialist systems, dynastic power and communist ambitions are the main hindrances in Asia's path. They must be combated or overthrown through peaceful struggle, constructive work, and the vote. Asia must renovate itself. Without internal change, the best of foreign policy in any Asian country condemns itself to futility", Lohia said.

"The dominant impulse in the international relationship of the modern world is conformist", Lohia said. "and foreign policies of the great powers at least stem from that impulse. More than communism, more than capitalism, this disease of conformism is disabling the world. The Atlantic camp wants the world to confirm to its foreign policy. So does the Soviet World. These two monstrous structures of the Atlantic and the Soviet camps, had been unable to produce a world apart from the one that exists today, a world of evil and poverty and war and destruction. Each accuses the other but with the accusations, the misery also. The politics of socialism with a new internal and external outlook, although it might also introduce conformism in politics, should be given a chance, so that at least it may take the world away from its present moorings and set it on a different course".

He said that the principles and objectives of socialism in Asia would have to be considered from two view points. The first viewpoint is the application of socialism to the local Asian scene, and the second, the necessity of universal ideology and concepts. Countries believing in the concept of the third camp should also enter into mutual security pacts so that aggression upon one automatically became aggression on the other", he stated.

Exposing the hypocrisy in the advocacy of coexistence of Soviet Russia and the U.S., Lohia said that both of them been trying to suck the people of Asia into their camp. Naturally, the elements required to move the third camp are available in a larger measure in Asia. Capitalism and communism do not have the capacity to achieve economic reconstruction of Asia, because both believe in the use of identical technology of large scale industries and large scale concentrated production. This is totally useless for Asia in view of its too many people, too little land, and too few forces of production. Asia's density of population varies from the 300 persons per square mile of India, to Java's 600, while its productive equipment averages at Rs. 150/- per person. "The Asian socialist conference would have to be build a third force, based on the system of political and technological decentralisation", he said. "This is not to say that concentrated capital and large scale industries are entirely ruled out. There must be, for instance, steel works or river-training projects. But the accent should rest on the other type", Lohia added.

Referring to the question of foreign aid, he said that any aid that is designed to tie up an Asian people with one or the other of the conformist systems must be rejected summarily. Some of the aid may be in the form of investments, bearing interest and reasonable profit, provided conditions of control and compensation in case of nationalisation are clearly defined. Such aid can be of use only to such Asian economies as have decided to revolutionise themselves, to become socialist and also to devise appropriate and new forms of reconstruction. For foreign aid that comes to capitalist economies serves to rouse expectations, to cause revulsion when these are unfulfilled, to give chaotic elements an added opportunity, and also to bolster up inefficient traditional or corrupt regimes. An effort should, therefore, he made to set up a world development authority to which every people would subscribe according to capacity and from which every nation would draw according to its need.

Lohia outlined his concept of a world parliament which he

said, should replace the U.N. He pointed out that human democracy would continue to be restricted as long as the adult vote determines and elects a national parliament without in any way determining and electing a world parliament. The powers of such a parliament should not be difficult to be in. The powers may be restricted to the right to impose peace and help drawn world reconstruction.

"What will present difficulties", he said, "is the adjustment of existing imbalance of strength to an approximation of strength among people of the world, and the delimiting of constituencies that will yield a world parliament not too far removed from the realities of power but removed far enough so as to achieve the new order and mechanism that adjusts itself and expands. Acceptance of progressive disarmament of nations and establishment of an international armed force are both dependent on the devising of a world parliament and world government that would achieve the ideal, without altogether departing from reality, and be also capable of expanding the content of freedom and equality".

"This is indeed a dilemma", he said, "but, should it prove insoluble, the fate of man is sealed. The peoples of Asia must strive their utmost to solve this dilemma, to bring into being a parliament of man, where there are no high or low castes, where man achieves the majesty of equal power, and whose judgement would be the conscience of mankind. They may, as an immediate necessity, offer critical support to the U.N. and its various agencies, with a view to correcting excesses of the existing semblances of power, but, more so, as a step towards achieving a new balance of an equal world".

"With a view to attaining a new world order, Asian socialists must forge links with like-minded world movements and forces. A distressing feature of world opinion is the entirely separate ways, which varying protagonists of a new order tread. To achieve a federation of these various initiatives for a world order should be the aim of Asian socialists and such a concerted opinion may ultimately slay the three monsters of hunger, slavery and war", he stated.

Lohia's exposition of this international policy produced a tremendous impact on the gathering. It was reflected in the joint statement issued by the secretaries of the Socialist parties of India and Pakistan after the meeting. Similar joint statements with Indian socialists were issued also by the parties of Japan and Lebanon and the International Union of Socialist Youth. All the statements stressed the need to build a third world force for reorganisation of the U.N. and decentralisation of political and economic power.

Lohia had worked hard for convening the Conference of Asian Socialists. It surprised many, when he did not attend the conference when it met in January 1953. The debacle of the Indian socialists in the general election in 1952, had created a feeling of frustration among party workers. Lohia placed before the party, a new comprehensive approach to the tasks and increased its strength and popularity by bringing about the merger of the Krishak Majdoor Party with the Socialist Party, resulting in the formation of the Praja Socialist Party. These efforts made by Lohia helped remove to a large extent, the feeling of despondency among party workers and infuse in them a new spirit of enthusiasm. It was at this time that Jayprakash Narayan and Ashok Mehta began to oppose Lohia's line. There was also a dispute on who should represent the party at the Asian Socialists conference.

In sheer disgust, Lohia decided not to attend it. Jayprakash led the party's delegation. It was expected that the Indian delegation would take the initiative in keeping Asian socialists away from the politics of Nehru and Mao. But what actually happened was quite the contrary. Jayprakash declared, in the course of his speech at the conference, that Nehru was a great man and the interests of the nation were safe in his hands. He also announced his intention to explore the possibility of cooperation between the Congress and the Praja Socialist Party.

Delegations of Socialists parties of some countries to the conference, particularly those from Israel, were pro Atlantic bloc. Israel, Burma and Indonesia had come under the influence of Atlee. They influenced Jayprakash and Ashok Mehta, too, with the result that the group plumped for Nehru's liberal policy and the conference strayed from its objective. Instead of defining its own independent policy and programme, it toed the Nehru line towards Asian affairs and the Atlantic bloc in the international sphere.

These developments at the conference disappointed Lohia. He hoped that the situation would improve, if there was a change for the better in the policy and approach of the Socialist Party of India. Lohia, therefore, devoted his attention towards improving the affairs of the party. He did not however lose interest in the

Asian Socialist Conference. Towards the beginning of 1954, Lohia felt that the party's political line had assumed a definite direction, and therefore, attended the session of the conference held that year. However, deliberations in the conference revealed that instead of becoming an instrument of world revolution, it had become a centre of the politics of establishment. It also became clear that the conference was inclined towards the Atlantic bloc. At the meeting of the Asian Bureau, Lohia moved a resolution advocating boycott of goods emanating from countries that were perpetrating atrocities against the peoples of Kenya and Tunisia. The resolution was not accepted. At that time the South East Asian Treaty and Defence Organisation were being set by the Atlantic camp. The conference was called upon by Lohia to declare itself categorically against the move, no matter how the resolution was framed, whether denunciatory or critical of the proposed SEATO. This proved to be unacceptable. Nor were Asian socialists prepared to support the idea of the world parliament based on adult vote. They could at least have demanded that the U.N. should franchise to all member nations the right to vote enjoyed by permanent members of the Security Council and the system of permanent membership itself should be scrapped. Socialists from Burma and Indonesia were scared of adopting any definite stand on any such issue. A delegation from Vietnam was admitted to the conference, though everybody wondered whether its members were socialist at all. The only consideration that impressed the conference in admitting it was perhaps its anticommunist record. Asian socialists were, however, unwilling to be similarly impressed by a slightly pro-communist record of the Lanka Samaj Party.

Meanwhile, Lohia began to realise that the affairs of his socialist party were not proceeding along the desired line. He had to give up his dream of improving the character of Asian Socialist Conference and organising socialists in Asia, as he had to devote his attention and energy to clean the augean stables of his party. Lohia also found that socialists from Burma and Indonesia and Praja Socialists in India were more pro Atlantic bloc, than the parties in the power in the respective countries. The tendency among Asian socialists to lean on the crutch of the Atlantic bloc, and the policy of the Atlantic bloc powers to corrupt political leaders of underdeveloped countries, had resulted in a progressive increase in the Atlantic bloc's interference in the domestic affairs of Asian countries. The debacle of the Asian Socialist Conference, as of that of international socialists, also profoundly pained Lohia. The unity of the workers of the world had ended with the first world war in 1914; and no element which could serve as an instrument of change remained in the Asian Socialist Conference after 1954. Lohia's view was that Asian Socialists imbibed the socialist doctrine as it was preached in Europe after the end of the first world war, and appears, as they were, they turned it into a more terrible caricature of itself.

Though the peoples of Asia are militant, the entire socialist leadership is moderate. The tyranny exercised by the big powers is self evident, but small nations are not prepared to stand up and resist it, he said referring to the behaviour of Israeli Socialists at the Asian Socialist Conference as an instance in point. "On every major issue of anti bloc or anti-imperialist import", he remarked, "Israel took the lead in stalling and delaying". Lohia said "I must confess today, my error of premature universalism. The somewhat socialistic settlement of Israel impressed me, but I deliberately overlooked the fact that they were artificially maintained by foreign money, and also hopefully believed that they would have an impact on the whole of Asia, at least West Asia".

Suffering can take or a people towards intrigue, diplomacy and narrow fanaticism, just as much it might incline them to a life of pure and undeviated harmony and undifferentiated universality. The Jews have suffered more than any other people on earth. Only those who are unmitigatedly coarse will refuse to stand with the Jews as their kinsmen. This is not a case of sympathy; it is a case of being one with them. To be one with a Jew, however, by no stretch of imagination, means to be one with Israel". A major obstacle to the growth of genuine internationalism lay in the attitudes generated by criticism, he said, and recalled how he was once barracked by a group of lovable young persons in an American university. They wanted him to take the lead in organising the international brigade of nonviolent volunteers who would transpose themselves between the warring armies of Korea. The young man who made the suggestion was utterly genuine. Some of them would probably have laid down their lives, had the suggestion matured. Lohia said he had told the young men that he could not assist their endeavour because he would not want to spend young lives or his own, trying to palliate a crisis of other people's making to intervene partially into forces, in whose maturing or denouncement, he had no part to play.

"A truly international mind must want to create a crisis of its own making. A crisis is, after all, the simultaneous existence of conflicting forces that are contending for mastery and are no longer able to live together in peace. Persons and parties that are wanting to create the united human race must continually create new forces appropriate to their aim, which, without doubt, clash with existing world and its constituents. Men of peace may only want that these crises are generated and matured in term of nonviolence", he said. Lohia stated that there seemed to be four great objects to which men could offer their continuing passion and even surrender his lives in time of trouble; self and its needs; state or nation; mankind and God; or woman, truth or beauty. Of these, mankind was still dormant and that of truth or beauty in the doldrums. Alone, self and state, move most of them.

A true internationalism could never come into existence until the object of mankind was given a concrete shape. The respective roles, functions and places of the state and the world parliament must be defined. Every human being must have the right to travel anywhere in the world without a passport; he must have the right to work and even die wherever he pleased; the world parliament should be elected by adult citizens of the world; a fixed percentage of the defence expenditure of every state must be pooled into an international authority and a world armed force established; the peoples of the world must vow to give themselves a world constitution, This would bring them in conflict with their nation state. They must then be prepared to practice civil disobedience. "What a great experience it would be for mankind, if masses of men in different countries of the world, simultaneously and civil resisted their own governments in pursuit of the common aim to achieve the world state", he remarked.

Lohia had always been making pointed references of the disparity between the world of the rich and strong whites and that of the weak and poor coloured. He said that after the 1962 war between India and China, both coloured nations of people who yearn for equality, irrespective of colour must unite. He urged that the leaders of the U.S.S.R. and the U.S. should regularly meet at an interval of six months to consider the question of making the world free from hunger and ending the exploitation of the underdeveloped part of the globe. He was sure that if they arrived at an understanding these two super powers would be able to uplift the underdeveloped nations. It was possible that they might unite on ignoring the demands of the under-developed, and added that he would welcome such a development. That alone would make the underdeveloped nations self-reliant. If these nations realised that there was none in the white world to aid them, they would either stand on their own legs or there would be revolution in those countries.

When Nasser nationalised the Suez Canal on 26th July 1956, Lohia said the day would go down in world history as a memorable day. It marked the beginning of the era of equality and prosperity in the history of Afro-Asian countries. Egypt wanted to build the Aswan dam for it's prosperity, but the western powers created difficulties in the way by denying aid to the project. This incident was the beginning of nationalisation of the foreign capital and the end of the domination of the west. Egypt had the right to nationalise the canal under the Constantinople Treaty of 1888, and the Anglo-Egyptian treaty of 1954.

Lohia said that India should have told Britain that an attack on Egypt would be considered by her as an attack on herself. Nasser had invited representatives of Indian newspapers to meet him. He wanted to place through them the facts about Suez Canal episode before the world. But the government of India remained silent. India should have quit the Commonwealth on the issue, but the Government of India remained inactive. Nehru's behaviour made one wonder whether he was the last victory of the British to cap them. Nehru complained in a letter to Marshal Tito that Nasser's action had violated a clause of the Briyoni agreement, signed by Nehru, Tito and Nasser, which provided for safeguarding "legitimate economic interest of the powers in the Middle East". "Surely, the clause was not meant to safeguard the interest of the White powers" Lohia stated. Arab and Soviet newspapers gave wide publicity to Lohia's statement.

When Khruschev attacked Stalin at the 20th Congress of the Soviet Communist Party in 1956, Lohia said; "The mass of the Russian people and even their leaders need undoubtedly to be reassured about their own safety and security. Living in insecurity and a state of arbitrary arrests and deaths, wangled justice, absence of law, general terror, deprived large sections of the people of the sense of secured well-being. No people can permanently stay in such condition, least of all, a people which has been progressing materially. The foreign relations of such a people are governed by suspicion and lawlessness, on its side as well as on that of the others. Such international relationships, polished by doubts and lawlessness became too heavy a burden, like that of a nightmare, for the people most isolated. The Russians people have, without a doubt been the most isolated among the world councils at least among the white nations. To dispel internal terror and external isolation has become a primary need of Russian leadership. This cannot be done except by cutting away clean from Stalin and the methods he practiced. The students of history will indeed recognise that it was precisely Stalin who brought Russia and her present leadership to the forefront of world affairs. In fact, the second weightiest place in respect of industry and armaments. Whether such a fast rise in material power would have been possible in any other way is a matter for speculation. What was unquestionable, was, that Stalin, a great Asian leader, when chance brought him at the head of a backward, but predominantly European people, and while he despised Europeans, and loved Asia, needed to whip and terrorise his own backward people, into matching and out racing all European advancement, used communism to increase Russia's strength and he brought the predominantly European people of Russia to the level of West Europeans and Americans". Now that Russia is as strong as the strong West European and American peoples and also because the internal terror and external isolation have become insufferable, a return to the European family was necessary, and has taken place. In some ways, it is also a return the human family, he stated. "The present leaders of Russia have been accomplices in Stalin's crimes. They are, in fact little jackals to the lion Stalin. They took part in every one of his black deeds, and anything else is patent gibberish", Lohia pointed out.

Discussing the impact of these developments on world affairs, Lohia said that the concept of unanimous reconstruction had forcefully emerged out of the Russian Communist Congress. "This concept", he said, "was valid only when communism became the government, and through the dictatorship of the proletariat. It has now been extended to cover all such countries whose governments may be non-communist or non-socialist but who largely practice a peace policy or a foreign policy sanctified by communism. This is only natural. In order not to weaken peoples and governments whose help is essential to Russia for the purpose of countering and outmatching America, and also to dispel Russia's international isolation, communism must practise the concept of unanimous reconstruction at least in those areas. Acharya Vinoba Bhave's concept of unanimous decision, Ashok Mehta's areas of agreement and Jayprakash Narayan's partyless politics, and the earlier communist concept of dictatorship of the proletariat and the present concept of unanimous reconstruction are all of one piece. That is why their doctrines must inevitably cancel each other, at least until one of them usurps the government of the land". Lohia further said that concept of unanimous reconstruction for countries pursuing a friendly foreign policy like India and subtler relationship with West Europeans so as to wean Americans away from positions of strength may give slight prestige, and a little strength, to international communism. "That will not be so. Communism through peaceful and competitive coexistence lacks the lustre of communism through conflict", he stated. He envisaged the possibility of Indian communists practising this concept of unanimous reconstruction. Until the 20th Congress, Communists liked Nehruism in all the world, Indian communists, he said were robbed of all self-respect and even that minimum pride which held the personality together. The Russians had sinned up with profit. Indian Communists had sinned without gain. They had, during the open rebellion of 1942, associated with the foreign rulers in treacherous suppression of their own people, they intermittently dishonoured the national flag, and they had learned to abuse Mahatma Gandhi. When they did this, they were sustained by the martyr's faith in the world revolution and its leader, Stalin. "That faith and leader are now dashed to bits, and the books of their world revolution are glorifying Mahatma Gandhi as a peoples' leader, like Lenin. One would have thought that Indian Communists would need all the sympathy of their countrymen to restore their self respect and broken personality though the leadership of the Indian Communist Party would not. "That would be communism through competitive coexistence and would lack the lustre of communism through conflict".

Commenting on the development in the Congo, Lohia said: "Patrick Lumumba was the first notable coloured leader who tried to fight back against the partitionist trickery of the twentieth century imperialists. While the great leader Gandhiji submitted to his Kasavubus and Tshomas, Lumumba, a much smaller man in other ways, combated partition of his country and died. The India Government's policy in relation to the Congo had vacillated between the Belgium-Kasavubu-Atlantic line on the one hand and the Lumumba-Soviet-Africa line on the other. This has resulted in the grave weakening of forces of freedom and unity and has encouraged separatist and pro-imperialist forces. History will never forget and forgive the fact that an Indian officer was in command of the U.N. forces when Lumumba was transferred from one prison to another and eventually murdered".

Russia invaded Hungary in November 1957. When the Russians suppressed the uprising of the people of Hungary and hanged the Hungarian leader, Imre Nagy, Lohia remarked; "The Hungarian experience has proved abundantly that communism, at least in East European countries outside Russia, is the creed of the minority and a cruel and ruthless creed at that", and added; "the creed must be reevaluated by the coloured peoples of the world".

"There was a time", he said, "when many people made the mistake as though the iron rod of Russian rule had destroyed all sentiments of freedom in East European countries. Let there be no such categorical assertions about human nature and it's craving for freedom ever again. Man will resist injustice as long as he lives. There may be brief intervals during which he goes quiet, but he will rise again and again, as long as injustice prevails in this world, no matter what truthless barbarians rule over him. The Hungarian episode has made it quite clear that Poland, Czechoslovakia, and probably Rumania also, would under certain circumstances undertake actions which would cause the collapse of the Warsaw alliance". Lohia said. His prophecy about the force of nationalism rising again and again in East European countries, undaunted by ruthless repression by Soviet Russia, came true when the armed forces of Russia and other Warsaw Pact countries invaded Czechoslovakia in August 1968.

"Communism outside Russia, particularly in Eastern Europe", he pointed out, "has shown a split between the orthodox and the heretic communists. These heretic communists, as is shown by the case of Imre Nagy, have not desisted from taking the assistance of other nationalist forces in their land. I wish to repeat again and again, that nationalism is today the most dominant force in the world, whether we like it or not, and that no internationalism and no ideology of one particular economic reconstruction or another, is strong enough completely to cancel this vital force of nationalism. On this basis, I conclude about the Hungarian case, that whether today or tomorrow Russia will have to withdraw from the eastern European territories. That Russia may take time to do and it may also be the result of bloodshed. But, there seems to be no doubt that, Russian communism is at war with the nationalism of East European lands and such a war can have only one consequence".

Lohia said that India's foreign policy must not be formulated according to the personal predictions and prejudices of the ministers for external affairs. It must be based on well-defined principles. India's external affairs ministry lacks creative ability, he said, "We have had enough shibboleths. The grand design of a free India, acting as a nucleus of creative strength for a new world, and away from both the Atlantic and Soviet camps, has emerged as a welter of clever words. But, only those words have power, which well up from the heart. India's foreign ministry has known how to speak clever words, not true words. It did not speak true words on defeated Germany and Japan, China and Tibet, or Kenya, Egypt, Hungary, Algeria and Israel, nor on non-violence and war, on disarmament, nuclear or unilateral, and, what is worse, bribed almost all the vocal elements to ventriloquy. Its attitude to Anglo-America has been one of oral disharmony but material compliance, and to Soviet Russia that of material disharmony but oral compliance, while a purposeful approach to both America and Russia would have been based realistically frankly, and harmoniously on India's estimate of her needs and those of the world's".

Commenting on the debacle of the Socialists in the elections held in Burma in 1960, Lohia said, "To most socialists the rout in Burma must have caused agony, as the defeat in England some months ago, was the occasion for sorrow or anger. Ever since Karl Marx, socialism has become a doctrine of environmentalism, which inclines the socialists to emphasise the environment and to minimise the individuals, to love humanity without loving man. Incomplete abstractions tend to cruelty or dictatorship. After communism appropriated the environment of socialism, preeminently the abolition of the private property, and practised it successfully, socialism had tried, as a counter move, to reduce or even forget it's environmental base. After having learnt to forget man, communism has at least been able to retain the love of humanity without being able to acquire love for man. Nothing, therefore is left for socialism, except to shake on the ice or moss of opportunism, to manoeuvre and intrigue, to make cynical calculations, which it calls realistic but which are generally wrong, and to ache for parliamentary and ministerial positions".

He added: "I am sorry for Ba Swe and others whom I have liked in the past, but I would ask them once again to break with the cynical realism of U. Kyaw Nyein or to persuade him to give it up. I also urge the Praja Socialists of India, perhaps for the twenty-first time now, to break with the unprincipled realism of their leadership, which is bound one day to destroy them physically as it has already ruined them spiritually".

Lohia described the action of the Khrushchev Government in removing Stalin's body from the Kremlin as symptomatic of its anti-Asia feeling. Stalin was hated in Russia because he was an Asian, hailing from Georgia. Lohia regarded preservation and display of the body of the dead as a barbaric tendency. He welcomed the removal of Stalin's body from this point of view, but he said, "the process would not be complete till Lenin's body also was removed from the Kremlin". He also expressed the view that no statue should be installed to perpetuate the memory of a great man till three centuries had elapsed after his death.

Referring to Khruschev ouster, Lohia said that the manner in which Khruschev was ousted from his office was improper. Freedom of thought and free discussion was impossible in Russia. It appeared that conspiracy and palace intrigues would continue to triumph in the U.S.S.R. in the future also. No doubt, Lohia used to raise his voice against injustice perpetrated against anybody anywhere in the world; but he had a soft corner particularly for the coloured. When communist China exploded the nuclear device, Lohia, though an avowed opponent of the red rulers of China, who were hostile to India, was somewhat glad that the monopoly of the white in the nuclear field had ended, but that did not mean he was in favour of a unity of the coloured, irrespective of ideologies. "I am unashamed of my insistence on the frontiers of skin colour, the rich and powerful white as against the poor and weak coloured, but, this has merely been the recognition of a fact, at no point has it been used as a plea for an unprincipled combination of coloured peoples", he said.

"Continental combinations irrespective of ideologies", he added, "have always been a sham. If some people still persist in them, even after the India-China war, some great mystery of interests is working behind the screen. Any coloured combinations to achieve equality with the white peoples is therefore, devoid of value. What may succeed in achieving equality between the white and the coloured, is precisely a combination of all those who desire equality, irrespective of their skin-colour".

16. SOCIALISM: DOCTRINAL FOUNDATION

The Socialist Party met at Panchmarhi in May 1952, under the shadow of its debacle in the first general election in India. The party had fielded a large number of candidates for the election. Some of the party leaders were not only confident of a spectacular success at the poll, but had also confidently expected that it would be returned to power in at least two states. But the result of the election gave a rude shock to them. The debacle had demoralised the party leaders more than its rank and file. The very existence of the party appeared to be jeopardy. From its very inception, the party had a band of brilliant and capable young men which any organisation would envy. About this time, leaders like Achyutrao Patwardhan, Kamaladevi Chattopadhyay and Aruna Asaf Ali left the party and Yusuf Meherally died. Besides, the party continued to suffer from several weaknesses. It had still not become free from the influence of Marxism. There still existed the belief in section of the party that the ultimate overthrow of the existing order could not be carried out except through force. The strike of textile workers in Bombay and the agitation against the bifurcation of the Vindhya Pradesh were the only two struggles organised by the party during the previous two years. The textile strike in Bombay and the "break-the-Iock" satyagraha at Hyderabad were also symbolic in nature. Some leaders of the party still continued to regard Nehru as their leader. Half-baked Marxists in the party leadership pooh-poohed Lohia's struggle for social revolution and his criticism of the inadequacy of the Marxist doctrine. Lohia was the only leader of the party whose poise was not affected by the electoral setback. It had become necessary to lift the party from the slough of despondency and re-invigourate it, outlining, in clear terms, its basic principles and policy and a programme of a action. Against this background, it was in the fitness of things, therefore, that Lohia was chosen to preside over the Panchmarhi conference. His inspiring address at the conference justified the choice in full measure.

He said in the course of his address: "Socialism, the only hopeful doctrine of the age, was in a bad way. Torn between the worlds of capitalism and communism, socialism is unable to evolve into a doctrine which would reconcile the claims of stability and change, which would serve the needs of stability without strengthening the status quo, as well as the needs of change without fomenting chaos".

"Socialism", he said, "is a newer doctrine than capitalism and communism. That will explain some is its failings and also give hope. Faulty application and organisation is another cause. But the career of socialism is impeded most by its inability hitherto to secure a doctrinal foundation. No living doctrine is ever fully founded or closed. The Day will be dismal when socialists cease to complain of their inadequacies. But there must be adequate doctrinal foundation of consistent logic, that gives socialism it's direction in thought and action, and saves it from confusions that disperse and scatter. Socialism must ever be a doctrine that grows, but it must also ever seek the principle that holds its various limbs together. Socialism should cease to live on borrowed breath. Too long has it borrowed from communism its economic aims and from capitalism or the liberal age its noneconomic and general aim. An acute disharmony has resulted. To explore once again the economic and general aims of society and to integrate them in harmony should be the high endeavour of the socialist doctrine. "

Capitalism, he pointed out, is a doctrine of the individual and of free enterprise that leads to ever changing application of science to industry and agriculture. In its economic aims, it seeks mass production, low costs & profits to owners. In its general aims, it seeks democracy and morality, through adjustment of diverse interests, and peace, through balance of power. This capitalist integration held good for one-third of mankind to whom the benefits of its revolutionary technology have strictly been confined. Although it has led, even amongst them, to periodic crises and wars. But it has produced the graver contradictions between the massive means of production over one-third of the earth, and the decaying apparatus over the rest. The contradiction has, like a knife, cut the world into two. Peoples living more than 40 degrees north of the equator, have at least bodily comfort, while the much vaster numbers of others are submerged in misery. This whole other world bleeds. Capitalism has imposed the peace of death on Asia and elsewhere, and caused their population to grow and their economic apparatus decay.

Lohia further observed; "The people of Russia & America live in densities of under 50 persons per square mile, and although some parts of Europe have reached high densities, they have their vast production apparatus and still have the vast colonial hinterland of Africa and Asia to fall back upon. The coloured peoples, inhabiting two-thirds of the globe on the other hand, have already attained unbearable densities, for instance, 300 persons to the square mile in India and 600 in Java, while their productive apparatus is so woefully meagre as to compare Rs. 150 worth of tools per person with Rs. 5000 to 8,000 worth of tools per person among the white people. The task of capital formation in this two-thirds of the world is far too colossal for private capital to accomplish. The efforts to spread capitalist integration, which has hitherto been of local application among white people, to all mankind and make it universal, is foredoomed to failure. Poverty and war have been the two monstrous progenies of capitalism, poverty to the two-thirds of mankind, and war for the rest, and it is powerless to destroy these two. In the midst of such appalling poverty of the coloured peoples, morality through free enterprise, and democracy through adjustment of interests, are impossible to achieve.

Lohia urged the need to appreciate the practical disasters of communist victory in these areas of high density and low technology. He pointed out that communism inherits from capitalism its technique of mass production; it only seeks to smash the capitalist relation of production, by liquidating private ownership of property and complete state control over the means of production. To turn a peasant of India, Java or China into a tractor driver with the concentrated capital of modern technology will be a cruel and barren effort. Land areas averaged at around 15 acres for every agricultural worker in Russia before collectivisation and the tractor brought them somewhat at level with American agriculture. Where land areas average, between acre and a 1/1 acre, as in India and China, the communist modernisation of agriculture would throw tens of crores of people out of work. They could not be absorbed in modern industry, for that, too, would require a unachievable capital. "Over half the population living in two-thirds of the world is unemployed. This unemployment is indeed concealed because almost everybody appears employed, though they are chronically underemployed. To secure employment for such great numbers, a capital :investment running into more than Rs. 50,000 crores for India, and five times that amount for all the underdeveloped areas would be necessary. A mere statement of the requirements reveals its fathomless absurdity", he remarked.

"Currently, on the basis of the outlay of India's five year plan and taking the multiplier factor into account, a period of 75 years would be needed. A bigger capital investment under communism, made possible through ruthless suppression, may, at best, reduce the period to 50 years. During this period, famine and other tensions would cause untimely death by tens of millions, unheard of brutality, and certain ultimately collapse. Communism would indeed know how to abolish unemployment by concealing it under the guise of under-employment, a practice which it has followed in Europe, and which is too familiar in the under-developed two-thirds of the world, but it would not be able to conceal that, the few more Calcuttas and Kanpurs it might build would rest on the dry bones of tens of millions dying in numerous hamlets and towns in the country", Lohia continued.

"Is there then no way out?" he asked, and said; "there is none, if the accepted modes of rationalisation, common to capitalism and communism, are pursued, and the mind refuses to display its intelligence and ingenuity. A new mode of rationalisation and a corresponding mode of ownership would have to be devised. The small-unit machine run by electricity or oil was the answer. Technology, which the modern world had kept ever-changing, would have to make a revolutionary break with the present. The problem will not be solved by going back to earlier machines, discarded by modern civilisation, but by inventing new ones with a definite principle and aims. These machines shall be available to hamlet and town as much to city; it may be built on the principle of immediacy in operation and output; and it shall not require a large capital investment. Such a machine is the embodiment of the whole principle of decentralisation, in space and in time, so as to avoid complexity and achieve immediacy. This machine will not only solve the economic problem of the under-developed world; it will also enable a new exploration and achievement of the general aims of society" he said.

"This is not to deny altogether", he stated, "the heavier machine in steel works or in river-training projects, but emphasis must heavily rest on the small-unit machine. On the basis of investment assumptions made earlier with regard to five year plans, rationalisation carried out through such machines may well provide employment to ten, instead one, million persons annually. This immediacy in science and planning must be matched with immediacy of ownership and political control. Private property must of course go, except such as does not occasion employment of one person by another. Ownership of property by the state, exclusively at the centre, goes with mass production and is disastrous both for bread and freedom; property of appropriate types must be owned by the village and the province, as much as by the centre and by cooperatives socialism must irrevocably reject all doctrines of restricted capitalism and mixed economy", he stated.

Lohia said that "Socialism must develop forms of struggle and organisation which would aim economically at a technology that rationalised economy, not sector by sector nor regions by region, but, as far as possible, in all sectors and regions at the same time. The aim of immediacy in science and planning should be matched with the aim of immediacy in democracy and power. Remote tests often sacrifice the declared principles. Not remote, but immediate tests, should be applied to every act in present. Each act in the present should contain its own justification. Its immediate quality must be such, as makes it pass the test of general aims of society. It must not justify present lies by future truth, an immediate bureaucratisation by remote democracy, a present sacrifice of national freedom by a remote one world, or an immediate murder, by future health".

He referred to the wide-spread notion, that ascribed the cultural deficiencies of communism to certain elements and traits of the Russian people. It was argued that the older cultures of India and China, or the democratic conscience of the British people would soften communism. "The reverse might will be true", he said, "at the first touch when communism starts rationalising Indian agriculture, which does not possess the wide scope that it's Russian counterpart did. Already, China's terror has surpassed in some ways, that of Russia, and should the average one and half acre per agricultural worker be pressed into the moulds of communist rationalisation, there is no knowing as to what lengths the spirit of man may have to be oppressed. Soviet Russia would then appear to have been civilised in the process".

No greater disaster could befall socialism, he pointed out, than if the historical peculiarities of its career in Europe were sought to be universalised and reproduced in the other two-thirds of the world. Socialism in Europe has been gradual, constitutional and distributive. Socialism, henceforth, and in the rest of the world, must be drastic, and unconstitutional when necessary, and lay accent on production. The great deeds of European socialism in the sphere of the welfare state must remain an inspiration and a model, but Europe's socialism had a reservoir of massed forces of production, which Europe's capitalism had built, and from where it could distribute. Socialism in the rest of the world must build the reservoir as much as it has to distribute it's contents justly. It has to set up the investing and capital—forming community, before it can achieve the welfare state. Where such a situation has yet to be created, socialism must needs to be drastic, and in order to be that, it cannot always adhere to the slow processes of constitutionalism.

He said that "Constructive work be supplemented by resistance to injustice, but urged that the modes of resistance to injustice must be peaceful. Doctrines which enable violence are incapable of achieving a classless and casteless society. Socialism must learn to distinguish itself rigorously from such doctrines".

"Socialism must ever denounce the advocacy and organisation of violence, and it must strive for such a basis of peaceful struggle, as will lead to increased individual initiative and responsibility and not to concentration of power. Organisation of violence inevitably leads to concentration of power", he argued and advocated "organisation of satyagraha and civil disobedience to resist injustice. The spade, the vote, and the prison should be the troika of social revolution. In that context he referred to the party's activities in Maharashtra under the auspices of the Sane Guruji

Seva Pathak while hundreds of men and women had courted imprisonment in the satyagraha organised by the party against the pricerise of foodgrains.

"When socialism is able to unfold continuous programme of construction and struggle", he said, "the winning of votes, will naturally follow. No one should minimise the importance of the vote, for it is the grandest expression of the people's will. This expression may sometimes go counter to the doctrine and programmes of socialism, but it will not be good for the party to blame the people, or deride the vote. Both the people and the party are at fault in such an event, for if the people are not sufficiently enlightened, the party is not sufficiently matured. A major defect of socialist agitators is to look upon themselves as teachers of the people. They must realise that they are students as well".

Lohia said; "A two-way relationship of students and teachers should be established between the people and the party. Whoever is aware of such a relationship will look upon an electoral reverse as a spur to efforts for improving the party and enlightening the people. The majesty of the vote should never be derided, for there is no alternative to it. In another sphere, the alternative is between peaceful struggle against injustice, and organisation of non-violence, and between peaceful revolution and armed insurrection. 'Ballot or Bullet' is a wicked presentation made by capitalism and communism; the choice is 'Satyagraha or Bullet'", he averred. While communism is a doctrine of hate, Sarvodaya had hither to been an inadequate doctrine of love. Only when love and anger, love for all and anger against injustice, find a combined expression through a revolution, will humanity be able to make the next onward move. A fancy opposition has been allowed to grow between satyagraha and class struggle. There is in fact no such opposition and a genuine class struggle is civil disobedience.

No society is completely free from injustice, but India and other under-developed territories abound in misery and repression. Issues of national freedom and of discrimination between men on the basis of the colour has also come to the fore. "Shall these be decided by the organisation of violence?" he asked and said; "there is ample scope in the U.S. for the exercise of civil disobedience on the issue of discrimination between whites and Negroes and on the problem of citizenship, and a similar scope on the issue of caste system and citizenship in India. The day may come, when the exercise of the civil disobedience in numerous countries of the world, produces it's effect on the peoples living under communism.

The tensions and emptiness of modem life seem difficult to overcome, whether under capitalism or communism. Capitalists expected their ideal kingdom to arise out of each's man self interest operating under a perfect competition, communists still expect their ideal kingdom to arise out of social ownership over means of production, but their common fallacy has now shown up; that the general aims of society do not invariably flow out of certain economic aims, but an integrated relationship between the two sets of aims has got to be set up. If previous civilisations broke down under the weight of spiritual equality coupled to a social inequality, modern civilisation appears to be cracking under the weight of social equality couple to a spiritual one. Modern civilisation came to the end of its voyage some decades ago. Man is no longer at peace with himself. He must move away from existing civilisation in both its aspects of capitalism and communism. He is in exile, in search of his home. "The long pilgrimage of socialism has been to end the exile of man; his agonising self-alienation. That pilgrimage asks, in our time and in our country, a new direction. To offer that direction is the only way to keep it alive", he said.

Lohia said that conservatism and communism have strange identity of interest against socialism. Conservatism holds socialism as its democratic rival and does not fear communism, except as a threat of successful insurrection. Communism prefers the continuance of a conservative government and is mortally afraid of a socialist party coming to office, for its chances of insurrection are then dimmed. Until communism revolts successfully, it is a doctrine of succour and support to the bourgeoise.

The high priests of communism have rejected all notions of absolute morality and have raised evil behaviour into a noble virtue, as long as it serves the cause of revolution. Sacrifice of national freedom and treason become a commendable virtue, if practised for the international solidarity of the working class, as expressed through Russia or China. Democracy or parliament is utilised alone for its destruction and, what is perhaps worse, the hierarchical spirit and cult of complete obedience to the party leads to the abandonment of all responsibility and democratic conscience except such as is expressed through the highest committee. Mass violence and purges are necessary instruments. Above all, communism denies reason and has no faith in the capacity of the people to reach a decisively clear judgement, except through civil war. A doctrine such as this, which does not trust the people fully, is never reciprocated with adequate confidence of the people. A communist government through the vote for the whole people is, therefore, a contradiction in terms. Until communism achieves its problematic victory through an insurrection, its chief role is to split the socialist vote, thus to assist in the continuance of a conservative government, he pointed out.

Both the Congress and the Communist Party would, therefore, very much like to see the Socialist Party out of existence, for it is their essential foe. Nevertheless, there is some truth in the accusation that the Socialist Party does alternative service to the Congress and Communist parties. The party must definitely abandon its facing both-ways policy in doctrine as well as in programme. It should never be an auxiliary team of the Congress party. As long as the doctrinal foundation of socialism is not secured, the Socialist Party will continue to be torn between the Congress Party, which will often appear as the instrument of democracy and national stability, and the Communist Party which will as often appear to be a party of change. Between the stagnation of the Congress and the chaos of the Communist Party, The Socialist Party must ever appear to intervene like an enveloping power. The Congress Party is indeed to some extent a coalition of conservatives and radicals. Contrary to popular estimate, such a coalition does more harm than good and confuses the public mind with regard to radical views and forces. The two elements of democracy and national freedom, which go into making the Congress party, give it an advantage over the Communist party. In long run, the Congress party is without doubt, superior to the Communist party, for one may reasonably expect it to act democratically and nationally within certain limits. In the short run, however, the Congress is a party of famine and corruption and of disguised capitalism. The radicals in the Congress do more harm than its conservatives. There can be no question of the Socialist party treating them with consideration or wooing them.

He said that the general election had, for the time being, resulted in the fragmentation of the nation's political life. Besides these three parties, a large number of parties and groups have appeared on the scene. If the split occurs in the coalition of conservatives and radicals, it would be due to the pressure of events in the country, the Socialist party can increase this pressure by intensifying its own constructive action and peaceful struggles and initiating political moves in a big way.

Three broad types of parties and groups had appeared on the scene; one represented by groups like the Forward Bloc, the Peasants' and Workers' Party, the R.S.P., and the Scheduled Castes Federation; and the third by the Ganatantra, Mahasabha and Ram Rajya Parishad, while the Jan Sangh seems to share the characteristics of both these types. While the second type has blurred the line between radicalism and conservatism, it may under favourable circumstances, add its weight to the growth of a massive radical party and the third type under similar pressure, join the Congress Party. The youth of the Jan Sangh may travel either to socialism or communism, and its leadership, to the Congress. There is a need now to work out a political line which would, in time, break up the coalition of the Congress Party, and send to it groups represented by the third type and some elements of the second type.

"The Congress party will then become in outward form what is already in actual reality, a clean and outspoken party of Indian conservatism. This political line must also consolidate groups represented by the second type and elements of the first with the Socialist Party, so that this party becomes in time the clean instrument of Indian socialism and radicalism, and is able is absorb all other radical elements, when they split away from their organisations. The communist party will, in such an event, lead, as it should, an isolated existence of extra-territorial loyalty and of doctrinaire hair-splitting and unfructifying calls to general strike and insurrection. The Socialist Party must be able to unfurl a political movement which, with its wide sweep, achieves such a consolidation", he said.

Referring to the party's electoral set-back, Lohia said that the Socialist Party of India should know that the reasons for their reverses are removable. If it frets and fumes, and tries artificially to capture attention, it will be but one of many other parties, without rudder and compass. The great test for the party comes when it suffers adversity. Can the Socialist Party take it? To take it would mean to bide one's time and prepare to strengthen one's base and doctrine, and further train the spirit. He declared; "The Socialist Party may perish, many a time, fighting its own kind of battles without pollution from the twin masters of the age. The Socialist Party will rise again, for man will live. Victory shall belong to socialism".

Socialists had never examined the economic aims of communism closely. Some of the leaders of the party had, in fact, had been devotees of Marxism and of the economic ends of communism, right from the party's foundation in 1936, to its Panchmarhi convention in 1952, they took pride in calling themselves Marxists. It was their firm belief that it was necessary to faithfully follow the tenets of Marxism, if they were to believe in scientific socialism. Many of them even claimed to be more genuine Marxists than the communists themselves. They criticised the absence of democracy under communism. But they had failed to grasp the fact, that the existence of dictatorship, and absence of democracy, were the twin progenies of economic concentration under the system of communism.

Lohia had grasped these contradictions inherent to the communist doctrine long ago. Every theoretician acknowledges the heritage bequeathed by his forebearers, while developing the doctrine further by removing its inadequacies. That is why there is some measure of similarity in different doctrines. But this similarity is like the one between one man and another. Though all men are similar physiologically, each of them has a distinct personality of his own. Likewise, Lohia's Panchmarhi address was not a critique of either Gandhism or Marxism. It was a statement of an independent, integrated system of his own. It provided a sound, lasting, and well defined basis for the socialist movement, which had been hanging in the air like a Trishanku.

Leaders of the Socialist Party had, till then, been all praise for Russia's five year plan and used to ridicule the concept of decentralisation propounded by Gandhiji. Lohia had his doubts about the success of the Russians plans. He was not prepared to accept Marxism as the complete truth, nor to adopt it as the basis for the socialist movement. One who propounds a new system is seldom understood by his contemporaries. More often than not, he becomes the object of their hatred. His philosophy or doctrine is subjected to severe attacks. Lohia met with similar treatment.

Some of the delegates to the Panchmarhi convention, who had all along been under the influence of Marxism, could not stomach Lohia's criticism of that doctrine. Some of them remarked: "Marxism is a complete gospel, a bible, a new testament. It is the height of audacity to try to propound a new doctrine to replace it. Lohia is trying to swallow more than he can chew". Another exclaimed: "Reject Marxism? Impossible! Marxism can be the only way to end India's poverty". Though they liked Lohia's attack on Stalin and Indian communists, they could not relish his attack on Marxism, their article of faith. Contrary to the normal practice. Lohia's presidential address was discussed at the Panchmarhi convention. Replying to the debate, Lohia said: "I do not want to apply the tests of Marxism to my speech and examine it in that light. I am not interested in that, I am interested in stating the truth as I see it". He said that he was neither anti-Marx or pro-Marx, and that equally applied to his attitude towards Mahatma Gandhi. "I have been told", he said, "that I have rejected Marxism. I do not quite see how this question arises. But those who talk so much of Marx and are loud in their in profession of Marxism do not realise that some of Marx's fundamental formulations are incomplete. Marx's theory of evolution of capitalism, for example, is inadequate. Socialists the world over believe that capitalism, in its growth, leads to concentrated capital on the one hand, and on the other, to the integration of the relations of production. These relations of production produce within them a tremendous social force, and tensions between the forces of production, and the obsolete relations of production, develop into a conflict and socialism is born out of this conflict. I used to believe this. Even today I do, but will it be a complete statement? Then, will it also be correct to say that once capitalism was progressive, but today it is at an impasse?"

"If we must understand the theory of the evolution of capitalism, then such incomplete statements will not do. If we say that capitalism has engendered the clash between the forces of productions and relations of production, we must complete this statement by saying that in the wake of it's evolution, it also created two worlds; one on whose people it bestowed the benefit of its revolutionary technology, and the other, on whose people it bestowed poverty, misery and incalculable suffering. To one world it gave massive means of production, while to the other a decaying apparatus of production. Can this truth be denied in the face of facts and figures and the trends of history?"

"A conscientious Marxist will always endeavour to complete a half truth. But there are very few conscientious Marxists", he remarked, and added; "Marx also has a place in my tradition, which goes very much back in history and even beyond Marx, and is intimately connected with human integrity. Even Marx was bound by his hoary tradition and its endless quest across the waves of time. This talk of being Marxist or Anti-Marxist is futile and irrelevant. What is relevant is correct thinking and an integrated approach. Our mind must ever be on the quest, a quest for the essence that lies under Gandhiji's and Marx's thoughts. Quest, and not entanglement with tradition, can help us do this". Barring the few who reacted adversely to the address, the delegates to the conference were profoundly moved by the integrated ideology and programme of action outlined in it. Jayprakash Narayan hailed it as a classic of new thoughts. Ashok Mehta's comments were, however, cautious. He described Lohia's address as a new turning point in the pilgrimage of socialism, and so it was. Lohia had lifted the socialist movement from the old rut, provided it a distinct identity of its own, and given it a new direction for its onward march along the road of self-reliance.

Lohia presided over the conference of Uttar Pradesh Party held at Hardoi from 13th to 15th June. Acharya Narendra Dev, known as an ardent votary of Marxism, had not apparently liked, like other dogmatic Marxists, Lohia's Panchmarhi address, questioning the validity of some of the formulations of the orthodox Marxist doctrine. "We alone have kept Marxism on the right track and should not feel ashamed to call ourselves Marxists", he said, and advised the delegates to undertake a deep study of the philosophy instead of resorting to a "Shock Therapy" as Lohia had done. Lohia's address to the Hardoi conference was virtually a postscript to his Panchmarhi address. In it, he dealt with the antinomies: spiritual and material, present and future, religious and nonreligious, individual and social, bread and culture, to which he had not referred to, at Panchmarhi. Most political doctrines, including traditional socialism, have got tied up in rigid philosophies, that mangle these antinomies with disastrous result to thought and action. A political doctrine and organisation must be able to contain a variety of philosophies, but that would be possible only when they are shorn of dogmas and rigid querulousness.

The attempt must be to confront the antinomies and overcome them into a working unit, he said. "Any sensible person would want to be a materialist in spiritualist company and a spiritualist in materialist company. This is the debacle at which the human mind has arrived. Needless to say, this is due to the one-sideness of most current philosophies and the effort to fit the facts of life on the rack of a close notion", he remarked. He observed that, "Spirituality appears in many guises. It's most revolting form is the practise of gainful miracles and the calling to shape and speech, persons who are dead. Only slightly less revolting is its second guise, in which it leads a ceremonial half hour existence in a life otherwise of callous self and totally divorced from it. A third manifestation of spirituality is the advocacy and the justification of the existing order, of its proper relationships between rich and the poor, of the caste system nationally and internationally, of the inferiority of women to man, and generally, of hierarchies of high and low".

Lohia propounded that, Spirituality has also appeared in two other forms, noble though ineffectual. It is to be felt in such messages as those of the Upanishads and the Bible, of Lao Tse and Socrates, or even Erasmus and Jefferson. These messages have at best, acted as amendments and rarely as substantive propositions. They have been unable to alter the main flow of life, whose source has lain elsewhere. A fifth form of spirituality is the pure investigation into the mind and the soul and its working, and the disciplines of compassion or contemplation that make man feel one with the universe and everything. Such disciplines profess to be timeless and ageless and claim no connection with a specific form of society. Of the five forms of spirituality, the first three are totally unsatisfying, while the other two raise a regret and curiosity if they could not be made more effectual. Even the materialists have rejected all forms of materialism save one. Dialectical materialism seeks to explain the world and reality, not only by interpreting it, but also by changing it through the doctrine; that being determines consciousness and that consciousness in all it forms-religion, poetry, jurisprudence, economics, and the like,—is an ideological superstructure thrown up by the mode of production prevailing at a time, and therefore, values and spirituality of an abiding character do not exist. It may here be pointed out here, that the answer to the question; whether mind or matter is primary, would still not settle a question of primacy. Even if it were some day established that mind is a product of matter, which has not so far been done, it would settle the question of chronological sequence, but the problem of logical sequence or equality will still remain. That matter and mind, may both be logical sovereignties traceable to the principle, which includes them both and expresses them in sequence, is a theme that has often recurred in Indian philosophy. The relation between being and expression of consciousness, between mode of production and expression of consciousness, has not been studied in any detail, or in its totality.

Marx had said that men indeed make history, but only within the environment in which they are born. This is a true statement, but its meaning is as elusive as that of any other great saying. All being is no doubt becoming, but through all becoming runs also a pattern of being. Every moment is no doubt a passing link in the great flux, but it is also an eternity in itself. The current age of man has laid great stress on achievements and little on being. Forgetful of the twofold character of the moment, it has raised the antinomies of the material and the spiritual, which should never have been done... The moment as flux is material, while the moment as eternity is spiritual. Expanding knowledge and the method of dialectical materialism may reveal the flux, contemplation or compassion, or the method of spirituality, may reveal the eternity. But the two methods must inform one another. . . Man must live for the future, but he must also live in the present. The twofold character of the moment settles the relationship between the material and the spiritual; to the realm of dialectical materialism belongs the moment as the future; to spirituality belongs the moment as the present. While old time socialism denounced religion as opium to man, the modern attitude seems to be one of indifference to matters of religion, and, belief in secularism. This is not a complete attitude.

Religion appears in four different ways. It breaks out as quarrels, sometimes bloody, among various religions. It defends and upholds the existing order with its mode of property caste and women. It is also an ethical and social training in good conduct. Finally, religion, at its best, appears as the discipline of compassion and contemplation. The first two expressions of religion are indeed an opium to the people. Instead of making politics religious, and thereby softening somewhat the clashes of power, religion itself becomes political and thereby adds fanaticism to intrigue. Such religion must of course be denounced, but the other two expressions of religion cannot be a matter of no concern to politics or to socialism. While a socialist may be a believer or an atheist or even an agnostic, he cannot stay unconcerned about religion. The opposition between the individual and the social is resolved as soon as the twofold character of the moment is borne in mind. For the moment as the link with the past and the expression of the future, the individual is the product of environment and the instrument of its change. For the moment as the expression of the present, he is the executor of his human destiny and the mouldier of the environment. The individual is both an end and a means; as an end, he is the unfolder of love unto all; as a means, he is a tool of revolutionary anger against tyranny. All problems of the individual and the social, of ends and means, fall in their true perspective. Good means must not be postponed until after the advent of revolution, and the revolution must not be postponed until all men have become good.

Instead of arguing the antinomy of bread and culture in the abstract, it should be related to the situation which obtains in the hungry two-thirds of the world. Bread and culture here, are inseparable. If one is asked to wait, the other must wait as well. The taste and quantity of bread depend upon the quality of culture and vice-versa. With hungry stomachs, and due to other reasons, an almost insurmountable sloth has overtaken this two-thirds of the world. This is not to say that the people do not work hard; they sometimes work harder than elsewhere and are turned into beast of burden. But hard and regular work voluntarily undertaken is lacking. This lack must be removed before plentiful bread can be had. To dispose sloth, the people must feel that a new age of equality of opportunity and of sacrifice has dawned. They must also be provided with the tools which make their labour rewarding. These two requirements of the spirit and technology can be fulfilled in the situation where bread and culture become warp and woof of the same cloth.

In order to enliven the moribund village, to dispel the indolence of the high caste and the sloth of the low caste, land must be distributed, but land redistribution may turn into a nine day wonder and degenerate into a paper transaction, if those to whom the land is distributed have no say in the administration of the village, in the fixing of procurement prices and government revenue, in the recruitment of military personnel, and generally in the exercise of the sovereign power of the state. Socialists must undoubtedly pay as much attention to constructive work as to satyagraha. Struggle without construction is like a sentence without a verb. S.M. Joshi is a remarkable embodiment of both construction and struggle and if he becomes a model for other socialists to follow, the Socialist Party will well mean something for all the world, Lohia felt.

Redistribution of land, minor irrigation projects through land volunteers, and a food army for uncultivated areas, are the essential ingredients for a right food policy. All trade in good crops may well be taken over by the state on its multiple levels. The political economy of the days of Mahabharat also ordained it. Existing agencies in food crops will not, by and large, refuse to be integrated into a system of State trading, he observed.

Later, presiding over the conference of the Gujarat Socialist Party, Lohia expounded a new interpretation of history. He elaborated it in a series of lectures he delivered subsequently under the auspices of the Nava-Sanskriti Sangh at Hyderabad. He said in the lectures, that man and civilisation had not progressed in any particular direction without interruption. A particular civilisation reaches its peak and begins to decline. All the civilisations in the world had passed through such vicissitudes; when a civilisation is progressing, internal social relations are dynamic and flexible, but these relations become rigid when its decline begins, and urge for progress is replaced by a rigid system of jurisprudence and stratification, which can be regarded as a caste system. Centres of strength and prosperity shift from one region of the globe to the other, when a civilisation in one region decays and a new civilisation is born and blossoms in another. He said that socialists would be able to realise their objectives if they succeeded in ushering in a new world civilisation, based on humanism, free from the distinctions of caste, class and colour, and which would promote all round development of man and society.

17. WILL TO POWER

Through his addresses at the Panchmarhi, Hardoi and Gujarat conventions, Lohia provided a distinct doctrinal foundation and a new perspective to the Socialist party. Meanwhile, Acharya J.B. Kripalani, Dr. Prafullachandra Ghosh and T. Prakasham had left the Congress and formed the Krishak Mazdoor Praja Party. In the first general election, that party, too, had been routed all over the country, except some parts of Madras and West Bengal. The Socialist Party had a Marxist tradition and the K.M.P.P. was Gandhian in outlook. Lohia still believed that a merger of the two could provide a strong alternative to the Congress and worked in that direction. The two proposals were considered by the general council of the Socialist Party at its meeting in Bombay, on the 25th and 26th September 1952. The merger proposal was approved at a joint meeting of the two parties on September 26, and the Praja Socialist Party was formed.

Jayprakash Narayan was the sole leader of the Socialist Party till its Kanpur convention, held in 1947. In subsequent years, Lohia's influence on the party progressively increased. At Panchmarhi, he was chosen as the ideologue of the Socialist movement. However, the party elected to head it's organisation, leaders who did not whole heartedly subscribe to Lohia's formations, particularly his conception of a third force in international affairs and his endeavour to integrate the various like-minded elements in the country into a broad-based non-Congress, non-Communist force. While Lohia advocated a dynamic political line, Jayprakash Narayan pursued the line of supporting Nehru, both in international and domestic spheres. This situation undermined the homogeneity of the party's leadership and affected its rank and file too. It created amongst party workers a unreal conflict between their loyalty to the ideology and loyalty to the organisation. Then followed a series of developments which proved disastrous to the socialist movement. In the meanwhile Jayprakash undertook a soul-purification fast for twenty-one days and declared his decision to disassociate himself with socialist politics and activities. The same time he made it clear that he has lost faith in Marxism and advocated "partyless politics of good people". Through speeches and newspaper articles Lohia tried to remove the confusion these developments had created among party men. "The greatest test for any political party", he wrote, "lies in its will to power. A curious obscurity has been allowed to grow around. The will to power is considered in our country as if it were a sin or at least ugly. The new party must end this enfeebling hypocrisy. It must be shot through and through with the will to power. After all, a political party exists because of policies and programmes, which it believes essential for the nation and the world, and which it must equip with the force of the government. The will to power must indeed be a chaste and vigorous will, as far away from perversity as it should be from weakness. A healthy will does not make use of lies, deceit and violence", he added. The will to power, of a person or a party, is best measured by the will to react to situations, old and new, he pointed out, and said that the two parties which were coming together (S.P. and K.M.P.P.) were not sufficiently alive to situations. A primary test for the new party would lie in its ability of swift reaction to old and new challenges, he said.

"For example, unemployment and malnutrition were dreadfully increasing, particularly among artisans, landless labourers, the middle-class and the educated youth of schools and colleges. These are precisely the sections which have no voice nor organisations and no political party has yet tried to reach them or to bring them to the stage of day by day history", he said. "The Praja-Socialist Party will have to react to all such situations, old and new. To react is primarily to be aware and then to think out solutions and finally to act in constructions and combat. Parties which are alive, react and kick in all directions. It is a false notion to imagine that one line or accustomed lines of work economise energy. A live party expands energy by expending it". Lohia pointed out. Lohia was trying to provide a militant orientation to the party's line of thought and actions through his writings. The Congress, its sympathisers within the P.S.P., and in the country, as also vested interests, could not naturally relish the prospect of the P.S.P. developing into a genuine, militant, opposition party. They tried to work to undermine Lohia's effort. As soon as he sensed the danger he wrote: "Like many members of the Praja Socialist Party, I have followed the varied reports of cooperation with the Congress party, with some concern. The people of India, and the socialist movement are plagued with a curiously indecisive and split attitude towards the Congress. While they have tended to look upon the Congress as a party of famine and corruption, the president of that party has continuously succeeded in blurring their vision. The P.S.P. must strengthen its own hands and not someone else's".

In February 1953, Nehru invited Jayprakash Narayan for talks and sought the party's cooperation. Nehru later had a similar meeting with Acharya Kripalani and Acharya Narendra Dev also. At the beginning of March, Jayprakash Narayan and Ashok Mehta formulated a fourteen point programme to serve as the basis for cooperation between the Congress and the P.S.P. and sent it to Nehru for consideration. When Jayprakash saw Nehru again on March 16, the Prime Minister ended the game of talks for cooperation, which he appeared to have initialised for his own amusement. He wrote to J.P. to say that the fourteen point programme was just a catalogue of attractive items and suggested that he should meet him (Nehru) frequently to exchange of views. He also expressed the hope that he would have the cooperation from Acharya Kripalani and Acharya Narendra Dev as well. Nehru did not want the P.S.P. to function as a genuine and strong opposition party. He wanted it to be a weak and paralysed party which would regard him as it's leader and would, at the some time, enable him to claim the world over that democracy functioned successfully in India. Jayprakash Narayan and other P.S.P. leaders walked into the trap cleverly laid by Nehru for the purpose.

Ever since his return from the Asian Socialists Conference held at Rangoon, Jayprakash Narayan had begun to urge that all parties and the people not belonging to any political party should collaborate in the task of nation building. He had also being advocating the formation of an all party government, as in his opinion, the task was beyond the capacity of a single party. He even pleaded that all political parties should be dissolved as their existence only creates lust for power among the people. He was so much influenced by the *Bhoodan* movement as to predict and it would sweep out of existence all political parties in the country. It was a surprising stand for any party leader to adopt. It bewildered party workers and created doubts in the peoples' mind about the party's future. In the welter of confusion created by these developments, Lohia took a firm stand and gave clear lead to the rank and file of the party. Writing under the caption, "I am an anti-coalitionist", he said; "The P.S.P. is as distant from the Congress party as it is from the communist and the communalist parties. If the communists & the communalists are parties of chaos, the Congress is a party of status-quo. The P.S.P. must increasingly distinguish itself from both, in thought as well as action. I do not have to add that the P.S.P. adheres to the similar theory of equidistance from the Atlantic and the Soviet camps. The P.S.P. does not recognise that there is a clash between party interest and national interest In fact, parties are formed and grow in the service of national interest. When the weight of custom and decrepit institutions oppresses the people, new ways of life become just as necessary in politics as in religion. I am sure Gautam Buddha's first speech at Sarnath, and the activities of his faith for many years thereafter, must have been denounced as a sectarian and party bigotry, by contemporaries to blur a new way of life. To avoid the search for a new way of life, out of fright of such denunciations or a search for a sloppy goodwill, is to surrender to the dead past. The accent on good people against parties and their ways of life can only end in a political dictatorship a la Hitler and Stalin, or a moral dictatorship in the style of Cromwell. The belief that good people must come together and blur the outlines of the parties must be combated. The P.S.P. is ever engaged in refining its programme of national reconstruction, which shall be both time bound and concrete. Should such a concrete and time bound programme of the P.S.P. find favour with the Congress or any other party, there will still be other obstacles in the way of an alliance or a coalition. Only when the people vote a programme into power, is there sufficient enthusiasm in the millions and an appropriate agency is created. The P.S.P. should stave off the threatened disintegration of the country not by becoming a shield but by continually acting as a sword. I will like the Indian people to relieve Nehru of his office and place Jayprakash Narayan in his place by voting for socialism".

The Congress had stated at almost regular intervals of six months, five different ideas such as classless society, cooperative commonwealth, a state without 'isms' and a welfare state. The Bhoodan movement had become lifeless as the Bhoodan workers insisted that it was the only solution to all problems. Further, it was being used to soften the opposition of the P.S.P. to the Congress. Lohia drew pointed attention of the people to these aspects of the situation. About the present 'monstrous' five year plan, Lohia said; "it is likely to result in a large scale famine". Thus the two big leaders of the party had in reality started striking at the very foundation of the party. The differences between Lohia and other P.S.P. leaders went on widening increasingly. They could not be attributed to the merger of the Socialist Party with the K.M.P.P. The leaders who fell victims to Nehru's charm belonged to the old Socialist Party. Through his thesis on the "compulsions of a backward economy", Ashok Mehta provided a theoretical basis to Jayprakash Narayan's policy, for cooperation with the Congress and the eventual coalition with it.

The party met in special conference in Betul in June 1953, against this background. Lohia was asked to speak before Jayprakash Narayan. He requested J.P. and the delegates to "forgive any sharp phrases that I utter and to take note only of the basic ideas which I will try to put before you". After criticising the moves for cooperation and coalition with the Congress, he said: "to the Indian people as a whole, the unmasking of the Congress is taking place gradually, and for all I know, the increase in vote for our party in the bye-elections is the result of this gradual unmasking, rather than any desire for coalitionist politics". He referred to the formula placed before the party workers, by those favouring cooperation between the Congress and the P.S.P. because of their common adherence to nationalism, secularism and democracy, and said; "If such common features are to be detected from time to time, what would prevent some people from detecting common features with the Communist party such as nationalisation of industries or redistribution of land?" The political object of the P.S.P. could not be to reform other parties, he remarked. Assailing the fourteen point programme formulated by Jayprakash Narayan, Lohia said "Vagueness and meaninglessness is a characteristic fault of Indian thought. We are always fond of talking of first principles and of philosophy, but seldom take good care to put meaning into our talk". He alluded to the view held by some persons that the acceptance of the programme by the Congress would change its character and create conditions in which national reconstruction would be possible and said: "This is taking too easy a view of successful programmes. Not one, but three, factors are necessary for the successful execution of a programme; one; well defined items which are concrete and time bound; two; appropriate agency; and three; corresponding atmosphere. There has been talk, here, of the political compulsions of a backward economy. It has also been suggested that heavy burdens and unpopular taxation have to be imposed on the people, in order to make national reconstruction possible. For such heavy sacrifices to be undertaken by consent, and not through dictatorship, it is felt necessary to achieve cooperation among the two largest parties in the country. This is a faulty and mechanical reasoning. The consent of the people depends not on summit cooperation among the parties but on the nature of measures undertaken, and the character of the government. One might wonder why the Congress government finds it necessary to extend such ridiculously frequent invitations to the people of India and their parties for cooperation. I am inclined to think that the less deserving a government of people's cooperation, the more frequently it extends invitations for cooperation. If the government were deserving and undertook satisfactory measures in a satisfactory way, the people would not wait for invitations in order to cooperate with it, and their political parties would do so with speed. Even a single party government, such as the Congress with its overwhelming parliamentary majority, would have the largest measure of consent if it only chose to undertake satisfactory measures. One may suspect that these frequent invitations for cooperation are either meaningless, or are extended with dubious intention of entangling the opposition in the failures of the government".

"Far more dangerous than the achievement of cooperation or coalition", he remarked "is the attitude of mind it generates. The search for areas of agreement, somewhat removes from sight the very much wider areas of disagreement. In a country where a hundred million people have to live on one meal a day, where near famine stalks from state to state, and full famine is threatened, where ejectments, police repression, unemployment and other injustices continually prevail, the party will only stultify itself by shutting its eye to them. There are sweeping areas of disagreement with government party. Let us not forget that we are still a young democracy and many democratic conventions and practises that are so natural to maturer countries, have yet to be secured by us and in the process many protests and fights will have to take place, which the European peoples no longer find necessary to undertake".

Lohia referred to the "moral and spiritual compulsions" which were being talked about, and said; "It is being said that good people of all parties should come together, that the party system leads to wasting and frittering away of national energy and that a clash exists between party interests and the national interest and that good people must, therefore, ever rise above party interests. All this has no meaning in politics, unless, it is meant to lead to a break up of the existing parties and to the creation of a new one, or to increase the strength of a the party of one's choice. I can well understand the effort to remove the deficiencies and weaknesses of a party, but I cannot understand the decrying of the party system altogether. I have in the past emphasised, more than any one, the defect of negativism externalism, electionism, and insurrectionary, that is obtained and still obtains in our party. But than a party is only a way, and to destroy the party that is to destroy that way".

"But", he pointed out, "goodwill is both a philosophical concept and a political recipe and it would be dangerous to confuse one with the other. As a philosophical concept, goodwill must permeate every act as far as possible and ever be at the back of the mind. It is then a universal feeling and its effects must not be restricted. This philosophical or emotive background of good, must bring within its purview the Communist Party and the Jan Sangh as much as the Congress Party. To restrict it to any one party, to the exclusion of others, is to distort the feeling of goodwill and, unconsciously perhaps, to adopt it as a political tactic". He went on; "Some comrades are holding me responsible, so I am told, for the recent happenings in the party, because they believe that by seeking to destroy the Marxist basis of the party, I, more than any other, have brought it to such a pass. I admit that I have been relentless in criticising Marxism, but it was not merely a negative criticism but a positive effort at building up of a new thought".

It was the general belief that Nehru had made a definite

offer of cooperation at all levels. But in his letter to Jayprakash Narayan occurred the sentences; "I did not think of any precise method of doing so. It was rather the general approach that mattered. I had not thought of what is called merger of parties. I felt that if there was a mutual realisation of the necessity of the cooperation, other things would flow from it. When you or Kripalaniji asked me for greater precision, I said that I was prepared to consider the question at all levels, including both popular and governmental". Commenting on this, Lohia said; "It is obvious that the Prime Minister has only made a vary vague request for cooperation. He was not clear about the precise method. Our colleagues asked for a greater precision. I am afraid that the Prime Minister on some day find it necessary to use this sentence against the party. Even if the programme had been presented to him, there was no need for our colleagues to have so precisely offered their cooperation on the level of the government in the event of his acceptance of their programme". Lohia suggested that the conference should appoint a commission for the purpose of framing the programmes for the party, both when it is in opposition and when it is office, as a way out of the crisis. However, Jayprakash Narayan, Ashok Mehta and other office bearers of the party resigned from the party's executive, even before the debate on the coalition and cooperation with Congress had concluded. The situation was tense and called for firmness in policy together with the avoidance of a split. In his shortest speech ever, Lohia asked the delegates to extend to him two privileges; "one, to speak on your behalf and two, none among you may speak after me" and said "on behalf of the convention, I request my esteemed colleagues to continue". The proceedings of the convention continued after Jayprakash Narayan had said: "Lohia's request will be considered". At the end of another speech at the convention, Lohia said; "People have talked of clarity of policy and unity of the party. I hope that this party will never split. But let us not forget clarity is as essential as unity".

As per Lohia's suggestion, a policy commission was formed and Lohia thus succeeded in postponing the evil day. Though the convention had rejected the move for cooperation and coalition with the Congress, some leaders still continued to think on those lines. The inclination to enter into electoral adjustments with other parties was the corollary of this way of thinking. Cautioning the partymen against this tendency, Lohia said; "In all areas where the parliamentary situation does not consist of a simple struggle among two parties one of capitalism and the other of socialism, a strong temptation to political piracy exists. Principles and programmes become subsidiary to the expediency of adjustments of personalities. In order to avoid such political piracy, the Socialist party must evolve for itself a firm and unwavering policy.

In the meanwhile, the Congress ministry in Travancore-Cochin toppled after the state assembly had passed a no-confidence motion, tabled jointly by the P.S.P. and the communist parties. The P.S.P. National Executive outlined the policy, its unit in that state should pursue, in the election to the state-assembly which followed the fall of the ministry. The policy was to achieve electoral adjustments with the United Front of the Leftists, without actually entering into an alliance with it. The policy had a threefold objective; (1) non-return of the defeated government, (2) non-increase in the communist strength and (3) expansion of socialists strength and governments. Lohia hoped that ". . . the P.S.P. of Travancore-Cochin would not go beyond the line drawn for them. In all areas where socialists are strong and are becoming the alternative, to the party of capitalism or mixed economy, there is no need for an electoral adjustment", he added. In this context Lohia propounded the theory of supporting the government from outside and without joining it. Lohia hoped that it would be possible to curb opportunism, but was also aware of the danger of partymen falling prey to lust of power. The Bombay party executive passed a resolution, criticising the decision of the national executive regarding the Travancore-Cochin unit, urged it to withdraw the permission given to the Travancore-Cochin unit for electoral adjustments with the Leftists. Lohia hailed this resolution of the Bombay executive as a "sign of health" and welcomed that the Party committees freely passed resolutions on problems of national importance.

Kisans of Azamgarh district in Uttar Pradesh launched a land satyagraha on the 9th August 1953. Entries in the government's land records were incorrect. Kisans fought valiantly for their rights. Hundreds of them had been imprisoned. The chairman of the U.P. Party, Gopal Narayan Saxena, was sentenced to nine month's rigorous imprisonment. The police lathi-charged even women satyagrahis. Lohia toured the district, studied the situation first hand and listened to the account of police atrocities. Dalsingar Dubey, secretary of the P.S.P. Ghazipur district, was severely beaten up by a dozen persons, in the dark of night, on a village track, when he was returning after addressing a meeting held to condemn government atrocities. Lohia hailed him as the hero of Ghazipur. The police had opened fire on students at Lucknow in a wanton manner. About the same time, the police had humiliated the party's Manipur leader, and M.P., Rishang Keshang, and had even slapped him. All this became intolerable to Lohia. He asked; "Why does not the party rise from its stupor?" The policy commission of the party met in Bombay from 27th to the 30th of November 1953. In the course of the discussions, Lohia asked "Why are not even party ranks, leave aside leaders or the national executives, moved by an incident like the slapping of Rishang Keshang or vindictive imprisonment of Pardy and Azamgarh satyagrahis? Why do some of us, within a week or fortnight of launching the movement or going to jails, begin to search for solutions? During the freedom struggle, many of us used to search for news of talks in newspaper columns, but surely not for the first six months of the fight. Why had this will to fight acts of injustice aggressively, to react to issues of national importance, deadened?" During the deliberations of the commission, Lohia referred to the programme the Party should undertake when in office. He said; "India has around 41 crore acres of land. Of this, 26.5 crore acres is under cultivation and 15 crore acres remains fallow. Of the 26.5 crore acres of the land under cultivation, only 6 crore acres are irrigated. Our governmental programme in the five years should be to bring one crore acres of additional best cultivable land under cultivation. "I propose that a good army of one million persons be recruited to undertake this task. The aims of the agrarian policy ought to be; (1) increased production, (2) increased employment, (3) greater economic equality, and (4) strength of the state". He added; ". . . private enterprise, in most of the large scale industries must go. It must be borne in mind that in poor countries, various such industries are interlocked, and nationalisation of one is impossible without nationalisation of other interlocked industries. No doubt, nationalisation is bound to lead to bureaucratisation and a way out has to be found to eradicate the evil". The commission entrusted to Lohia the task of preparing its report for the Party convention.

The first convention of the Praja Socialist Party met at Allahabad from the 29th to the 31st December 1953. The conferences held at Panchmarhi and Betul were special conventions. The one held at Allahabad was, therefore, the first regular convention of the party since 1950. The report of the policy commission, presented by Lohia to the convention, outlining a well defined and a concrete programme, envisaging, among other things, a four pillar state based on decentralisation of power, and enunciating a policy of development of agriculture and industries that could ensure economic equality. The convention adopted a six-point election policy which posed the danger of increasing the tendency of opportunism and lust for power in the party. It had become clear that there existed two divergent views in the party, but effort was being made to compose the differences and continue the activities of the party with determination and vigour. That had made it imperative for Ashok Mehta and Lohia to work shoulder to shoulder.

Lohia agreed to become the Party's General Secretary under compulsion of events and pressure from friends. However, he expressed to a colleague his doubts as to how he would be able to function successfully in that capacity. The Party had to be saved from the dangers inherent in the policy regarding elections. The task of ensuring clarity of thought, militancy in action and preserving unity in the party was far from easy. The party looked forward to Lohia's tenure as its general secretary with great hopes and expectations.

18. SUCCESSFUL STRUGGLE

In an open letter to the members of the party, written in early 1954, which was also the beginning of his tenure as Party's General Secretary, Lohia referred to the reports received by him the about acts of injustice perpetrated by the government against the people. He said that all those acts cried for resistance and called upon the partymen to set in motion the "wheel of satyagraha" to fight injustice everywhere. He pointed out that there was no conflict between construction and combat and welcomed the satyagraha campaigns launched by the party in Rajasthan, Vindhya Pradesh, U.P., and Bihar. The Congress government in U.P. had enhanced the irrigation cess sevenfold in 13 districts of the state. The burden was beyond the capacity of the peasants to bear. The state government had resurrected the U.P. Special Powers Act, a draconian measure enacted by the British, to put down ruthlessly any resistance to the increased levy. The executive of the U.P. unit of the party met on 14th & 15th May, to consider the situation. Lohia was present at this meeting. Besides opposing the enhancement in the levy, the executive condemned the State government's resort to the Special Powers Act and decided to launch a satyagraha in the 13 districts from 15th May.

The government unleashed a reign of terror in the state to suppress the agitation. By June, 1500 persons had been arrested in connection with the agitation from 12 districts. Lohia toured the state to mobilise support from the campaign. He urged the people to express, through satyagraha, their anger and resentment against the injustice meted out to them. He was scheduled to address two meetings on the 4th of July, at Kayamganj in the evening and at Farukhabad at night. Lohia was arrested by the city magistrate of Farukhabad and the sub-divisional magistrate of Kayamganj, under the Special Powers Act, at the place where he had been for dinner in Kayamganj. The police remanded him to custody for two days. Two days after the arrest, the magistrate went to the prison where Lohia had been lodged and wanted to hold the trial there. Lohia opposed the proposal, which he described as strange, and submitted an application that he should be tried by the Allahabad High Court under article 436 of the constitution. The request was granted.

Lohia wrote a letter to the Chief Justice of the High Court. In it, he contended that; (1) he should be tried in an open court and not in a prison; (2) he was produced before the magistrate 48 hours after the arrest; (3) He had sent a telegram each to the Chief Justice of India and Chief Justice of Allahabad High Court, immediately after his arrest, seeking their intervention, but the city magistrate did not forward it to them, and told him (Lohia) the next day that he did not do so because it was for Lohia to bear the telegram charges. He had pointed out to the magistrate that by not doing so, he had committed contempt of the court, but he had ignored the warning; (4) it was unjust to arrest a person in a free country just for having delivered a speech. The government's offence would be all the more grave if the speech did not contain incitement to violence. The U.P. Special Powers Act violated article 19 of the constitution; (5) he did not know which of the issues raised by him came under the jurisdiction of the Supreme Court and which came under that of the High Court. Even so, he prayed that the supreme court should take up the issue raised by him about the validity or otherwise of the Special Powers Act. He submitted that every hour of his detention in custody constituted an encroachment on his fundamental rights and an encouragement to violence for 1500 to 1600 persons who were undergoing severe sentences under this unjust act; (6) prisoners in the ordinary class were being supplied unwholesome food; (7) he said that he had despatched the letter on July 7.

Lohia was transferred from the Fatehgarh prison to the Naini jail. Speaking to newspaper reporters who met him at the Allahabad station on the way, Lohia said; "After arresting political leaders, Sardar Patel had at least the decency to keep quiet and not to talk too much, but the Prime Minister must talk on all occasions and on every matter. He ought to know that we too had a hand in placing him where he is today. Small men, whom luck and Gandhiji pitchforked into high positions in one of the most ancient and populous countries, are tragically proving that they are really small men and the verdict of history will also record it".

Though he was ill, Lohia was taken to the prison in an old ramshackle van. From the Naini Prison, in a letter to the President, Dr. Rajendra Prasad, he wrote; "As a citizen of the republic over which you preside, and as one who was first put in prison and later hit below the belt, at least three times—at Nangyal, Allahabad and Mirzapur by your First Minister, I am writing to you, not in expectation of a remedy, nor even in the hope of publication of the wrong done to me unless it be through some fortunate chance, but only to go on record. Your first minister has observed that the practise of civil disobedience in a free country is senseless. He may have specifically meant conditions of democracy and the adult vote. Even in that case all war-resisters, all tax-resisters and all peasant and labour fighters, from whom he earlier drew inspiration, have been senseless. The illiteracy of the Prime Minister's remark can only be matched with its astonishing irresponsibility, the scattering away of this contribution and the invitation to violence in place of civil disobedience. The law under which I have been arrested makes signs and gestures, for instance, the open palm uplifted so usual with Mahatma Gandhi, punishable with imprisonment of six months and a fine. Your ministers, Sir, have no conception of *Maryada*—or limited authority. Your ministers are using against us a law which was called the black law by Mahatma Gandhi. Your First Minister has justified without shame this trampling under foot of the Indian constitution and the guaranteed liberties of the republic. The tyrants do not even care to conceal their tyranny. Your First Minister has forgotten, too soon, that he is where he is, not alone by virtue of what he and his companions did, but also because of what we did. This ungrateful person has proved that a stung liberal can be worse than a blunt conservative. There was a time when the Congress Party also spoke in too many voices and then it was alive. Today it is dead. It speaks with the voice of Nehru alone, who has successfully stifled all voices. I have only two wishes and ambitions. One is to travel throughout the world without a passport. Secondly I wish Your first minister to live along, so long that the people send him again into a prison for his numerous offences against the Republic. I do not like being in a prison, I have always disliked prisons and hate them now. They are a mortifying reminder to me of my impotence; the impotency of the justice against injustice. As long as tyrants roam the earth, prisons will be filled with those who hate them. I apologise for writing to you at such length, and more so for writing it in a foreign language that I do not know well enough. But I remember the fate of the People's Charter, "which was written in Hindustani, and your government obviously, transacts most of its business in a foreign language".

Lohia's arrest caused resentment among the people in general and in the Party in particular. Newspapers also criticised the government's actions in arresting him. The British Labour Party leader Fenner Brockway wrote to Nehru expressing his distress over Lohia's arrest. But the Socialist Party failed to channelise the people's resentment and anger. It directed its units all over the country to observe "Lohia Day" on 18th July. Some state units decided to send jathas of Satyagrahis to U.P., but some of the party leaders like Jayprakash were opposed to the agitation against the enhancement in the irrigation cess. An attempt was also made to see that the agitation did not develop into a massive popular struggle. When Acharya Kripalani met him in prison, Lohia urged the Acharya to intensify the struggle. Kripalani's reply was astounding. He asked Lohia: "should I commit a murder to court imprisonment?" The subject of intensifying the struggle was raised at the meetings of the party's General Council held at Indore in the same month, but no decision could be taken. Madhu Limaye, joint secretary of the party wrote to Lohia on August 4th; "I have an impression that some of our colleagues are not serious about the U.P. struggle. Kripalani did not even want our all India day to be observed; and as for jathas, he does not like the idea of outsiders offering Satyagraha in U.P. The party and people have responded enthusiastically and a record number of meetings was held throughout the country on the occasion".

The hearing of Lohia's petition began before a divisional bench of Justices Chaturvedi and Desai on 26th August. A huge crowd had gathered to hear the proceedings. Lohia was brought to the court under heavy police guard. Lohia's counsel Shri. Khare, addressed the bench first. He was followed by the advocate general. Lohia made his statement on August 28. He said; "I have come here not as a offender but as accuser. I am an accuser, and the government the defender. Whether the Special Powers Act (1932), is offensive to the Indian constitution or not, is the issue before this Court". He said that between August 15, 1947, when India became free, and July 4, 1954, he had been arrested several times. But then he was comparatively certain about his personal freedom, because he had been arrested on all those occasions for his acts in disobedience of the law. He had never before been arrested on the charge of making a speech, he pointed out. The Special Powers Act, he said, was "a rusted sword that the government had dug out from the armory of the British suppressive laws". The Advocate General had in the course of his address, contented that as the civil disobedience affected law and order, it was necessary to impose restrictions on personal freedom. Incitement by an individual could cause the beginning of civil disobedience. Lohia referred to the argument and asked; "Has, or has not, any political leader preached civil disobedience or refusal to pay a tax in a democracy before?" He cited three well known examples in that respect, one each from India, the U.S., and Greece. The three men he was referring to, Mahatma Gandhi, Socrates, and Thoreau, were universally acknowledged as great men. Two of them were assassinated and the third courted imprisonment. Each of them was far greater than all the persons, whom the Advocate General had quoted in the court, put together, Lohia remarked. He said Socrates was tried by magistrate who was a great believer in democracy. After he was awarded the death sentence, Socrates's friends had prepared a plan for him to flee Athens. But Socrates refused to flee. Athens was then a free and democratic state. He was the first great man in the world who called upon the people to disobey bad laws, but insisted that they must obey just and progressive laws. Thoreau called upon the people not to pay unjust taxes. He contended that if they found the laws enacted by the government, which the people voted to power once in five years, meaningless, the people must defy such laws. Even if 999 persons out of thousand supported such laws, the remaining solitary citizen could resist such legislation. This was Thoreau's conception of social civil disobedience, Lohia said. Mahatma Gandhi was the greatest man born during the last five centuries, not only in India, but also in the world. He was never unequivocal in expressing his views. He had said that to refuse to pay a tax was man's most ancient birthright. It was his view that the people had this right not only under an alien rule, but they had this right irrespective of the character of the regime. It became the people's legitimate right to refuse to pay a tax, if the levy was oppressive and all other means available to secure its withdrawal had proved of no avail. Civil disobedience was Gandhiji's legacy to humanity for all time to come. Its gospel must be spread all over the world, Lohia said. He also referred to satyagrahis like Pralhad and Charvak in that context. He said that humanity had progressed from Socrates to Gandhi after a long and arduous journey. Only select persons resorted to civil disobedience before Gandhiji's advent on the world scene. Gandhiji made the weapon available to millions of the common people.

Lohia said he made a distinction between the preaching and the practise of civil disobedience. Socrates, Thoreau, Gandhiji, and others like them willingly underwent the sentence imposed on them for disobedience of the unjust laws. But none of them had been penalised for having preached civil disobedience. On the contrary, their writings preaching of civil disobedience are available in book form. Section 3 of the Special Powers Act sought to prohibit the preaching of civil disobedience, and that he would have no objection to the provision, had it sought to prevent violent resistance. He pointed out that under that section of the act, the government would be able even to proscribe the works of Socrates, Thoreau and Gandhiji. Lohia told the Court that he spoke quite openly before thousands of Americans, against the law then in force in the U.S. discriminating citizens on the basis of colour. He was not prevented from doing so, as long as he restricted his opposition to the law, to its verbal expression. He referred to the Advocate General's contention that civil disobedience could not be practised against a democratically elected government and said that to say that civil disobedience had no place in democracy amounted to denouncing Gandhiji's legacy of satyagraha to humanity. India had become barren in political thought and action after Adi Shankaracharya. For the first time since then, India had contributed to the world thought, through its practice of satyagraha on a broad, mass, basis. Closure of the avenue of peaceful civil disobedience would amount to an invitation to a violent insurrection he pointed out to the court, and submitted to the judges that they are custodians of the entire legal system of the country, and not merely of section 124 of the I.P.C. He said that he was perhaps the first satyagrahi to be tried for having preached civil disobedience. He had not actually committed breach of any law through any action. He said that freedom of speech also meant the right to make a wrong speech. A speech which a government and the people regarded wrong or improper today, might be regarded as right and proper after the lapse of some time. The weapon of civil disobedience was invaluable. Its practice would cause no harm to the nation. Lohia pointed out that he had remained in prison for more than 50 days, and said that it was necessary to lay down rules to facilitate expeditious disposal of *habeas corpus* petitions.

The judgement of the bench was postponed to 12th August. The two judges constituting the bench could not reach unanimity. Justice Desai held that the Special Powers act was *ultra vires* of the constitution. He was of the view that, when actual refusal to pay the irrigation cess could not undermine public order, mere incitement not to pay it, could not bring it in jeopardy. Justice Chaturvedi, however held that section 3 of the act, as amended, did not offend the constitution and, therefore, its violation constituted a grave offence. The matter was, therefore, referred to Justice Agarwal. He struck down section 3 of the Special Powers Act as *ultra vires* of the constitution. He agreed that abiding by the laws was a basic necessity for the success of democracy. But one could imagine circumstances, when the most law abiding and the greatest believers of truth among the people, would find it necessary to disobey unjust laws and might consider it as their duty to disobey them.

His Lordship referred to the martyrdom of Socrates in the cause of freedom of thought and expression, and to the advice Socrates gave to the citizens of Athens at his trial. He also alluded to what Thoreau had said while preaching civil disobedience, as also to Gandhiji's concept of civil disobedience outlined by the Mahatma in the course of his deposition before the Hunter Committee in 1918, and said that though a person practising it was liable to conviction, it did not mean that a civil resister must necessarily be convicted in every case. The preaching and practise of civil disobedience was an action in exercise of the right to freedom of expression. This freedom could be curbed only under circumstances contemplated by section 2 of article 19 of the constitution, he said, and observed that in his opinion, the constitution protected the right of every citizen to preach satyagraha. Allowing Lohia's petition, the court also ordered the state government to pay him Rs. 500/- as costs.

19. STORM THAT SHOOK THE PARTY

The High Court judgement was a triumph for Lohia. It had upheld the contention that the people had the right to preach and practice Satyagraha under the constitution. As a result of the judgement, the contention, of the apologists of the establishment, that civil disobedience or satyagraha had no place in democracy also stood rejected. The huge crowd that had gathered outside the court hailed the verdict with jubilation. As Lohia emerged out of the court building, he was profusely garlanded by the people and the party workers. He told the newspapermen who greeted him; "My first obligation is to my several thousand comrades in the state, who have so far been illegally detained and will be released today due to the High Court's decision, and I have to have a little consultation with them. My second thought is for the Andhra civil resisters who are in jail. For the rest, my illegal imprisonment for two months has seared my soul, or whatever that place be called, which gets seared in such cases. The balance between anger and sympathy has been upset. I have to retain the element of sympathy somehow, although anger may predominate for a longer time". All the satyagrahis arrested under the Special Powers Act were also set free, following the judgement.

To pacify himself, Lohia proposed to go to some place and rest. Not a rest at some secluded place, but a storm was in store for him. In fact, the victory was followed by events which caused him profound distress and anguish. Other leaders of the party began to treat him like an undesirable criminal and he had to prepare for an ideological confrontation with them immediately after his release. The storm which rocked the party had already begun to gather while he was in prison .On August 12, he received the news that the P.S.P. government of Travancore Cochin had opened fire on the people, resulting in four deaths. The same evening, Lohia sent a telegram to the chief minister, Pattam Thanu Pillai, from the prison, which read: "Although rioters may be entirely in the wrong and have precipitated, the ugly situation, police firing resulting in deaths is wholly unjustified except in insurrection or killing. Recommend appointment non-official enquiry, suspension of officers and simultaneous resignation government in assertion this principle. Best regards". He sent a copy of the telegram to the chairman of the party, Acharya Kripalani.

The P.S.P. chief minister rejected Lohia's advice. He came to know, that Pillai had asserted with the arrogance of an autocrat that the allegation that the police had committed an excess in the use of the force had first got to be proved. But neither Pillai nor Kripalani replied Lohia's telegram. Lohia, therefore, wrote to Kripalani on 17th August, resigning from the general secretaryship of the party, as also from its executive. "Ever since my arrest, and due to my consequent absence from the post, I have often thought of resigning from the General Secretaryship of the party, as well as the membership of the executive committee". Lohia wrote. He referred to the telegram he had sent to the Travancore-Cochin chief minister, and said; "The recommendation was, of course, personal, and had no such force as an official communication would have, but it had naturally all my force. I have to date received no reply from the Chief Minister. He was, of course, not obliged to reply. But the chief minister has made a public reply after visiting the area where the police had killed people. The chief minister said that 'it was necessary to steer clear of an excess in exercise of force. The police had acted as leniently as possible.' The time has not yet come when an Indian minister may deserve to act as his own judge. For the rest, the first socialist government in India has not done well to make use of such meaningless and dangerous generalisation about force and leniency. Tyranny always hides behind such generalities. If I were out, I would have the executive consider this question at once. If the executive took an opportunist line, I would have called the general council to attend to it. One has, of course, to modify one's advice to suit the taste to whom it is to be given, but there is a limit which should never be transgressed.

I may be told that I don't know the facts. Those who say that, would demonstrate that they are unprincipled charlatans who are prepared to buttress themselves in office with scraps of so-called facts. One such fact, I understand, is the allegation that the rioters were communists. Whether they were communists, or communist-inspired, or congressmen, is of little relevance. However, it is a standing marvel how opportunism can continually oscillate between the kissing of communists or any others. I concede, of course, that the rioters were an exceedingly undesirable lot and some measures were indicated. But firing? No; not unless there is an insurrection".

The formation of the P.S.P. ministry in Travancore-Cochin was an event unique in the history of democracy. After the party's debacle in the 1952 general election, nobody had dreamt that it would be called up on so soon to accept office. But this strange phenomenon was the outcome of the mid term poll in the state. Neither the Congress nor the Communist Party could secure a clear majority in the state assembly. The party wise break of the result was: Congress—45, P.S.P.-19, C.P.I.-23, Kerala Socialists-3, T.T.N.C.-12, R.S.P.-9, and Independents-6. Neither the Congress nor the C.P.I. could form a government without the support of some other group. In this situation, the 19-member P.S.P. group came to hold the balance of power.

The P.S.P. had joined the united front of the other opposition parties to defeat the Congress in the midterm poll. When the results were declared, Lohia had expressed the view that if any party other than the Congress formed the government, the P.S.P. would extend its sympathy to that ministry and would tolerate its regime as long as the government pursued policies which would promote national interests. But the party would not join the ministry. The National Executive of the P.S.P., meeting after the poll, declared that the P.S.P. was prepared to form a ministry, if invited. If the K.S.P., R.S.P., and the T.T.N.C. agreed to join such a ministry, the leader of the P.S.P. group in the state assembly would consider the matter. The Executive also stated that if the United Front of the leftists formed a ministry, the leader of P.S.P. group would decide, in consultation with the chairman of the party, whether or not to support it. There was hectic political activity in the state and moves and countermoves for combination of groups to form a government. The chairman of the P.S.P.'s state Unit and the leader of the party's group in the Travancore-Cochin Assembly, Pattam Thanu Pillai, was keen on becoming the Chief Minister. He had been carrying on negotiations with the leaders of different parties and groups in the Assembly. Some informal understanding was reported to have almost been reached. Meeting against this background at Madras on March 11 and 12, the National Executive unanimously decided to allow the party's state unit to form a ministry. In the end the P.S.P. minority ministry with the outside support of the Congress was formed under the chief ministership of Pattam Thannu Pillai in the state.

Though the decision of the National Executive to allow Pillai to form such a government was unanimous, the approach of the different party leaders to the issue was not identical. Both Jayprakash Narayan and Ashok Mehta knew that the P.S.P. ministry would be required to lean on the Congress party in the Assembly. Ashok Mehta looked forward to it as an opportunity to experiment his policy of searching areas of agreement with the Congress. Lohia's approach was quite different. He felt that if the P.S.P. led ministry implemented a progressive programme, it would be able to enlist the people's sympathy and support, and though technically a minority in the assembly, it would be able to mobilise behind it massive support of the people outside the house. To realise this objective, it was necessary for the ministry to formulate a radical programme for change and to implement it with earnestness and determination.

It was futile to expect other leaders of the party to resist the temptation the situation offered. Lohia alone could have saved the party from the disaster the step involved. Perhaps, moved either by the desire that the party should achieve something spectacular, or due to excessive optimism, he too was tempted to pursue a mirage. The experiment proved too costly for the party. The P.S.P. chief minister functioned like a power-hungry bureaucrat. The ministry had neither the imagination nor the drive necessary for building a distinct image of its own, as Lohia had fondly hoped. The P.S.P. ministry instead chose the existence of an object dependent of the congress. Before long, it began to pursue retrograde policies, including the use of the Preventive Detention Act and anti-labour measures, culminating in the opening of fire on industrial workers resulting in deaths.

The Allahabad policy statement of the Party had outlined

its conception of the relations between the police and the people. It was adequate enough to serve as a guideline to the ministry on the issue. The ministry ought to have resigned on its own, as the police firing had violated the code of conduct enunciated in that document. When the Madhya Bharat Congress ministry opened fire on student demonstrators at Gwalior in 1950, Mehta had, in his capacity as General Secretary, asked Baleshwar Dayal, Convener of the Action Committee, to demand the resignation of the ministry and institute a judicial enquiry into the firing and to launch an agitation in support of these demands. The agitation that followed had resulted in the change of the ministry. Again, when the Congress ministry of the state opened fire at Indore on July 21, 1954, about three weeks before the Travancore-Cochin ministry resorted to the police firing, the party demanded the resignation of the ministry. But the P.S.P. leadership was not prepared to use the same yardstick to judge the behaviour of the ministry of its own party. This double standard governing the party's functioning made Lohia uneasy. No notice was being taken of his communications, nor was a meeting of the party's executive being convened to consider the issue.

Lohia, therefore, sent in his resignation. After the news about his resignation was published, an item circulated by the Delhi bureau of the Press Trust of India, purporting to be an interview given by the P.S.P. spokesman appeared in the newspapers all over the country. The spokesman sought to make out that there was contradiction in Lohia's stand on the issue. Lohia wrote another letter to the party chairman from prison, following publication of the spokesman's 'interview'. "I refuse to believe", he said, "That you had anything to do with this. Some small town politician, who is able to pretend to a national status because of general lack of talent, and who is low enough to hide behind anonymity in relation to internal party differences, has imagined that such a serious matter as a police firing could be dealt with on the level of a petty court lawyer". He went on: "I am told I could not simultaneously demand both a non-official inquiry into the firing and the resignation of the government without awaiting its report. The two acts aim at entirely different purposes, one complimentary to the other. The government should have resigned for asserting the principle that police firing, resulting in deaths, in situations other than an insurrection or killings by a crowd, is undesirable. Who ordered the opening of fire, whether the government or officers, can have little meaning for a democratic government. To assert this principle, no facts, other than those already known, are necessary. No blame or motive could have attached to the government, if it had resigned, but by refusing to resign, it has made itself guilty of bad administration and bad intention. The suspension of the officers concerned, and the appointment of the non-official enquiry should have been the last acts of the government before resigning. This inquiry could have been assigned to record the relevant facts and also their sequence, as truthfully stated as possible, so that it could be known as to who went wrong where, and various agencies would in future know somewhat better how to act. I am also told, that I cannot simultaneously demand the resignation of the Travancore-Cochin government and submit my resignation from the National Executive. I demanded the government's resignation on the 12th August and I submitted my resignation five days later, after the chief minister, and some others as well, had already spoken. I am imprisoned. Those who think that government should stay in office have freedom to act and organise; for me, no other course is open to me except to resign"

Lohia added in the letter: "I am somewhat worried by those in the party who call themselves men of Gandhi or men of Erasmus-Gandhians and humanists. . . . If others kill people, that is wanton, indiscriminate and reckless, but if we kill people, irrelevant questions of facts and procedure are raised. Both you and the Congress party make Communists and antisocial elements responsible for your firings. When the Congress party does so, you call it the search for scapegoats, and when you do it, of course, you are men of Gandhi and men of Erasmus. I do not know what to do. I appear to be the only one in your crowd of the party publicists, who is worried about such things. Who knows you may be right. But I believe you to be wholly wrong. Therefore, let me go from your executive".

After his release, Lohia received two letters from Acharya Kripalani, but neither of them contained any reply to the issue raised by Lohia. In one of them, there was sarcastic reference to the allusion made by Lohia to Gandhi and Erasmus, while in the other, the Acharya had said that Lohia had a good case on the firing and suggested to him that he should place his viewpoint before the National Executive. In fact, all the other party leaders, including Acharya Kripalani, Jayprakash Narayan and Ashok

Mehta, had understood very well Lohia's stand on the subject. They agreed with him in principle, but had no desire to take the action that would logically follow. Lohia commented in disgust "Either I am useless by nature for an official post in the party or the party is still useless for me to be its secretary".

Lohia undertook a drive to educate party workers in particular and the people in general on the issue he had raised. He said that the 90% of police firings in India since the advent of freedom had been resorted to, not with a view to maintaining law and order, but with a view to stamping out certain ways of thought. He urged that such killings should be understood in their proper perspective, and observed; "If the principle of 'life for life' could be followed in regard to 'judicial murder', that is, capital punishment, it should also be adhered to in case of 'administrative murder' that is, killing by police firing". He recalled that Nehru had said many years ago that governance of India was like riding a tiger, and remarked; "that is how most Indian people think of the Indian people—that they are wild beasts who should be shot before they behave".

"All this bungled reasoning", he said, "can be traced to the existence of the caste system in India which did not regard some forty percent people as human beings. Human life has no worth in India. The question is whether the people of India are human beings or mere files. India might take twenty years to provide the people with food, clothing and shelter, but India must forthwith regard them as human beings. Indians are much less violent than Europeans. In 1919, in Vienna, the police did not open fire on the crowd even though four policemen were killed. The assumption that the Indian people would indulge in sabotage and violence, if the government right to use rifles was limited, is wrong. . . . preventive firing cannot be justified".

"There is in India today", he remarked, "a continual talk about Mahatma Gandhi and continual action against everything against all that the Mahatma stood for. I want the weapon of civil disobedience to be used against social injustices". In the last week of August industrial workers from Ernakulam wrote to Lohia, congratulating him on the stand he had taken. They said that the Pattam Thanu Pillai government was autocratic and not socialist in behaviour and sought his intervention. In an identical letter to Lohia and Kripalani, a journalist from the area which was the scene of the police firing, wrote; "I am a Malayali residing in a

Tamil locality. We have been living together for centuries in fraternal amity. Disturbances occurred in this area, when Pattam Thanu Pillai was the Congress chief minister, and they have occurred again when his is the Socialist Party's chief minister. Who is to blamed? Neither the Tamilians nor the Malayalis, but this unimaginative chief minister".

The National Executive of the party met at Delhi on 4th and 5th September to consider the issue. Reports were current on the eve of the meeting, that Jayprakash would try to find a way out of the crisis. Ashok Mehta, Sucheta Kripalani and H.V. Kamath appeared to have come to the meeting with the set purpose of having a showdown with Lohia and defending the Travancore-Cochin ministry. They were, perhaps, afraid that Jayprakash might soften in his approach to the issue, unless they adopted a hard line from the very beginning of the discussion. They sought to isolate Lohia and treated him like a criminal. All sorts of irrelevant points, regarding the language he used and the procedures he followed, were raised by them. He was asked to explain why he had sent the telegram to the chief minister of the Travancore-Cochin government from prison and why he did not write to the party chairman before doing so. Lohia was told the National Executive alone was competent to ask the chief minister to resign and that he had better stop his activities to split the party. This was too much for Lohia to stand. He walked out of the meeting. In the course of the discussion at the meeting, Ashok Mehta urged that the Executive should not demand institution of an inquiry into the firing without consulting Pillai. Jayprakash almost endorsed Lohia's stand on the demand for the resignation of the Travancore-Cochin ministry. He said not only the ministry, but also the Executive was responsible to what had happened. If there was to be any resignation, then both the executive and the ministry should resign. The first day's discussion ended with a request to Jayprakash to produce a draft resolution.

The next day Jayprakash placed his draft resolution, which was clearly impressed by Lohia's views, before the Executive. It did not ask for the resignation of the Travancore-Cochin ministry. Even so had the Executive adopted it without amendments, the differences in the party leadership would have been resolved and it might have led to the withdrawal of Lohia's resignation. The 'practical politicians' in the Executive however started to mutilate the draft through amendments. The following significant sentences were sought to be omitted from the draft; "(1) the crowd however unmannerly, had not before or after the firing, taken toll of a single human life; (2) fire should be opened only in case of armed insurrection or when the crowd had actually indulged in killing. Under all other conditions, the Executive could consider police killing as unwarranted and contrary not only to the values of socialism and democracy, but also the those of civilisation itself; (3) judging by these principles, the Travancore-Cochin firing cannot he considered justifiable and must stand condemned; (4) it is the failure of the movement to clarify these issues and to educate itself and public opinion that is responsible for the failure of the Travancore-Cochin ministry to set a new code of conduct for its police and ensure its observance; (5) in future, no socialist government—though this should hold good for all governments—should be justified in remaining in office if it violated these guiding principles; (6) the executive would accordingly recommend to the Travancore-Cochin government the immediate appointment of such an inquiry commission together with the announcement that it would abide by the commission findings". What was most surprising was that Jayprakash Narayan remained a silent spectator to this mutilation of his draft. This made one wonder whether he had spoken on the subject without conviction at the meetings the previous day. The amendments were carried and the resolution, sans its very soul, was adopted by the executive, with three members recording their opposition. After the resolution was passed, some members sought to censure Lohia for what he had said about the Prime Minister and his colleagues. Objecting to the move, Madhu Limaye said that it was none of the Executive's business to criticise what their colleague had said about their opponent, and pointed that Bevan and Shinwell had used much stronger words about Churchill, who undoubtedly was a greater man than Nehru. The move was then dropped. Lohia's resignation was promptly accepted. Madhu Limaye then pressed for acceptance of his own resignation as well. He said that he had not been very happy during the past few months and it was clear to him that the Allahabad compromise had not worked. The discussion went on for some time but Limaye could not be persuaded to withdraw his resignation.

When Limaye met Jayprakash the same evening he asked

Limaye not to resign, but he remained unconvinced. At that stage, Jaiprakash suggested to him that a special convention of the party should be held to discuss the issues confronting it, including the firing in Travancore-Cochin. "Let it also discuss equidistance" he remarked. Limaye replied that equidistance could not be discussed in the abstract. "It means a vigorous policy of opposition in relation to the two blocs internationally, and to the Congress and Communist parties nationally". Jayprakash further suggested that the debate on the policy statement adopted at Allahabad might also be reopened. He said that he would attend the convention and participate in the discussion. It was ultimately decided to hold a special convention of the Party at Nagpur from November 26 to 28.

20. NAGPUR CONVENTION

The special convention of the party met at Nagpur from 26th to 28th November 1954, against this background. The storm triggered by Lohia's resignation had served to focus the attention of the partymen in particular and the people in general on the issue of the police firing. It had provoked, for the first time since the advent of freedom, a national debate on the broader issue, underlying the controversy, of how a democratic government should deal with popular agitation. Police firings on angry demonstrators had become far too frequent in the country. Is it not necessary that the functioning of the ministry of a party, wedded to democracy and socialism, be distinguishable from that of the Congress governments? Should the approach of the socialist ministry to the people be as cynical and callous as that of a Congress ministry? Is it necessary for the Socialists Party to lay down norms of behaviour for a government which would be in consonance with democratic values? What was needed to answer these posers was to undertake an agonising reappraisal of the situation created by the Travancore-Cochin firing. But the National Executive of the party had instead chosen to skirt and confuse the issue. The delegates had gathered at Nagpur in the hope that the convention would define, in clear terms, the Party's policy on the subject after a free and a frank discussion on all its aspects, when the national executive's resolution came up for consideration.

But to the utter surprise of the delegates, the Executive resolution on the Travancore-Cochin firing was not placed for consideration before the convention. Instead, Ashok Mehta very ingeniously moved a resolution seeking the convention's approval of the Executive's Delhi resolution on the issue. The only alternative it left before the delegates was either to accept the Executive's Delhi resolution in toto, or reject it. While commending his resolution to the convention, Mehta told the delegates that the resolution sought their vote of confidence in the Executive. This manoeuvre created a tense atmosphere at the convention. The delegates were bewildered, and confronted with a dilemma. They did not approve of the Executive's Delhi resolution in toto, however, they were not only denied an opportunity to discuss and amend it, but were also asked either to approve or face the prospect of the Executive's resignation. However, a clever delegate found a way out of this difficult situation. He moved an amendment to Mehta's resolution seeking to add to it the words; "and this convention directs the Travancore-Cochin Ministry to resign". That at once relieved the tension and threw the doots open to a discussion on the issue raised by the firing. The discussion that followed brought into the open the divergent views prevalent in the party on the subject. Pattam Thanu Pillai defended the firing with the arrogance of a bureaucrat. P.V. Raju startled the convention with the disclosure that Pillai himself ordered the police over the telephone to open fire on the crowd. With tears in his eyes Jayprakash Narayan tried to appeal to the delegates emotions. He expressed the hope that there would be change of heart in Pillai and that he would tender resignation of the ministry on his own. Dr. Lohia urged the delegates not to mix up the issue of his use of a strong language with the question involving principles and criticised the executive for its delayed reaction to the firing, because it met 20 days after the incident to discuss it. He wanted the convention to differentiate between the judicial equity and the ministry's resignation. One was the judicial act, while other related to the party's approach to the question of police firings.

"As far as judicial inquiries are concerned", he said, "even Congress ministeries are in the habit of ordering them. A judicial inequity will concern itself only with the action of the police and the magistracy within the frame work of the existing law. It will pronounce no judgement on the action of the ministry". He stated that a police firing itself was an admission of failure of democracy. Even granting that large scale destruction of property could justify a firing, he pointed out, the damage caused by the crowd to property amounted hardly to Rs. 50. Once the principle of an automatic resignation of the ministry after such a firing is accepted, political workers in the country will have to revise their thinking and take a lead in establishing democratic relations between the crowd and the police". He said that the convention should reject the National Executive's stand for three reasons; (1) to tell the people that the socialists will behave the same way in and out of office; (2) for them, an Indian is a human being and not a fly; and (3) to declare their unflinching faith democratic values.

Dr. Lohia's speech not only placed the real issue before the delegates in a proper perspective, but also exposed the hollowness of the postures of Jayprakash Narayan, Acharya Kripalani and others who swore by Gandhism and Sarvodaya. Before putting the resolution to the vote, the Chairman warned the delegates not to split the party by rejecting it. The official resolution was carried by 303 votes against 217. The anxiety to avert a split in the party impelled the majority of the delegates to vote for the resolution. Despite this vote of confidence, members of the National Executive tendered their resignations from the body. The delegates found themselves in an unenviable position. They had subordinated consideration of principles to their loyalty to the party's executive, in their anxiety to prevent a split in the party. In the bargain, most of them felt guilty of having forsaken principles, but in actuality paved the way for a split in the Party, which they were so eager to avoid. Some of the delegates approached Acharya Narendra Dev with a request to find a way out of the crisis. He had just returned from a tour abroad and had stated on the eve of the convention that he had come to the gathering without any bias, as he was not well acquainted with the events in the party that had occurred during his absence. When pressed to accept chairmanship of the Party, he replied that he would accept the office provided Dr. Lohia agreed to join the National Executive. Normally, Lohia would have agreed to do so, but what had happened at the convention was not the success or defeat one usually met in a democratic debate. Support to the official resolution had been sought as a vote of confidence in the Executive. By voting for it, the convention had expressed its lack of confidence in him. Lohia felt that his joining the Executive was, therefore, out of the question. But the Acharya did not stick to his position, he subsequently indicated the willingness to accept the party's chairmanship, if any one of Lohia's supporters proposed his name for the office. The Acharya had issued a statement, while away on the tour, condemning the arrest of Dr. Lohia by the U.P. Government under the Special Powers Act. It was difficult to imagine that a person of his stature was unable to grasp the situation created by the Travancore-Cochin firing and the controversy it had touched off in the party. Those developments were not shrouded by mystery needing any special effort to unravel it. Narendra Dev ultimately accepted the post without making any effort to avert the developing crisis in the party. This was followed by circulation of inspired reports that the Acharya did so under pressure from Lohia himself. Lohia described the reports as "an absolute falsehood". He said; "the facts are that he had asked me to persuade Madhu Limaye to second his nomination. In all the confabulations of the previous day and night, I had no part. The present chairman (Acharya Narendra Dev) sent for me and I came down to the conference. The talk between him and me lasted barely two minutes in full and open view of the entire conference. The chairman came to me on the morning he was leaving Nagpur and told me of his four selections for secretarial posts. I am not in the habit of objecting to anybody's selections in such matters, nor does a person of normal behaviour do so. Such listening to another person's selections should never be taken to mean approval".

The subsequent developments in the country vindicated the stand taken by Lohia on police firings. The resort to police firings by Congress governments almost became a daily occurrence. When the communists came into power in Kerala after 1954, they followed in the footsteps of Congressmen and opened fire on demonstrators. Thus Congressmen, Praja Socialists and Communists came to have the blood of unarmed people on their hands. Had the first socialist government resigned, following the firing in Travancore-Cochin as urged by Lohia, it would have set an ideal pattern for a political party's behaviour in office and given future developments a new turn. But the temptation to stick to power proved stronger than the need for adherence to principles. Missing rare opportunities provided by history has been a tragic feature of the socialist movement in India.

As the number of police firings on unarmed civil resisters went on mounting in India, Lohia bemoaned: "it is a murderous irony of fate that the practice of police firing should increase in consonance with professions of nonviolence. . . . The state in India, born out of civil disobedience, has been most disrespectful to its mother. A child had never so kicked the womb out of which it was born". "This total disregard of civil disturbance and its small degeneration by the crowd", he remarked, "have largely been possible because of curious relationship between the people and the government that has been allowed to grow in the past few years. The government and the people behave towards each other as murderous parents and irresponsible children would. A certain type of parent, who may be normally quite affectionate, becomes murderous when he feels his authority flouted and what is slapping and beating in the case of the individual parent, takes the form of police firings in the case of the Government parent. But children do not remember the beating after some time or they think it best to forget and normal relationships between parent and child are restored. Such children may occasionally engage in pranks or reckless acts. The Indian people have slid into the role of such irresponsible children, who infrequently throw stones or burn buses and who are ruthlessly beaten up by the police firings by their murderous parents. Normal relations are soon enough restored. Localities and crowds which became the victim of ruthless police firings are found, not very much later, according a tremendous reception to their own murderers in the same fashion as a reckless child, who had earlier been beaten, clings to the legs of his murderous parent". He added: "Not until this relationship between the murderous parent and the reckless child is brought to an end, not until the Indian people put themselves under the rigorous discipline of civil resistance which admits of no stone throwing or bus burning, not until they learn to acquire enduring contempt, and anger against governments which school down their own people not until the people and the government learn to respect each others personality and its limited authority, would there be rational regulations of crowd and police relationships.

Police firings in Kerala and at places like Lucknow and Ahmedabad in 1958, again impelled Lohia to deal with the subject. He said: "A government that loses confidence in its ability to command the loyalty of the people will lose its sanity. Governments can be sane without being believers in non-violence. A government confident of itself and its right to the throne will not shoot or unarmed citizens. A government which loses confidence forfeits its right to power in a democracy; that is why the demand for immediate resignation of a ministry that kills unprotected men logically follows from the tenets of democracy alone, leave aside the high ideal of nonviolence. The ultimate consequence of such police firings can be disastrous in the shape of civil war. The feeble minded and weak-kneed governments in India may find a temporary relief after having dispersed the ghost of their doom at gunpoint. But a mode of behaviour in never confined to one side, it becomes reciprocal. A government that is violent to the people will turn the people violent. A governments that uses guns to face the people will engender the use of guns in the people. The common weapon of violent mobs, at present in India, is the stone, but continuous firings will turn it into bullets. The only safety valve against the explosion of the Indian situation into a civil war is the abjuration of violence and common code among the political factions in India".

The tendency on the part of the Congress governments to resort to police firings only progressively increased in the years that followed. It, in its turn made the people retaliate with greater ferocity, as Lohia had feared. The angry people who are earlier content with hurling stones and brickbats at the police in reply to their bullets, began to resort to other forms of violence and incendiarism. Lohia's visit to riot torn Calcutta, in March 1966, provoked him to condemn the acts of violence indulged in both by the Government and the people. Condemning the acts of sporadic, senseless and ineffective acts of violence resorted to by the people who had come to the conclusion that the Congress government could not be toppled except through violent means, Lohia urged the people to give up their methods of burning buses and jeeps and killing some innocent people. "Let them prepare for four or five years, if they so want, to take over radio stations, Sachivalayas and arsenals, instead", he said. He however added that he had not yet come to any definite conclusion on the subject of organised and open violence.

The P.S.P. leadership refused to adopt a firm, principled stand on the Travancore-Cochin firing with the sole object to save it's state ministry. It could not, however, survive. The Congress withdrew its support to the ministry in 1955 and the government fell. The desperate effort to save the ministry even at the sacrifice of the principles for which the party had stood all along, was in vain. Its exit, unwept, unhonoured, and unsung, only tarnished the image of the Indian socialist movement. However, the

Travancore-Cochin firing served as a blessing in the disguise. For, the debate provoked by Lohia on the issue marked the beginning of a campaign to cleanse the party's augean stables.

21. STORM BURSTS

"The long arm of free speech and the strong fist of controlled action" was Dr. Lohia's conception of party discipline. It proved inconvenient to some leaders of the party and led the party to a storm that rocked its ranks at the beginning of 1955. It had along been Nehru's policy to adopt tactics that might throw socialists into disarray and weaken the socialist movement. He indulged in a new gimmick at the plenary session of the Congress held at Avadi in January 1955, when the general election was drawing nearer. He persuaded the session to adopt a resolution, defining establishment of "Socialistic pattern of society" as the party's objective. Even the rightists in the Congress voted for the resolution, knowing, as they did, that adoption of a resolution did not involve a commitment on their part to implement it. That had become the normal pattern of functioning of the post-freedom Congress.

But it had its impact on the P.S.P., as desired by Nehru, and particularly on that section of the party which had been anxious to see "areas of agreement" with him and the Congress, under what it described as the "compulsions of a backward economy". This section of the Praja Socialist party had been smarting under its defeat at the party's Betul conference and had been lying low since then. The Avadi resolution of the Congress provided an opportunity for this faction to raise its head again. Its leader, Ashok Mehta, in an article published in the special issue of the *Janata*, the Socialist Party's mouthpiece, hailing the Avadi resolution, said: "I welcome the Congress party's adoption of new social objectives. I feel happy that between the two parties, a few new points of contact have emerged and that areas of agreement have become clearer. . . . We now press not against locked doors but those that are opening".

Dr. Lohia had been condemning the Congress as the party of corruption, famine and status quo and said that under its regime, "the three professions of rickshaw-pullers, that tribe of half man half-horse, beggars and prostitutes have rapidly been on rapid increase, and that the common man's life had the value of only a fly. Mehta had never liked this criticism. Expressing his optimism about the success of the five-year plan and about the ability of the Congress to realise other objectives, Mehta deplored the tendency of diffidence and doubt which the criticism reflected, and had a dig at Dr. Lohia; "If man is not a fly or a half horse, he should neither be a ostrich" he remarked. When Mehta's article welcoming Congress's Avadi resolution appeared in the *Janata*, Andhra Pradesh was scheduled to go to the polls and the P.S.P. was in the fray. The Andhra Pradesh Congress took out thousands of copies of Mehta's article and distributed them among voters to the utter embarrassment of the P.S.P. in the state. The defenders of Mehta's policy set out vigorously propagating the need for elimination of political conflicts, and differences with the Congress, & create a congenial atmosphere by mutual trust. In a Bombay meeting Mehta declared; "P.S.P. should give up the hope of becoming an alternative force to the Congress. P.S.P. is now more nearer to the Congress". Madhu Limaye, a prominent member of the Bombay P.S.P. committee came out with scathing attack on Mehta's policy in a speech. The attempt of Mehta and his supporters to reopen the question of seeking areas of agreement, which had been finally settled at Betul, sparked off a fierce controversy in Bombay. Nine P.S.P. members of the Bombay municipal corporation came out with a statement criticising Limaye. They said that describing the Avadi resolution as a fraud would amount to denial of reality and called upon the P.S.P. to be prepared for cooperation with the Congress. They urged that a special convention of the Party should be held to consider the subject. A meeting of Bombay Committee of the P.S.P. was convened to express confidence in Mehta, and to consider the question of taking disciplinary action against Limaye. At the meeting M. Harris said that "Dr. Lohia is an arch enemy of the party and was ruining it". A meeting passed a resolution, suspending Limaye from the party for the period of one year and recommending the National Executive to take suitable further action against him. Limaye appealed to the National Executive against the Bombay Committee's action. But the Executive, instead, confirmed the step. Dr. Lohia came out to fight this act of injustice against Limaye. He said: "I, and others like me, would no doubt consider it a very grave act with possibilities of very grace consequences. Questions of policy as well as decency are involved in it. These partisans of paralysed socialism from the tallest downwards have been over the past several years, it's worst villifiers. I shall only state that disciplinary action should follow, if absolutely necessary, an act of indiscipline of behaviour and should never be connected with any indiscipline of speech making". He added; "Meanwhile, we should want all committees and organisations, which are run by advocates of militant socialism, to invite Madhu Limaye to speaking engagements. To Madhu Limaye, himself. I offer what little solace there is in the fact that many big men have been, at one time or another, expelled from their parties in their search of effective action and that the idol of paralysed socialism, the present Prime Minister of India, was once expelled from the League Against Imperialism of which he was then the vice-president". The action taken against Limaye created a sensation among units of the party all over the country. Many of them passed a resolution urging the National Executive to reconsider its action: The executive of the U.P. party announced its intention to invite Limaye to address the Party's state conference. The General Secretary of the party, Triloki Singh, asked the chairman of the U.P. party, Gopal Narayan Saxena, why disciplinary action should not be taken against him for having invited Limaye, against whom disciplinary action had been taken, to the conference. At its meeting held at Delhi on May 4, the National Executive suspended the U.P. executive, and the chairman, Acharya Narendra Dev, appointed an adhoc committee to replace it. It also banned the U.P. state conference of the party scheduled to be held at Ghazipur. Disciplinary action was taken against the party's Delhi unit too. This spate of suspensions of party units and members provoked, '*The Times of India*' to remark; "It is too difficult for the P.S.P. leaders to see that disciplinary action is no substitute for the ideological cement that alone can hold the party together". This controversy raised the issue of democracy within the party and freedom of speech to party members. Dr. Lohia said that the totalitarian tendency which these actions betrayed must end and the functioning of party must be improved forthwith. Otherwise, the people would have to forge a new instrument to work for ushering in a socialist society in the country.

The party had begun to function like a bureaucracy in which lower units merely carried out the orders and instructions issued by the higher authority. The relations between the National Executive and the units of the party at different levels had been reduced virtually to that between the collector and the village officers. The initiative and the capacity among the members and the party units had been stifled. The belief had grown among partymen that expression of views at variance with the decision of the National Executive was wrong and constituted an act of indiscipline. Triloki Singh went to the extent of declaring that no unit of members of the party could criticise a decision of the National Executive. The National Executive had, in fact, begun to regard itself as a sovereign body.

Dr. Lohia challenged this contention. He said that the issue of internal democracy must receive greater attention of the people than it had so far done. "While it is not always possible for an outsider to understand all the processes of a debate in a party, which some times appear winding and torturous to him", he stated, "the entire refusal to consider and evaluate happenings inside an organisation can have deadly consequences. Democracy dies outside in the country only after it has first died within one or more major organisations of the country". He said that the party units, and party members at the different levels, must function within the jurisdiction laid down in the party's constitution. Public issues must be publicly debated. Private issues may be discussed within the four corners of private rooms". Discipline should mean the long arm of free speech and the strong fist of controlled action. It has hitherto meant the short arm of disciplined speech and the loose fist of free action. Members of political parties, including leaders, have been free to do as they please and note is taken of alleged transgressions only in speech".

He added: "the Praja Party, that once tried to be socialist and still claims to be such, violated all principles of internal democracy and its own constitution and took disciplinary actions of suspensions and expulsions by the hundreds on the single score of undesirable speech. An event, unparalleled in the annals of political parties in the whole world took place; he whole state conference of delegates elected by over 30,000 members, or one-sixth of the total membership of the party, was banned by the Executive of no more than twenty-five. What was done by Praja Socialist leaders is lot, after all, so dangerous to democracy as no single voice of conscience in the country was raised against it, and that the agencies of opinion met it with silence, or even with jubilant satisfaction, because disciplinary actions were taken against elements severely hostile to the government party. The people of India must learn to examine the internal working of their political parties, for these ultimately determine the external working of the state. "Suspensions and bans promulgated by the National Executive of the P.S.P. are in violation of law as also of good conduct, and unless defied, will help ruin outward democracy because these actions were taken not under a constitutional clause or rule but under a code of conduct, which is entirely non-justifiable. The Geeta is certainly a higher law than the penal code, but no same person could contemplate legal action under it. Tyranny has always used agent provocateurs as agencies for achieving its own brand of discipline. The same National Executive which refuses to reopen the Bombay action on the ground of constitutional incompetence, responded to Andhra cases of discipline thereby proving that what was involved was policy not discipline. Such shameless acts were possible because the National Executive banked on the popular but erroneous belief that discipline means obedience to higher orders. Such absolution in beliefs combined with majority rule must inevitably turn democracy into a monster worse than the worst monarchy".

The U.P. state party informed the P.S.P. central office that it would withdraw its resolution on the Limaye episode, cancel its invitation to Limaye, and its chairman would even tender an apology, if the National Executive reconsidered its action against Limaye. But the National Executive remained adamant. Many of the leaders threatened to resign from the body, if that suggestion to resolve the crisis was accepted by the Executive. The dominant group in the Executive protested that they were being charged with an intention of joining the Congress. But that had never been the charge of Dr. Lohia and other militants in the party against these leaders. As Lohia himself stated, "My charge against the present executive is not only that some of them are cooperationists, or that, the executives as a whole tends, unknowingly or otherwise, to strength the cooperationists, but that it is paralytic and guilty of inaction". Lohia's criticism was that both the old Congress Socialist Party and later the P.S.P. had almost been functioning as a transit camp for persons ultimately joining either the Congress or the Communist party. He observed; "Faulty notions of discipline and democracy cover up the socialist leadership's utter failure in the triple spheres of action, thought, and organisation. Four-fold ideas of merger, coalition, coalition on terms, and cooperation, each succeeding idea being more dangerous, because it looks more innocent, are effectively paralysing the party of socialism. In a democracy there is a limit to one's powers. Everybody and every authority high and low has its limitations, for in democracy the power is shared by all committees at all levels of organisation. Sita was saved in so far as she stayed within the line drawn for her by Laxman, but when she transgressed the line, she was kidnapped by Ravana. Similarly, every authority when it functions within the limit set for it, will be accepted. But when even the highest authority transgresses it, it is a signal for defying it and a fate similar to Sita must overtake it. Otherwise it tends to be fascist and crushes the soul of the people".

Though they were themselves guilty of adopting totalitarian methods, the dominant leadership accused Lohia of dictatorial behaviour. Jayprakash Narayan branded Lohia as a "splitter" and said that if he had been the Congress president he would have awarded a gold medal to the doctor in recognition of his activities, calculated to split the P.S.P. The National Executive declared that Lohia did not deserve the P.S.P. platform. This whole campaign against Lohia was being conducted while he was under detention in Manipur in connection with the party's agitation for restoration of a representative government in the former princely state. Before its merger with the Indian union, Manipur had an elected assembly and a ministry, but after the merger, the government of India scrapped the assembly and the ministry and replaced them with an advisory council. The people of the territory had been agitating for restoration of the representative assembly, under the leadership of the P.S.P. since five years. After all other efforts to persuade the government of India to grant the demand. They had launched satyagraha to secure it. Two P.S.P. leaders. Sucheta Kripalani and Hareshwar Goswami had visited Manipur to study the situation there and submitted to the party a report which had revealed the atrocities perpetrated by the administration against the people; more than two thousand people had been put behind bars. In view of the strength of the popular movement and the misuse by the administration of section 144, besides other repressive measures, to suppress it, the Manipur unit of the party naturally expected that some of the senior leaders of the party should participate in the movement. Lohia visited Imphal in April. The P.S.P. unit there wanted him to address a public meeting. They sought the district magistrate's permission for the purpose. The magistrate sought from the organisers guarantee that there will be no disorder. Besides demanding such guarantee in writing, the magistrate also verbally asked for an assurance that no slogans would be shouted and placards exhibited at the meeting. The organisers naturally declined to give any such guarantee and the magistrate refused permission to hold the meeting.

Lohia addressed the meeting, defying the ban. About three thousand people attended it. Lohia and six others, including L.E. Achawsingh—who presided over the meeting, A. Surendra Sarma and Thakur Chandra Sekore Singh, were arrested. Seventy volunteers of the party who joined Lohia and other Satyagrahis were refused bail and were remanded to judicial custody for 14 days. They were manhandled and ill-treated in the jail. They were all placed in the 'C' division and put in a cell meant to accommodate only one person. Lights, both in the cell and outside, were put off round the clock. The food served to them was not wholesome, and no proper facilities for bath were given to them. Surprisingly, Lohia who had blood pressure, was not allowed to take his medicine inside the prison. Newspapers, other than the *Statesman*, and books, even on non-political subjects, were not permitted to reach him. He was, however, subsequently permitted to take his medicine inside the jail.

After he had undergone the ill treatment for three days, Lohia and his co-prisoners refused to be locked up in the cells. The jailor flew into the rage, pushed them about and dragged them into the cells. On 13th April, Lohia wrote to the Vice-President that their "arrest was tied up with the issue of the gravest importance to national unity and the democratic well being of India and it is these issues that I should like to note before the government has completely obscured them with its customary skill". He said: "Our officers in the frontier areas should learn economy in the use of force and irritating words. After 15 days, remand to jail custody, of persons who did not offer bail, for they should almost be tried on summons, is not a magisterial but a revengeful act. Such laws of remand are disgrace and no sensible Magistrate would apply them to persons who are not out on bail and whose case is so simple that even if the offence is established, the sentence would probably fall short of the remand period". He went on: "Imphal is our eastern most city and Manipur with its capital is so aptly called, 'India's Eastern Lion's Door' Imphal is a poem in statesmanship and in taste. In relation to its tiny population, it has far more theatrical houses for drama and dance, compared with any other town in the whole world. But today there has been a considerable falling off in taste and foolish hands are toying with the stagecraft of our ancestors". He added; "Anyone who has a slightest experience of a crowd could straightaway tell that continuance of prohibitory order on meetings in Imphal is certainly against the maintenance of law, also not for the preserving of order, but either for vindication of prestige or prevention of a meeting of a public exposure of governmental misdeeds. Nobody likes to break up and disturb his own meeting. No Indian would like to challenge the validity of the state's integration, for it was in itself a good act, but to have coupled it with the dissolution of a sovereign legislative assembly was an attempt to sidetrack the real issue", he remarked.

Lohia and his co-prisoners filed a petition in the court on May 3 challenging the validity of their arrest and detention. However, they were all released before the petition came up for hearing before the court. Achaw Singh, Chairman of the Manipur P.S.P. and former M.P., who had been arrested along with Lohia, filed another petition in the court for having detained him in prison even 12 days after the court had ordered his release. The court allowed the petition and ordered the Manipur district magistrate to pay Achaw Singh Rs. 25, as compensation. The government later withdraw the order under section 144 which had been in force at Imphal for a number of days. Lohia thus succeeded asserting in the people's right to freedom of speech. Meanwhile when Lohia was involved in the Manipur struggle, the party's National Executive in its meeting passed a resolution condemning Lohia for his 'indiscipline' etc. Earlier a directive was also issued from the Party's central office to its provincial units asking them not to invite Lohia on any P.S.P. platform. The first annual conference of the Samajwadi Yuvak Sabha was held at Puri from the 26th to the 31st May. Madhu Limaye presided over it. Other leaders of the P.S.P. like Acharya Narendra Dev, Ashok Mehta and Lohia had also been invited to the conference, but the general secretary of the P.S.P. issued a directive that no member of the party should attend it, as Limaye was to preside over it. In fact, the Samajwadi Yuvak Sabha was an autonomous organisation of the socialist youth and had no organisational connection with the P.S.P. It was therefore beyond the Party's control and a subject of discipline. But Mehta wrote to the general secretary of the Samajwadi Yuvak Sabha to say that disciplinary action had been taken against Limaye with object of denying any party platform to him. No leader of the P.S.P. would therefore, attend meeting or the conference where Limaye was present.

In the course of his speech at the conference, Lohia, besides dealing with the political situation prevailing in the country, analysed the ideological crisis in the country. He said that in doing so, he was not referring to the common failing—the gap between precept and practice. Always the ideal suffered somewhat during its translation into practice. Emotions like greed, selfishness, anger and the like influenced man's thinking and action and give rise to what might be termed "errors of emotions" or fault of character. "But a fault of character is wholly different from a fault of understanding", he said. "When the character is just about going wrong and has not yet formed into a habit there is always the possibility of remorse and repentance. But a faulty understanding knows no mode of correction beyond itself. One of the beliefs prevalent particularly among the socialists in the country was", he said, "that there should be unity between theory and practice. The ideal and the actual were two separate identities. But there was sometime a tendency to see the "ideal" in the "actual". This fallacy of the idealisation of the actual often crept into man's thought. One should never identify what is with what ought to be. The ideal appeared in the human minds in two shapes—the abstract and the concrete. An abstract ideal had a concrete shape, although it remained an ideal still. If an ideal abstract failed to get a concrete shape it became meaningless. The consistent interplay of the particular and the general must become the habit of the mind. 'The ideal in its abstract form motivated thought and, its concrete form, motivated action. Equality for instance, a highly generalised and abstract principle—timeless, and ageless, is eternally and universally true. In order that such generalised principles may become relevant to life and action, they must always appear in a concrete shape to the meditator The absence of concrete images is primarily responsible for the ideological crisis in our politics. Only when the concrete meaning that we put into these generalised concepts is brought to the fore, that differences reveal themselves", he remarked.

"The gap between precept and practice will never altogether disappear as long as the agency to realise the precept is human. The European mind has tried to deny this gap between precept and practice and has, in fact, given it a thorough, theoretical scaffolding. But the Indian mind is different, in the process of explaining the gap between precept and practice, it has achieved a complete divorce of the ideal from the actual. Shankaracharya truly represents the Indian mind. In a stupendous sweep of mind, he differentiated between the worldly truth and the absolute truth and thus made it possible for the human mind not only to distinguish a stone from a man but also a man of caste from a man of another caste and yet believe in the Advaita and undifferentiated absolute", he added, He said that the primary task of young socialists in India was to put an end to this sorry mental condition. They must unfold such a vigorous and widespread mental activity all over the land that the division of the Indian mind into an abstract and a concrete compartment ends. At present these two compartments were visibly there; when the compartment opened up, the other closed up completely. The distinction between the aspects of the ideal must be there, but the passage between the two compartments always be open and unclotted. The five general principles of equality, non-violence, decentralisation, democracy and socialism, which had become the seemingly supreme aims of political endeavour in India, must be continually subjected to this treatment of interplay between the general and the particular. He observed further; "Otherwise, the tongue will continually spin the charkha and the hands will continually set up textile machines; the tongue will sing of non-violence and equality, the hands will practice inequality and use of the gun. The tongue will praise decentralisation, and concentration of power both in vast secretariats and in mass production factories and in wealth, will go on. The present gap between the tongue and the hands, the most characteristic simple feature of Indian life today, is not all due to dishonesty, greed or selfishness. The larger part of it is due to error of understanding. Young socialists must set before themselves the task of removing this error of understanding".

The U.P. state conference of the P.S.P., which had sparked of the confrontation between the militant and "paralysed" elements in the party, was held at Ghazipur from the 11th to the 13th June. The conference passed a resolution calling upon socialists to fight the totalitarian tendencies which sought to destroy the internal democracy of the party. Speaking on the resolution, Lohia said that it was sought to be made out that "militant socialists claimed that they had ideological differences with the other faction in the party, only to justify the acts of indiscipline. This charge could be countered by referring to the fact that the charge of indiscipline being levelled against militant socialists had been designed to obscure the differences between the two sections over ideology, actions, and approach to the issue facing the movement". He said the party's leadership had failed in all respects—thought, action and organisation—because of their faulty conceptions regarding democracy and discipline. The ideas of the merger with the Congress, a coalition or cooperation with it on certain conditions have all proved to be disastrous. They had paralysed the party. Opposition parties had developed the tendency to remain silent on vital issues, while they raised their voice on minor and unimportant issues. The creation of an organisation that would fight injustice and work for socialism was the need of the hour.

The campaign unleashed against Lohia after the Ghazipur conference exceeded all bonds of decency and restraint. Acharya Narendra Dev had claimed that he was neutral in the controversy between the two sections in the party and only a custodian of party's principles & programme, and no more, when he assumed the office of the chairman, but he gave up that pretence and openly allied with the section seeking areas of agreement with the Congress. He declared in a statement that he did not subscribe to the policy of equal irrelevance of communism and congressism, outlined in the Allahabad thesis of the Party. He even advised the leaders of the P.S.P. in Andhra Pradesh to seek an electoral understanding with the Congress.

The Acharya extended an invitation to Lohia to attend Party's National Executive meeting to be held at Jaipur in July, to consider the issue of the indisciplined activities of Lohia & others. Lohia received the telegram of invitation. He wrote a letter in reply to the telegram his inability to attend the meeting; ". . . . to expect him to attend the meeting was strange as those who constitute the Executive and blow hot and cold at the same time when they encourage such uncivilised acts as cancelling an invitation to the Tamilnadu Party Conference & openly proclaim that we do not deserve P.S.P. platform. They can also issue further invitations and publish in the press the we are the top invitees to the meeting". A rumor was also set in circulation that Acharya Narendra Dev had sent a letter to Lohia requesting him to meet him (the Acharya) in Delhi before the Jaipur meeting to discuss informally the whole issue. But Lohia in fact had not received any communication from Narendra Dev except the telegram of invitation for the Jaipur meeting. Lohia clarified his stand saying: "It is not that I must go as soon as I am called by somebody, but my relationship with Narendra Dev is such that I could not have refused his invitation for a talk".

The National Executive's meeting was held in Jaipur as scheduled in July. Very few members of the Executive were present in the meeting for the first four days. Lohia's letter expressing his inability to attend the meeting was not placed before the meeting. Jayprakash Narayan who had earlier publicly disassociated himself from the party activities was surprisingly invited to the meeting. Jayprakash arrived at the meeting on the fifth day. He was requested to draft a resolution suspending Lohia from the Party. This resolution was carried. The Chairman, Narendra Dev who was on the sick bed approved it. And on 10th July, Lohia was suspended from the party.

Lohia's virtual expulsion from the party created an unprecedented crisis in the P.S.P. and evoked comments from leading newspapers, questioning the wisdom of the step. *The Times of India* said that "the tactics adopted by Lohia may not be happy but his charge that 'the party never had the confidence to stand on its own legs' and that 'it sometimes turns to the right and sometimes to the left' is not without justice". *The Free Press Journal* commented that "the suspension of Dr. Lohia does not resolve the crisis in the Praja Socialist Party. It merely shows that the National Executive of the Party will tolerate democracy within the Party only so long as the opposition is not vocal. Democracy is in short supply and is an article for export only. The *Indian Nation* was of the view that "the harsh reality is this; that with Lohia out of the P.S.P., the pro-Congress elements in the P.S.P. will grow stronger. True, the P.S.P. will continue to be theoretically an opposition party, but realistically, it will be loosing, under the pressure of circumstances, its opposition teeth. The P.S.P. loves to bark but it does not like to bite the Congress party". 'Republican', a columnist of the *Hindustani Standard,* remarked, "there perhaps are many things that can be said for and against this dependence of the P.S.P. on Nehru. The first is that Nehru is no longer a young man and his party had not been schooled in socialist traditions the way he has been. It is doubtful that, in his absence, the Congress will be able to continue along the path that he has mapped out. It is also doubtful that the P.S.P. leaders will be able to step into his shoes". He added; "the second factor is that, even were the future of socialism safe in the hands of Nehru and the Congress, no democracy can afford the luxury of a one party system. The existence of a powerful opposition is no less essential than that of the party that rules. And no strong opposition can ever arise anywhere unless the men who lead it really do oppose. It is this that gives a certain timeliness to Lohia's announcement that he will now certainly form a new socialist party. Inasmuch as the old socialist party (P.S.P.) seems to have lost much of its will to live and refuses to be rejuvenated it is an inevitability that a new party should be formed. Dr. Lohia, who seems not to share the attitude of his former comrades towards the Prime Minister, is perhaps the best man in India to undertake the formation of such a party. It could have passed to less competent hands".

At a public meeting in Hyderabad called for propagating the founding of the new party. Lohia reviewed the socialist movement and said, "From 1935 to 1946, the socialists participated in the freedom struggle as a group within the Congress. This was a period of action. Thereafter from 1946 to 1951 was a period of illusive hope and a false bubbling over of socialism. The period from 1951 to 1955 was a period of indecision and inaction. The present deadlock has arisen out of confusion of thought as to whether the Socialist Party is an alternative to the Congress or just a party for correcting it". Being attracted towards the Congress by its five year plans and the external glitter and grandeur of those plans, Ashok Mehta became engrossed in the praise of Nehru. For pulling the socialists out of this maze, Lohia said about so called progress; "In 125 years of their rule, the British built up one mile of railway per day, one station in three days, one textile mill in four months and one sugar factory in a year. They planned watersupply schemes and founded cities. Big cities like Bombay, Calcutta, Madras and Delhi are landmarks of this kind of progress during the British regime. From this point of view the figures of achievement during the Congress regime are mere handtricks".

According to Lohia this was not true progress, but exploitation of the common people by the government in league with the capitalists. In this so called progress during the Congress regime there has been no limit to corruption, misuse and extravagance. Lohia further said, "Congress is trying to ape the European type of industrialisation. As a result, the country is required to put in more efforts without a corresponding increase in production and handful of people are receiving the benefits of planning, while the vast majority is getting only promises". While talking about the new party Lohia said, "I hope this socialist party will not resort to tactical manouevers, intrigues, casteism, money and opportunism. Let us form a party of which the country will be proud".

The revolt of the militant socialists began to spread. Party units at New Delhi, Mysore, Madhya Pradesh, Madras, Manipur, Bihar, Bombay, and Hyderabad, welcomed the new party. Lohia gave party to be born a slogan: "Power to within seven years". But at the same time Lohia took care to warn the would be leaders and workers by saying. "This would be possible only if we have courage, character and ability. As a mark of courage, the socialists should go to jail for two months in a year. Those who fight against injustice when not in power, can alone form a good government after the capture of power. We must show our skill through constructive work".

The socialist mind which has been saddled with fear that the socialist movement would crash after the decision to form a new party was now relieved. New confidence was born. But along with this enthusiasm, it was also observed that even stalwarts tottered when the moment of decision arrived. People are generally not prepared to leave temptation, personal loyalty, selfishness and power lust. But it was observed that even in such conditions several brave socialists girded up their lions, to carry out radical and revolutionary work of the newly formed Socialist Party. A new flame started blazing in Indian politics.

22. NEW FLAME

A large number of P.S.P. units and the partymen from all over the country condemned the action of the National Executive in suspending Lohia from the party. The executed reacted to the nationwide outbursts of protest with the spate of suspension of Party units and members for this act of "indiscipline". Expressing grave concern over the ideological and organisational crisis in which the Executive had plunged the P.S.P. numerous party units and members pressed for an immediate national conference to settle the issue. The feeling among these partymen was that though the dominant group in the National Executive professed its continued commitment to the policy and programme outlined in the Allahabad thesis, it had been making persistent efforts to blur the separate identity and distinctive features of socialism evolved by the party, and that the constant talk of coalition and cooperation with the Congress had tended to paralyze the Party's will to achieve power and create a new society. They saw in the suspension of Lohia, the architect of militant socialism and the author of Allahabad thesis, and other militant socialists, a sinister design to eliminate all militant elements from the party with a view to succeed in the dominant faction's search for areas of agreement with the ruling party—a bid frustrated by the militants at Betul. The party was fast heading towards disintegration, a calamity which only a national conference could avert.

These feelings found expression in the resolutions adopted by a number of party units and statements issued by members, and legislators from different areas. They pointed out that such suspensions, amounted to virtual expulsions and denial to them, of all opportunities to participate in party discussions and activities.

But all these pleas went unheeded. The Executive was in no mood to convene a National Conference and seek the party's verdict on the issue. The only alternative left for Lohia and his followers in the party, under these circumstances, was either to retire from politics or to form a new party of militant socialism and accept the challenge of the hour. They chose the latter. News poured in from all parts of the country about meetings and rallies where party units and partymen announced their decision to severe connection with the P.S.P. and join Lohia. Lohia himself addressed some of these rallies. Addressing a meeting at Hyderabad, Lohia said, "The central issue at present is whether the P.S.P. should function as just corrective to the Congress or an effective opposition, with an objective of being an alternative; of replacing the Congress and forming a new government in the country. It is this dilemma that has brought the party to the present crisis".

The new socialist party was launched at the convention of militant socialists held at Hyderabad from the 28th December 1955. Lohia presided. In the course of his address, he referred to the march of events from Panchmarhi to Hyderabad. He alluded to the issue of internal democracy which led to large scale suspension and expulsion of militant socialists from the P.S.P. and culminated in the decision to form a new party. He said that the socialist movement should learn an unforgettable lesson from these developments.

Reminding the people that democracy dies in the country only after it had died within one or more political parties in the country, Lohia said; "No law or court should be expected to obligate political parties into democratic functioning, although certain requirements concerning public accounting of party funds and the like are a healthy practice. What the law may not compel should, however, be achieved by an alert public opinion, so that parties that weaken and destroy their own internal democracy should be denied approval and the vote". Members of political parties, including leaders, he stated, "have been free to do as they please and note is taken only of alleged transgressions in speech. This is partly understood, because the staple diet of Indian politics is speech, much more than action, and uncomfortable speeches tend to disturb an otherwise placid existence. Discipline should henceforth mean the positive doing of what should be done and non-doing of what should not be done. The concept of the limited personality will then be the ineffacably engraved on the Indian mind. A limited personality always strives to be free of thought and controlled action". He said that leaders of limited authority would naturally be somewhat saddened but would never revolt or fall, if they lose on a resolution or in an election. Democracy must mean the earnest striving to win but also the ability to bear defeat. It must mean the desire to hold together, for a people as well as political party, in the hope that the next encounter would be more favourable.

Lohia stated that the socialist movement would be well advised to call its creed by the simple name of socialism instead of wasting its mental energies on disputes of grammar relating to one word or another, and should concentrate on an increasingly simple statement of the fullness of its tenets and beliefs. Such a statement is clogged at the outset by disputes between Gandhism and Marxism, "so beloved to a certain class of socialists". The desire to adopt one teacher or another and wave the banner of the doctrine arising out of his name, he remarked "is also a search for a tribal charm, and it gives peace of mind, makes things easy and avoids the perpetual need to think. It had led to a variety of schools of interpretation, so that there are actually several Gandhisms and several Marxisms, every school automatically believes that it is the inheritor of the teacher. .... Gandhism and Marxism are, in fact, being reduced, by and large, into curiously anaemic doctrines". While a sterile Gandhism has come into existence which concentrates almost exclusively on changing the heart of the well placed, to the utter neglect or the poor's man's change of heart. "Marxism, which has in India become another name for class struggle, furiously preaches the doctrine of class struggle, but always tomorrow and never or only rarely today".

He said that socialism need not proclaim itself as Gandhism or Marxian on the one hand and as anti-Gandhi or anti-Marxian on the other, for, "this would only substitute thought by a charm". Lohia referred to the pursuit of peaceful methods as against armed rebellion and said; "the debate of violence in a revolution has hitherto been corrupted by concentration on the single question whether the method of armed rebellion should ever or never be used. The use or non-use of violence in the last stage of revolution is a matter of such accidental relevance or secondary detail that the dispute about it is like arguing about the funeral of one who has yet long years to live. Such foolish disputes could hitherto take place because the world knew of the lone alternative between parliamentary and insurrectionary means. A new dimension in the shape of individual and mass civil resistance has now been added. The question now relates not to the use or non use of violence in a revolution but to whether the revolution shall be organised on the basis of non violence or that of violence. "Not the ultimate use, but the continuing organisation of non-violence or violence, should be the central theme of the debate on revolutionary outbreaks. While a revolution may regrettably erupt into violence in its last stages, particularly when the decaying Government seeks to dispense with democratic forms, participants in the revolution must definitely resolve to organise on continuing base of peaceful methods. Mankind will ever hurtle from the hands of one tyranny and irresponsibility into another, if it continues to seek and organise its revolution through violence". He added that in the concept of a non-violent revolution both non violence and revolution had equal importance. Socialists must be wedded to both. Characterising the different opposition parties in India, he observed that, "there was a complete absence of an opposition party that aspired to oust the Congress government. Some organisations took up from time to time single aims, narrow, restricted and partial. The Communist Party of India also pursued a single aim, partial and restricted to the foreign policy. Ever since the chanceries of Delhi and Moscow achieved coordination, however negative, of their foreign policies, the communist opposition fizzled out also in respect of internal matters. While the P.S.P.'s modes of action are so paralysed that it will be, like some mythical animal who is half man and half beast, half government and half opposition. An obstruction against radical politics is the notion of progress prevalent in the country, particularly among the vocal elements of both the government and the opposition. Against this prevalent notion of progress, certain indisputable facts must be noted; Of all the seventysix countries of the United Nations, India is the seventy-fifth country in respect of her average food consumption per head; she obtains fifteen hundred calories a day per person which is lowest in the world. Of all countries participating in the Olympics games at Helsinki, India was placed thirty-second. Qualifying objectives such as 'the greatest in Asia', are exceeding misleading".

"The dams of Bhakra or Tungabadra or Damodar and the

factories of the Chitraranjan or Sindri, are being quoted and looked upon as demonstrative evidence of progress. Well could the British had claimed to have brought progress to India in that, during the 125 years of their rule, they laid one mile of railway track every day, built buildings of public use every fourth day, helped set up one textile factory every four months and one sugar factory every year, and, on top of it, built the largest cities of Calcutta, Bombay, New Delhi and Madras. In reality, British rule brought economic, political, cultural and spiritual ruin to the country" he remarked, and pointed out that even with such inflated rates of expansion, as the government of India claimed, India is placed at the lowest rung of the ladder of developmental world progress.

Referring to the colossal split in the thought of the vocal classes and the mass of the people that had made itself manifest, he said that "more than any other country in the world, the existing Indian civilisation is middle class and supervisory. This civilisation had produced a remarkable situation in which the worth of an opposition politician is measured not so much by his radical politics as by his capacity to recommend to, and help secure some crumbs from, the tables of the ruling party. If the middle class intellectuals in the socialist movement should only consider themselves as manure for the growth of leaders out of working men and the lower castes, India would truly become a socialist land. One who patiently allowed himself to be used as manure over a number of years might himself in time grow into a uniquely pleasant flower.

Anger towards those above and aloofness from those below is not socialism; the oneness of sympathy and anger against exploitation, can alone combine to produce right socialism. Political parties that only provoke and do not consolidate through continuing integration, mentally and physically, of the leader and the led, become like rival shops to which the people go for small and temporary profit. It may be, that the divorce of the lower middle classes from working classes, and the lower castes, except in temporary periods of struggle, which the socialist movement has so far represented, has occasioned this malady of excitement without fulfillment, of provoking without consolidating. The Indian socialist movement must now learn to provoke as well as consolidate, excite only as much as it can fulfil, to provoke as much as the situation currently demands. And, after having consolidated the gains, to provoke and excite again and more, until the last battle against exploitation or the last provocation is won. ... The socialist movement must begin to act, and it must give up the old habit of reacting continually to situations of others making. When the socialist movement would keep on building a nucleus of steady thought and action, unmindful of the temporary opinions of the people, the rest is only a matter of time". Lohia said.

He referred to the stupendous welcome accorded by the people to the Soviet leader, Mr. Khruschev and Mr. Bulganin during their visit to the country and said; "The welcome is an indication of the sense of adoration of strength which always exists in the people. Soviet visitors placed themselves exceedingly handsomely, even more than the Indian government ever did, on the side of India in respect of Goa and Kashmir. While fools alone would neglect the possibility of the Russian government turning turtle in a trice and espousing the cause of Pakistan, should their global strategy so demand, it would be foolish not to admit that Russians need friends, that they are emotional, that the warm welcome of the Indian people really touched them and while they are friends, they are very good friends".

Towards the realisation of the Party's national and international objectives, the conference adopted a seven year plan to power. He said that a seven year plan to power was not an analytical foretelling of what would happen in the country "It is a willed plan of a phased programme of socialist action. In view of the immensity of the task, a period shorter than seven years, would surely open the door on opportunism and manoeuvering and considering the urgency of the situation, a longer period would make the plan somewhat irrelevant. Too long has the socialist movement lived from hand to mouth and in expectation of the rose-tinted dawn always on the morrow, a tomorrow that never comes because it is only a feeble and excited wish and not a serious determination to mould events. In its inception, the plan rejects the pious humbug of professedly not wanting power but in actual practice pursuing it out of egoistic impulses and openly calls forth for power for socialism and, only to that extent, to its agents and spokesmen. Such plans may never have been formulated elsewhere, for belief in insurrectionary methods, on the one hand, and exclusive reliance on parliamentary practice without the practice of civil resistance on the other, does not make for such confidence in willed action "and added that seven year plan to power is an attempt of striking a balance between an ugly eagerness for power and a hollow desire for it without accumulating corresponding strength".

"The Socialist Party" he stated, "has already acquired the reputation, and rightly so, of being a militant party of fighters. Even more than that, it is a party of builders. It wants to build canals, roads, youth centres and other constructive projects, while in opposition, and appropriate factories and farms and dams, when it becomes the government. Above all, it wants to build the mind of India. Out of such militancy and the desire to build, the seven-year plan to power derives its substance". Outlining the plan of action, Lohia said that the two years of 1956 and 1957 must be treated as emergency years of plan, when much would have to be done on the footing of sturdy war measures. It would be followed by two years of consolidation and 1960-61 would again be years of expansion. The plan made 1962 the year of decision. Other items of the programme included a weekly study centre in every constituency and, when possible, in smaller units; while four major study camps of national scope would be run in the first year, to be gradually expanded into a permanent camp site and school of socialism, the end of 1956 would see the establishment of, at least 500 study centres on the constituency level, 1000 in 1957 and, between 1960 and 62, the number would be expanded into 3,000. While study centres would directly concern themselves with a pervasive mental development of tens of thousands of persons, he said, the particularised forms of generalised principles of social reconstruction such as the demand of no-tax on profitless agriculture or unemployment insurance would be reached agitationally to the mass of the people. Apart from these willed agitations against permanent evils, there would other agitations forced upon the people by new laws and orders of exploitations and injustice. While individual civil resistance may be expected to become the characteristics of the more active socialists, local, state or zonal struggles would take place when the situation was urgent, people's strength somewhat adequate and all other means of redress have been exhausted.

Lohia placed before the party the aim of enrolling five lakh members in the first year, ten lakh in second year and increase it to 20 lakh in 1960, and reach the target of 30 lakh in 1961-62. With every active member becoming the nucleus of 20 to 50 ordinary members, the entire party organisation would be steeled through agency of functioning constituency committees on the one hand and the active members on the other. With the establishment of 1,000 committees in the first year and 1,500 in the second, the target of 3,000 will be achieved about the end of the plan period. 6,000 office bearers ringed around by 3000 committee men who would, in their turn, be controlled by 3 lakh councillors, who would form the unbeatable core of organisation. Elections to legislature and other representative institutions would only be fought in constituencies where the organisations had reached the required level. He expected socialists to try to build and expand affiliated organisations of peasants, labourers, youths, women, artisans, professional classes and the like and evolve a corresponding seven year plan also for them. Lohia concluded his address to the foundation conference of the party with the call to members—"So, onward to give lakh members, one thousand constituency committees, five hundred study centres, agitations where possible and struggles where necessary and construction everywhere in 1956.

The foundation conference was attended by a large number of delegates from all the states. Their enthusiastic participation in the proceedings of the conference made one think that the new party meant business. Lohia's fresh thoughts and new approach immensely influenced the thinking of the delegates and made them reappraise the traditional beliefs they were entertaining about socialist thought and action for about two decades. For example Lohia's concept of discipline: "Free expression and controlled actions shattered the old beliefs about the internal discipline of a political party. Some delegates even suggested that there should be some restrictions on free expressions on members of the party. Lohia was so shocked and perturbed at this suggestion that he vacated the chair and expressed his inability to continue to guide the proceedings of the conference further. This suggestion to restrict freedom of expression was a deadly stroke on the very foundation of the new party which was born out of the struggle for the establishment of the right of a party member for uncontrolled expression of thought. The suggestion was however withdrawn after some discussion.

Lohia was elected chairman of the party. He devoted all his energies to the attempt to fashion the Socialist party into an effective instrument of socialist revolution. He resisted the nomination as best as he could but at last succumbed to the number of his close colleagues pleadings of friends. Lohia's election to the chairmanship of the party was in a way quite natural as he alone was the architect of the new experiment in the organised socialist movement. The situation then prevailing demanded Lohia's leading the party and leading the socialist opposition which was facing a life and death struggle. Lohia immediately set forth to lay down a sound foundation for a principled discipline and a militant socialists party with the introduction of a number new experiments in the party organisation. He knew that sound principles and militancy alone do not make a party which can deliver the goods. Harmful old habits should be eschewed and new habits helpful to the running of an efficient and disciplined organisation should be cultivated. He warned the workers to get rid of having excessive personal ambitions, pleaded to avoid imitation of the life-style of the few; severely criticised excess in smoking, drinking and other habits. Not the leaders but common workers according to Lohia were the real pillars of the party organisation. He regularly sent circulating letters to the party workers which were expected to be read and discussed collectively. Through these letters Lohia expressed himself on various problems facing the party and the country and tried to enthuse the workers for action. Lohia wanted to finish the traditional gap between the leaders, legislators and members of higher bodies of the party and the common workers in the sphere of the actual party organisational work. He therefore fixed up a certain quota of organisational work for the leaders and others of their class and wanted them to fulfil it without exception. Lohia himself enrolled primary members, collected contributions for the central office, and attended study camps as an ordinary worker of the party.

It is during this period that Lohia started his monthly English magazine '*Mankind*' from Hyderabad. *Mankind* was a collective voice which will not call itself Gandhian, nor Marxist, nor after any other man, although many will be it's teachers, in its effort to achieve a world mind. Apart from the publication of this magazine, the central headquarters of the party, under Lohia's guidance, started publishing a variety of socialist literature. Existence of a principled and militant socialists party was being effectively felt in the country by a number of actions undertaken by the party in various states. The great Kisan march on the Lucknow secretariat in March, 1956 exhibited for the first time after the Hyderabad conference, the party's hold on the peasantry in U.P. In U.P. again, the socialists were conducting a mass satyagraha for the entry of Harijans in the Kashi Vishwanath temple. Bihar party was also engaged in the civil resistance battle with the government in which more than five thousand resisters, the majority of whom were poor peasants and of depressed classes, courted arrest. In Maharashtra there was the popular movement for formation of separate linguistic state. Socialists though comparatively weak there threw themselves in the agitation with vigour.

The ensuring general election to parliament and state legislatures in 1957, posed a difficult and testing situation for the party. Opposition to the united front and go it alone election policy of the party, made it inevitable for the party to fight the elections on its own ticket only. Consequently there would be fewer candidates of the party in the field. In a majority of the constituencies there would be no Socialist Party candidates. What should the party members and party symphathisers do in those constituencies? Whom would they vote? Lohia stated "Not to vote out of carelessness and laziness is against democracy, but to return a vote when there is no candidate of one's choice is a great duty of the voter. This situation, of course, must not continue for long. We must, at the earliest, show up as a party which would fulfil the wishes and aspirations of the masses.

Though Lohia was striving hard to infuse the party with the spirit of collective socialists action, he did not get the extent of response he expected. He was somewhat disillusioned and distressed. He commented, "may be the horse is dead long back and I am whipping it to get up and run in vain. The party is half dead. Getting at the causes at this will not suffice. The remedies will have to be found out". Doubts were raised by some prominent party leaders about the party's 'go alone' election policy. Politics of summit manoeuvreing and of short cuts to power was again found visible at some levels of the party. The gap of inequality still existed between the leaders and the workers. The dependence of lower committees of the party on higher committee, and on the leaders, still continued. The lower committees still failed to achieve initiative in thought and action. Traditional disregard for organisation and the party building was there as of old. Lohia had to fight against all those ills in the party. Lohia fought with determination and incurred the wrath and discontent of many of his colleagues.

His term of chairmanship terminated when the first annual conference of the Socialist party was held at Sihora (Madhya Pradesh) in December, 1956. In his presidential speech in the conference, Lohia drew attention to the growing symptoms of the party returning to the old ways of thought and action, and warned the party: "Politics of manoeuvering will not bring revolutionary change in the country. Revolutionary change of mind must precede revolutionary changes in the country. The longer path is, in the long run, the shortest path". The credit of whatever success the new Socialist Party gained during the next ten years, goes without doubt to Lohia's one year in office as chairman of the party.

23. THREE PILLAR STONES

For any political party, the period of a general election is the most crucial period. For a party with a pronounced ideology, however, it is the time of an acid test This is a period when a party is likely to break up. The Socialist Party had entered the election area in its maiden year of existence and had fielded 33 candidates for the Lok Sabha and 335 for the various Vidhan Sabhas. However only 9 of them were elected to the Lok Sabha and to the Vidhan Sabhas. This success fell far too short of their expectations.

In a public statement of assessment of the results of the elections, Lohia said; "Thus the people of India are not prepared to elect any of the parties, Socialist, Communist and Jan Sangh, in preference to Congress. It is clear that they have not yet made up their mind as to who should replace the Congress. I wished the Socialist Party could secure this position. However, at least this time, the verdict of the people has been otherwise. The Socialist Party has doubled its strength in the Lok Sabha It is moving ahead slowly and has secured a foot-hold in Ganga-Godavari region. After the fall of the Congress, perhaps the Socialist Party will be the only party capable of taking care of the country. This is the only party in the country which has fought single handedly. An ideology is always characterised by singleness of purpose. Other parties had fought this election not for any principle but just for securing a fair number of seats".

Government had done injustice to small parties and independent candidates. Voters lists had been given gratis to the Congress, the Communist, Jansangh and the Praja-Socialist parties. Each of them had been allotted a single symbol over the entire country. Speaking against this, Lohia's said, "This is contrary to the principle of equality of justice as enumerated in the Indian Constitution. The government has violated articles 14 and 326 of the constitution. Thereby small parties and independent candidates have not only suffered losses but have suffered from injustice also. The Congress is a party on the decline. It is a collapsing edifice. When a big party becomes static, it is the sign of its retrogression. In politics, neither a man nor a party can remain static at any point. Although the Communist Party is the ruling party in Kerala, it has received a set-back on all-India level. It has not done anything revolutionary for fear of incurring the wrath of the centre or the displeasure of the people. What can one say about the P.S.P. which has not been able to save itself, even at the cost of selling its soul and loyalty? Inspite of this, had it doubled it's seats in the Lok Sabha and Vidhan Sabhas, one could have applauded it's successful tactics without approving its policies. Thus a sin has been committed without getting a chance of enjoying its pleasure. Even the crime has become insipid.

Lohia severely criticised even his own party. He lauded the Maharashtra unit for having held its soul and loyalty intact even in the inidst of the powerful sweep of the linguistic agitation. It had not slipped into the trap of united fronts. In this context, Lohia said; "A party, led by principles, even if destroyed temporarily, is reborn and becomes successful". Defects like selfishness, disloyalty, laziness, lack of brotherhood, etc. had crept into the Socialist Party also. Referring to them, Lohia said; "Dishonest individuals playing petty politics should quit the party. Can love and respect for an individual be reasons for pursuing unscrupulousness? A party must be run on moral principles, rules and regulations. Things like mutual love between workers are irrelevant. I have observed that when a house catches fire, everyone tries to save his own life. He does not bother at all about others. Mutual love and respect are unreal". Lohia had refused to contest the election in 1952 and afterwards also. But in 1957, he decided to stand for election, in order to share the sorrows of defeated candidates. Lohia contested from a U.P. parliamentary constituency. He was defeated by about 30 to 35 thousand votes. Nehru and the Congress had resorted to all possible means, fair or foul, to defeat him. Lohia accepted the defeat with an open mind. He said; "The better person has won. The man and the party who had no good organisation, have lost". Still the defeat had it's effect.

After the defeat, Lohia expressed, "One's mind is greatly disturbed on such occasions. One cannot escape one's duty. But the mind fails to understand what is happening in the country. We all of the socialist party must imbibe the courage and tenacity of Mohammed Ghori. Even after being defeated consequently 17 times, Mohammed Ghori stood up in challenge eighteenth time and won".

Life came back to normal, as soon as the elections were over. The river of degradation and corruption flowed freely. Lohia got agitated. He said; "On the one hand the government talks about simple living, but on the other, the daily expenditure incurred by Nehru is huge enough even to put an emperor to shame. The administration of "South Avenue Managing Agency Unlimited" with which the Prime Minister and the President are associated is one of the extravagance and irresponsibility. This agency is more extravagant than the Clive Street agency of Calcutta or the Wall Street agency of New York. So called intelligentsia and white collar workers are being corrupted by the Government. Many instigations like Bharat Sevak Samaj have accepted slavery of the government and the entire society is permeated by fear, selfishness, subservience and weakness. Instead of raising the level of the whole country slowly but simultaneously, the government appears to have adopted the policy of making a handful of people modern in turn. This is the real cause of the degeneration of the country. There is far more disparity within the Indian society than between America and India. If motor car, radio and telephone are taken as yardsticks it appears that in India there are 2½ lakh persons using motor cars, 3 lakh using telephone and 8 to 9 lakh having radio. Thus on the one hand there are few lakh elite, while on the other there are 40 crore poor people. When foreign visitors see these elite, they say that our country is on the way to progress. The really 'progressive' aspects of things are kept hidden deliberately. The fact that the grandson of a peon and the son of a lawyer became the Prime Minister of India is a thing which would arouse the confidence of the common man. However, the Prime Minister suppressed this fact and glorified his father as "the son of progressive epoch".

While clarifying the economic policy of the Socialist Party, Lohia said; "The Socialist Party will put an end to this elitism and try to raise the economic level of the entire society. Expenditure is incurred on three accounts; allowance and amenities, two prices of the same thing, and misuse of public money. The Prime Minister gets from the government a house with a monthly rent of Rs. 3000 and furniture worth Rs. 1300 per month. Besides he also gets allowances for motor car petrol, guests, medical treatment and other facilities. At the government canteen attached to the Prime Minister's residence, a cup of tea costs just one anna. However, at Ashok Hotel, which is not prestigious as the Prime Minister's residence, the same cup of tea costs two rupees. Once bouquets and flowers worth about Rs. 200 were carried from Calcutta to Gauhati by plane for presenting them to the Prime Minister, similarly, for a public meeting an expenditure of rupees fifty thousand to one and a half lakh is incurred for the security of the Prime Minister and other items".

During this time Lohia launched the 'Remove English Movement' since English had been accorded the status of the state language, although India had become independent. Thereby Lohia placed before the people a healthy policy about the language problem. While elaborating his language policy Lohia said, "I am opposed to English, not because it is a foreign language, but because it is the language of a handful of people, barely one percent of the people. In the entire world, India is the only country where official transactions in Lok Sabha, and Vidhan Sabha's as well in law courts, laboratories, postal department, factories, railways, etc. is carried out in a foreign language not understood by 99% of people. English must be banished from the public and the social life of the country. If at all it remains, it may do so only as an optional subject. Nobody is demanding it's removal from England and America, or from libraries. It will remain as one of the languages of the world. The conception that it is the world language is incorrect. Alongwith French and Spanish, Russian has also now made an advance. Out of the 300 crore people in the world, only 30 to 35 crores speak English. It is because of his slavish attitude to English their the learned man in India shows a lack of fundamental thinking. It is the English language that has been responsible for recession in industry. For bringing about industrialisation, India needs one million engineers and scientists and one crore foremen and supervisors, how can this need be satisfied if our education is imparted through the medium of English? Countries like Japan, China, Rumania, etc. bought industrialisation through their mother tongue only. Indian army will not become people's army and the country also cannot be protected unless the domination of English in the army is ended. It is not possible to regulate the stomach unless the mind is regulated. The development of regional languages can be attained only through experiment and usage. Indian languages are rich. Whereas there are about 5 to 6 lakh words in Hindi. English had only half that number, Sanskrit, the mother of all Indian languages is an ocean of words. English is the last tool on holding on the power, used by the Congress and through it by the handful of upper class men who have raised their standard of living, with the help of the Congress. Conflict is unnecessarily being created among the fourteen regional languages, and between the north and the south. Students are suffering since English had been made the compulsory subject. Boys and, girls work hard in studying English and neglect other subjects. It is quite possible to get science textbooks translated by one lakh and odd professors in the country. It is a misconception that it will not be possible to attain scientific knowledge without English. Countries like Germany, Russia. China, Japan etc. have made progress in science through their own languages only. English has created among our people a sense of inferiority complex. An Indian language can be learnt with the lesser effort than English. "On the one hand, one sees people's language, people's dress, people's food and the people's home while on the other are seen the language, dress, food and the homes of the privileged. Thus there has been an abominable division of the Indian life. At one time only a handful of people held fast to Arabic, Persian and Sanskrit. Similarly, in the present generation also only a handful are holding fast to English. These handful of people feel that their traditionally privileged position will be jeopardised by the removal of English. Democracy will be crippled without peoples languages".

Besides language policy, Lohia placed in the hands of the socialist one more weapon viz.; his policy towards caste. While analysing this revolutionary policy, Lohia observed; "Casteism is the dirty legacy of Indian life. The tenacious hold of casteism is a great obstacle in the way of the establishment of equality. Thousands of years of casteism have created in the society certain practices whereby the society is split into caste divisions, which are perpetuated in practice, from generation to generation. Handful of upper caste people are cultured and cunning. The lower castes are stagnant and lifeless. Upper caste people do not number more than 5 to 10 crore but due to the influence of thousands of years, they have become intelligent and influential; it is only approximately 50 lakh of people of the upper castes, who have become rich in the true sense, and are currently holding the means of power and wealth of the country. 80% of society, while neither holding any wealth nor wielding any power, has been living in a suppressed state for thousands of years just due to being born in low castes. They intellect has rusted due to lack of opportunity for using it. Only the work requiring manual labour has been forced on them and, the flowers of leadership of the upper classes in all the spheres of life, have blossomed at the cost of the lives of the suppressed people. Some castes appear to have been created merely for doing such dirty work only". While suggesting the way of removing this extreme disparity in Indian society, Lohia said, "Congress, Praja Socialists and other parties and intellectuals, talk about 'equal opportunities for all.' This language is deceptive. It is intended for maintaining the status quo. It should be stopped and 60% of the posts should be reserved for Adivasis, untouchables, Shudras, women, and low-caste Muslims, irrespective of whether those persons are deserving or not. These sections of the society should be given special opportunities. The plea that the privileged and the unprivileged should both be given equal opportunities is an unjust and unequal competition. The privileged class must sacrifice themselves in order that backward classes should flourish".

Lohia didn't sit quiet by simply propounding his caste policy. He established contact with Dr. Babasaheb Ambedkar and started an exchange of views with him. But for Ambedkar's sudden death, the two leaders would have met each other and perhaps the Republican Party might not have been seen as an independent party as at present. Besides Gandhiji, Lohia considered Dr. Ambedkar as a great personality of India. According to Lohia, Dr. Ambedkar represented a symbol of hope in the struggle for destruction of casteism. Lohia corresponded with the president of the Indian Backward Class Association, Ramlakhan Chandrapuri, and brought him within the fold of the Socialist Party.

On 23rd January 1958, Lohia met the old leader of the Dravid Kalagham, Ramaswamy Naicker. Naicker was then in jail, but on account of deterioration of his health he had been removed to a hospital. He had been charged with inciting his followers to violence. While he was undergoing the trial in the court, Pandit

Nehru had said in his speech at Trichinapalli that Naicker should be declared as an insane person and awarded the maximum possible punishment. This was an injustice. Lohia told Naicker that he stood against this injustice. He admired the 'anti-casteism movement' of Naicker. At the same time he made it clear that he was opposed to the anti-North stand and the demand of Dravidistan by Naicker, his anti-Hindi agitation, burning the portraits of Gandhiji and the violence against individual Brahmins. Lohia also said, "I think burning of the constitution is improper. But I may tolerate even that since the Congress government is violating the sanctity of the constitution by transgressing constitutional limits". While expressing this view, Lohia concluded his interview by expressing his desire for the cooperation of Naicker.

During this period Lohia tried to give some solid content to his idea of economic equality. From this point of view he demanded a total remission of land revenue. He expressed that if this remission was granted, crores of people would for the first time have the experience of freedom. He also stated, "Prices of commodities and their production are the two wheels of the chariot of life. If one of these is broken, life is ruined. Whereas the prices of commodities gallop, production increases with the speed of a donkey". So Lohia put forth a policy for controlling the prices. In his own words this policy was as follows:

(1) Between one harvest and the next, the price of grain must not vary by more than about one anna per seer.
(2) Price of an essential factory—produced commodity must not be more that 1½ times its cost of production.
(3) The prices of agricultural products and machine products must be balanced.

In this way, Lohia developed a policy in respect of language, caste and prices which later on became the foundation of the socialist thought. He encouraged the socialists to build movements by taking up varied programmes like "Give work or give allowance". "Food-brigade", "Land-brigade", "Literacy brigade" etc. Lohia propounded that "The highest test of a civilisation is the type of it's latrine. Arrangements must be made about clean drinking water and closed latrines for women. Modern and American styled localities like 'Panch Bangaliya. Dakashinpath, Wall Street etc. are growing in big cities like Delhi, and Calcutta. On the other hand 6 lakh villages are still sunk in filth".

Lohia also drew attention to the laws and the judiciary system. Citing as an example an event which had taken place a few days earlier Lohia recalled; "A rickshaw-puller of Nagpur. Baburao Kochale, was sentenced to 6½ years' imprisonment for having displayed an open rusted knife before Nehru. The punishment for such an offence is normally an imprisonment of 6 months. But the offence of Kochale was not that simple, he had displayed the knife before the Prime Minister, and hence was arbitrarily punished more".

Lohia picked up the rusted Gandhian weapon of Satyagraha and restarted its propaganda. He said, "In Satyagraha there is a wilful union of intellect and physical strength. In ancient times Prahlad and Socrates had resorted to this path. A 'New Man' having chosen this path, will say, 'I shall not surrender, nor shall I hit back'. There are two ways of facing injustice, either always surrender meekly like a cow, or sometimes attack violently like a tiger. Instead of this, the alternative suggested by satyagraha is one in which a common man can show his courage. The test of this alternative lies in winning over crores of people and enhancing their courage". After describing the greatness of Satyagraha, Lohia put forth the idea of eternal Satyagraha and said, just as in a relay race. When a runner is tired his place is taken by the next one and the relay race continues. So also a similar relay race of Satyagraha must go on through all the states in India. And the relay race of Satyagraha as anticipated by Lohia did take place in the country; Struggles were organised in practically all states under the leadership of the Socialist Party. About sixty to seventy thousand men and women broke the law and about twenty-five to thirty thousand were imprisoned for breaking law and pressing the demand of the people.

Thus the socialists-men and women were carrying on their party work facing various difficulties, encountering dangers and struggling all alone. They were intoxicated by there party ideal. They were fired up with unprecedented frenzy and stubborn will. However as the party was dizzy with idealism, it had to face a different type of danger. This was most unexpected. The unexpected thing happened on the 2nd June 1956. On this day Jayprakash expressed, through a letter, his desire to see Lohia. That moment marked the beginning of the ideological ruin of the party. Even in the Socialist Party itself there were some weak-kneed and power-hungry people. But they had been forced to remain quiet due to the pressure of the circumstances. However, after the Jaiprakash-Lohia meeting, their malady of dissension developed further.

At their meeting at Lucknow on 15th July, Jayprakash and Lohia unanimously agreed that it would be better to have a single party of democratic socialism. At this meeting Lohia clearly warned that "The basis of unity would be the constitution, policy and programme of the Socialist Party. Only the convention of representatives will make changes if they consider them necessary. The laws and bye-laws of the constitution will be considered as part of the constitution itself. There will be no condition of vacuum till the convention is held. The Socialist Party Committee will be formed for carrying out enrolment of membership and elections". Jayprakash wanted the new party to function under the name of 'The Socialist Party'. Lohia accepted the flag and election symbol of the P.S.P. for the new party. However, it was also made clear that the convention of representatives would make whatever changes they might deem necessary. Both the leaders disapproved of a system of merger which is based on bargaining. Jayprakash sent a report of his meeting with Lohia to Ganga Saran Sinha of the P.S.P. He also endorsed a copy thereof to Lohia and added that he feel relieved of a long-standing burden on his mind. Lohia sent a reply to Jaiprakash, reiterating some of the points discussed in their meeting. At the end of the letter he wrote, "We had also started talks about your own self. It is essential that they are carried to a conclusion". Jayprakash admitted that his interpretation of the talks at Lucknow meeting had been different from that of Lohia and wrote to Lohia on 12 August saying, "I regret that I could not understand properly what you said at Lucknow". On 12th August they again met at Calcutta. In the meantime there had been a number of developments. Those in the P.S.P. who stood for a united front did not want a merger. Some members did not favour strong opposition to Congress. Some were afraid that the merger would entail a curb on their licentious activities and opportunism. Thus Jayprakash received no support from the P.S.P. This is reflected in his letter of 12th August. The working committee of the P.S.P. deputed Triloki Singh to apprise Jayprakash of its views. But Triloki Singh did not mention anything about it to Jaiprakash. So Jayprakash thought, "I have no right to talk on behalf of the P.S.P.

But I feel P.S.P. will not generally disapprove of what I find reasonable. I do not desire to be drawn into the politics of power or party". This was the background the Calcutta meeting of 12th August. In this meeting, Lohia said to Jaiprakash, "Considerable dissension seems to have arisen. You also appear to be disinclined to enter politics. So it is better these talks are ended now". But Jayprakash did not desire that the talks should be ended, so they again met for the third time on 13th August. Jayprakash urged Lohia to find out some way of achieving unity. Lohia advised Jayprakash thus; "Ask the P.S.P. to study the constitution, policy and programme of the Socialist Party and thereafter convey to the Socialist Party, in writing, the modifications that it would like to make in the Socialist Party proposal". To this Jayprakash replied, "I have not read the policy etc. of the Socialist Party, however, it must be good since it has been drafted by you". Thus the third meeting between Jayprakash and Lohia ended on a hopeful note.

On 22nd August, Ashok Mehta told news reporters at Madras, that the its between the P.S.P. and SP had failed. This was strange. The news about the failure of negotiations between Jayprakash and Lohia was announced by a third man instead of the persons directly involved in the negotiations. Lohia was altogether unaware of this. After his meeting with Jayprakash on 13th August his feeling was that unity was an accomplished fact. In fact, work initiated by Jayprakash should have been completed by him alone. When a man faces pulls in several directions, he is completely at a loss to know even his own mind, leave aside his knowing the minds of others. Even then there is some substance in the letters, of Jaiprakash. In one of his letters to Lohia, Jayprakash wrote, "I expressed a desire to meet you and accordingly met you at Lucknow. I feel this was interpreted wrongly. Personally I shall not feel sorry about bowing before you or anyone else if some good is likely to emerge out of it". In another letter he writes, "The question of negotiations about unity is now over. I have no desire to do anything more about it".

Lohia wrote to Jayprakash, "You should have initiated this task more carefully. Let me give you a piece of advice regarding the letter in which you had written about your willingness to bow down to anyone if that should help in the emergence of something good; you should not form your opinion on the basis of whispers and gossips. Really speaking opinion should be formed, not on incidental happenings but on the steady direction and movement".

Such was the tragic end of the efforts for socialist unity. Who was responsible for this failure? The socialist movement was never a disciplined system. Some persons used to carry out certain responsibilities but there was no definite common outlook behind it, nor any specific direction. Summit diplomacy had become an essential part of the policy. Ordinary members desiring unity never took active interest in the efforts for such unity. They always remained silent spectators, Consequently for several years the leaders acted as they liked and the entire party suffered the consequences. However in the present case at least Lohia's party stood behind him. The party never disregarded him. But the P.S.P. betrayed Jaiprakash, and Jayprakash too absolved himself merely by stating, "I understood the Lucknow talks differently!" He himself stopped the game he had initiated. But it had lasting effects both the parties and the entire socialist movement. In fact in his report on the Lucknow meeting forwarded to Gangasaran Sinha, Jayprakash clearly wrote, "It is Lohia's desire that the basis of the new party should be the constitution, policy and programme of the Socialist Party. I asked him whether these are unchangeable. Thereupon he said, "No, and yet I would not like any fundamental change". Thus you will see that Socialist unity depends on the constitution, policy and programme of the Socialist Party and that is as it should be".

Lohia's desire was not limited to the merger of the P.S.P. and S.P. parties only. He desired that many parties should come together, exchange their views, discuss and form a single powerful party of democratic socialism. Jayprakash had expressed in his letter that he agreed with this idea of Lohia. Under these circumstances the plea of Jayprakash that he understood a 'different meaning' is a lame excuse. In fact it was clear that the person responsible for the failure of these talks was Ashok Mehta. On one hand these people were clamoring that the Communists are getting stronger, and on the other, they were forming a united front and getting communists elected in Bengal and at Kanpur. Gwalior, Bhopal, Indore, Bombay and Coimbatore. Jayprakash had said that after the merger, the Maharashtra unit of P.S.P. being a constituent of the United Front would severe its connections with the Socialist Party and the Bengal Unit would leave the United Front. Of course, this was not the reason for the breakdown of negotiations. As soon as the negotiations were over, an attack was once again launched against Lohia. Ashok Mehta said, "The talks failed because Lohia tried to strike a better bargain". Moreover, he charged Lohia without giving any justification, of being a dictator and indulging in character- assassination. To these charges Lohia's reaction was; "Most of the leaders of P.S.P. are individualistic, stunted in outlook unprincipled and pygmies. They are charging me with character assassination but I have never indulged in this. Very often I wonder if these people have any political character at all worth the name, which could be assassinated and in any case. I am not interested in their personal character. As soon as unity talks failed, wordy attacks were levelled against me. Abusive language was resorted to. I am not worried about the abuses, since I have always been a target of abuse am not pained at being called a dictator since I have been a victim of dictatorship. Some people say that I should not have acted so hastily when disciplinary action was taken against Madhu Limaye. They say I should have waited for the decision of the National Convention. But I am convinced that had I shown looseness in respect of Madhu Limaye's case, those persons, who have been fighting today, while remaining in the Socialist Party, would have been suppressed. As a result, democracy and socialism in the socialist movement could not have been saved".

Some members of the P.S.P. expressed that 'their party had no differences with the Socialist Party regarding ideology or policy. Yet the unity between P.S.P. and SP could not be achieved because of one man, Lohia, whose behaviour had been uncontrolled and undemocratic'. In fact Lohia had stated much earlier; "I say openly that, should necessity arise, we may have to form another party. A party is an instrument for achieving an objective. To join a party or leave it, is not a thing of great concern. The basic thing is the ideology. Even then, I am prepared to satisfy those who hold that 'I am a thorn in the path of unity.' I am prepared to leave the Socialist Party and alongwith it politics also. I say this in all seriousness since there are many other things besides politics which greatly interest me. I place before P.S.P. a proposal that if they are prepared to accept the constitution, policy and programme of the Socialist Party. I shall give up the socialist movement. If this challenge is not acceptable to them, it will mean that they are dishonest. It will mean that their talk holds no water and their only intention is to condemn others".

Evidently nobody answered Lohia's challenge, since the P.S.P. was not at all prepared to get itself bound to any constitution, policy and programme. How could those who were accustomed to unfettered freedom of action—action even against the resolutions of their own party—accept any restrictions of behaviour or rules and regulations. The question that arises is; Was not Lohia aware of all these things? If he was, the why did he entangle himself in the maze of socialist unity? The reasons are found in his own words; "Even in the P.S.P., nearly half the people are militant, by habit and nature. They have become crippled due to defective leadership, and hesitancy. Similarly even in the Socialist Party there are cripples by habit and nature". Lohia desired to bring together the militant persons and control the cripples in both the parties. But this was not a problem of just addition and subtraction. The ways of all the socialists, whether militant or non-militant, were not simple and straight-forward. There were may who were mentally linked to certain course, but physically to another. They could not severe old relationships, or bonds of friendship. Moreover, they were bound by the fetters of selfishness. There was every possibility that the coming together of the filth in the two parties might have resulted in the dominance of these very people.

24. SATYAGRAHA CAMPAIGN

On the 2nd November 1957, Lohia was standing in the verandah of the Sales Tax office, Lucknow. When a postman arrived to deliver mail, Lohia told him, "Please do not enter this office. Sales Tax is the cause of soaring prices of food items". Immediately Lohia was arrested for threatening, violence and obstruction, none of which was involved in his action. He was taken to the district jail with a fortnight's remand.

Lohia's offering of satyagraha was a part of an all India campaign for redressal of various grievances of the people and certain other demands. One of these was the removal of statues of the earlier British rulers in public places. The U.P. government conceded this demand and declared that the statues would be removed before the 15th August 1957. Earlier, Raj Narain and other socialists were arrested in an attempt to offer satyagraha for this demand. Logically, following this decision, those who had sought arrest for this demand should have been released from jail. Lohia said: "If Raj Narain who demanded removal of statues gets 18 months of jail, surely Sampurnanand who ordered it should get sentence for 29 months". Over five thousand Satyagrahis had been jailed in this movement, since May 10. Kamesh Prasad Rai had died due to police torture, Ramsingh died for want of medical aid. Satyagrahis had been given two to two and a half years' imprisonments. In Lohia's opinion peaceful demonstrators should never have had to undergo jail terms longer than 6 months. Hence his counsel was that appeals against the injustice perpetrated by governments and courts were in order if made after six months. Earlier announcing his decision to court arrest, Lohia said in a public meeting". Of late, courts, particularly at lower levels, have become unreasonable and shameless. True, socialists should not have appealed. But judges of higher courts have themselves remarked that sentence of lower courts were extreme and severe.

The 16th of November was observed by party branches as Lohia day. His arrest was condemned and the state government's repression was placed before the people as also the significance of the path of satyagraha. Lohia had been remanded after arrest without being presented before a magistrate. He was given copies of warrant as well as remand order on the 16th. Lohia wrote to high court, seeking redress. He said, "Seventh clause is neither constitutional nor in force in U.P. Further it becomes operative only after a declaration under clause four, and it is not applicable to government offices. A remand has to be just and granted in the presence of the accused. A remand granted in his absence is illegal. Remand has come into being for the convenience of the accused as well as prosecution".

It was clear that remand was granted in Lohia's absence. Refusing to appear in court on 18th Lohia remarked: "Judicial and jail authorities run a remand factory in collusion. Undated blank forms are kept in readiness and any dates are written according to convenience". Thousands had been put behind bars under clause seven of the criminal amendment law. While this unconstitutional law was being used for months and thousands were being arrested under it, Parliament and other self styled civil rights organisations had not lifted a finger. To Lohia all these institutions seemed stagnant, lifeless and meaningless.

On November 30, the magistrate visited the jail to take up Lohia's case. Neither Lohia nor his attorney had been advised of this, so Lohia would not come into the jail verandah to participate in the court proceedings. In the afternoon the all superintendent accompanied by warders and prisoners approached Lohia and informed him that orders had been received to present him before court forcibly. Lohia replied that the court may please be reminded of his petition filed in the high court. If, inspite of this, they wish to force things, it will be another matter. The Superintendent withdrew but returned with 30-35 prisoners and 18-20 warders. They mounted a cane charge on the Satyagrahis around Lohia. More Satyagrahis gathered on hearing the noise around Lohia. The attackers also called for reinforcements. Satyagrahis were thrashed severely. Some even got hurt on their genitals. After all the Satyagrahis were pushed into their cells, Lohia was tied in chains and carried to the magistrate. When Lohia would not even speak his thumb impression was secured on a piece of paper, by force. As the news of all these events reached outside, Raj Narain approached justice Randheer Singh of Lucknow bench of high court and filed a petition on his advice, with Justice Beg, for permission to act as an *amicus curiae*. He ordered the civil surgeon of Lucknow and his assistants to examine the Satyagrahis and submit a report.

Lohia's *habeas corpus* case to the high court for hearing on the 3rd, 5th and 6th December. Judicial magistrate Jayaswal explained to Justice Beg and Mulla that because Lohia twice refused to attend the court, the third time around he had to be bought to the court and his thumb impression secured by force. Justice Mulla queried as to the need to secure the thumb impression. The government prosecutor replied that this was because Lohia would not answer any questions. Justice Mulla exclaimed, "How ridiculous! And the magistrate was a silent witness to this episode? Taking a thumb impression by force is sheer stupidity and utter impropriety!" On 5th December Lohia himself participated in the proceedings with the court's permission. He narrated the whole story beginning with the illegal remand. The city magistrate replied that he could not recall whether the reasons of arrest had been explained to Lohia. The argument made on behalf of Lohia was that Article 22 (2) of the constitution and Articles 344 and 367 of the I.P.C. had been violated. The remand was illegal and hence the accused should be released forthwith, Justice Mulla asked if a second order for Lohia's detention had been issued after the expiry of remand on November 16th. The government prosecutor replied that magistrate's calling the case for hearing is deemed as a remand order. When Justice Mulla asserted that an explicit order was essential, the prosecutor only replied that the tradition of the U.P. jails was being followed. Justice Beg commented that detention of an individual was a serious matter and the tradition seemed a dangerous one. When the prosecutor continued to defend his point Justice Beg thundered: "What preposterous tradition! How does the court tolerate this? Mr. Prosecutor you better destroy the constitution itself so that every thing will become legal. Are you a law unto yourselves? If these things continue the courts will become superfluous. Your entire affair seems fabricated". After examining the warrant register of the jail Justice Beg said, "This is indeed a long series of misdeeds. Every law has been transgressed here". Similar was the reaction of Justice' Mulla. Justice Beg told the argumentative prosecutor that his justification amounted to yet another link in the same chain. "This is a vicious circle of glossing over errors". Lohia argued in the court that in his case Articles 22(2), 22(1), 19(1), 19(A) and 21 of the Constitution had been violated. Describing his entire experience Lohia remarked: "I am not given to habitual law-breaking. But the government arrests men in an erroneous manner. My only hope is the high courts of the country, not as a leader, but as a common man it is my request to the court that the encroachment upon civil rights may not be allowed. 1 hardly enjoy jail terms. I have suffered enough in the British Raj. Now even a minute's detention becomes unbearable. But I am helpless. Having been brought up in the Gandhian tradition I cannot but resist injustice and exploitation". Justice Mulla interrupted Lohia and told him that he was only indulging in demagogy. 12th December was the day of the verdict. Justice Beg opined: "Lohia's arrest is illegal. Even if all the irregularities in the matter are overlooked any further detention of Lohia would be against law. There is no provision by which he could be kept in jail". Justice Mulla however found Lohia's arrest a normal matter. Due to the difference of opinion the case was delegated to the third judge.

On 13th and 16th December, the case was heard by Justice Raghuvir Dayal. Lohia was present to make a statement, inspite of his illness. Article 341(i) of the constitution provides that the language of the Indian government is Hindi and Article 351 specifies that spread of Hindi is a duty of all governments. Lohia calling attention to these articles began to address the court in Hindi. But Justice Dayal taking advantage of Article 343(2) which makes English the language of transactions in high courts for 15 years, forced Lohia to switch to English. Lohia repeated the whole story. But on 17th Lohia's habeas corpus petition was rejected. A writ petition was filed in Supreme Court on 21st December challenging this decision. The government chose to retreat on the eve of the Supreme Court hearing, by releasing Lohia.

The Socialist Party was somewhat jubiliant. Jail authorities had forced Lohia's thumb down, but it was Lohia who had the last laugh. Ram Sevak Yadav in the Pairliament and Raj Narain in the U.P. legislative assembly strongly protested the government's actions against Lohia. In the aftermath Raj Narain's membership was suspended for three days. During the episode Lohia's health deteriorated. Dental and ear complaints arose, and his blood pressure went up substantially.

About the same time a minor storm developed within the party. Symptoms of a disease endemic with the socialist movement began to appear in the new Socialist Party as well. A dissident faction had crystalised since Lohia took a stern approach to the question of indiscipline. Lohia was insistent that the party central office must not use English in its working. This was not being followed by the office bearers nor was the rule, that all office bearers and committee members must join satyagraha, being taken heed of. The rule that, if once defeated in an election to the Vidhan Sabha or Lok Sabha, party members must not seek to join legislative council or upper house of the parliament through indirect elections, had also been ignored. A widespread feeling was that rules need not to be taken too seriously. Lohia's attack on this attitude provoked resistance from the vested interests. The impending explosion took place during the second national convention of the party at Sherghati in Bihar between 26th and 28th April 1958. On behalf of the disgruntled souls Surendra Saxena tabled the motion of censure against Lohia. That saw the end of the self-restraint of delegates. Karunesh who was about to address the gathering in support of the resolution was hooted out. Lohia criticised this. In his opinion, delegates should rather have indicated their preference through voting.

Lohia toured many provinces including Orissa, Kerala, M.P., Rajasthan, U.P. and Bihar. Many states were under the spell of a drought. Lohia sounded a warning; "Those who preach that the food problem should be kept above politics are either naive or unscrupulous. The first task and content of politics is feeding the people. Governments must open free kitchens. Today 150 million people in the country can afford only one meal a day and 45 million can eat only once in two days, they must be fed. The outlay necessary to run free kitchens for 3 months is about 1 billion rupees. Every year the combined expenditure of central and state governments is 27 billion rupees of which almost half is over a show of extravagance. In such a set up my proposal of allocating Rupees one billion to free food for the people, seems trivial. When traders, bureaucrats and the ruling elite join hands, corruption is the inevitable outcome". Lohia made house to house calls to get an overview of the drought stricken people's plight.

Meanwhile an incidence took place on the floor of the U.P. legislative assembly which shocked the traditionally held notions of parliamentary protocol and propriety. Raj Narain tried to table an adjournment motion to highlight the condition of drought and the arrest of over a thousand Satyagrahis. The chief minister, Sampurnanand, countered by proposing that Raj Narain should be disallowed on the floor for the fortnight. Raj Narain's response was a similar proposal for Sampurnanand with double the period. With the brutal majority of the government, Raj Narain's motion was defeated and Sampurnanand's motion passed. When Raj Narain refused to leave the house he was dragged out. A few other opposition M.L.A's suffered the same fate for no particular reason. Referring to this incident Lohia commended Raj Narain as the first dynamic legislator. Describing basic principles of parliamentary behaviour and conventional etiquette, Lohia raised the question, "After all what is parliament? A place for representatives and the speaker to sit together. Rules are for everyone. All must abide by them. Indeed, parliament is only a reflection of society. Here the authority of the speaker is discretionary. He has to be above board. The notion that 'A Speaker never errs' is unfounded. Our parliamentary conventions and rules have been adopted by mimicking foreigners". Lohia argued that the total length of all sessions of the assembly was only around four to five months. If the venues for airing the grievances of the masses remained closed for months on end, the wheels of democracy could hardly move effectively. He argued that Raj Narain had made an important contribution towards ameliorating the parliamentary modus operandi.

Lohia was in Calcutta in October 1959. He sensed the growing Chinese threat. He sharply criticised the government policies towards tribal and hilly area communities on the frontier. After his visit to Imphal on October 27, Lohia revealed that the Nagas had demanded a separate state within the Indian Union, in the third Naga convention, but the demand was totally ignored by the Government. There was harassment of the people of the Manipur. Repression and violence was the order of the day. In point of fact, 150 Naga rebels had led down annas in response to a call by the Socialist Party. Lohia warned: "The machinations to neutralise the socialists had invariably helped Fizo and his seditious band". The government had exacerbated the Manipur problem. The secretariat was flooded by outsiders. The people felt that being a part of Burma would be preferable to their present state. Indeed it was very essential to placate the communities in the frontiers and secure the border. But the government mismanagement was boundless. Critical areas remained vulnerable while citizens were subjected to block-headed regulations which are quite unnecessary, such was the border policy. A particular action of Lohia brought these topsy turvy attitudes of the government into sharp focus.

The story was this: During the preceding year, i.e. 1958, Lohia had toured Assam in November. He arrived at Jayarampur to enter NEFA after visits to Gauhatti, Nangoan, Golpatra, Vorhat, Dibrugadh etc. The guards would not allow him to enter NEFA without a permit. Permission had already sought from Governor of Assam, telegraphically. The Governor had asked Lohia to call on him. To Lohia, it was sheer madness to impose restrictions on an Indian citizen's right to travel freely in his own country. It was unconstitutional, too. But at that time Lohia agreed to abide by the regulation. However he announced that after a year he would certainly visit NEFA again.

And now, in 1959, Lohia he was at the gates to fulfil his promise. "I own neither a palace nor a garden. That is why I enjoy viewing the picturesque beauty of my motherland in all its facets", he said. He surmised that the former adviser to the government on tribal affairs, Father Verrier Elvin, was perhaps behind the ridiculous system of entry permits. This gentleman had propounded the thesis of reserved forests for tribals. This was tantamount to keeping them untouched by the outside world, like lions in the wild. He cited an example of this in which a visiting lady teacher was not allowed to many a tribal damsel. But she was so bent upon it, that after three unsuccessful attempts the wedding did take place the fourth time around. Till only recently pictures of Lord Shiva, Goddess Durga, Gandhiji, or even Nehru could not be displayed in shops in NEFA. Maybe, the Padri was afraid that this would corrupt the people.

In point of fact Lohia was going to NEFA neither to buy land nor to exploit the tribals. He could not possibly be suspected of trying to liaise with Chinese, Burmese or Russians. No meaningful case could be made for detaining him for his own protection. Assam was flooded with Chinese agents and the governments had done precious little about it. In 1953-54 China had distributed photographs of Mao, 80 miles inside from the border. On November 12th, 1959, Lohia made the following statement: "I have no intention to break the rules or undertake satyagraha. Inspite of the years intimation the government had failed to issue necessary permit. Such exclusivity would only make the tribals an easy prey to alien influences".

Finally, on November 23rd, Lohia entered NEFA. He was arrested and released in Dibrugadh. On 27th November, Lohia attempted reentry at Namsingh, about 38 miles from Tinsukia. His night halt was at Deomali. The armed guards here informed him that he could not enter the area without official permission. The Divisional Superintendent and two judges had also arrived. Lohia was arrested near the Superintendent's office under Clause 3 of Bengal and Eastern Frontier Regulation, 1873, presented before a magistrate and brought to Dibrugadh.

Lohia's arrest was unconstitutional. The gravity of this event and the profound thinking behind the satyagraha were not appreciated even by his socialist colleagues let alone the man in the street. His actions were described as wanton provocation or even lunacy. However, his thinking was vindicated by the Chinese aggression in 1962.

25. DUTY IN DESPAIR

The Socialist Party had enhanced its popularity and its members had won praise for their toughness of character and devotion to principles. Still the party had not yet gained sufficient strength. Naturally Lohia was toying with novel ideas in his mind to infuse new life in the party. In December 1958, in one of his speeches at Bombay he presented an unusual idea, saying, "If we cannot keep vigil over all the levels of the party, let us try a new experiment by disbanding the party units, at all-India, state and district levels, and maintaining only those at lower levels. It may be argued on this, that lower committees might behave in a libertine manner. Even then, I think they should be allowed that freedom. Results thereof would be visible after 1½ to 2 years and the tower committees would automatically become aware of the situation.

He noted; "At present the power of the people is not built up from taluka to district, thence to state and thereafter to all India level. It is built just the other way round. The top leader trains the man next to him, who in turn follows suit and this goes on right down to the bottom. This is a great drawback among the political parties in India. Power of the people must surge up from below. That is the only way to make an organisation powerful. We must cast off our age-old practice and think a fresh along the new line for building up an organisation from below". During this period Lohia laid special stress on the policies relating to caste system, language and prices of essential commodities. He considered these as three aspects of one and the same thing. He looked upon this trinity as a tool of feudal exploitation. It was his conviction that a new society cold be built up only by persistently attacking this trinity. With this aim in mind he gave a call for "the formation of committees like "English Removal Committee", "Caste Abolition Committee" and "Price Fixation Committee". He had also suggested that elections be fought on behalf of these committees.

Many people considered this suggestion as a hint for the formation of united front in disguise. While refuting this charge, Lohia said: "This criticism is wrong. A united front is formed by bringing various parties together. In the committees proposed by me there is no place for oraganised political parties. Instead they will consist of individuals supporting specific policies like 'English Removal', 'Caste Abolition' and 'Price Fixation'. Regarding the discussion about an impending split in the party, Lohia expressed; "I don't attach much importance to this discussion. In a revolutionary party like the Socialist Party split is never ending, just like satyagraha. This is an age of selfishness, in which priority is given to individual progress. In fact, more importance should be given to mental discipline and self restraint. We must not be afraid of the failure. We are forming a ladder for a future generation. If we go on building it, those who will come after us can complete it. We must do our duty even in despair. We must be prepared to accept an occasional failure. Ours is a revolutionary and militant programme. Those entrusted with the task of its execution are, however, middle-aged. But even the young are no better than elders in outlook".

Lord Krishna gave the message of deed without desire in the Geeta. Various people have explained this principle in as many ways. Lohia gave a very novel slogan; "Duty in despair". Work without desire is difficult, but deed with desire is contaminated with greed and selfishness, so Duty in despair was the real thing. Explaining his approach Lohia said: "We must be ever ready for temporary setbacks. Our party has a revolutionary programme but the people supposed to pursue it are half-hearted. Young workers are no different. Generally one expects youth to be more idealistic and less pragmatic. We must think about strength and not positions". 'Duty in despair' became the entire philosophy of Lohia. He considered three levels of despair; national, international, and that of mankind as whole. His explanation of national despair was: For the last millennium and a half, the Indian people have never revolted against the internal repression. This defeatism is given the name of conciliation. This has made us satisfied and incapable of taking any risks. Consequently revolution had become unlikely. In India, a genuine firebrand of a man is hard to find". Inequities inherent in a caste ridden society make revolution unlikely. "There is time of despair in the life of every nation. There is time for enjoyment and then there is time for duty and responsibility. In some ways the pre-independence era was the time of the sacrifice, hardship and responsibility and revolution. Following freedom came the era of hedonism. The king changed, but the entourage, that is, the bureaucracy, remained the same.

Lohia said that international despair was of two types. One due to weapons and war and second due to machine. The white man owns the world, and he is distinguished by his technology which is revolutionary. It is continually increasing its productivity. White man's world is a world of plenty. Similarly weapons are becoming irrelevant. Whether we make new weapons or not, the U.S. and the U.S.S.R. can, and will, if they so desire, destroy each other and the world. Either mankind will eliminate weapons or weapons will wipe out the human race. International inequities are a great injustice. Siberia, Australia or Canada have a density of population of 1 per square mile, in California figure is 7 or 8, but in India it is 350 per square mile and in Kerala and Eastern U.P. it is over 1000. International inequities in productivity go hand in hand with colonialism U.S. and U.S.S.R. have a per capita income from 8 to 14 thousand rupees while in India it is four hundred rupees. Thirdly there is a intellectual imperialism. Fourth is that of weapons and fifth of currencies.

In white countries the disparity between the rich and the poor is 5 to 7 fold, while in India it is 300 to 500 fold. Every white country improves its per capita income annually by a couple of hundred rupees. India can only raise the per capita income by 8 rupees. What takes an Indian an hour to do, is done by a Chinese in 40 minutes, a Russian in 7 or 8 minutes and an American in 3 minutes only. In the U.S. and U.S.S.R. daily consumption of milk or orange juice is half litre per capita while in India, it is a bare teaspoonful. In the global population, whites are 70 crore while coloured people are 250 crores. Regarding despair on a global level, Lohia said; "as organisations become stronger, idealism is on the wane. The must be a balance between the fight against injustice and power gained through satyagraha, and injustice. On ascending the throne, a philosophy of defeat may change into philosophy of victory. Social change and power are related.

Thus Lohia's ideas of duty in despair did not mean inaction. He clarified his position quite early. "Some people see in my discussion the despair of a tired and defeated man. It is true that in general people of my type would be judged as defeated, but you might want to consider the possibility that I am, what I am, by choice. Despair in such a case is not the consequence, but the cause of defeat. The person refuses to be tempted by the mirage of hope but rather prefers to do his duty in despair. This philosophy of defeat may one day prove to be philosophy of victory". To remain defeated by choice is a hard assignment. Conciliation, and comprise with evil are great temptations. It is a vicious circle. Lohia knew this and wanted to break the vicious circle by abandoning the path of Mansingh and following the footsteps of Pratap.

Lohia's success in the canal-water agitation in 1954 was an eye sore for the government. The Uttar Pradesh government appealed to the Supreme Court against the decision of the Allahabad High Court. The appeal was to be heard on 10th August 1959. Lohia attended the court accordingly. However he was informed that the appeal had been postponed to some date between 21st and 25th September, and that the exact date would be communicated to him in the due course. However the appeal was taken up by the court on 25th September without any pre-intimation to him. He himself pleaded the case. The moment he started speaking in Hindi, Justice Kapoor brought to his notice that the language of the Supreme Court was English. Thereupon Lohia said: "In that case, I shall have to discuss the entire constitution itself. Although Indian constitution has given me that right, I am not forcing you to speak in Hindi. Similarly your Lordship also should not force me to speak in English". Justice Sinha, who had become Chief Justice lately, permitted Lohia to state his case in Hindi.

In the course of his speech, Lohia complained to the court as to how he had lost his time in going to the court four times, since he had been intimated in advance about the date fixed for hearing. Justice Sinha said, "You will have to come to the court even 20 times when called". To this Lohia retorted, "In that case, you can decide the case ex-parte. Henceforth it will not possible for me to attend the court unless I am informed about the date of hearing two months in advance". On 5th October Lohia received at Hyderabad a letter from the Supreme Court dated 25 September, saying: "The Supreme Court's language is English. Please do not waste the time of the court by writing letters in a language other than English". The greater the vigour with which Lohia conducted his English Removal movement, the greater was the tenacity with which certain people, who wielded power due to English clung to the last bastion.

A 3 day session of the fifth national convention of the Socialist Party was held at Chennimalai in Tamil Nadu from the 29th to 31st December 1959. A few days before the convention, Lohia in a party workers meeting at Bombay, had put forth a revolutionary & basic idea about the administrative and executive set up of the Party. Since then the idea was also discussed a little among the party members. Many were annoyed & restless. But Lohia's idea about holding in abeyance the organisational work of the party at Central state and district level, did not figure before the convention at all. On the very first day, while addressing the delegates. Lohia said: "I do note desire to impose on you any decision against your will. However I shall certainly participate in the discussion". But the convention decided by a majority not to discuss Lohia's ideas. It was essential for the party that the reins of power passed from the upper classes to the lower classes. One way of doing this was suggested by Lohia, that could have developed initiative, decisiveness and decision making efficiency of the village units. To a certain extent this would have been useful in loosening the strong hold of the parliamentary group over the party organisation. All those who opposed this view were not necessarily opposed to the development of the lower classes. Some members opposed mainly due to their long attachment total organisation, built by them. Whatever it may be, Lohia expressed regret that the convention did not even discuss his ideas.

The convention passed the resolution about launching a countrywide movement for securing the demands of the party. Accordingly Satyagraha movement started in various states under the leadership of the Socialists Party. Lohia again toured the whole country. On 17th April 1960, he announced at Allahabad that about one lakh volunteers would be participating in Satyagraha. Lohia addressed several mammoth meetings and adivasis and poor people attended them everywhere in large numbers. The satyagraha campaign was launched at Manipur. Teargas, lathi-charge and firing were resorted to by the police. It appeared that the government was determined to suppress the countrywide struggle with unlimited violence. The satyagrahis were beaten up severely. Some of them even died in jail. A woman satyagrahi died in Thandla. According to the estimate of Lohia, out of the approximately one lakh people who participated in Satyagraha, forty thousand were arrested, of which 500 were imprisoned. A strange incident took place in this campaign. Once Lohia wanted to halt at the circuit house in Kanpur. The watchman refused him accommodation. Lohia forcibly entered the circuit house and halted there. Lohia's stand in this satyagraha was that places like circuit houses and dak bungalows were after all government rest houses. So even ordinary people must be as much entitled to stay there as ministers and government officials. Later he was prosecuted for his unauthorised entry into the circuit house and was fined Rs. 100. Lohia refused to pay the fine.

When Lohia was addressing a public meeting at Coimbatore in connection with satyagraha, stones were thrown at him for having spoken in Hindi. Supporters of the DMK were also among the stone-throwers. Referring to them Lohia said that DMK supporters had participated in such dirty things. Of course the real fault lies with the Central Government. The entire public life of the country has become corrupt since the government has never adopted a clear and definite policy about the language problem. "As at Coimbatore, stones were also thrown at Lohia's public meeting in Bangalore, because he spoke in Hindi.

Along with 'English Removal' Caste Abolition and 'Price Fixation' movements. All India conventions for the same had also been held. By organising such programmes, Lohia tried to make the Socialist Party more broad based and more popular. Another effort in this direction was Lohia's idea of organising a grand 'Ramayan Mela' rally. This idea was also an attempt by him to set right the relationship between politics & religion. While analysing his idea about holding such 'Mela' at Chitrakut in February 1961, Lohia said: "The relation between religion and politics has been vitiated. Religion is long term politics, and politics is short term religion. While religion fights for achieving the external good for the people, politics fights against the various evils imposed on them. Today whereas religion has become lifeless in its fight against unholiness, politics has become full of conflicts and meaningless. The aim is organising 'Ramayan Mela' is to give the Indian people vision for discriminating between the 'gold, diamonds and pearls' in the Ramayan and the worthless rubbish in it".

Lohia had planned to organise the 'mela' on a grand scale. He thought this could show a way to wipe out the racial differences like Aryans, Dravidians, Mongolians etc. created among the Indian people by foreigners. Lohia looked upon it as an experiment for resolving the North-South conflict and achieving unity of the country as well. According to him, while Krishna was a God symbolising East-West unity, Ram represented North-South unity. He expected a 'stream of peace and joy' to flow through this 'mela'. Ramayan loving people from ancient islands Indonesia, Cambodia, etc. were to attend this 'Mela'. Lohia had a planned to stage a variety programme comprising dramas, music etc. in Tamil, Marathi and other Indian languages, all based on Ramayan. But all these turned out to be castles in the air. Mela committees requested the railway authorities to grant concession to the participants in the 'Mela'. But the ministry of railways turned down the request on the ground that such concessions could be given only to the participants in cultural conventions not to those participating in religious and sectarian programmes. It became clear that the government was coming in the way of organisation this function. Everywhere Lohia could see an atmosphere of lack of cooperation, so ultimately he had to drop the idea of organising the 'Mela'.

At about the same time, the second 'English Removal' convention was held in January 1961 at Ujjain. Queen Elizabeth of England was also to visit India just then. Lohia gave a warning in clear terms saying: "I do not wish to insult a foreign visitor and certainly not a lady visitor. But at the same time the foreign government and its offices must not interfere in our internal affairs. It is not proper that advantage is being taken of Queen Elizabeth's visit to propagate the continuance of English". India's High Commissioner in England, Smt.Vijayalaxmi Pandit, called the 'English Removal' movement, a 'movement of lunatics'. While inaugurating British Library at Pune, the, British Deputy High Commissioner expressed that English was essential for the development of India. The Ujjain convention condemned these developments. In his speech at the convention Lohia said: "so long as wealth and respectability are linked with English, it is difficult to make the people stand against English. Awakening the people is the only way of achieving this".

As the confrontationist approach of the Socialist Party developed, the treatment given by the government changed too. A socialist worker Chandrashekhar Tewari was murdered at Kanpur. Avadh Sharan, Siyaram, Ramsingh, Damu Ramu, Keshav, Sukharam, Birjubai joined the ranks of the martyrs. Margo Skinner, a member of the editorial board of *Mankind* was knocked out by two female police and two A.C.P.'s in Hyderabad in 1961. She considered herself a world citizen, and the government in a vengeful mood deported her. Lohia and his party now faced a full governmental attack.

At the end of November 1961, Lohia undertook 15 days tour abroad. He visited Turkey's ancient city Byzantium, the Greek capital Athens, the Italian capital Rome, and the Egyptian capital 'Cairo'. Athens was hosting a peace conference of world politicians, to which Lohia was an invitee. While he was leaving for it, someone said: "So you are going to the country of Alexander". Lohia replied; "No I am going to the country of Socrates". But even in Greece, Lohia observed that Alexander was in general more admired than Socrates. Lohia remarked; "One was a great philosopher and the other great general. But the verdict of history appears to be in favour of the general. In Greece there are cities like Sikandara and Alexandra named after Alexander, but there is no place named after Socrates!" Lohia was more or less disappointed with the atmosphere at the peace conference which was attended by the world celebrities including Justice Douglas, Ex-Chancellor Robert Hechinza of Chicago University of Cambridge, Prof. Jack Ilulu of Bordeaux, novelist Ruth, diplomat Scott Buchanan, Prof. E.H. Carr, and veteran humanist Jean Thiobald. Lohia held the view that weapons arise out of injustice. This view was accepted by the conference, in general.

While addressing the conference, Lohia for the first time propounded his famous theory of 'Seven Revolutions' on a world platform. Lohia said, in clear words "In order to free the world from armaments, and make it based on justice, it is necessary to bring about following seven resolutions; (1) Equality between man and woman, (2) End of political enslavement and imperialism, (3) National and international economic equality, (4) Abolition of the caste distinctions by providing the downtrodden with special facilities for development. (5) Protection of individual's life from undue intervention from the state, (6) Following the path of satyagraha while striving for disarmament, (7) Recognition for racial equality irrespective of the skin colour and acceptance of the corresponding standards of beauty. The disparity between the city and the village is much less in Europe and America than in Afro-Asian countries. Inequality grows in poverty and slums. In Europe, one could come across bewildering brightness of affluence. There are restaurants and shops with dazzling lights. Ultramodernism of woman is beyond words. Speed of progress is enormous. The magnificence of Europe and America is based on the wonderful skill of modern technology. Black nations are imitating the glitter of the white nations. But they possess neither knowledge nor skill of modern technology. The Socialists Parties of Europe have become traditional. The only exception to this is the Italian party".

After the convention Lohia met the general secretary of the Italian Socialists party, Pietro Neni. They had a mutual exchange of views. Thereafter a joint communique was issued for publication, sponsoring new internationalism and supporting the seven revolutions. Lohia could not return as scheduled and could not attend programmes in Bihar. Partly the reason was the aeroplane. Air travel in backward countries often gets bogged down in technical problems. Lohia was very upset. He felt that we should take up air travel only after we begin to manufacture our own plane.

Meanwhile, back in India, the Third general elections were round the corner. The Socialist Party joined the fray with it's programmes such as equality, caste, language, prices, agriculture etc. All the non-Congress political parties were hopelessly disarrayed, and the ruling Congress Party was using all methods fair or foul to break them. The attitude of all parties towards each other was dogmatic, and seemed at times unreal. In search of a solution, Lohia visualised a new political party of socialism, nationalism and internationalism based on all round equality between all nations, revolutionary yet believing in non-violence too, and which would participate in the great endeavour of bringing about seven revolutions in the whole world. Just before the elections Lohia issued a statement calling for the formation of a single opposition party. He put forth his idea about the new party in following words; "The aim of this party should be socialism and it should be as involved in internationalism as well as nationalism.

It should I be much non-violent as a revolutionary. Similarly, it should participate in the seven revolutions of the world. If Jan Sangh leaves it's opposition to nationalisation and the Muslims, it would be a valuable asset to the new party. Similarly, if the Communists leave their false internationalism, eschew violence, take to democracy, showing the same kind of revolutionary attitude towards caste, language, etc. as they do towards private property, they also can be of help to the new party. Just forming united fronts does to appeal to me. My ideas should not be distorted".

Election drums started beating Lohia drafted the election manifesto of the Socialist Party. This manifesto was unique in many respects. While analysing the opposition parties in the country, Lohia said in his manifesto: "Congress is a body of half dead mass. The Communist Party is a party of disruption and partial radicalism. The Jan Sangh is a party of narrow nationalism, and the P.S.P. is a group of sheer opportunists. It has become just a ladder to secure vantage seats. The Swatantra Party and the Congress Party are both parties of the capitalists. Whereas the Swatantra Party is made up of dethroned, distressed and thrifty capitalists, the Congress is composed of ruling extravagants and careless capitalists. The Socialist Party is the only party which stands for radicalism, democracy, nationalism arid socialism. It alone can defeat the Congress". In this context, after discussing the disparity between the income of the rich and the poor, craze for modernisation etc. Lohia said; "In white countries this ratio is between 5 to 7. But in India it ranges from 300 to 500. It is under such a situation that cosmopolites have appeared in this world. An artificial world unity has manifested itself bringing about uniformity in the standards of a handful of people of certain sections in various countries. The cosmopolite is either a regionalist or a hypocritical universalist, not a citizen of his nation. "One universalist, Marx, aimed at uniting the workers of the world. Another one, Gandhi, wanted to unite the people of the world. Fake universalists in the world want to unite the bureaucrats and capitalists of the world. While Nehru and Nasser are examples of cosmopolites, Marx and Gandhi are examples of universalists.

In the party manifesto, Lohia also discussed questions like the Chinese aggression, northern frontier of the country, Nepal, Bhutan, Pakistan, etc. and thereafter stated "that all these questions have remained unresolved, since India's foreign policy has not been creative". The seven revolutions of the world had also been mentioned in the manifesto.

Lohia himself stood against Nehru in the elections. While stating his reasons for this, he said: "Pandit Nehru is enjoying the grandeur of the President and the power of the Prime Minister. Hence it has becomes imperative to defeat him in the election. He is feeding the people with the opium of the dreams of future benefits of the 5 year plans and thereby blinding their vision. In our country, a sweeper gets 2 rupees per day and farm labourers get only 10 annas per day. On the other hand the expenditure of the Prime Minister is about 25000-30000 rupees per day. Gandhi era had been an era of devotion to duty, simplicity and sacrifice, but the Nehru age is an age of grandeur, fashion and extravagance. For the good of India the defeat of the present Prime Minister is very important".

So far only communalists or reactionaries had been Nehru's opponents in the elections. However, now for the first time, the electorate of Phulpur had in Lohia a candidate of a balanced political thoughts. His election symbol was the tree. In his election appeal, 'The story of a banyan tree', Lohia said; "The common and the poor people in India consider me as their own. This is my only asset. It is with the help of this only that I am fighting against the old rock. Progress has to be assessed by comparison with others. Every white country is increasing its annual per capita income by 150-200 rupees. In China this increase is 70-80 rupees but in India it is only 8 rupees. In a new country like Ghana also, yearly per capita increase in income is 25 to 30 rupees. Lohia lost the election, but in a way he had won it. In all respects he was a man without means, while the Congress had at its disposal vast resources government as well as otherwise. In this contest Congress used all their dirty methods to win. Even then Lohia proved that Nehru was not invincible. In 43 poling centres. Lohia secured more votes than Nehru. The *Times of India* wrote in its editorial notes: "For every pair of voters for Nehru, there was one for the socialist leader".

Although the militancy of the Socialists Party and its policy regarding casteism, language, etc.. had become widely popular the Socialist Party did not get the expected success even in the 1962 elections. Lohia, of course, was wedded to doing his duty even in despair. Immediately after his defeat, he attended the party study camp at Gorakhpur from 11th to 15th June 1962, and awakened the workers about the drawbacks in the party organisation and called upon them to launch a powerful movement all over the country for demands relating to caste, language, and prices. The third 'English Removal' convention was held at Hyderabad form 12th to 14th October 1962. It was inaugurated by Prof. Satyan Bose, National Professor and presided over by Mr. Maganbhai Desai, Gandhiji's colleague in Gujarat. Lohia had attained some success in getting for this movement the sympathy of learned men from the various states in the country. An idea which appeared as impossible and improbable had now taken firm roots. According to the Indian Constitution, use of English in the administration should have been stopped after 1965. However, the government intended to continue English indefinitely as an associate language. The attempt of the government to retain English permanently under the pretext of the opposition of South Indians to Hindi, was totally unacceptable to Lohia. In order to blunt the edge of this powerful weapon in the hands of the government, Lohia made a practical compromise in respect of his stand on English. In Southern states and Bengal opposition to Hindi had been a reality. Taking this into consideration, he suggested various alternatives as follows: (1) The state language at the Centre should be English. However, non-Hindi people of the coastal states should be given protection for the next ten years in respect of the gazetted posts of the Central government. (2) The administration of the Central Government should be carried out in more than one regional language. (3) If none of these alternatives is acceptable to the non-Hindu states, the country should be divided into two regions on the basis of the practicability of the state language. One region will consists of those states which have no objection to Hindi being the state language of the centre. All the government work in such states will be carried out compulsorily in Hindi. The other region will be composed of those states which are opposed to making Hindi the state language. All the government work in such states should be carried out by the Centre in English as long as those states desire.

By this suggestion it became clear that Lohia did not desire to impose Hindi on non-Hindi states. However, he did not want that English should be forced upon those whom Hindi which is acceptable, under the pretext of the opposition of the non-Hindi states.

Lohia knew that the problem was more of restraining English

and not of imposing Hindi. He felt that once states adopted regional languages in administration and the centre adopted Hindi, those regions which recognise Hindi will make definite progress. This will influence those who stick to English, in the non-Hindi states. In these states, 90% of the people do not know English in any case whereas familiarity with Hindi is increasing due to various reasons such as cinemas, compulsions of business, or dealings with Hindi speaking people. However the handful elite who control wealth, power, prestige, knowledge and science would never allow elimination of the English.

26. RESTLESS SOUL

20th of October 1962 was a dark day in Indian history. On this day Chinese armed forces violated India's borders. Congress government proved itself incompetent to defend the motherland. The nation was humiliated, all it's prestige in the community of nations was wiped out. The Chinese army ran over bases at Dhola and Khinazmane and continued their victorious drive. Walong and Bomdila fell on 10th & 20th November. The Chinese army was within 80 miles of Tejpur in Assam. The panic, desperation and debacle were beyond compare. Senior government officials, the very people responsible to boost people's morale, ran in shameful panic. On 19th October Nehru addressed the nation on the air in a most gloomy and defeatist tone. It made one conclude that Nehru had written off Assam.

Witnessing this, Lohia could not hold his revulsion and anger. This was only to be expected. He had warned the government of the Chinese the menace, when not only Congress government but even socialist leaders like Jayprakash Narayan, had swallowed the bait of Chinese friendship. In 1949, the Chinese yellow grip wrung the neck of tiny Tibet and Nehru put a stamp of consent under Panchsheela on the act. Indian soldiers in Tibet were withdrawn and the post and telegraph as well as twelve rest houses were handed over to the Chinese free. On top of this the issue of six crucial passes such as Shipkala, Mana, etc., was left unresolved. Later by 1962, the same passes became disputed. In 1946 as Tibet was being overrun, Lohia was in London. In a press conference Lohia had said: "India should stop this infanticide". Three dayslater the communist daily from London, *Daily Mirror* published a statement of Jayprakash Narayan. He had opined that Chinese claims of sovereignty over Tibet were completely legitimate. Lohia was humiliated by his own colleague Jayprakash Narayan who was then the general secretary of the Socialist Party.

Later Lohia warned the government and the people when the borders were threatened, and when the Indian Government eulogized communist China that had carried out liquidation of people by the millions, Lohia had said: "The Indian government has become an agent of the Chinese". The official visit of Chou En Lai to India began on 25th June 1954. The two Prime Ministers signed the Panchsheela pact of mutual friendship. But, right afterwards in July, the Chinese objected to the presence of Indian Army units in Baraholi area of U.P. claiming it as Chinese territory. The diary of those events makes revealing reading. As the Indians were busy trying to secure the U.N. membership for China, the Chinese indulged in a series of mischievous and provocative acts. In 1954, Lohia warned the government in a statement when the Indian government accepted the Panchsheela principle of coexistence with China. In that year Chinese commenced the construction of a hundred mile road in Aksai Chin. In 1959, the Chinese occupied Spangoor in Ladakh and Long Ju in NEFA. Lohia was furious when Nehru described the area occupied by Chinese as rocky and uninhabited. "What kind of a premier is he?" Lohia demanded in public meetings, "Traitor! Traitor!!" responded the people. This was the kind of acceptance that Lohia enjoyed with the masses. In the parliament socialist and other opposition M.P.'s demanded to know the reason for concealing from parliament and the country, the construction of the new Chinese road. Lohia roared, "Is the Delhi government in it's senses or in the grip of some narcotic?" He rejected the McMahon line, marked by the British imperialists, as wrong and declared that Kailas, Lake Manas and the eastward flowing section of the river Bramhaputra as constituting the Indian northern frontier. Lohia brought to light the fact that the village Mansar sixty to seventy miles north of Lake Mim paid taxes to the Indian government till 1954. Nehru took no cognizance matter even after it was unearthed by Lohia. On the contrary he said: "It was an Indian village no doubt but the tax amount collected did not every cover the expense of collection". Such was the indifferent attitude of the government. Lohia denounced those who wanted to divide the Indians into racial groups such as Aryans, Dravidians, and Mongolians. He demanded that Tibet which was more akin to India in many respects including script, language, religion, way of life and thought, must remain free. When, even after India suffered complete humiliation on the Indo-China border dispute, the Chinese premier Chou En Lai was invited to visit India, Lohia commented: "The government is committing a blunder".

When the Indian representative defended the case of Chinese membership of U.N. on 26th October 1962, the naked Chinese aggression on India not withstanding, Lohia remarked, "My soul suffers, in desperation". For a decade Lohia had argued that India should support recognition of the two Chinese; that of Chou as well as Chiang. But the government continued to pursue its suicidal policy. He appealed once again: "Be loyal to Himalaya and alert about Jambudweep". He launched a campaign for the following demand: Tibet should be freed, borders of August 15, 1947, should remain the Indian borders, military service should be compulsory, a truly independent foreign policy should be pursued, masses should be enthused with revolutionary actions, hesitancy abandoned and war taken to the plateau of Tibet. He organised a number of 'Save Himalaya' conferences. He argued that the masses were the arm-military the fist, and hence the need to strengthen the masses with equalitarian policies. It was Lohia's opinion that nations participating in the Colombo conference have fallen prey to foreign politics and therefore their Colombo plan is an uncivilised act. He said India should never pardon these States for their intervention. He recommended that the Dalai Lama government should be recognised. But all in vain!

Around this time Socialist Party faced a another crisis. On 13th December 1962, S.P. & P.S.P., MLAs in the U.P. assembly, flouting their respective central leadership and in contravention of party rules, came together to form the S.S.P. and were promptly given the status of an opposition party by the speaker of the assembly. This merger with no basis in principles and policies naturally caused a turmoil in the Socialist Party. However, major leaders of the P.S.P. welcomed the news heartily. Some leaders of the S.P., immediately arrived in Lucknow and warned the party MLAs that they have either to seek ratification from their P.S.P. colleagues for policies and programmes of the S.P or face disciplinary action. The combined group accepted election manifesto of the S.P. as the basis for the merger. This averted the crisis temporarily.

The Socialist Party had paid a heavy price in the issue of socialist unity. Lohia himself had suffered mental torture. It had been resolved in the Gorakhpur National Executive meeting of June 1962, that negotiations with P.S.P. regarding merger are futile and impossible. Lohia maintained complete silence this time. There was a reason for this. At the beginning of 1962, he had proposed that merger should be based on leadership of P.S.P. and programme of S.P., but the response was abuses like 'hypocrite' and 'dictator' the P.S.P. leaders always contended that not the policies of the S.P., but it's leadership was the obstacle in the merger. After Lohia's proposal, it was said there were differences in policies also, and hence joint discussions were necessary. To those who wanted Lohia to meet P.S.P. leaders, his reply was; " . . . such meeting is always interpreted as effort at organisational unification. Meeting with the leaders of the Communist Party or Jan Sangh is never interpreted this way. At best, people say it is a ideological exchange or discussions on common platform. I have fraternal feelings towards P.S.P. workers as well as pre-47 Congressmen, but as a party the P.S.P. couldn't be more worse. I appeal to members of the P.S.P. to join S.P. individually or collectively. If necessary new committees could be instituted. Those who want to bring about change through the plenary session have no time to lose. Programme must be made time bound. 80% of the P.S.P. leaders feel inclined to join the Congress to do whatever possible from within the conglomerate. 80% followers wish to have a distinct philosophy and organisation. Congress assimilates diverse groups from a position of strength. Willingness of the P.S.P. to join them springs from their weakness or power hunger. Barring the S.P., the socialist movement in India is demoralised. This weakness has come from ideological confusion. We can't emulate European example where there is a tradition of several generations of political parties and ideologies".

This was the background that had led to Lohia's silence. Inspite of this, he was called as 'the main obstacle in unification'. The sixth plenary session of the S.P. was held in Bharatpur from 28th to 31st December 1962, in the shadow of all these events and circumstances, As usual it deserved to be called historic and critical. Madhu Limaye tabled the resolution on unification already carried by the National Executive of the party. The resolution expressed regret over the actions of MLAs from U.P. defying the party directives. It acknowledged the fact that subsequently the Socialist Party manifesto was accepted as the basis for the merger in U.P. assembly. Another resolution authorised the National Executive to take necessary steps for merger of the two organisations, provided the P.S.P. accepted the manifesto as the basis of wider unification. This revolution encountered considerable opposition. Addressing the gathering Lohia remarked; "Initially the action of the U.P. MLAs was undoubtedly that of total departure from party policy. However, later, on December 16th they secured support for merger with the acceptance by the P.S.P. of our election manifesto. Nevertheless, do not suppose that the basis of the merger is strong and sound, because after all, all the developments took place flouting party discipline. If ideology is abstract, manifesto is its concrete form. By their very nature, ideological positions are very general and loopholes can always be found. On the other hand, a manifesto is specific and includes well defined short term programmes. Good things don't last long in the quagmire of the Indian politics. Someone who is trapped marginally can be helped out. But there is no way to help those who are deep in it. On the contrary, one who comes to their aid, risks his own neck".

Lohia felt that the process of unification may take even two or three years. "Meanwhile", he said, "I shall be with you. But I won't participate in the related meetings. For one, thing I am past the age of hectic bargaining, and secondly, I am always blamed for rocking the boat".

In his speech following the passing of the resolution, Lohia said; "I share the feelings of the 62 delegates who voted against the resolution, but I have no desire to form a new party now. If they do it I shall join them. Hold fast to the manifesto as the basis of merger. Be firm. Resolve not to yield further".

In January 1963, the national committees of the both the parties met separately in Delhi. The whole socialist movement waited for the outcome. The Executive Committee of the P.S.P. declined to accept the Socialist Party manifesto as the basis of the merger. A committee was appointed to examine the issue of the merger and was asked to report in February. The Socialist Party expressed in a revolution, its disappointment and regret at the decision of P.S.P. Indeed, all those who had agreed on the merger formula following the events in U.P. were disappointed by the stand of the P.S.P. executive. This included state committees in Rajasthan and Tamil Nadu as well as many leaders and branches of P.S.P. in Maharashtra and Bihar. Beginning from a stand that there was no difference of principles, P.S.P. leaders opposed virtually all the basic policies of the S.P. The Socialist Party did not recognise the McMahon line, P.S.P. accepted it was the legitimate boundary They conceded to accord English the same status as Hindi. Their policy on caste was also ambiguous. Like the Congress, they talked of equal opportunity, rather than preferential treatment to backward classes. They held that specific programmes on caste and linguistic issues, attitude towards planning etc. needed further consideration. The policy of joining hands with all opposition parties in elections and mass movements was a point of disagreement as was parliamentary protocol. The National Executive of the Socialist Party highlighted the double talk of P.S.P. leaders and called upon branches of that party to join the S.P. individually.

On 22nd February 1963. S.P. and P.S.P. workers in Maharashtra gathered together at Pune. They appealed to the two parties to expedite steps towards merger and settle all differences by discussion with the seven-member committee instituted by P.S.P. It was clear that the socialist rank and file all over the nation was earnest about merger. Nonetheless, the matter did not seem to get off the ground. In March, the President of India, gave his inaugural address to Parliament in English. The socialist MPs staged a walk out in protest of this. Going beyond his jurisdiction the President requested the Speaker to take necessary action against the MPs who staged walk out. As a matter of fact, a walk out is a generally accepted mode of protest, but it was intolerable to the fuming Nehru, He said: "This was a humiliating episode, it calls for strict penal action". His desire was to suspend the concerned MPs for one year. He was outraged that unlike other opposition members, the socialists members refused to dance to his tune. He manoeuvred to appoint an inquiry committee though there was no basis for such action. However opposition, as well as some Congress MPs sided with the Socialists. Surendra Dwivedi of the P.S.P., was the lone supporter of Nehru. One more incident which indicated the non-existence of a unified approach to certain issues took place in the U.P. assembly. On 22nd March 1963, 22 Socialist MLAs of the U.P. lower house were forced out of the house by the marshal.

The P.S.P. members did nothing to resist this. Consequently Ugrasen, the leader of the newly formed S.S.P. in the legislature, immediately informed the speaker that the new group had split into its original factions.

The endeavours for socialist unity thus all came to a nought. Lohia stuck to his decision of remaining aloof. He was dismayed by the Indian debacle vis-a-vis China. On 12th March 1963, Lohia arrived in the border region to get a first hand view of the situation. On the road passing through Bilasipada—a village in the district of Gualpada in Assam—he was arrested for refusing to give the police his personal information. A truck load of policemen were at hand. He was released after a while, and the tour proceeded further. After visiting Bomdila, Tejpur, North Lakhimpur, Jecro, Dibrugad, Deerang, etc., Lohia felt, "Are we really so incapable of waging a war?" The people appeared thoroughly depressed. They sole desire seemed to be to survive; to somehow or the other keep body and life together. Lohia exclaimed; "What has the Indian man come to? We must examine dispassionately the nature of this rot that seems to have set in. The main culprit is this hidden lust for existence. There was hardly any battle at Bomdila or Darang. What else can you expect when no one will put his life at stake? The Indian mind is behind times and decadent. All changes are superficial. Even at a time of national calamity there is no awareness of the co-related nature of a military disaster and social inequities. How can one hope to conquer the Chinese while all social barriers of inequality remain untouched? The victory will be possible only through eliminating all kinds of discrimination. A healthy man can save others along with himself. When an Indian troop went to exchange prisoners of war, a Chinese told them: "Your soldiers were better trained and better equipped. But they were on the run". The real challenge is make the Indian mind healthy and strong. The present corrupt government is only the external manifestation of the rotten core. To complain of outdated armaments is hardly reasonable. The Chinese came only with rifles while we had giant tanks and latest kinds of arms".

Lohia learnt during his sojourn in Urvasium (NEFA) that the Indian army was running at the rate of thirty miles a day in fright of the Chinese. The rout was total. By the 12th November, the airport at Tezpur was already in shambles, and the morale of the air force officers was very low. The top army brass had proved themselves incompetent, unfit and even treasonous. The tactic of evacuating a position implies an orderly retreat of women and children followed by citizens and finally soldiers, only after the defence of the position becomes untenable. Not here. The exodus had begun even before the commencement of fighting. In fact, Chinese forces were as far as eight to ten days march from Fam and Teji, and yet panic had prevailed there. Government themselves took to it's heels.

After reviewing this, Lohia said; "According to the Prime Minister", Bomdila and Walan fell on 18th November. But how can this be, since there was no battle? The Indian army had already abandoned these posts on the 17th November. So it is difficult to decide to whether the posts fell on 17th when abandoned by Indians, or on the 18th November when occupied by 'die Chinese".

The six months from October 1962 to March 1963 were a period of great national shame. Lohia described his state of mind thus: "My mind is gloomy and numb. But the Premier is remorseless. All he tries is whitewash. He claims victory even in defeat. First step towards rectifying errors is repentance. But he lacks it totally". It was clear that the Prime Minister had given false information to the house. The real and grave blame is on that ill-famous circular for the withdrawal. Describing these facts Lohia said: "The chief of army staff should be court marshalled. The Prime Minister has overstepped his prerogatives, Parliament must discuss this question".

Inspired by Lohia, the 'Save the Himalaya' convention was organised in Patna in October 1962. In the convention, former President Rajendra Prasad said: "Tibet should have been defended while China was still trying to annex it. But we did not do that, and are now paying for it. We must free Tibet as our own freedom depends on it". Jayprakash Narayan said that the Chinese challenge is not merely a military challenge. It is a challenge thrown by a revolution. The only language the Chinese understand is that of force. Our appeasement policy had boomeranged. It is India's duty to recognise the Tibetan people's right to freedom, and a logical conclusion of this would be to recognise the Dalai Lama as the leader of free Tibet. "As early as 1949 Lohia had argued that Tibet is completely free and should remain so. It is not a province of China. Shared language, script, land, life style, religion, history and desire of the masses make India and Tibet brothers. Lohia pointed out that Tibet was never a part of China, but instead held sway over it at times. He argued that we should recognise the Dalai Lama as the leader of free Tibet and break the aggressive designs of the Chinese by launching a counter attack".

Lohia was saddened by another incident that happened at this time. In March 1963, Rajendra Prasad, India's first President passed away. Prime Minister Nehru was absent at the funeral. Nehru had put aside all engagements to attend the last rites of Bidhanchandra Roy and Sardar Patel. Thus it was a surprise that he could not attend the funeral of Rajendra Prasad. Yet there may be one explanation, during the Chinese aggression, many differences of opinions had arisen between Nehru and Rajendra Prasad. Perhaps the fact that Rajendra Prasad addressed the socialist inspired convention for, liberation of Tibet, might have disturbed Nehru, Lohia thought that this explained Nehru's absence at the funeral. Lohia's comment was; "Of course differences of opinion can separate friends. But to stay away even at the last rites, after an association of over thirty years, is inhuman. It only points at his intransigence, pomposity and arrogance".

An incident that gave a new turn to Indian politics, particularly parliamentary affairs, occurred at this juncture. The national humiliation during Chinese aggression, defeatist attitudes of the Congress government, sky rocketing prices and food shortages had led to a sense of outrage among masses. Either because of this or as a windfall for the nation, the impossible became possible. The over confident Congress government decided to hold bye-elections in the parliamentary constituencies of U.P. It was decided that Lohia would contest the Farukhabad seat. In all, there were three vacancies. Acharya Kripalani was to contest from Amrohi as an independent and Deendayal Upadhyay of the Jan Sangh stood from Jaunpur. Farukhabad became the battlefield for the socialists. Thousands of activists from all provinces gathered together. The whole party experienced a rejuvenation. All began to urge the people of Farukhabad to exact vengeance for the humiliation of the nation; this was the opportunity to settle scores with the Congress Government that let foreign aggressors annex parts of the motherland and people should make the most of the opportunity. The response of the masses was whole-hearted. Love for Lohia, anger against the Congress and a desire to take revenge on behalf of the whole nation manifested themselves intensely. Masses of Farukhabad rose up to all the expectations of an angry nation.

Lohia won with 1,07,816 votes, defeating his Congress rival by a margin of 15,588 votes. The Congress had spared no means, fair or foul, to defeat him. But no one was carried away by the bribes, wild promises, threats and other mean tactics. The masses gave the boot to the Congress with all its might and power. A wave of victorious celebrations and jubilation spread throughout the socialist movement following the news of Lohia's victory. The candidate of P.S.P. was totally forgotten.

It was in this very electioneering that the seeds of later disputes within the Socialist Party were sown. All the three bye elections, Farukhabad, Amroha and Jaunpur were treated by Nehru as prestigious contests, a challenge to his power. Lohia was equally determined to defeat the Congress. He had the support of Jan Sangh and Communist Party. While the support of Jan Sangh was not conditional upon reciprocity, it was expected that Lohia would campaign for Deen Dayal Upadhyay in Jaunpur, Lohia too felt that it was his duty. Alongwith Kripalani's Amroha constituency, he undertook an election tour of Jaunpur also. However some in his party were perturbed that this was contrary to the long standing policies of the party. The issue was raised in the National Executive at Bombay, in June, following the elections. There was much debate. Finally, the Executive passed a resolution approving Lohia's action. It was resolved that the party could support a suitable anti-Congress contestant. Lohia was present at this meeting and argued forcefully that nothing could be done unless Congress was wiped out.

This was a volte-face in the socialist election policy. It was proudly held that the Socialist Party is the only genuine opposition party, all others fight the Congress with the tacit understanding not to seek its ultimate elimination. This contention was held with as much vehemence as any other policy stand. Socialists in Maharashtra and Bengal had paid a heavy price for it. Electoral alliances, negotiating seat adjustments, were tantamount to political corruption. Thus the new stand of Lohia gave a jolt to big section of the party. This section held political struggles and principled electioneering as an issue of prestige and pride for the party. Naturally they experienced a traumatic shock to see the father of these policies turn his back on them.

Indeed, Lohia had not suggested the revision casually. He had expressed his mind very clearly in a meeting of party workers in Bombay. India's humiliation at the hands of the Chinese had thoroughly outraged him. He was now convinced that the Congress government was incapable of guarding the national interests and was a national disgrace. But no single opposition party was, or was likely to be, strong enough to counter the Congress. He saw clearly that the Congress, inspite of polling only a minority of votes ruled because the opposition was divided.

He commented, "It is a great folly to equate the ruling and the opposition parties. Congress has at its disposal the one and quarter crore strong bureaucracy as well as fifteen hundred crore rupees. If our party were strong, who would have sought electoral alliances?" On another occasion he said later; "Prior to independence, the Congress was a broad based national front solely confronting the British Raj. Such a broad based anti-Congress alliance must now be forged and Congress boldly asked to quit government".

The gravity of the situation was ever deepening. Socialist unification was getting nowhere. A stalemate had been reached. In May 1963 a plenary session of P.S.P. was held in Bhopal. The party appealed to the country to dislodge the Congress government & demanded Nehru's resignation. It was resolved that the party will contest elections independently without alliance with any group. When it became evident that it had taken a staunch anti-Congress line, the S.P. called upon MPs of the P.S.P. to table a no-confidence motion in parliament and offered an unconditional support. In the plenary session, S.M. Joshi was elected the president of the party in place of Ashok Mehta. These were good omens. A tug of war between conflicting attitudes and analysis was on in the P.S.P., there were some signs of dynamism. On the other hand, at the same time the party approved Ashok's Mehta acceptance of a post on the planning commission, which was clearly a demoralising act. Ashok Mehta had obviously flouted the anti-Congress line of Bhopal by accepting the deputy chairmanship of the Planning Commission. The argument offered was that the Planning Commission was not connected with government policy and administration, but like any other commission of inquiry. This was hog-wash. It was clear as daylight that planning commission was the part of government and enjoyed no autonomy. The P.S.P. thus ended up demanding Nehru's resignation, and offering him cooperation in the same breath. This led to considerable unhappiness in the rank and file. Some demanded Ashok Mehta's expulsion from the party. The P.S.P. executive considered Ashok Mehta's overt membership of the P.S.P. and simultaneous covert membership of the Congress an embarrassment, and asked him to tender his resignation The party appealed to the country to dislodge the Congress government & demanded Nehru's resignation. Mehta refused to oblige and challenged the P.S.P. Executive to expel him. He even advised an enmass joining of Congress.

27. IN THE LAND OF LIBERTY

Lohia's increasing popularity became a sore point for the ruling party. Lohia's maiden speech in the parliament was highly praised by the '*Hindustan Times*' a prestigious daily in Delhi. As the rumour goes, government's displeasure for publishing and praising the anti-Nehru speech was communicated to the editor who realised his error and fell in line. Later the *Hindustan Times* ostracised Lohia. In this period, Lohia thoroughly exposed the Nehru government's treason during the Chinese aggression, in all his speeches in tours. Naturally he was an eyesore to the government. In Punjab he was threatened with arrest and trial, but the Punjab government could not muster enough courage.

For four days between 28th and 31st December 1963, the seventh All India Convention of the Socialist Party was held in Calcutta. The main issue was adjustment with opposition parties in elections and mass struggles. The mass support of the Congress government had eroded further. And yet a political force capable of wiping out this government had failed to emerge. Lohia said that forging such a force should be the first priority of all political parties. "In each state, we must make friends with the party which is second in strength. These are the DMK in Tamil Nadu, the P.S.P. in Mysore, the Jan Sangh in M.P., the Swatantra in Bihar, and the Communists in Bengal. Further we must consider joining hands with such parties as the Revolutionary Socialist Party, Forward Bloc, P.S.P., Republican Party, and the PWP" Lohia stated, and added; "All parties, including the Socialists, have become hotbeds of opportunism, nepotism, squabbles and laziness. This discourages potential entrants and even the old cadre is put in despair. The Socialist Party adheres strongly to its goals and policies.

It should not matter much whose company you keep as long as you are on the right path. If the associations last long enough perhaps our companions may change. Accepting a new thing does not mean abandoning the old policies. It means a new experiment on a new path".

The main resolution, to the effect that the Socialist Party should cooperate with other opposition parties in elections as well as in mass agitations, was passed with 103 votes in favour and 35 against. Amongst the dissenters, representatives from Maharashtra were the largest group. However resolution faced at least token opposition in most states. In his concluding speech Lohia said: "A policy, no matter how good, is of no use if those who implement it were powerless. I feel that the socialist path is good but has failed to attract enough followers. It is futile to put the blame entirely on either the masses or the socialists. Both deserve an equal share".

Earlier, in his inaugural speech Lohia had said: "There is a world of difference between the conditions before and after October 1962. After October 1962 the people realised that the government had put the nation to shame. Earlier the masses supported the Congress who polled nearly half the votes, today that fraction has declined to a third. Congress had lost its hold on the minds of the masses. I have suggested two things; electoral alliances and supporting a candidate with the maximum electoral merit and having the best programme". Lohia argued the need for maintaining an even keel between summit level politics and grassroot level politics, between electioneering and mass struggles, between cooperation and independence in election strategy. Lohia believed that "...if the path towards the ultimate goal is correct one, need not worry who the fellow traveller is. It is possible that he would reform himself during the journey with one. In my opinion we must be ready for give and take to facilitate formation of such party while not losing sight of the fundamental principles. Defeat of the Congress moves the people and makes them receptive to revolutionary ideas. Let the masses feel confident that the Congress governments can be changed It is of course possible that the government that replaces Congress may not be good either. Then it will be for the people to dethrone the new government in its turn. That time things will be easier, for the people will have learnt their lesson that they can change the government".

Lohia stressed the need to cultivate the habit of equal vision and a sense of proportion and a state of mind where there is both snow like peace and heat of fire. Lohia was confident that if the party workers develop these two qualities in their minds, they will surely bring about the revolution they desired. He further stated; "It is said that I am leaning towards communists. Let me make it clear that communism remains to me, as irrelevant and bad for India and the world, as ever before. But some Indian communists have certainly changed. So think of communists and not communism. Some people say there are pro-Moscow and pro-Peking groups among communists. The real distinction is between those who are apologists of Nehru and the Congress government and those who are against them. While, I was a student in Europe, there were Chinese too. Then we used to dream of a time when all oppressed people, coloured, Chinese, Indian, & Africans, will destroy the international feudal order. Australia, Siberia, California are regions with few people and plentiful land, but these are held by force by the white feudals. A time will come when we will knock on their doors and say these lands are for all mankind to be shared and not just for you. But the dream has withered. Instead of Australia, Siberia, and California, the Chinese chose to annex the Himalaya, for it was weakling. Though I advocate electoral adjustments with the communists, I still hold the view that the problem is that Marxism is unable to undo the inequality between races, between white and the coloured, between countries. The Chinese don't appreciate it, nor do the communists in India".

About socialist unity Lohia said: "I want it, but I see no reasonable way to it. P.S.P. leaders and members should suggest a modus operandi". The decision of the Socialist Party, to cooperate with opposition parties in a elections gave an excuse to the section of P.S.P. opposed to unification in any case. A sudden wave of commitment, "to our ideologically pure election policy" arose. It was argued that the Calcutta resolution of Socialist Party had put the P.S.P. in an embarrassing situation. They had resolved, in Bhopal, not to join any electoral fronts and the Calcutta decision was exactly the opposite, electoral unity of different parties with distinctly different policies, Lohia stated: "It is a formidable task no doubt. But not so difficult if we have a little more broad mind & discerning intellect". Lohia had long before said that a drop of treason by the government is more serious than even a series of treasonable acts by communists, likewise, even a shade of communalism among Congressmen is more dangerous than anything the Jan Sangh would ever do, because treason & communalism in state power have a greater capacity to do damage to the nation than they have being out of power.

In January 1964, Executive Committees of the P.S.P. took the decision of cancelling the party membership of Ashok Mehta and tried to put an end to the fifteen year old debate on whether to act in cooperation or in opposition to the Congress, and to be a complementary or a competitive party. The Socialist Party's stand regarding electoral alliances and cooperation and P.S.P.s demand of Nehru's resignation and the disciplinary action against Ashok Mehta were a series of jolts to the socialist movement, and gave it a sudden new turn. Lohia's announcement "SP and P.S.P. can merge without any precondition" made simultaneously in Bombay and Ahmedabad was the latest in the series of the shocks. It meant that Lohia had shifted from his earlier position, that the 1962 election manifesto must be the basis of any unification. He went even further and said; 'sooner the better' and he hoped it should materialise immediately. He added, "If the Calcutta resolution is the stumbling block, it should be annulled. I shall be only too delighted if the election manifesto of SP can be the basis for unity, but if this is not acceptable, leadership of the two parties should search for an alternative".

In a meeting in February 1964, the National Executive of the P.S.P. welcomed the proposal of the SP for an unconditional unification and elected a five member National Committee to conduct further negotiations. The SP committee resolved in a meeting at Lucknow on 14th February, that it agreed with Lohia's advice that the SP-P.S.P. merger should be pursued unconditionally and appealed to the P.S.P. to expedite the process. A sub-committee was appointed for this. The SP Executive invited the P.S.P. to participate in the 'Janwani Day' demonstrations planned by the SP on 13th March in Delhi.

The P.S.P. did not reciprocate, nor did they participate in the massive morcha on March 13. Some P.S.P. leaders expressed the opinion that certain issues related to unification must be thrashed out beforehand. Disagreements about the process of unification began to surface. An early unification following Lohia's advice would have been welcomed enthusiastically by the whole nation. Mutual acceptance of the idea of unconditional unity had created the atmosphere of hope. If it had materialised, a party of the masses would have been born and the Indian political scene would have changed. The hope was that a strong party wedded to democracy, socialism, radicalism and nationalism would emerge. The enthusiasm began to wane with the delay. Only a fog of unity remained. Lohia's reaction was; "If unification is delayed further, there might be further division in socialist groups".

About the process of unification, Lohia's feeling was that there should be a fresh start with a clean state. Unity first; doctrines and programmes can be discussed later. If ideological wrangling begins, unity won't be possible. As far as the five member committee for unification appointed by the P.S.P. national committee was concerned, Lohia was of the opinion that policies of the new party must be thrashed out in a plenary session. A hidden danger in appointment of such a committee is that these handful of people may frame policies first and later make their acceptance by the party a prestige point.

In fact the P.S.P.'s procrastination was unpardonable. While Lohia's pronouncement had temporarily averted the likely mass exodus to the Congress along with Ashok Mehta, the tendency could have resurfaced after seeing the fate of the proposed unification. One wonders why the P.S.P. leaders failed to perceive how self-defeating their actions were. They proposed that the five member committee should print the membership forms of the new party. The two factions should continue to function separately and enroll new members independently. Lohia remarked, "This is even more dangerous. The parties might enrol bogus members just to secure a majority in the general convention. If there is no unification, the SP will function as it is. Dissolution is out of question. Those who wish to crossover to the P.S.P. are welcome to do so" warned Lohia, and added; "If the new party is ambivalent on such issues as language, caste, foreign policy and starvation, and planning, it has no future. The new party must have firm direction and commitment. No one should anticipate its electoral policies. No one can be spokesmen for it. There are two views about this among socialists. An open session shall chose between them. We must ensure that the union does not cause a rift in the anti-Congress bloc".

The Janwani morcha of the SP was highly successful inspite of the non-cooperation of the P.S.P., SP workers broke the nose of

Lord Irwin's statue in front of the parliament. This same Lord Irwin had sent Bhagat Singh to the gallows. Lohia led the morcha. The intention was to encircle the parliament building, but the number was not adequate. In his address to the morcha, Lohia said: "Had there been two lakh participants I would have advised a gherao to the Parliament, let us postpone this and organise it better on 13th March next year". The atmosphere of Delhi was permeated with slogans, and demands from enthusiastic and aggressive socialists.

Prime Minister Nehru's health had taken a definite turn for the worse. The left side of his body was crippled. Even in such a condition either the Congress continued to exploit him, or perhaps he desired demise while in office. His general disability had repeatedly become obvious during parliamentary proceedings. Finally Lohia reminded the Lok Sabha of an anecdote in Jadunath Sarkar's book. He read out the relevant passage; "The condition worsened. Lower limbs were swollen, tongue gone dry. The daily routine of public appearance was discontinued. The courtiers could no more visit him by the bedside. Only Dara and his confidents reached that far. Interests of the state demanded of the ailing Shahjehan to act, but without physical & mental vigour sound conduct of the state was not possible". Lohia warned repeatedly that an ailing premier of an active nation should step down. "This is in the interest of Nehru himself also", he said in a public meeting.

On 16th April 1964, Lohia began his second world tour, 13 years after the first. By April end he was in U.S.A., having visited earlier, Thailand, Cambodia, Vietnam, Philippines, Australia, Fiji, Samoa, Hawaii etc. He was in U.S.A. for 2 weeks. On the way back he visited Italy, Greece, Lebanon, Mexico, Turkey, Iraq and Iran. In the U.S.A., Lohia was to give a talk in Arizona university. On 28th April, he landed at Tucson International Airport on his way to the University. He was welcomed by Richard A. Haiville of the university and Dr. Ruth Stephen, founder of the Ruth Poetry Centre. In his lecture at the poetry centre, Lohia said: "My understanding of Gandhiji has become a little deeper with the years. I sometimes feel that he sacrificed India at the alter of the world". He added; "In his pursuit of non-violence and civil disobedience, Gandhiji did a number of things which have temporarily brought harm to the country. But if the tenets of non-violence and civil disturbance become universally adopted, this temporary harm to India would result in the good of the world and Gandhiji would be remembered alongwith Jesus and Buddha. Up to now we have had a Jesus or a Gandhi of non-violence" he added, "Now the world is set for the Bismarck of non-violence. If President Johnson aspires to become the Bismarck of non-violence, he should ask for a summit conference with Khrushchev not for any negative issues, but positive issues like the removal of the poverty. I have no criticism of America's motives in foreign aid, but I am somewhat sceptical of the west's ability to distinguish between modernisation of production and modernisation of consumption. Aid to foreign countries should be based on how these countries use the aid they receive and what those countries need".

After discussing issues such as Indo-Pak relations, Goa etc. Lohia launched a vitriolic attack on Nehru and the Congress Party. He said, "Prior to 1947, Nehru was a national leader of some stature, but now he is the leader of one party, and the successor of Nehru will be no better". Lohia attacked Nehru's foreign policy in his lecture in the Physics-Mathematics auditorium at Arizona university. He opined; "It is a policy of subservience to both U.S.A. and U.S.S.R. in turn. Internal policies of the Congress are total failures, how can we call a country free if it cannot guard its freedom? "he added. When asked about Pakistan's overtures to Red China he" said; "They are cutting of their nose to spite their face".

It was the 26th of May. Lohia was in Jackson, a town in Mississippi. This southern state was notorious for its extreme poverty and racialism. While going from Jackson airport to Touguloo college along with the writer friend Ruth Stephen, the President of the college, Mr. Beitles, his wife, and Lohia stopped at the Morizan Cafeteria for lunch. Looking at the black man, Lohia, the manager of the Cafeteria declined to serve him food. Lohia was naturally full of indignation and full of a feeling of resistance. But he calmed himself and intimated the manager, "I shall come back tomorrow". That night discussions in the Tougaloo college with agitating students, Beitles and Edwin and Janet King on the situation in the state went on till late. After this Lohia announced his intention of going out to the cafeteria next day. It was explained to him that he might get arrested in New Orleans or Atlanta, and that there was even the risk of facing a blazing gun.

Lohia agreed to face the risk. He told his friends, "Backing out now would be against my notion of non-violence. If I stay it will mean I am coward and unconcerned about the treatment meted out to the blacks".

The next day officers of Morrison company were intimated. The Kings escorted Lohia to Jackson. Students and friends waited at a distance to watch. Lohia in his Indian dress entered the restaurant as planned. The white manager told him, "We do not wish to do business with you. This is private property. Please leave the place". Lohia firmly but politely refused to oblige. The police lieutenant asked him if he heard the manager asking him to leave. Lohia reiterated his stand upon which the police officer announced that he had no choice but to arrest Lohia. The police van was just outside. Lohia extended his hand in a friendly gesture towards the officer who curtly brushed it aside.

Lohia was taken in the police van. The van left the place but did not go to the police station. Instead it drove aimlessly through the streets of the town of about an hour. Obviously the police officials of the town were still undecided whether they should arrest Lohia or not. Probably they were consulting the Home Department in Washington. At last after some more time Lohia was released.

In the press conference Lohia said: "I want to make it clear that my purpose was not at all that of highlighting a dark corner of American life. Such retched places are everywhere including India. Normally I would promptly leave a place where I am not welcome. But in this particular situation to leave America while the upheaval is going on is to encourage injustice and oppression. If entering a public place is a breach of law by all means arrest me. I break such a law deliberately as member of the human race. I have therefore not intimated my consulate or parliament". This was his act as a world citizen, he said and added: "The relevance of my action is obvious. I shall always practice civil disobedience. I bow to the welfare and inspiration of United States which is squarely facing the challenge of apartheid".

A prolonged discussion between Lohia and some young activists developed that night. Many young participants of the Mississippi movement had gathered to attend the conference on civil liberties at a house on Beach street in Jackson. Volunteers and citizens exchanged ideas and experiences of the mass movements. Lohia was all praise for the non-violent efforts for social change. His interest in their movement pleased the audience. Lohia enquired about the future plans and advised them to be conscious of the past as well as future. After the first round of discussions. Lohia sensed a restlessness among the young activists. So he invited questions about India. But no one knew enough to ask anything. Realising this he narrated the thrilling story of the Indian freedom movement, enunciated non-violence as its strategy as well as a philosophy of life and explained the limitations of the movement and its victories. During the discussion a black woman asked him with surprise how Lohia could describe Nehru and his great contribution to the Indian freedom struggle in such glowing terms when Lohia had suffered an electoral defeat at his hands. Lohia smilingly explained that he knew Nehru and his associates very well and hence was their severe critic, but this by no means implied that their good deeds should not be appreciated.

Lohia advised the activists about the need of careful conceptualisation of the objectives of their movement strategies and long term perspective. These must stand the test of time. Edwin King, his wife Janet and their associates in S.N.C.C. were highly impressed. The discussions continued into the late hours, the participants absorbing many ideas. Lohia remarked that perhaps he may return to U.S. to join the movement. On receiving the news of Lohia's arrest, Under Secretary of State, George Ball, issued orders to the Mississippi state government for his release and sent a regret note to the Indian Embassy. Officials of Foreign Ministry contracted Lohia on the phone and apologised for the mistreatment. Lohia's response was typical. "I expect the same treatment as American citizens. If my experience in Jackson is that of a common black American citizen, I want nothing else. "News came from New York. Adlai Stevenson, the U.S. representative in the United Nations would meet Lohia and discuss the latter's arrest. Lohia laughed and said", I will ask Stevenson to apologise to the Statue of Liberty' Lohia asked; "Why apologise to me? President Johnson should similarly offer apologies".

In a public meeting, leaders of various sections criticised Lohia's arrest. Lohia had made his own small contribution to the antiapartheid movement in which Kennedy had become a martyr. Following Lohia, Martin Luther King was arrested alongwith 17 associates. The struggle was getting intense, and consequently, on the 20th June, the U.S. Senate passed, by a thumping majority, the historic civil rights bill to put end to discrimination in American public life. The bill empowered the government to take all necessary steps. Blacks were to get every right enjoyed by the whites, thus at least on legal plane the demand for equality by blacks was conceded. Gandhi's civil disobedience was thus victorious and a true Indian Gandhian participated in it as a world citizen.

In India on the 27th May 1966 the death occurred of Prime Minister Nehru. On 28th May 1966, Lohia sent to his condolences from Jackson. "I am grieved by the demise of Prime Minister Nehru, the premier leader of the Indian National Congress. I mourn the death of one who led us once upon a time with an endearing style. He supported certain revolutionary actions. I share the grief of his bereaved daughter. Reminiscences may become distant but their imprint remains. I shall call upon the mourning Indian masses to break the chains that restrain revolution. I make this statement rather belatedly since as the news came I was busy struggling against a certain injustice. A salute to the pre-1946 memories of that fighter has strengthened my will".

As Lohia reached the airport for his flight to London from the U.S.A. he realised from the letters from home, that a conspiracy against him was about and the parliament some newspapers and the PTI correspondent in the U.S. was party to it. These people had suppressed Lohia's message of condolence. Lohia, realising the viciousness of this, wrote to the Asst. Secretary of the party from London, "I do not approve of criticism of policies when the person in question had just expired. As a matter of fact in my press conference in New York on 2nd June, I had vowed silence for the next six months. Perhaps some journalist was hurt since I opposed English as well as lavish government spending and his colleague advised him not to go into the details of Indian politics. Indians must learnt not to react without first hand evidence. For someone like me without any means, communications with the masses is difficult. At least I should not have to face mudslinging".

Perhaps no one even in Nehru's intimate circle had offered such glowing tribute to his memories as Lohia. His satyagraha in the U.S.A. was indeed the most appropriate homage to Nehru. But some vested interests affected by Lohia's radical politics found here a golden opportunity to condemn him. And the message of condolence of May 28 from Jackson was shamelessly suppressed while the press conference on June 2nd was given publicity. The PTI correspondent who covered the press conference, ignoring Lohia's own statement, chose to report lustily on some distorted questions from mischievous journalists.

The scheme of character assassination was not yet ended. Lohia addressed a large rally of Indian students in London on 12th June in the Mahatma Gandhi hall. The London based '*Peace News*' report of this rally read thus: "After being introduced as an ideal opposition parliamentarian in a democratic government, Lohia delivered a very effective and sarcastic talk on "Present Indian Politics". A student asked some questions rather pompously but had to resume his seat after being answered in kind. A sharp answer by Lohia to one of his questions was received by the audience with wild applause. The student was crest fallen and silenced. While this was the reality, in India, the *Amrit Bazar Patrika* of Calcutta published a mischievous letter according to which Lohia faced his 'Waterloo' at the tondon rally, as the students harassed him with catcalls and abuses, all of which was patently false and distorted.

Lohia reached Paris on June 19. On June 22nd he was back in India via Brussels, Vienna, Rome, Istambul and Teheran. His impressions about some of the countries visited were as follows:

Cambodia:

> There is feeling of kinship with India, but the feeling is on the wane. Some fundamental errors are responsible for this. They must be amended.

Vietnam:

> Women here (Saigon) are very delicate. For a millennium a war between freedom and slavery is going on here. I am confident that freedom will prevail and slavery will perish. I hope that women here, dressed like queens, shall enjoy equality with males without having to lose their femininity.

Philippines:

> Men here (Manila) wear embroidered shirts. Senators here are comparable to American Senators in all but their accents. Americans have undone in 60 years the Spanish traditions of four centuries. For that this country has established closer

ties with Pakistan and Indonesia rather than India. A superficial and fake policy is practiced hert.

Australia:

This is a living monument of the Europe of exclusiveness. The place is full of vagabonds, thieves, murderers and criminals from Europe. It is a powerful nation of the South Pacific with level of living compared to that of Americans. But to nonwhite people who have hardly any opportunity to enter it, Australia appears such a peculiar nation.

Fiji:

Australian and British capitalists and bureaucrats have deprived the majority of the people here of their rights and self-determination. 44 of the population is Kuwaitis who came to Fiji nearly five hundred years ago. 52% are Indians whose ancestors came to the island 100 years ago.

Samoa Pago Pago:

Seas and skies embrace each other here. Added to this is the matchless beauty of South Pacific that eyes cannot but worship. One feels lonely on this piece of land surrounded only all sides by the vastness of the seas; though not as much as on the icy peaks of Himalaya.

U.S.A.:

Alongwith competitive growth and opulence, one encounters dissensions between racial groups. This is a great white country with lively politics. Elsewhere one finds politics bogged down in polished routine debates. In U.S. there is idealism albeit among only in a few. Freedom here is not just an empty shell of legalities; people appear inspired to search a new path towards constructive equality and resistance to dictatorship.

A reformist view prevails in both governmental and non-governmental fields, and hence the nation is without big ideals and incapable of big decisions. Sometimes it gives into the rising tide the fiery spirit of idealism. This makes one vaguely hopeful that tradition bound Russians with their dubious ideals might accept the leadership of their idealist minority. If this materialises, a happy world without armaments, will become a distinct possibility. In America where Mississippi government arrests me and Washington D.C. government apologises, I joined the idealists in their work and received warmth that I had never experienced in my earlier visit in 1951.

Mexico:

Revolution is a phrase encountered more in night club songs, and guns and shooting mostly in ballets. Here the party in power provides the leaders for opposition parties. Spanish people have destroyed the Aztecs. The population is friendlier here than anywhere else on earth. Even now the country needs a revolution.

England, North, Ireland, France, Belgium, Italy:

The affluence has wiped out politics here. Nevertheless there is a remote chance that the pacifying pleasures or slump as in Italy may push these societies towards wider and egalitarian horizons.

Delhi:

The fish is back to its pond. The water is dirty, but either on the Pacific or in Europe, it always craved to return to the same dirty pool.

28. BIRTH OF THE S.S.P.

While Lohia was away on world tour, the attempts for socialist's unification were getting nowhere. Those who favoured unity were trying hard to expedite the process while those against it were busy with rumour mongering. Thus, *Janata* the weekly of the P.S.P. reported that socialist members of the Bombay Municipal Corporation have become affiliated to the P.S.P. Cadres of both the parties were in a state of total confusion as a consequence of the uncertain atmosphere and had become inactive. Many party branches fed up with the stalemate had passed resolutions demanding unification. Finally representatives of both sides came together in a meeting in Delhi on the 7th and 8th May 1964. A five point plan of the process of unification was agreed upon. It was decided to set up an adhoc committee with 14 members from P.S.P. and 11 from S.P. after the national conventions of both parties ratified the decisions regarding the name, flag, election symbol, constitution and policies of the new party. It was also assigned the task of organising a national convention, at end of 1964, by electing delegates on the basis of previous membership strengths of the two parties. The adhoc committee was to act on the basis of broad consensus till then.

By the end of May, national conventions of both the parties ratified the unification and members of the adhoc committee were elected. The P.S.P. was not careful in selecting its representatives. These should have been chosen only from among those who had supported the party's Bhopal resolution wholeheartedly. However, barring one or two exceptions, the representatives chosen for the adhoc committee were either ambivalent or outright antagonistic towards the Bhopal resolution. Seeds of the later disaster were sown right at the start. The first meeting of the adhoc committee was held at New Delhi on 6th June 1964, and an official announcement of the formal founding of Samyukta Socialist Party was made. The new opposition party was born in the twilight zone between the Nehru Era and the Shastri-Kamaraj Era.

Lohia was on his way back to India. It was by no means certain that Lohia would get along with the S.S.P. His caste policy was not implemented while selecting the members of the adhoc committee as well as national and state office bearers. Some former P.S.P. members were extremely and unnecessarily resentful of Lohia. To them even his very name was an anathema. Naturally the adhoc national committee had taken no cognisance of Lohia's satyagraha in U.S.A. in their meeting of 7th and 8th June. Perhaps Lohia never perceived this and decided in his forthright and generous way to work within the S.S.P. He commenced his work as an S.S.P. activist with a statement issued jointly with Surendra Dwivedi (MP) "Depose this government if it does not eradicate rise in prices with a firm policy". In a public meeting in Jullunder on July 4th, Lohia said "The target of the S.S.P. is not merely defeating Congress candidates or driving the Congress from power, but the very liquidation of the Congress. Revolutionary changes and socialism are impossible without this. For defeating the Congress, the opposition parties must come to an electoral agreement and field only one candidate against the Congress".

Party joint-secretary, Prem Bhasin, attacked Lohia's statement: "The aim of the S.S.P. is not destruction of Congress but elimination of exploitation of man by man and of a nation by another nation, in economic, political and cultural fields. The means to be used are democratic and non-violent". Regarding the association between S.S.P. and Dr. Lohia, Prem Bhasin said; "It would be in the interest of all, if the nature of this relation is made explicit". He also criticised Lohia's election strategy. While Lohia was discussing a possible strategy, others talked as if a particular strategy had already been agreed upon. It was indeed a folly particularly for a joint secretary to take such posture before a strategy was finalised. In fact Bhasin wanted to eliminate free discussion. The old malady was again raising its head. He had forgotten even the fundamental fact that the ultimate aim of any opposition party is always removal from power of the party in power.

At this point of time, price rise, scarcity of commodities and starvation were unprecedented. Lohia expressed the opinion that the S.S.P. had failed in organising people's discontent towards the deadly food shortage. The S.S.P. had decided to lead anti-starvation demonstrations on 1st August, but according to Lohia this was 'too late'. "This is like playing games with the masses" he said. Ritualistic satyagrahas were hardly effective. More radical actions were the need of the hour. Lohia suggested, "Advance intimations of morchas are quite unnecessary. Our demand for provision of wheat at the rate of 8 annas a seer, acceptable to the poor, is in itself a notice". Elaborating his nation of a grand 'gherao' said; "Perhaps ten or twenty thousand people will die. In any case what is the bravery in dying of starvation? The deaths during resistance will at least avert the future starvation deaths. Give a call to all parties and masses in large to participate in "sell wheat for 8 annas a seer" programme. People of a village in M.P. took over a godown and sold all grain keeping detailed accounts. This must be emulated everywhere".

The nation faced anarchy. Reports of looting surfaced inspite of attempts to suppress such news. Lohia went to Bihar in the first week of July. He addressed huge mass meetings of lakhs in Patna, Pharbisganj, and few other cities. People were very receptive to Lohia's revolutionary speeches Congressmen were however thoroughly outraged. They campaigned; "Teach him a lesson for condemning Nehru in U.S.A. Receive him with black flags". The capitalist press carried on a systematic propaganda to incite people against Lohia. The Congress weekly in Bihar '*Himalaya Sandesh*' allegedly published fictitious letters to the editor to stir up the people. "Black flags are not enough for him, welcome him with shoes; boycott his meetings", said the letters. Even more it openly preached violence imploring the people to "make sure that Lohia never leaves Bihar" but to no avail. To those who had come to break his meeting under the pretext of his condemning Nehru, Lohia challenged "For whose sake you raise this hue and cry against me? For him who gave jewels to his relations and ashes to the nation?" There were ripples of laughter in the audience "Is it good to spread ashes in the air?" asked Lohia.

In fact the P.S.P. had made election pacts even after the Bhopal resolution, which opposed them. What is more, they were participating in united fronts too. In Trivandrum they were cooperating with the communists, in Poona Corporation with the Hindu Mahasabha, in the Maharashtra Ekikaran Samiti with the communists and in U.P., and in M.P., the politics of united fronts was being practised everywhere. Lohia could not bear with these double standards. He made a full statement. "The recent behaviour of office-bearers of the S.S.P. has confirmed me in my resolve that I can best serve the S.S.P. by not joining it. The trouble arises because its office bearers are unable to define their relations with me. These leaders and chiefs come to me for help and guidance. Their members and units approach me. They must henceforth exercise enough discipline on themselves so as not to come to me. Let no one be afraid. I have no more stomach for a split. I wish to warn those who may be heading towards one and assure those who are nervous that I shall have nothing to do with a split either before or after its occurrence".

Some leaders had made statements from Jullunder, Bhopal and Lucknow, that the S.P.P. will not work with communists and communalists. Lohia warned that party policy in these matters was not decided yet. He said: "Office bearers who act as sole custodians of a party's virtue tend to become prigs. If the S.S.P. is so docile as to allow its office bearers to issue threats of estrangement in its name, what decent person would want to be connected with it? The S.S.P. office bearers are quite good at arranging alliances and agreements with other parties. But there is a difference between what they are continually doing and what I wish to do. Their agreements are impromptu, on the spot, personal, and designed to ensure the election of this or that individual or group. I want to have agreements that would be impersonal and comprehensive so as to heat the people and defeat the government. When all arguments fail the old trick is used and I am accused of inputting motives. I had only talked about the consequences of a certain type of policy. If men may take exception to the phrase 'unprincipled alliances' and 'opportunistic politics', I may say that I have no use for pompousness or perks and hurts and forked tongues of equivocal and inactive people and if these must ultimately prevail, in that event the party will have no use for me either. I have earlier declared that I would campaign only in a constituency where there was one opposition candidate or a serious effort had been made to achieve this condition. Introspection is not strong point of the P.S.P. After deciding in Kerala on electoral adjustments and even alliances, it moved further dangerously and dictatorially to the point of coalition government, not for principle or programme, and just under authorisation of the national committee. If my policy is implemented emphatically and persistently, who but the S.S.P. can emerge as the most in potent force out stick united fronts? I am criticised for taking a negative approach. But I claim to be a socialist with the most constructive and concrete ideas in India or elsewhere. I never discuss motives, but only the consequences of the specific policies. To me, the criticism about the sharpness or propriety of the language do not manner, but ambiguity and inaction are simply too much for me".

Some leaders of the P.S.P. attacked Lohia's election policy while others tried to avoid the issue by proposing postponement of the discussion. But the party was faced with imminent 10 Lok Sabha by-elections, 40 state-legislature bye elections and Kerala general elections. The election strategy just had to be finalised. The adhoc national committee meeting on 16th and 17th August could not come to a decision on the controversial question of cooperation with the parties in struggles. Later Kerala branch passed a resolution regarding electoral adjustments, in a special state convention. Lohia made his position clear: "If the S.S.P. is 51% acceptable I shall join it I am willing to compromise my principles to the extent of 49%". But this bargaining attitude was ridiculed. A certain group began to assert that Lohia and Mehta were anti-socialism to the same extent. Finally Lohia declared, "It is better that I stay away from the S.S.P. in view of the atmosphere of belligerence and suspicion. I shall not become a member of the S.S.P. at least until I know what it wants. I shall serve the Party from outside".

Even the S.S.P. MPs did not cooperate with Lohia. He had a bitter experience once. Lohia moved an amendment to a proposal tabled by the Food Minister Shri Subramaniam. The amendment concerned lavish government spending, enormous food imports etc. all acceptable to S.P.P., but the S.S.P. members abstained during voting on the amendment. Lohia was shocked at this. In the adhoc national committee of S.S.P. there was no unanimity about any policy matter. Everytime the 11 former S.P. members differed from the 14 former P.S.P. members. The main controversial point regarding cooperation with other parties in election and struggles could not be decided upon. Nor was the national convention being called. Even the fact that George Fernandes and Madhu Limaye as representatives of the Hind Mazdoor Panchayat had a meeting with a communist leader, Com. Dange, on invitation, became a point of dispute. The S.P. and P.S.P. members could have acted according to their own judgements till the adhoc committee settled the policies, but even this was being disputed. On top of this stagnation there were the important Lok Sabha by-elections. For opposition these were the prestige seats. A straight fight with the Congress was essential. But Jan Sangh fielded a candidate in Phulpur and Monghyr. A compromise with Jan Sangh could have been arrived at earlier. But when Lohia negotiated, it was too late. In his opinion the S.S.P. was to blame in this matter and hence lost the seat. But Lohia was held responsible for the Phulpur defeat. To this Madhu Limaye retorted, "If Lohia is to get the blame for the Phulpur defeat, he should certainly get the credit for Monghyr victory ".

The anti-Lohia smear campaign had reached a climax. '*Time*' the American weekly published a newsletter under the title 'Nehru's return to politics'. In this issue several mischievous and patently false allegations were levelled against Lohia. Statements he never uttered were attributed to him. Thus for example; "Do not be carried away by the beauty of Vijayalaxmi Pandit. She is pure poison", or "Vijayalaxmi Pandit has undergone plastic surgery" were some of the quotes attributed to Lohia. Lohia demanded an explanation through a legal notice and filed a libel suit. The compensation asked for was 10 paise.

In December 1964, Lohia had to face a very peculiar situation, while engaged in the proper pursuit of his parliamentary work, for the first time in his 15 months in the Lok Sabha. The so-called elite who wanted to condemn Lohia had been waiting for an opportunity to pull Lohia. They had been very concerned about protocols and conventions in the Lok Sabha, but they were disappointed, Lohia unearthed many injustices, electrified the Lok Sabha and managed to work through the tangle of all the laws, customs and rules, thus foiling them. However this particular situation was too much even for his battery of techniques and he was compelled to use the weapon of satyagraha.

The case was as follows: Prime Minister Shastri had accepted the suggestion of withdrawing jeeps from community development blocs. Later some minister said that this was impracticable and a good idea was shelved. On 16th November, Lohia tabled an adjournment morion for failure to act upon the Prime Minister's declaration withdrawing jeeps from community development areas. It's consideration being refused, Lohia raised the matter on the floor of the house on November 17th on the plea that declarations that are not followed by action constitute clowning and fowl debate. A restructured resolution in the form of a motion to censure the Prime Minister was tabled. The speaker admitted the motion for discussion. The parliamentary affairs minister told the house that the motion would be taken up when the Prime Minister returned from his foreign tour, but even fifteen days after his return the motion was not taken up for discussion. It was clear that the government was trying to avoid it. There were only three days left for the closure of the session of Lok Sabha and it was not to meet again for two months. Lohia uncompromisingly insisted upon immediate discussion on his motion. He said: "I would wait for the right action till the last day". But the speaker expressed his total inability. Lohia declared: "Unless and until you do not compel them to act upon their assurances in this House, discussion henceforth is meaningless. I am unable to be a party to it. This issue that I have been trying to raise is not just this or that declaration, it deals with the mind of the people behind it". The speaker was not prepared to agree and Lohia was not ready to give up. Lohia's young colleagues Madhu Limaye. Kishan Patnayak, Ramsevak Yadav, Mahiram Bagdi rallied around Lohia and supported their leader with loud voices. The speaker did not even listen to the pleas made by senior members of other parties like Nath Pai & S.M. Bannerji. The situation became very tense. Meanwhile Vidyacharan Shukla tabled a motion to the effect that Lohia's membership should be suspended for the current session. The speaker disallowed any discussion on this. S.M. Bannerji still insisted that Lohia had repeatedly raised this question before the house and yet the minister for parliamentary affairs had not made up his mind. Nath Pai had also argued that the house had awaited the discussion patiently but the minister had been careless. The Speaker conceded that the matter was serious. H.N. Mukherjee demanded that the treasury benches should be represented by a senior leader. Instead an upstart was proposing suspension of Lohia's membership. Prakashveer Shastri joined him in the feeling that presence of the Prime Minister for parliamentary affairs would have been useful. Shukla's motion was passed (179 in favour and 36 against) Lohia then left the house. The S.S.P. members Madhu Limaye, Ramsevak Yadav, Kishan Patnayak and Maniram Bagdi left the house too. This provoked a controversy. For Lohia was not a member of the S.S.P. and the action of other S.S.P. members was not done in consultation with the leader of the S.S.P. in the house.

At last the date of the national convention that party workers were clamoring for, was set. It was scheduled from 29th to 31st January 1965, at Varanasi. There was all round discussion as to whether Lohia would attend. Lohia had developed a feeling of isolation since the expulsion. It was clear that a large section of the S.S.P. was very vocal in criticising him. His kind of politics was totally unacceptable to them. Lohia was far from interested in waging an interparty struggle in the S.S.P. He said; "I have therefore no intention of using the little energy left of me for internal squabbles. I have only one opponent and that is the present government; which is continuing to ruin the country". Lohia therefore announced; "If the Varanasi conference chairman of the reception committee wishes to hear me, it will have to pass a resolution to that effect, and I shall accept no invitations from any office bearers or committee".

There was a suggestion that Lohia should meet S.M. Joshi. Lohia's reaction to this was; "As an old comrade of the 1942 uprising, and as a human being, S.M. Joshi is always welcome. I have not been able in the past to deny such meetings, even though I knew that they would do no good. If the purposes of this meeting is to strengthen or improve the S.P., Joshi should meet Shri Raj Narain or like persons. If the purpose is to restore personal relations, unhappily suspended six months ago, I would be happy to have it". Commenting on the policy of the left Lohia said: "Nanda and Shastri are about as good or as bad patriots as Gopalan or Rama Murthy. If the latter displayed Mao's photograph at their conference, the former sent messages of success and prosperity to Mao's government. The disease is wide spread, for the national will has weakened and as a nation we lack self-respect. I have no intention whatsoever of leading either a section of the S.S.P. or the whole of it and people insult me when they offer me its leadership. I am today perhaps the most stranded and helpless person in the country and all I want is taking politics to over 95% of the people, who are today without any politics at all".

The founding convention of the S.S.P. opened on the 29th January 1965, as scheduled with S.M. Joshi as the president. For the first time in the history of the Socialists movement there was a record turnout of 1700 delegates and 5000 observers. The socialists from all corners of the nation had gathered with high hopes. The delegates marched in a procession. Both pro-and anti-Lohia slogans were given. There was some exchange of words and even punches. These minor incidents were blown up out of proportion by the press and vested interests. Some former P.S.P. members who had joined Congress were camped in Varanasi in these days. Newspapers in Poona and Bombay even carried bannerlines of exaggerated news of an impending split. The convention proceedings commenced after the procession. Prabhu Narayan Singh referred to Lohia's name in glowing terms and the chairman of the reception committee expressed his regret at Lohia's absence. At this time the P.S.P. leaders lost their tempers and left the pandal. Nonetheless S.M. Joshi's presidential's speech was delivered in a quiet atmosphere. The session began on 30th afternoon. In the meanwhile senior members from both groups, particularly S.M. Joshi strove for continued unity. This was astonishing. There was no justification for the schism. No one pressurised the gathering to invite Lohia. In fact the proposal had come from Vimal Malhotra (P.S.P.) and priority status was sought for it by Prem Bhasin (also P.S.P.). The former S.P. group had not canvassed for this, even though they held Lohia in highest esteem. The P.S.P. proposal regarding representations were also agreed upon. The third point of difference was strategy and programme. A sub-committee was appointed to settle this, of which N.G. Goray was a member. The sub-committee examined three drafts sent by Madhu Limaye, Prof. Mukut Biharilal and the U.P. executive council of the S.S.P. It was agreed that a combined new draft be prepared after giving careful consideration to all three. Any issues on which the committee was divided were to be placed before the general body. On 29th after a night long sitting, the committee was close to fulfilling its objective. But the second day i.e. 30th January, indicated some signs of the impending crisis on the 31st January, the third day of the convention. The Chairman & erstwhile P.S.P. leader S.M. Joshi, declared at the very commencement of the proceedings that 12 out of the 14 P.S.P. members of the adhoc national committee have expressed their desire to quit the convention. This was true. H.V. Kamath, a P.S.P.

member placed before the convention a statement stating their decision to quit. Some untoward incidents during the procession were sought as the reason of their decision to quit. The delegates gave patient hearing to Kamath. After reading his statement Kamath alongwith some other P.S.P. members left the convention. The departure of the dissidents affected nothing. The programme proceeded as scheduled. Only Samar Guha demanded a discussion on Kamath's statement, but once Kamath and his group left the session there was no point in a discussion.

Earlier the Kerala State unit of the S.S.P. which had a total membership of 30,000 (of whom 20,000 were P.S.P. members) had in its general council meeting endorsed unanimously the proposal for electoral adjustments with all opposition parties. This recommendation from the Kerala unit was accepted by the national convention. The statement about election strategy was also passed. Following this the president gave an inspiring and spirited speech. "I am not a general who abandons a battle" thundered S.M. Joshi in his brilliant and intense speech, referring to Lohia's walk out from Parliament, "The democratic spirit is what counts, technique is secondary", he said. Referring to the allegation of a Lohia cult he retorted. Cult of an individual is detrimental to democracy, but character assassination is equally condemnable. I happen to know Lohia for the past three decades. I see nothing wrong with feeling grateful to him for his fundamental thinking which has given Indian socialists philosophy an ideological foundation". About the rift, his reaction was, "Some leaders of the splinter group had really made up their minds even before the Varanasi convention. A whispering campaign was on for nearly month and a half. "Referring to the suspension of Lohia from parliament S.M. Joshi said: "Even after the speaker admitted the protest motion, some attempts were made to prevent it from getting a berth on the programme schedule. Under such circumstances can we condemn Lohia's attempts to seek redress as unparliamentary? In a sense he was offering a satyagraha".

N.G. Goray, President of new P.S.P. made it clear in his article in *Sadhana* a Marathi pro-socialist weekly that the reasons of the split are far beyond idiosyncrasies and personalities. The differences are fundamental. To me defeat of the Congress is not the foremost objective. In fact, it is awakening of the people. And if the Congress is defeated who will replace it?" S.M. Joshi also made it clear that the real issue was not about propriety in parliamentary behaviour or usefulness of united front tactics. The crux is the strategy vis-a-vis the Congress. The P.S.P. people are worried about 'After Congress who? Hence they are not committed to ousting the Congress from the seat of power. A half hearted resistance will only hamper the socialist movement. I shall appeal to the P.S.P. cadre to see beyond personal relations and limitations and make up their mind about the policy.

The Kerala unit of former P.S.P.,17 of the 22 MLA's of P.S.P. in Bihar, 16 out of 19 in U.P., entire Rajasthan P.S.P. unit, 80 out of the 90 representatives from Bengal. 9 of the 11 MLA's from Maharashtra and many others stayed with the S.S.P. The claim of the P.S.P. that the entire former P.S.P. group had split away was pure and simple falsehood. It was held in some quarters that Lohia was responsible for the rift in the Varanasi Convention. Lohia praised S.M. and other leaders in a statement, after the convention. He said that the political decisions of the convention made him change his mind about staying out of the party. He hoped that Peasants' and Workers' Party and Forward Bloc would also merge with the S.S.P. He further said, "The decision to join the S.S.P. would have been so much easier had popular leaders like N.G. Goray, Triloki Singh and Thakur Niranjan Singh decided to remain in the S.S.P. I am proud of S.M.'s dignified image".

By this time the Kerala elections were over and left Communists emerged as the largest single party. The S.S.P. had contested 29 seats and won 13. Kerala emphatically voted anti-Congress in this election. But the Congress flouted all democratic norms and conventions. They made it clear that, to them, it was democracy if we are in majority and dictatorship otherwise. 29 of the 40 elected CRI(M) MLA's were put under detention. All options suggested by the S:S.P. were rejected and President's rule was clamped on the state. Lohia's reaction was. "It is clear from these actions that the Congress in Kerala is no different from Communists and Fascists. Inspite of all my ideological differences with the left communists, I have no hesitation to say that their detention under Defence of India rules is totally illegal. If at all any people were to be detained under that law they are the defence minister, alongwith all the ministers of the Indian Government who had shamelessly accepted the Chinese stand that Long Ju Tishul etc. on the Northern Indian Border, that they were disputed areas".

29. A VOW FULFILLED

On 19th May 1965, Lohia left for a tour of East Germany along with Madhu Limaye, at the invitation of the East German Parliament. Describing his experiences in Soviet Russia and East Germany he said: "In the U.S.A. I can freely condemn President Johnson. I couldn't enjoy such freedom in East Germany and Soviet Russia". Lohia addressed a public meeting in Berlin. The audience applauded his statement: "East Germany deserves international recognition" halfway through, he completed it with the words: "Just as Formosa deserves it". The addendum made the audience very restless. Lohia was not to get any further opportunity of interacting with common citizens in Berlin. Nor could he deliver a speech at the Berlin University, where he was invited as an alumnus, even though it is customary for visiting alumni to do so. Perhaps a premonition of such things that had prompted Lohia to turn down the earlier invitations from the East German Government. After East Germany, Lohia visited Russia for the first time. There he got the chance of discussions with Russian friends in an Institute devoted to the study of Asian affairs. Lohia realised that the Russian protest against the mountain of Chinese misdeeds was no stronger than calling the Chinese "medieval". During the course of discussions Lohia pointed out: "We Indians have a different opinion of China". But it seemed no one was interested in pursuing the point.

At the end of the short foreign tour, Lohia was disgusted. He remarked; "These foreign tours are pointless. You have to be a yes-man. They are no good for the intellectual. Ministers, big government bureaurocrats and capitalists are the right 'caucus' people for foreign visits". A redeeming feature of the otherwise disappointing tour was the opportunity of a leisurely meeting with Abdul Gaffar Khan (Sarhadi Gandhi) at Kabul. Tears rose in Lohia's eyes when the latter warmly embraced him. There were free discussions on many problems such as Indo-Pak relations, Pakhtunistan etc. Lohia urged Sarhadi Gandhi to visit India. Afghanistan was to go to polls. Lohia welcomed the announcement and said that granting adult franchise to women, and too at one stroke in a country where the purdah system prevailed so far, is a grand achievement. I look upon these elections as an exercise in infusing new life into the people. He also held out a suggestion: "If the Afghan government puts up a proposal for regular half-yearly meetings between the Soviet Prime Minister and the American President, it will go a long way. Kabul is like a pearl inset among jewels and I hope trees like chinar, cherry and the like would be planted on the hills overlooking Kabul. Lohia was out of India for just 18 days. However, leaving out the three days spent by him in Kabul, he was up against some trouble or the lather every day. Commenting on this, Lohia said: "This goes to show that something is basically wrong either with me or with society or with both".

War had already broken out in Kutch border area even before Lohia left on foreign tour. Pakistan had attacked India's outposts at Chhadbet and Biarbet on 24th/25th April 1965. Since then Lohia had been grilling the government by persistently pressing for a stem action in war. Earlier China had committed an aggression against India and inflicted on it a crushing defeat. This disgrace was pricking Lohia's heart. So he now took up a challenge to save India from ignominy. He raised a storm. He knew that being a silent spectator or voicing a verbal protest, was of no avail. It was necessary to wage a relentless war. Lohia launched an offensive from within the parliament and also from without. On the floor of parliament he asked the government to clarify whether it was a real war or a sham showing off. The government had already lost a good deal of territory by surrendering Long Ju, Barahoni, Ladakh. Aksai Chin, Kashmir and now Kutch.

The government was saying that rains were due and soon there would be water logging, making all military operations impossible. Lohia was wild with rage over this policy of the government and said: "I am not a war monger. I do not like weapons. But there is no other alternative. Moreover, we are at war. However, Shastriji has made his government an 'earthworm Government' which is as purposeless as the life of earthworm during monsoon. I think I am a useless fellow in as much as I cannot overthrow this government. This government has become so spineless that even after continuously losing territory after territory, it has not yet made up its mind.

Ever since the artificial partition of India, Lohia had started thinking more intensely about Hindu-Muslim problem and Indo-Pak relations. At the beginning of 1950, he had focussed the attention of the people to the repression of the minorities and barbarism in East Pakistan. He raised a voice against the exploitation of East Pakistan. However, government of India always remained passive towards neighbouring countries and named that passivity 'non-alignment' or 'neutrality'. Lohia reminded the government of the warning given by Stalin to India's Ambassador to Moscow, K.P.S. Menon and said, "I am an admirer neither of Stalin nor of communism, However, this is what Stalin said to Menon, I hope you have not come here to talk about Korea etc., as I would like you to talk about India and Pakistan, about how your country was artificially partitioned and how it can be reunited". Lohia alone raised at the time a slogan about Indo-Pak federation and Hindu-Muslim harmony. He organised conferences, took up the ancient practice of 'Raksha-Bandhan' and launched an intellectual movement. He said: "Jarasandh was formed by uniting two pieces of human body. Similarly, Pakistan is made of two unnatural divisions of a country. After all what is Pakistan? It is a prison-house of several communities—Pathans, Baluchis, Sindhis and Bengalis. Fatima Jinnah is up against Ayub regime. Pakistan is like a sand castle. It will fall apart on mere touch. In India we must set up a society in which not only a Hindu and a Muslim be equal but every Hindu will try to become at least half a Musalman if not a full one and vice-versa. To bring down Pakistan, the Muslims will have to be roused. Many people desire to bring about a reunion of India and Pakistan. But that is considered an empty dream. It is asked whether a body, once cut into two, can be joined into one. However, a reunion of India and Pakistan will be reality even if the people of India alone are willing. Under the present circumstances I desire unity between Hindus and Muslims, which could prepare a basis for India-Pak reunion. Women can play a great revolutionary role in this task of uniting the two countries. Whoever looks at Indian Muslims with suspicion strengthens the roots of Pakistan. Suppose a situation arises such that a life of one Muslim cannot be saved without taking the life of one Hindu. Even then the life of that Musalman must be saved. In Indo-Pak conflict we must be harder than steel, but in Hindu-Muslim we must softer than the flower".

Before embarking on the tour of East Germany he organised rallies after rallies at which he propounded that the only way to peace was to create among the people of India and Pakistan a desire to get united by putting an end to the artificial partition. "In the Indo-Pak federation, the two topmost posts viz. the posts of the president and the prime minister will be shared between Pakistan and India. Once a loose federation is formed, questions like Kashmir, East Pakistan and the like will be easy to solve". Formation of a United Bengal is also possible, he said. From 1950 itself Lohia drew attention of the people to the impending repression of East Bengalis. "There is no contradiction between recapturing Kanjar-kot-Biarbet in Kutch from Pakistan and forming an Indo-Pak federation. I am not a warmonger. Yet I am determined to liberate our lost land. While doing it either I may go through with it or I may be no more. Then from my ashes will emerge a new-country". Lohia declared. Lohia's mental agony and unusual imagination again came out. Wall-posters appeared all over Delhi in Lohia's handwriting with the slogan, "Pool all grief". The atmosphere was electrified by this catchy slogan. Lohia not only held martyr Hamid in high respect but regarded him as symbol of Indo-Pak federation and Hindu-Muslim unity.

However Lohia's role was being deliberately distorted. The two big countries—Russia and America did not want India with her six hundred million people to become a powerful nation. As a result their spokesman in India, spoke out their master's mind. Subhadra Joshi, an M.P. demanded in parliament that Lohia be arrested for having raised the question of Indo-Pak federation at a time when the two countries were engaged in war. At this very time Pannalal Dasgupta, an old revolutionary, writing in *Yugantar*—a widely circulated Calcutta daily called Lohia warmonger because he elaborated on the critical military situation in East Pakistan.

By the time Lohia returned from abroad, government had already signed the black 'Kutch Award'. Lohia's mind was overwhelmed with emotions and anguish, anger, agitation, irritation, rage. He had become restless of third time surrender before foreign intruders in Kutch. For one, India had been defeated on her own soil, and for another she could not send troops to her own territory, now held and patrolled by Pakistan. Government contended that it was not a major border dispute, but just a minor one of border adjustments. This contention had already been disproved. So now a move was afoot for setting up a tribunal. While highlighting the situation arising out of Kutch Accord, Lohia said. "So long as there is no thorough consideration of all round relationship with Pakistan, India will slide down from surrender to surrender".

At the emergency meeting of the cabinet subcommittee it was decided that should the aggression the intensified, India would bring in the Air-Force. However, in the course of a few meetings India got a warning from Britain that should India take recourse to air action in pushing back Pak aggression, Britain also would have to act in deference to her commitment to help Pakistan under SEATO or CENTO military agreement. This foreign intervention was unbearable to Lohia. There were number of things which he wanted to bring up. So he requested a debate on Kutch in the parliament. He held that India had a unique weapon, the like of which, Pakistan had none. That weapon was parliament. He said: "Today only the guns of India are roaring, but parliament is silent". As a result of his efforts, parliament became lively. His mental agony gave way to his contemplation of long years broke into words: "Shastriji is tongue-tied, since he is in power. So let me speak out. In the present situation we the opposition parties, are alongside the Government, with the country, and firmly behind the army. This will be highly helpful to Shastriji".

Talks on ceasefire were in full swing. America, Russia and England were exerting their influence. Lohia threw in a point of caution that Britain's Prime Minister Wilson was not a man to go it alone but a man working in close collaboration with America's Johnson. If America were to lose 20,000 square miles of her territory, would any American say, 'Don't defend our land, don't resort to air raids'? So long as question arises about coloured and weak people, these powerful countries do not care or bother whether a particularly territory goes to one country or the other. Britain desires to weaken all countries. The Security Council passes resolutions on weak and helpless nations but none on Vietnam, America, Hungary or Russia. The Prime Minister should make a clear statement that there will be no ceasefire unless our lost territory is regained".

The Prime Minister gave an assurance that he would not surrender even an inch of territory whatever the circumstances, nor would be lag behind in doing the needful. However, when talks were held between the Prime Minister and the Secretary General of the U.N., a suspension lurked in Lohia's mind. He gave a warning in the Lok Sabha: "Talks on cease fire are in progress at the moment. I do not desire to say anything on that, nor have I any strength to do it. My word has no value. However, action for crushing the military arrogance of Pakistan must go on, till a ceasefire is announced. If China attacks and drops atom bomb we shall fight even if alone. If we survive, we shall start over life anew. If we don't Role shall cease to be for some time".

Newspapers had commented that in the event of our capturing Lahore, we would not be able to feed the 20 lakh of people there nor would we be able to administer that city. To this Lohia replied: "Once we were out in the field, there must be no hesitation in our mind nor any fear in our heart. We must catch hold of whatever we can, put an end to 'that India which is Bharat', and finish off Pakistan to once again bring to our mind the image of our cherished ideal of Hindustan".

After the government signed the 'Kutch Award', Lohia said in the Lok Sabha, "This war has thrown up just one sentence which can be remembered arid shall be remembered as a noteworthy sentence. That sentence is: "No longer shall India go from one cease fire to another". This was a grand lofty sentence no doubt. But it turned out to be a mere meaningless gabble. As before we continued to go from one cease fire to another. The word 'secularism' came to be widely used during this war. I am to be kindly excused if I say that very few people have understood its meaning. Unconcern with religion is just a small aspect of it. Secularism means worldliness".

According to Lohia the war between India of 40 crore and Pakistan of 10 crore population, was like a fight between an elephant and a buffalo—an absolutely insignificant manner. Hence, while opposing the impending danger, Lohia said: "Sometimes I begin to feel that Ayub Khan or Bhutto on the one hand and our fellows on the other have possibly have got some unwritten or unspoken understanding between them, that for sometime they should put their countries at war and then for sometime under tension so that during the period of tension they can tighten the grips of their parties in their respective countries. Don't say only that, 'we shall not surrender even an inch of our territory nor grab even an inch of the other's territory', say also that Pakistan belongs to Bharat.

Regarding the land of Pakistan, Lohia said, "It is not the land of the enemy. It is our land. Don't trample on it. Love it. The government there is atrocious. But the people there; men and woman are ours". Lohia regarded 'the border of the country as analogous to the skin of man. He contended that just as scratching of the skin makes one uneasy, so also nibbling at the frontiers of the country should make one restless.' In parliament, he said, 'Just as two rivers meet at a confluence, the sight of which gives us delight and which therefore becomes a holy place, so also the border between two countries becomes either a holy place or battlefield. But the government of India had no appreciation for such hair-raising delight. Neither did it make the border a place of pilgrimage nor save it from becoming a battlefield. Instead it left it, as it was, as a desolate, depopulated, desert".

While talking about 'Border Roads', Lohia cautioned the government against smuggling, since the border area had become a base for smuggling operations at several points. He was so much in anguish over the incidents in the Rann of Kutch that he broke his vow. Lohia continued; "When for the first time after independence, people died due to famine and I was teargased in the capital, I took a vow not to meet the Prime Minister of India on my own. Excepting the vow of not sitting on a man driven rickshaw, I have broken all other vows. Similarly today also, forced by necessities of foreign policy, I broke the vow of not meeting the Prime Minister. According to my experience, the Prime Minister is the modest man with serious nature, pleasing disposition and amiable character. However, I do not know whether or not all these qualities will have any influence on anything. I prefer a short tempered man, capable of flexible approach, to a modest man of just moderate ability. I hope the Prime Minister becomes as active as he is modest".

Prime Minister Lal Bhadur Shastri specially thanked Lohia for his sounds suggestions. Shastriji expressed this in English. Thereupon Lohia asked him to talk to Ayub Khan in Hindi. Shastriji was to visit Soviet Union on an invitation from Kosigyn, the chairman of the council of ministers of the Soviet Union. Lohia made Shastriji some suggestions for being conveyed to Ayub Khan at Tashkent. In a speech in the parliament but meant for and addressed to the Prime Minister of the Soviet Union and the Presidents of America and Pakistan, Lohia said: "I desire to convey to the Prime Minister of the Soviet Union that when there is no possibility of settlement on Kashmir alone, the only alternative left is not that of the security council, namely cease fire, then withdrawal of troops to the positions of 5th August, and finally mutual discussion on Kashmir, but the formation of some sort of a federation, even a loose federation of both countries. Similarly I shall appeal to the President of Pakistan that he should change the policy followed by Pakistan last 18 years, so that our united country, will be the most powerful one not only in Asia, but in the entire world. Looked at from another angle, India will be the biggest Islamic country in the world. "I appeal to the American President, Mr. Johnson, that, without entering into any kind of competition, his country, undoubtedly the most powerful in the world, should somehow change it's policy of the last 18 years and bring to this country such prosperity that the entire world will hail the real peaceful co-existence between American democracy world and Russian communism and proclaim that these countries have transferred this world into a fine place by putting an end to the reviling relationship and setting an example for the world to follow".

The S.S.P. observed general strike on 1st August. Copies of 'Kutch Accord' were burnt. 'Win the war' week was observed. The President of the S.S.P., S.M. Joshi, announced that volunteers would be sent to the Kutch border. Similarly, a movement was launched on a large scale demanding supply of foodgrains and prevention of starvation deaths. The movement became as powerful as the 'Quit India movement' of 1942. Everywhere Satyagraha, bandh, gheraos started, accompanied by a chain of arrests, lathi-charges and firings. Lohia visited the Rann of Kutch at the end of July to inspect the advance posts there. While going there he made an announcement: "If the government shamelessly disregards the feelings of the people and does not change its policy then after 31 December 1965, the people will try to fulfil their pledge of pulling down the Government with their entire organised strength. "Before the end of 1965, either my pledge will be fulfilled or I shall be no more. If the Government holds fast to selfish party interests, we shall have to brave the bullets. Many volunteers have expressed their resolve to uphold the honour of our country. They will face the bullets of the Congress government but will not move away from the Parliament".

At this very time China threatened an attack on India. Lohia called China the 'Hitlerite Germany' of this age. While emphasizing the need to become steeled for fighting the Chinese power, he said: "A man like me would like to say that after the attack, the savage beast of Peking must be hunted out of the caves of Tibet and finished off. Our armies must chase that beast out of our country and capture the caves of Tibet, just as our armies had done by going right up to Sialkot or Lahore. This Kutch accord will be followed by a chain of surrenders and wars. If we go on voluntarily parting away with parts of our land one after another. A time will come when India will have no land left for further Bhoodan. Can we expect such a cowardly government to fight? Some people ask, "What is there in a desert or a marsh?" I would like to ask, Why do the British not give away their rocks of Dover? New York is a small Island. Why does America not give it away to somebody? If something happens in Cuba or Panama, a call is given for a world war, since it's heat may reach America. So let us resolve that India will not be allowed to be mutilated. This resolve alone will bring about a revolution. People ask why all our outposts are deserted. Our volunteers will occupy them. The alternatives before us are clear: Federation or War".

In those days the enemies of the S.S.P. tried to bring about a split between S.M. Joshi and Lohia but they could not succeed as there was the perfect agreement between the two of them. The President of the S.S.P., S.M. Joshi said, "On 25th November, the Parliament will be 'gheraoed'. This time their the demonstrators will not dispose unless their demands are conceded. The Parliament will be submerged in the vast ocean of the people. The S.S.P. volunteers will occupy deserted outposts".

Lohia addressed two crowded public meetings at Bhuj and Anjar near Kutch border. Government extended all possible facilities to its; Indian and foreign friends for visit of the border. However no facility was given to Lohia although it had been promised by central minister earlier, that the facility of the motorcar or an aeroplane would be made available to him as far as possible. On returning to Delhi from Kutch, Lohia made a statement: "With the garrulity of the Prime Minister about peace, non-violence and arbitration and his attempt to play double of the saint and the Prime Minister, war is coming nearer. After Kutch is surrendered to Pakistan, peace will last at the most for about a year. Then war will break out for Kashmir. After giving away Kashmir, there will be peace for only six months. Again there may be a war for a corridor across our country between East Pakistan and West Pakistan. Even after surrendering our and for the corridor, there may not be peace even for 3 months".

The entire country had become a battlefield. Cities looked like military camps. The Army was being used to suppress people's struggles. Non-violent people were fired upon at Patna, Indore, Kolhapur and other places. Thousands of people were detained in jails. 9th August was observed as 'Patna Bandh' day. The struggle became intensive. Government tried to suppress it with the help of mounted police. Food grains in Bihar were being sent to the Chinese enemy by smugglers, while people were dying of hunger, however, no action was being taken against smugglers. In Patna, the movement became violent. Lohia addressed a public meeting of lakhs of people. He exhorted the people to eschew violence and carry on the struggle by peaceful democratic means. Even then, Lohia was arrested on the 9th August, under Section 30 of the Indian Security Act and kept in Hazaribagh jail. Large-scale arrests were made in Maharashtra also. Prominent leaders and workers were imprisoned under Indian Security act. The movement was particularly strong in Bihar, Bengal and U.P. On the 16th August, Parliament was going to have debate on Kutch accord. Lohia sent telegrams to the Lok Sabha Speaker and the Chief Justice of India requesting release so as to enable him to participate in the debate. In the telegram, Lohia had alleged that his arrest had been motivated by an intention to prevent him from participating in the parliamentary debate. He had further requested that his telegram itself might be treated as an application for his release since under the prevailing circumstances it was impossible for his petition to reach in time under normal procedure. The action taken against Lohia was not for the defence of the country but of the Congress government itself. The height of the situation was that two organs of the government viz. the non-gazetted employees and the police were at daggers drawn, and attacking each other. After the arrest Lohia was made to sit on chair from midnight to 6 o'clock in the morning and taken thereafter to a place 150 miles away in a police van in which had been accommodated 10 armed police and 5 prisoners. Ram Iqbal Singh and Revatikant Singh, the president and ex-president respectively of the non-gazetted Government Employees' Union, had been arrested. This was a representative organisation of the majority among the 1,80,000 Class III and class IV employees of the Bihar government.

While arguing over the petition against his arrest on 26th August 1965, Lohia asked for permission to speak in Hindi. Justice Mudholkar said: "If you so desire, it is perfectly justified. However, it will be better and more convenient for the court if you address in English since most of us here do not understand much of Hindi".

While accepting the suggestion of the court, Lohia said, "I had taken a pledge that in public matters I would speak in Hindi only, so if I break my pledge now, it would be negating my belief. But I am not a free man. My freedom of self expression is in fetters". Lohia said: "My arrest" under Security of India Act is an indication of the conspiracy between the government of Bihar and the Central government. I have been arrested on 4 counts: (1) to punish me for my statements against the ministers and officers of Bihar, (2) to stop me from appraising the people of Bihar of real situation, (3) to avenge my activities, and (4) to prevent me from participating in the forthcoming debate in Lok Sabha. I could not even imagine that I would be arrested under the 'Security of India Act' on a charge of threatening the security of my own country".

While discussing his constitutional position Lohia challenged the validity of his arrest under Section 30 of the Security of India Act and said: "According to Section 32 of the constitution every citizen has a right to submit a petition to the supreme court for the protection of fundamental rights". Lohia's petition had been under the consideration of the constitutional bench of the Supreme Court. The bench consisted of honourable Justice Hidayatullah, Honourable Justice Raghuvir Dayal, Honourable Justice Mudholkar and Honourable Justice Bachhavat. The hearing continued for 4 days. On the 7th September, the bench of judges ordered the release of Lohia. All judges except Raghuvir Dayal declared that the District Magistrate's order of arrest was illegal. It was pointed out that there was difference between 'public order' and 'law and order'. It was also pointed out that if anyone was kept under house arrest under the 'Security of India Act' and the attendant provisos, it was imperative that the law and provinces must be scrupulously observed, especially when a person was deprived of his fundamental rights When released, Lohia thought it better to spend a day at home and have rest instead of attending the parliament. He said, "I have already realised what prestige a small man like me has got in the biggest legislative body of India, our parliament. At least for a day I have got a right to show how much regard is left in me for the parliament. This was Lohia's second victory at the Supreme Court. This time the Supreme Court didn't give the Government of India a chance to avoid confrontation or to release Lohia under some pretext and claim credit. On the 18th September the victorious Lohia was greeted in the Parliament amidst thunder of clapping and tumultuous uproar.

The day of the fulfillment of Lohia's vow had come, the ink on Kutch Accord had hardly dried, when Pakistan attacked Kashmir again. Lohia's prophecy had come true. He had already warned earlier that although the Rann of Kutch was a swamp, the road to Lahore was clear, and circumstances had forced the country and the government to go that way. That was why for the first time on 6th September 1965, the Shastri Government launched a counterattack on Pakistan and replied the Pakistani aggression with the counter aggression. The persistent efforts of Lohia was crowned with success. Lohia and the S.S.P. were determined to get the government pledged to a definite policy regarding the Rann of Kutch. Lohia was pleased, and said; " I would have been pleased to adore the Prime Minister and pat him on the back. However, I am not doing so since he has already shown cold feet even before reaching Lahore and Sialkot".

Then a question arose about the Kashi University; which had been founded in Varanasi by Pandit Madan Mohan Malviya in 1916. This very name has been inscribed on the foundation stone laid in 1916. The words 'Kashi University' have been inscribed on every brick of the university. An attempt was being made by some persons to introduce the word 'Hindu' in the name of the university. According to Lohia such people, whether knowingly or unknowingly, are harming not only Hindus but the whole country. There is something basically wrong with their outlook or mental makeup. This is the part of the conflict going on between liberal Hindus and the orthodox Hindus for the past 1200 years. Lohia had no desire to enter into the dispute of Kashi University alias

Banaras Hindu University. However the Congress government—in Lohia's words the beautiful wife' first stirred up a conflict and then drew away.

The government got the name 'Kashi University' passed in Rajya Sabha but dropped it in Lok Sabha as soon as some trouble arose. Commenting on this trait of the government, Lohia very often used to say: "We should not rouse a snake, but if we do we should not leave it alive. These people have roused the linguistic feelings and done nothing to pacify them. For these 17 years these people rouse a snake but do not know how to kill it. "The name of educational institutions should not be indicative of religion, or caste, at least not of those receiving government aid. Kashi is perhaps the oldest city in the world. Like the names Mathura, Athens or Rome, the name of Kashi also takes you back to the grand history of ancient civilisation of man and his traditions".

After signing the Tashkent Treaty on 10th January 1966, the Prime Minister Lal Bhadur Shastri died of heart failure. The Tashkent treaty was an insult to the nation. It was a treaty of retreat. Whatever India gained by war was offset by the treaty. Not only had the outposts at Hajipur, Kargil been given up, but the one sided acceptance by India of non-interference in the internal affairs of Pakistan, was of the principle tantamount to the betrayal of Badshah Abdur Gaffar Khan. Pakistan looked upon Jammu and Kashmir as its own territory and continued infiltration into it. Lohia contended that by signing the treaty government of India had acknowledged the right of Pakistan to interfere in India and liberate Kashmir. While addressing the condolence meeting after Shastriji 's death. Lohia said: "I do not weep or mourn. However, amongst the aggrieved my grief is most profound. Every death is sad. But the death of a good man and that too of the Prime Minister of a great country is all the more so. The Prime Minister had stated 4 or 5 times in Lok Sabha and also outside that Hajipur would not be returned. I do not understand anything about a heart attack, but I do have some experience of the feelings of uneasiness due to excessive rise or fall in blood pressure. For the last 18 years the atmosphere prevailing in the country has been foul. However, it has neither been able to crush the spirit of independence or fearlessness. In 1965 this spirit appeared to be on the top and was in the winning position against the foul atmosphere. Then it looked as if the age of devotion to duty is coming, the name of Shastri had been associated with this upcoming age. In fact this had been his great fortune. Had he been able to understand this and courageous enough to grasp it then instead of being a mere spokesman he would have become a leader, and instead of sly manipulator, he would have become a pioneer. In that far-off country also he had his own servant, own doctor and own security personnel. However, when his heartbeat became feebler and 'feebler with pain become more and more severe, he trembled all over as he tried to get up from his bed. There was no arrangement attached to his bed for calling on attendant, neither a call-bell, nor a bell-switch, not even a bell rope. Such an arrangement was absolutely necessary. Since he was heart patient had already got two attacks earlier, and was engaged particularly strenuous work. Inspite of the splendid grandeur and unnecessary expenditure the nation sees its own reflection in the Prime Minister at the time of his death. Today I can well understand the grief of Smt. Lalitadevi, when she says: "Had I been there! "

After Shastriji, Indira Gandhi became the new Prime Minister. This had been prophesied by Lohia 8 years earlier when she became Congress president. To Lohia this looked like a link in the chain of selfishness. At that time he had also stated that under feudalism the heirship passed on to the progeny, but under democracy such an example is anomalous. After Indira Gandhi had become the Prime Minister in January 1966, Lohia said: "My reaction today is no different from that 8 years ago, that we would get an opportunity of seeing a beautiful face every morning. But it would be very tough going for Smt. Gandhi, since she would be required to carry on under the pressure of the sins of her father and Shastri. She has neither a sickle of morals to weed out wild grass, nor a compass to steer the boat of the country. Besides, she is more or less short tempered. It is my foreboding that there are bad days in store for her and the Indian people. Congress party is a cemetery of morals and a corpse of thoughts. It is a conglomeration of persons distrustful of each other".

Indira Gandhi was elected with a majority. The method of defeating a rival by securing a majority is healthy for an organisation only when the majority and the minority are at least partially influenced by thoughts and morals. While highlighting this situation, Lohia said: "Minor things apart, there is no one who has got outstanding personality with a distinctive characteristic of his own. A certain person may have a beautiful face. Another one may be adamant about prohibition. A third one may be particularly liberal in giving more posts to backward class persons, but all are of the same kind—petty selfish persons & conspirators and stereotypes continually changing patterns of collusion and collision all meant to serve; petty interests and aggrandisements".

30. IMPROVE OR QUIT

With the election of Indira Gandhi as the Prime Minister after Lal Bahadur Shastri, a rather a peculiar situation was created for Lohia. Prior to 1947, Lohia had close relations with the Nehrus including Indira Gandhi. Then again being an ardent crusader for the emancipation of women. Lohia naturally had a soft corner for women irrespective of their class, caste, party affiliation, etc. Hence Lohia wanted to wait and see how Indira Gandhi functioned before deciding upon his tactics to deal with her. After the few days Lohia declared in the Lok Sabha; "During the first three weeks, I was working under self imposed restraint because she is little younger than me and I wanted to give her some time to know her job. But her style of functioning suggests that she is answering question in the house like a robot. They are like a set of gramaphone records. One record says 'Yes.' Another one says 'No.' A third one says, "Government will not do anything against national interests or national honour". A fourth one says, 'Old policies will continue. We shall not flinch even an inch from them.' There are yet other records which go on blurting out such senseless stuff".

On another occasion, Lohia said, "The Prime Minister is virtually a living doll. She is also exceedingly sloppy in her ways of speech. It is difficult to think of thought in relation to her. Had she not spoken at all, things would perhaps have been better. Or else had she been just a doll at that and not a living person, her role as a talking-machine or a parrot could have been understandable. However, now it is clear enough, that neither has she any capacity to think, nor any ability to talk. In order to become a Prime Minister, one need not be a great thinker nor a good speaker. A Prime Minister can be great if he or she has courage, organisational skill and executive ability. The ability to give a lead to cabinet of 15 ministers and with their help to govern the country, is the supreme quality essential for donning the mantle of Prime Ministership. Leadership entails giving a proper orientation to the government policy, by instilling life into the people and leading the country in a specific direction with speed and strength. "Whenever the Prime Minister speaks, it is easily seen that her talk is devoid of direction, clearly enough, there is no governance in India. Whatever is there is nothing but administration. The country is administered by government servants and bureaucrats whose sole function is to look after the 48 crore people in the country".

Under the regime of Indira Gandhi, the ruling clique continued the legal lawlessness with falsehood, coercion and intimidation in the name of enforcement of law and order. The traditional modes of resistance such as satyagraha proved ineffective. The scattered incidents only gave an excuse to the government for further repression. The majority group denied the opposition any chance of reasonable dissent on the floors of the legislative houses, and the Speaker did not offer due protection to the rights of dissenting legislators. The economic situation had become fearsome; Rupee had been devalued under external pressures, inflated money supply had pushed the price line upwards. Describing this scene Lohia said, "Posterity will rightly criticise us that they have been burdened not with development loans but borrowing for day-to-day consumption".

The murder of justice continued unabated under the Indira regime. Violence continued ceaselessly as exemplified by the merciless killings in Bastar. Bastar is a district of Madhya Pradesh. It is situated in the far eastern part of the state and is the biggest district in India. 72% of the people here belong to scheduled adivasi tribes and other scheduled castes. Maharaja Pravinchandra Bhanjdev, the ex-ruler of Bastar, was declared insane in 1953, by the then Congress government of the state. The same Congress Party then got him elected to the state assembly in 1957. He contended that the Adivasis in Bastar were subjected to terrible atrocities. They enjoyed no freedom, no rights under the Constitution. The land there was being distributed freely to outsiders and the local adivasis were denied not only land but their traditional right to collect wood from the jungles as well. It appeared as though the government had entered into a conspiracy to convert Bastar into a future Nagaland by mercilessly suppressing the adivasis and exploiting them with help of the police,

Since October 1965, fire of hunger was burning in Bastar, It's northern part was caught in the grip of famine. Levy was being collected illegally. The Maharaja observed a hunger strike from 13th to 20th February to draw the attention of the government to the atrocities committed by the police and the government officers against the Adivasis while collecting the levy on 9th February 1966. Repression was let loose again on 18th March 1966. About 400-500 Adivasis-men and women were carrying logs from jungle for some religious ceremony. The policemen fell upon them and be laboured them. Pravinchandra Bhanjdev mediated between the police armed with guns and the adivasis armed with bows and arrows, and saved the situation. On 25th March, the police opened fire inside the Maharaja's palace compound. Hundreds of adivasis were killed. Pravinchandra Bhanjdev was implored to come out of his palace to pacify the crowds, and as soon as he came out, he was brutally killed by the police with 8 bullets. Authentic first hand information about this incident was conveyed to Lohia by Shri S.M. Joshi. Subsequently 6 adjournment motions and 18 'call attention' notices were brought before the parliament. The adjournment motions were rejected. S.S.P. MP's like Ram Sevak Yadav, Madhu Limaye and Kishen Patnaik, who repeatedly insisted on a discussion, were suspended from the house for 2 weeks. Ultimately the Speaker gave permission to an ordinary discussion on the motion of Shri Ranga. While talking on that motion, Lohia raised some fundamental questions. He demanded the appointment of a permanent commission for investigation of government firings and rioting, "It should be made the duty of the commission to visit the place of disturbance and carry investigate each rioting and government firing on such riots". The judge appointed by the state government for the investigation of the case was a relative of the Chief Minister and was partial. The Speaker did not allow any discussion in the Parliament since the subject matter was sub-judice. Thereupon Lohia said, "Though it is improper to have a discussion on the action of the administrative officer as the matter is subjudice. I should like to say that if the Prime Minister, Home Minister or any Minister in M.P. has got a hand in the incident, the House must have a right to expose him before the public, since it is a political responsibility. While discussing this point it has become imperative to discuss about violence also. Violence has a special quality to choose a weaker opponent to get beaten by a stronger one. I abhor violence. Even now I am not prepared to accept that people should resort to violence to counter government violence. The violent hand of the government assassin is already on the move in our country. This hand struck Bhanjdev, so also Sakharam Nagey. The killer of the people may be born and will be born see his hand advancing for rolling the head and piercing the chest of the Home Minister and also the Prime Minister".

In March 1966, people's struggle in Calcutta became violent. Lohia went round the city and with a heavy heart gave a warning, "If we want to save our country from ruin, we must eschew violence. What are we upto in our country these days? Boys of 12-14 years attacking a solitary policeman with brickbats and stones and mercilessly hammering his head! Cruelty has reached such a stage as to burn alive human beings by setting their houses on fire. All this goes to show that warp and woof of our national fabric are in bad shape and we must do something to save our nation".

At the Kota convention of the S.S.P. Lohia said, "This undesirable trend has to be checked, if possible by non-violence, and if ever necessary by organised violence. First of all we must stop the cruel killings in mob violence. Next, we must, if possible, halt violence by organised, all-out mass non-violence. If this also is not feasible, the third alternative to arrest violence would be to forcibly occupy the Secretariat, radio stations etc. by organised violence. Possibly, the day is not far away when the army will refuse to kill their won countrymen as the army is meant to fight invaders".

When compared with the power of the Soviet Union or the United States, power of the Indian Government is insignificant, however as compared to the power of the population, the government power is tremendous in the form of battalions and bullets. Highlighting this position, Lohia said; "The Home Minister always gets excited. One who wields power, must keep his head cool like ice. If he gets excited, he might become a demon".

On the 10th May 1966, the opposition members on the U.P. assembly brought the proceedings of the house to a halt. In 1950, the U.P. government had promised that there would be no further increase in the land revenue, however, now it had gone back on its word and enhapced the land revenue. The atmosphere had already become surcharged with various, problems like price rise, medium of instruction etc. Students and government servants were fighting for their rights with all their might. Lathi-charge and firing had become the order of the day. A call had been given for a U.P. bandh on 12th July. While he was on his way to Kanpur in connection with the bandh, Lohia was arrested on 11th July, under Section 144, and was sent to Agra Jail. At the press conference for the month of July, the Prime Minister Mrs. Indira Gandhi, called Lohia an advocate of violence. Since a case against him was already pending in the court, Lohia served Indira Gandhi with a legal notice asking her to withdraw charges against him, failing which he would proceed to the court of law for legal action against her. Lohia was released on bail. The hearing took place on 11th and 12th August. Lohia contended that Section 144 was already incorporated in Section 188 and both of them together ran counter to Section 19 of the Constitution.

When Lohia was in Agra jail he came across a prisoner named Tota alias Baba, who had been sentenced to death. Lohia tried to save him from the gallows. Lohia always used to say, "A man may be kept in jail for life but should never be hanged. What kind of creatures are we who take the life of others?" Lohia's efforts in saving Tota's life were of no avail. Ultimately he was hanged. When Lohia learnt about it he was restless for the whole day. A little earlier he had heard about the case of a doctor who had been responsible for the death of several persons and yet his sentence of death by hanging had been rescinded, since he was a big man.

Demonstrations, gheraos, bandhs etc. and along with them firings also reached an all time high in 1966. On 7th November 1966, sadhus held a huge demonstration outside the Parliament for a ban on cow-slaughter, they were indiscriminately fired upon. Countless dead bodies lay scattered all around. There was a big row over this in the Parliament resulting in the resignation of the Home Minister Gulzarilal Nanda. Shri Yeshwantrao Chavan became the new Home Minister. Incidentally a mass rally of students had already been planned in Delhi on 18th November. The new Home Minister's reacted with ruthless opposition. Early at night on 15th November, Lohia and three others were arrested under Sections 107 and 151. Delhi presented the appearance of a battle field, about 20,000 armed policemen had been posted in the city at various squares with orders to shoot at sight.

The fire of unrest was running riot in the student world. As a measure against this, government opened police stations within the university campuses and declared Section 144 of the Indian Security Act in those area. This added fuel to the fire. Most of the teachers and professors had only a limited aim of earning their livelihood, there was neither security nor charm left in their life. The ghost of unemployment was starting in the face, there were neither good houses to live in nor sufficient food to eat, everywhere students were treated like animals. This had greatly affected their minds hearts. There were no noble ideals before them. A very strange situation, a state of suffocation indeed! On the one hand, the government was entreating the students to remain aloof from politics, on the other their environment was rousing them to revolt. Lohia knew their pulse.

While explaining how the roadroller of repression had been let loose all around, he said, "An Indian is like a rather wretched creature. He is extremely unhappy, the whole day he hears the harsh words of his boss or officer, whether in the field, or the road, in the factory, or at the shop, and has no courage to return like for like. He spends whole day brooding over his miserable life and on returning home, fuming with rage, he lets loose his anger towards his wife, a poor soul indeed!, she cannot retort. The only way she can give vent to her anger is to slap her helpless children. This is a vicious circle which must be broken-Oft do I think, I sould build up a party of only children".

Lohia pinpointed the grievances of the youth; "An average student passing with a second or third grade cannot enter the college or university. But sons and daughters of ministers go to Europe or North America for further studies inspite of failing here. There is no justice in the world, only the whims and wishes of the big people prevail. What kind of impression all this must leave on the minds of the young people? There is no civilised country in the world in which failure rate is more than ten percent. Ours is the only miserable land where half or more of the candidates fail in an examination. What is the consequence? How does this affect the impressionable minds? They have worked for years, tried their best and yet failed. And these motorcar wallahs, the way they drive, it seems they are practising the art of splashing mud on pedestrians. These contradictions stand now out very vividly.

Women, backward castes, untouchables and tribals will all join the fray. Women's hearts are being trampled upon. Perhaps the Indian youth have lost some of the integrity, perseverance in studies or discipline, but on one count they come out with a better grade than the earlier generation, and that is fearlessness. We are all split personalities and the Government wants to split us further apart and make us into an incorrigible split society. The student movement or any other movement has no option but to develop further and smash this society devoid of justice and equality so that a new society may emerge in which the component parts are in harmonious complementarity. "The injustice manifesting itself has pained the hearts of the youth as it was bound to. So chaos and split are now inevitable".

Lohia filed a petition in the count against his arrest. The hearing was fixed by the High Court for 23rd November but government released Lohia on 22nd November itself. This was the fourth time that history had repeated itself in respect of the arrest and release of Lohia. He was arrested at Mysore in 1951. He filed a habeas corpus petition against this illegal arrest with the result that he was released before the court got an opportunity to take a decision on Lohia's petition. In 1955 also the government had released him in a similar situation. In 1957 when Lohia knocked at the gates of the Supreme Court against his arrest, the government ran away from the battlefield to save its face.

Members of the opposition in the Lok Sabha raised a voice of protest against the arrest of Lohia. Some time earlier, while ordering the release of Balraj Madhok of Jan Sangh the court had given a verdict that his arrest under Section 15 was illegal. So the members of the opposition had now raised a question in the Lok Sabha about the privileges of an MP. Several members criticized the government on this occasion. Nirmal Chandra Chatterji, a legal expert, by quoting a precedent from the House of Commons, showed that it was illegal to arrest Lohia for an offence other than a criminal one, within 40 days of either the commencement or the end of the parliament session. Lohia severely attacked the government for its policy of illegally arresting a person and then letting him off through cowardice on the persons filing of a habeas corpus petition.

Lohia encountered many difficulties in organising the opposition. He was opposed to any fronts, right or left. Whatever the strategy of a leftist front, in fact it helped the Congress and the government to defeat the right wingers. Similarly a non-communist front helped the Congress against the communists, whatever the strategy of the front. These strategies always seemed to spoil the opposition ethic. He noticed that leadership of all parties was again fast. The average age was 45. The age difference between the leaders and followers naturally created a communication gap between leaders and rank and file of the parties. Jan Sangh and Communist were similar in their tactics as opposition; both were dogmatic. Lohia said that the Jan Sangh had absorbed all the merits and demerits of Hinduism. It accommodated all contradictions in life, word, deed and strategy and still stayed in one piece. It played one against the other and managed to grow in the process. In life, disjointedness, in words, political and cultural unity of India, democracy etc., in tactics, opportunism and indeed petty selfishness. Communists have their own brand of international dogma. They are an example of the unbelievable extent to which such dogmatism can make you blind. They have no respect for nation's frontiers, at least not until some years after they have taken over country to them national boundaries are not sacred. In their thought process the focus is not India, nor the world at large but some external power. Once they are installed in power, matters will change. When China was eating away India's frontiers they were diverting attention to Cuba, and as Pakistan manoeuvred to gobble the Rann of Kutch, communists were diverting attention to Vietnam. All must understand that conceding of our territories to China and Pakistan and co-existence of lush green golf and racing grounds in New Delhi alongside 5 lakh hutment dwellers are two faces of the same social reality. I await the day when people will take over golf greens".

With the two programmes of "Indo-Pak federation", "Hindu-Muslim amity" and the struggle against the name of Banaras Hindu University and for changing it to Kashi University, Lohia had completely aritagonised the R.S.S. and Jan Sangh. R.S.S. had resorted to stone-throwing and other tactics of disrupting his meetings in Deoria, Varanasi, and Gorakhpur. Thus as Lohia assessed as hopeless the situation vis-a-vis communists and Jan Sangh, the internal affairs of the S.S.P. turned out equally painful. The S.S.P. had resolved that a candidate defeated in general election should not seek a backdoor entry to the Parliament via indirect election to Rajya Sabha. But Raj Narain who was very close to

Lohia did precisely that. Lohia held that upper houses of state and central legislatures were really meant to divide further, weak parties. He want on to suggest that indirect elections should be disallowed for these people.

Those were the days when every party was infected by groupism. Lohia called these groups subparties. They were not based on principles. And Lohia resented any activity contrary to party rulings unless and until such acts and splits were based on some dear principles. That is why he had opposed the move to quit Congress in 1947. Politics was in doldrums because there was not enough dedication around and politicians were desperate for positions of power. This twisted their minds so much that they forgot even the basic civil courtesies. Lohia knew that the very people who criticised the tactics of divide and rule, later resorted to it. He said, "India today needs upright people. We want a group that can combine understanding and patience. They must not be shaken by incidental happenings and must be able to concentrate on special change. If their leadership loses way they must bear with it with courage. I am afraid, all parties, the S.S.P. included, have failed to project a mature image, and failed to control the direction of events. Yet I believe that the masses will reach their goal inspite of the setbacks. This may of course take time. A ten day strike by government servants is an event unprecedented in the entire history of the country".

In such an atmosphere, Lohia was trying to build up opposition to the Congress. The S.S.P. had already been engaged from about two and half to three years in the tremendous task of preparing the people for bringing down the Congress. According to Lohia, the political parties in India could be considered as divided into two groups; the government party and all non-government parties. The government party has got an advantage of the services of 1,25,00,000 employees, a capacity to spend 5500 crore rupees a year and countless means of temptation and terror.

Lohia said, "Congress is well-versed in instigating the people to follow mutually antagonistic paths. Any party, when in power for several years, becomes more or less lethargic. Abandoning the path of ideas and ideals, it follows the path of convenience. Lohia felt that the dream of achieving unity between the opposition parties had withered away. All of them have long since abandoned all attempts to defeat the Congress and secure a majority. The opposition parties have always been fighting among themselves on various issue, like patriotic vs. unpatriotic, communalism vs. nationalism, leftist vs. rightists, democracy vs. dictatorship. Why can't they see that even the Congress has got all these differences in even greater measure and yet it remains as one cohesive party? Generally all parties are more or less influenced by the ruling party, which has multiple means of terror and temptation. Consciously or unconsciously they all try to imitate the ruling party. Thus every party, so to say, becomes an area for the clash of manifold ideologies. If it does not take to this pattern, there is a fear of its disintegration. Members are not able to understand to want extend the conflicts are of ideals or involved interests. Moreover, we are faced with the split mind of the Indian people and the unbearable pressure of the ruling party. The result is that these parties spend at least as much energy in infighting as they do in fighting against the Congress".

Lohia knew that a time would come when people would vote into power one of the opposition parties, which would stand for democracy, nationalism, material and cultural equality. However, that would take such a long time that by then the country would be completely ruined. The main point is that 50% of the people do not cast their votes. Barely 24% votes are polled by the Congress and the remaining 26% by the opposition parties. This means the formation of a minority government. And no other party has the strength even to make a powerful demand for proportional representation. We have to think within the present forms of election politics. "If the opposition parties do not fight among themselves, the defeat of the Congress is a certainty". Lohia observed and said; "The Communist Party and the Jan Sangh have become symbols of dogmatism. Hence it is essential to unify the ideologies of all opposition parties. In the context of the present situation, the integration of divergent ideologies would kindle the hopes and aspirations of the people and make it easier for the people to follow a proper path". Lohia had no doubt that distribution of seats alone would ensure the defeat of the Congress. He termed the opposition parties 'non-Congress parties'. He considered the struggle between the Congress and non-Congress parties as a tussle between status-quoism or stand-stillism, and radicalism. He desired to put an end to the twenty long years of dead silence. He said; "The so called stability of the Congress is the characteristic of the jungles and the mountains. The distinguishing feature of human society is change. If the results of the elections indicates the possibility of the formation of a non Congress government, it will become imperative to think of a minimum programme". In this connection, Lohia said, "No other thought has vitiated the outlook of the opposition parties as much as the idea of minimum programme. It is only after the possibility of the formation of a government arises that maturity and liveliness in thought appear. Then instead of talking in the air, one has to enter the realm of reality. Instead of being airy it would be concrete", Lohia further said; "In my opinion, all the, existing parties, born out of status-quoism, are treading a wrong path and will in the end be shattered with the risc of a real revolutionary party. So whenever a non-Congress government comes into existence, it will no longer be a single-party government but a coalition government. Within six months of its assuming power, it will have to act to speedily spread non-Congressism all over the country and keep the fire of revolutionary spirit burning. After wiping out the Congress, a powerful attack can be launched on against the disparities in all spheres of the society. Thereafter steps will have to be taken with lightening swiftness to make the people feel that the country is treading a new path. This is an important aspect of my idea of non-Congressism. A limit should be placed on expenditure of the Government, as well as non-government personnel. Such a programme will put an end to the power and prestige of money and luxuriant life. A revolutionary programme will fire the entire country with enthusiasm and generate in the minds of the people a will to carry out the revolution".

Lohia also put forward a proposal that the next Prime Minister should be selected from a non-Hindi state. "So far U.P. has given the country Prime Ministers, just as Rajasthan has given multi-millionaires, but the appalling misery of the common people in the Hindi region and the cruel injustice done to them continue unabated".

Lohia left no stone unturned to make non-Congressism effective. The S.S.P. tried to forge unity between all the rightists, centrists, and leftists by calling their meeting at Delhi. However the P.S.P., Jan Sangh and Swatantra parties did not respond to that call. Thus no front could ever be organised at the national level. Even then local electoral alliances were built up through the efforts of the S.S.P. Provincial parties like P.W.P., Republicans, D.M.K., and R.S.P. joined these fronts. Lohia's policy thus got partial success. Lohia prophesied that even if his dream did not come true in its entirety, the Congress would be defeated in Hindi-speaking states and the Centre. He himself contested from Kannoj parliamentary constituency. During his election speeches he took a definite stand on common civil code. A doubt was raised by the workers of his party that his speeches would alienate Muslims and he could thereby lose their votes. He reacted, "You people, do not know anything about the Muslim Personal Law. Whether I get Muslim votes or not, I am not going to change my stand". Congress propagandists naturally took advantage of this and told the Muslim voters that Lohia wants to interfere in their personal law. Indira Gandhi on the contrary, time and again publicly promised that she would not interfere in the Islamic personal code. Lohia toured all over the country, except his own constituency, with the slogan, 'Remove Congress & Save the Country'. He said that he was fighting the election of his party and opposition parties and not for his own personal self. After the campaign Lohia was listening to the election results as they were being announced. He was extremely pleased on hearing the news of Kamaraj's defeat. The news about the victory of the opposition candidates would make him elated while the defeat of his own colleagues would make him sad. His victory, by a small margin appeared to him like a defeat.

After the 4th general election to state assemblies, Congress lost power in eight states. In Bihar where there was only partial electoral adjustment and no united front between non-Congress parties, Congress met with a decisive defeat. Wherever there was partial understanding. The Congress was defeated and wherever there was no such understanding (e.g. Bengal, Rajasthan), there too the percentage of vote in favour of the Congress was less than in earlier election. Thus Lohia's strategy of mutual adjustments brought in good dividends to all the opposition parties. But, surprisingly, Lohia's own party the S.S.P. could not secure appreciable success in this process as a whole. In Bihar it emerged as the single largest party. In U.P. and some other Hindi-speaking states the role of the Jan Sangh helped the Congress get victory over the S.S.P.

Commenting in the result of the election Lohia stated, "For the next one or two years, democracy will have to function with maximum flexibility. Thereafter we may perhaps have break-up of existing parties and emergence of a new revolutionary parties or party of dictatorship under the guise of democracy. But I can definitely conclude that after 1200 long years of political stagnation Indian politics, an era of dynamism and change has set in. It is a matter of pleasure that the criminal house of the Congress is crumbling. All the same it is a matter of sorrow that no alternate better house is coming up its place. After the break-up of the Congress the country will oscillate between the hope and despair. A ray of hope here and there and then despair. This is what may happen". Lohia held that only revitalisation and reorganisation of different political forces would save the situation. The forces against progress and change have a long-standing tradition. The twenty year tong unbroken power monopolised by Congress has created a deadening atmosphere in which no dissenting voice is allowed and in which stability of a burial ground is preferred to a reformist dynanism. The other face of the regressive forces is represented by the millennium-old exploitative social custom which smother all reforms and withstand any progressive heat.

In Lohia's opinion there were two things instrumental in social change. First, the inspiration from within the human mind and second the enactment of law. Those who rely only on the first are saints and those who rely only on the second, promote a vicious dictatorship. An approximation is inevitable for social change. About the future governments Lohia said, "There will be attempts to topple these governments. Such attempts will have to be resisted firmly. Twenty years of Congress misrule has left a legacy of famines, rising prices, pessimism, oppression, tendency to shirk work, border violations, industrial recession, higher expenditure standards, national shame etc. These are the greatest obstacles in the path of non-Congress governments. If this disgraceful legacy is to be ushered out, something remarkable touching ordinary human life, has to be done as early as possible. Vested interests like high caste people, capitalists, bureaucrats etc. will put obstacles in the way of the government at every step and will not allow it to do any revolutionary work. Under such circumstances, if the governments surrender to the vested interests, they will be automatically destroyed. After the fall of the Congress, India will have to tread its path through lofty peaks of expectations and deep valleys of despair. The aspirations of the people suppressed during the twenty years of Congress rule will bubble up and if the non-Congress governments replacing the Congress fail to satisfy them, the people will fall into the valley of frustration and despair". Lohia suggested, "This situation can be faced by forming a people-oriented revolutionary government. Every living being has a natural tendency to continue to live. Similarly every government desires to continue to rule. However, no living being has a right to lead a purposeless life and be a burden on the people. Hence immediately after assumption of power, non-Congress governments must prove that they are not worthless and purposeless. If they become unsuccessful, I shall rouse the people to revolt against them".

Lohia expected that these governments would work for the uplift of our country, carry out routine administration efficiently and enact proper laws for bringing about necessary transformation within the stipulated period; whereby confidence would be created among the people. For doing this, the first requisite was 'a flexible mind and a firm determination'. Lohia was not very hopeful about the further governments. He said, "Governments which are assuming powers have no orientation as such and consequently they are leading in no specific direction whatsoever. But this is a stage of transition, these are hotch-potch governments. Within a short time or within 4-5 years at the most, people will get completely fed up with hotch-potch performance. As a result a bad government will come into power, or else a revolutionary urge may be roused. One thing is clear that the good and the evil cannot co-exist".

Famine conditions appeared in Bihar. It presented a great challenge to the new SVD government. Lohia said, "Non-Congress parties must be ready to assume the responsibility which has fallen on them. I am in favour of supporting all non-Congress governments for a period of 6 months, irrespective of whether the S.S.P. is a constituent of it or not". Lohia expected that the non-Congress governments would fulfil at least one of the following tasks within a period of 6 months. Improvement in police and general administration, abolition of land revenue, closure of costly schools, control of extravagant expenditure, cutting down the benefits and facilities available to the ministers, officers and big businessmen. Lohia said, "Political prisoners should be released immediately and enquiries ordered into firings. The conduct of the ministers should be such as to inspire the people with a feeling that the era of sensuous indulgence is over and the era of simplicity has set in".

The election of the President was due now. It was essential to nominate a man who had a flexible mind and firm determination and who was active in politics as an opposition candidate for that post. When some non-socialist admirers of Lohia expressed their desire that he should contest for the prized post, Lohia remarked. "Certainly I possess all these qualities in a much greater measure than any other man. However, the 4500 voters will not accept me. So I step out of the contest. However, I am saying this to make it clear as to what kind of a candidate the opposition parties should field. He further said; "If at all I happened to be elected to the Presidentship of the country my first job would he to disband the army". For the Presidential election the Congress put up Zakir Hussain as its candidate. The candidate of the opposition parties was Mr. Subba Rao. For Vice-Presidentship the candidate of the opposition parties was Prof. Habib. If however the opposition candidate were to win, the government at the centre goes. The fall of the Congress government would have been inevitable. Plans were formed and toppled during the discussions in the central hall of Parliament. Voting date for the election of President and vice-president was the 6th May. Lohia, the centre of attention was discussing various possibilities in voting, with some co-parliamentarians in the Central Hall. Around him were Radhakrishna Birla, Dr. Karni Singh, Bhupesh Gupta, Madhu Limaye and Tapadia, he argued that the opposition parties should be in readiness to form a government in case of the fall of Congress. Lohia invited Bhupesh Gupta to sign this one line resolution. Birla promised a gift of one thousand and one rupees. Bhupesh Gupta refused. The resolution never got off the ground because of the disagreement within opposition ranks.

Lohia held high expectation in this election. He felt that luck could suddenly take a turn. To make Subba Rao victorious, a call he had given a call to the voters before election saying. "A piece of luck is in your hands. The same piece is in my hand also Here affection and affinity are impelling me to write to you. I am not so arrogant as to give you advice. But my mind is bubbling up with joy that in this election we could achieve something which otherwise would have taken years to accomplish".

Prior to actual voting, hopeful signs were already visible. There was a lot of panic in government circles. Commenting on the defeat of the opposition candidate in the presidential election

Lohia stated, "America, Russia, Britain, China and France have their finger in every pie. They have their lobbies. The ugly foreigner is here with all his might and unwisdom. Communist leader Bhupesh Gupta has been unjust and rather harsh towards me. Sometimes I felt Jan Sangh desired change. However, now I think I was wrong. For me political strength is not just a matter of the parliament only but of the street as well. I had learned this lesson at the age of 7. I cannot forget it for life. A possibility exists that this interlude of the Presidential election may have proved a blessing in disguise. A very curious situation has come to exist. In an open voting the Congress is at a disadvantage. This is totally a new situation".

The total number of Congress MLAs in all states together was 1713. However Zakir Hussain got 1740 votes. Obviously a large number of MLAs belonging to the opposition parties had voted against their own nominee Subba Rao. Also more than 50 non-Congress MPs voted in favour of the Congress candidate. Lohia felt dejected by the defeat of Subba Rao. Perhaps he had great expectations knowing full well that there were supporters of the government in the opposition parties also. After this defeat, Lohia came to the conclusion that more time than necessary is wasted on Parliament and on those people whose interest in people's politics is of a secondary nature. He called upon all the people and particularly the youth who wanted to take to politics seriously, to think about the following 5 points: (1) socialist unity, (2) unity of all opposition parties, (3) joint demonstrations, (4) single-purpose platforms like 'fix the prices', 'remove English', 'abolish casteism' etc., (5) hard and sincere work for one's party and principles without imposition of any conditions. Lohia stated, "All the five points are complimentary. Lot of harm has been caused so far by distorting them. A large number of members of my party have wasted lot of their energy in trying to achieve unity of all the opposition parties without first developing a strength of their own party and principles. Sometimes the reverse of this has also happened. I think all parties have been victims of this type of behaviour".

The election of the President and the Vice-President showed that the forces of status quo are very strong in Indian politics. One reason for this is that the forces of change are scattered and unorganised. After having got same ministership and power, peoples representatives in legislatures totally forget the task of giving a proper direction to the people and organising them for bringing about the social transformation. There was a fear that the enthusiasm of the people who voted for change would whether away. Lohia hoped that the task of strengthening the forces of change would be taken up. However nothing of the kind happened. Lohia was rightly proud of some good work that was being done by non-Congress governments. He had expected much more from them, but he was disappointed. He said that one reason of the failure of the non-Congress governments in the States to do any thing big is that they are in many respects barren & shrivelled. Lohia pointed out; "Two ministers one of whom is a socialist, are more attached to each other than two socialists one of whom is a minister. This attachment to seats of power makes non-Congress governments vulnerable to the malicious machinations of the Central government. It must be born in mind that while the central government spends over forty-eight hundred crore rupees annually, the corresponding figure for the states like Bihar is two hundred fifty and for U.P. four hundred crores only. This gives the government in Delhi a strong leverage against non-Congress governments. The infection spreads through ministerial connections. As long as the primary source of infection namely the Congress government in Delhi is not shown to the door, there is no hope of the non-Congress state governments taking any fundamentally novel steps. The problem with ministers is that they only want 'to be', not to do'. I have seen the ecstatic complacency on the ministerial faces in Delhi. This contagion has successfully colonised a new host, the non-Congress ministers. I hope the good things being done by non-Congress governments will further harden the revolutionary, and determination of the people and ministers will improve. The only way is to strengthen the process of change. Before their fall the non-Congress governments will have to take some steps which will be remembered by the people".

Lohia wanted to rally all forces and concentrate all strength on isolating the Congress. Lohia regretted, "I wish I could kindle a new movement of the people but my means and my strength are not enough". As the non-Congress governments abandoned the revolutionary orientation, the socialist movement lost its momentum too. Those were the days of famine in Bihar. Lohia said, "In emergencies any distributed aid should be equitable not proportional to the purchasing power. In wartime Britain, a prince got the same ration of milk, eggs or fish as any pauper". Lohia reminded people of the six month moratorium granted to non-Congress governments in which they were to get some major efforts going. He said, "Shershah changed the face of this country in about four years. The question is of determination. We say the entire capacity for producing cars should be deployed during the next couple of decades to produce tractors, buses, trucks, and taxies. If even the rich have to ride in buses, concentration of wealth would be pointless. Air-travel should be totally disallowed. In these matters voluntary abstinence does not suffice, there must be legal blocks with provision for punishment". Lohia was deeply hurt when the Home Minister of Bihar permitted firings on mobs. Lohia demanded not only judicial inquiry of each case of firings but also resignation of the ministry. He felt this was end of one era and beginning of the second and he would not let his instincts loose even in such transitional phases. There is a dire necessity of bureaucratic and police reform.

The situation in U.P. was somewhat different. A non-Congress government had been set up there under the leadership of former Congress leader Charan Singh. Charan Singh, as well as Chief Minister of Bihar Mahamayaprasad (also an erstwhile Congressman) had never in the last twenty years shared the anti-Congress sentiments, Lohia said, "I wish them all the best, but they should bear in mind that events of 1967, were not a windfall but were proceeded by two decades of hard work and struggle". The Chief Minister of U.P. Charan Singh declared that the government of U.P. is a farmers government and will work in their interest. Lohia raised the question, "What does Charan Singh imply? After all who are the farmers? Does title to land make a person a farmer? Princes such as Jaipur or Patiala own thousands of acres of farmland. Are they farmers? In the same vein Birla also owns many farms. Can we count him among farmers? A government can claim to be a farmers government only if it can serve the interests of all farmers, and that means cultivators, not owners".

Non-Congressism became a dilemma for Lohia. He could not really call it off as long as Congress survived, but the instrument that emerged in the process could not deliver the expected results. In the October 1957 issue of Jan monthly, Lohia explained the situation, "Some people allege that non-Congressism is falling through. When someone declares a person dead before his death actually takes place, it only shows his desire for the person's death. Those who had a vested interest in the Congress Raj wanted to see non-Congressism dead the earliest. It is also true that non-Congressism finds itself entangled and cannot deliver the goods". According to Lohia one reason for the unproductiveness of non-Congress governments is the Congress power at the Centre. The village official is changed but the district collector is not. The non-Congress governments undertake some relevant programmes and the central government puts a spoke in their wheel. This will entail a centre-state confrontation. Lohia wanted this confrontation to be such that the people will see the central government as a hand maiden of the reactionary forces. Issues with the centre should be taken on matters which will appeal to the nation at large and which would bring people closer to the non-Congress governments, he felt.

"Though it was necessary to appreciate the good work of non-Congress governments", Lohia said, "they are no sacred cows never to be hurt or killed". Regarding the Bihar government he remarked; "Toppling the Bihar government would really be unfortunate. Bihar Ministry has put an end to the age old system of Malguzari. It is making progress in eliminating use of English in public dealings. It recognised famine and hunger where it existed and made some dent on the situation. I concede that more was possible and must be achieved. Any repression by the government, such as firing, must be subjected to scrutiny and justice must be given to untouchables, tribals, women, backward communities of Hindu or Muslim, reforms in bureaucracy and police are essential. But while Congress at centre is intact non-Congressism will face a dead-end".

The Deputy Prime Minister Morarji Desai challenged Lohia to develop irrigation facilities in a couple of hundred square miles of area in Bihar with voluntary workers. Lohia was tempted to take up the challenge but was hesitant. He confessed, "I don't know if we could do this. Everyone in our land shirks hard work. We can mobilise a voluntary force of thousands for resisting injustice and going to jail, but for earth work, I am not sure of a similar success". Lohia felt that contemporary politics was permeated by status quoism. People, workers and leaders all wanted to be someone. "Our politics seems haunted. There is the dread of being unseated and the reluctance to displease Congress bosses. We all feel obliged to them for our well being. This necessarily cripples our abilities to take any major initiatives".

One incident in Bihar outraged Lohia to such an extent that he even considered a step that might endanger the Bihar non-Congress government. B.P. Mandal a socialist, was elected to the Lok Sabha from Bihar. He was taken up in the state ministry and then got elected to the state's upper house. Lohia opened his barrage. Though Mandal was from a backward caste there could be no excuse for opportunism and power mongering. These very people later went on to from a new splinter group "Shishit Dal" which endangered the Bihar Ministry since they were 11 out of the 68 S.S.P. legislators. Lohia was ready to pay this heavy penalty for Mandal's shift from parliament to legislative council. Both these two S.S.P. seats would be in danger again. Further there was no compulsion to include Mandal in the ministry. Lohia publicly asked Mandal to resign immediately. This was Lohia's first and last attempt to restrain the lust for power in non-Congressist, before his demise. Lust for power like a wedge, once successful initially, would drown the entire organisation. Lohia could clearly see this dreadful vision. He was confident of being able to control this at least in the transition stage. But then came his untimely death. The voice of restraint was thus silenced. Consequently conscience, loyalty, vigilance and moderation were no more. Once the reins were loose it was all a mad rush. Fraternity and loyalty to principles, went down the drain while personal aggrandisement became the order of the day.

31. LOHIA IN LOK SABHA

"Parliament is the master whereas the Prime Minister is it's servant. The servant has to behave modestly and politely with his master". Raising the cudgel with these words Lohia on the fourth day of his debate in the Lok Sabha pointed out to Prime Minister Nehru his appropriate position. The day was 17th August 1963. The ruling party suffered a severe jolt by Lohia's admonition. Till then none had dared to comment in this vein in Nehru's Court and, with rare exceptions of the members on the opposition side, vied with each other in sycophancy. The Prime Minister was accustomed to listen to adulation and approval both from treasury benches and opposition. In the name of parliamentary procedure a semblance of opposition used to be enacted. It was a mutually agreed collusive combat of coalescence. The socialist members too had made themselves the target of ridicule.

Lohia had made the abominable and detestable debacle in the Chinese aggression as the main plank of condemnation of the government, during his battle at the hustings in the by-election. He roared disgustingly, "It is the most reprehensible government which brought the nation into disrepute" The voters deputed Lohia to the Lok Sabha to represent their feelings of woe and utter shame. Lohia confronted Nehru for the first time on the floor of the Lok Sabha as his political adversary. From his opening remark in the house it became absolutely clear that it would be very hard for the ruling party to face him squarely. Obviously a relentless opponent had arrived with the firm resolve to uncover the stark reality of the feudal style of functioning and dire lack of principled behaviour and direction, arbitrary and anti-democratic demeanour of those in power. Lohia's main objective was to direct the attention of the representatives to the basic national problems.

Lohia's presence in Lok Sabha was a queer paradox. A firebrand rebel was poised in the air-conditioned, cool, august Assembly Hall sparkling all around burning embers of potentially incendiary questions and highly explosive comments. Lohia had full faith in parliamentary politics as a sharp weapon of revolutionary logistics. Long back in 1937 he had rejected the offer of unopposed election to the central assembly, as it was impossible for him to take the oath of allegiance to the British Crown on attaining independence. Lohia was eager to wield the weapon of parliamentary politics as a representative of the people. He expressed his long-cherished desire in the Lok Sabha at the outset stating that "I had been waiting for this hour since the last fifteen years". He sought allotment of more time for the opposition in the debate. In support of his plea he argued that, "The government had availed of ample opportunity of blowing it's trumpet for the last fifteen years. It would not be appropriate to allot nine hours to its share now".

Prior to taking the oath in the house, Lohia wanted to observe that oath-taking had become just a formality devoid of any serious significances. But there was no occasion for his comments. After taking oath he fired the cannon so vociferously that the ruling party got panicky. He utilised almost all the available weapons including question, sub-question, adjournment motion, alteration-inviting-motion, two and a half hour debate, stop proceeding, privileges motion, etc. for the fight with treasury benches. However his parliamentary exploit got to a real start with his speech supporting the one line motion of no-confidence tabled on behalf of the opposition for the first time in the Lok Sabha as a sequel to Lohia's initiative and effort. In parliamentary history it is a red-letter day. On 21st August 1963, Acharya Kripalani moved the one line motion reading; "The Lok Sabha expresses no confidence in the council of Ministers". Lohia's speech on the motion was replete with dignified style, comprehensive outlook, foresight and immense self confidence. The house was spellbound by the historic speech. Several members of the opposition side readily granted their own allotted time to Lohia so as to enable him to give full voice to his views and comments. He could feel the impact of his outburst on members of the ruling party. Piquantly he commented, "The occupants of the benches of the ruling party went on stamping in favour of the government and in protest against my remarks. Nevertheless on returning home they will surely admit in private that Lohia frankly and unsparingly revealed the very feelings and concerns simmering in their minds".

In his thunderous speech Lohia vehemently lashed at Chinese incursion and India's shameful abject surrender. He also alluded to the food problem, the burgeoning prices of the necessities of life, the policy on foreign affairs and similar other burning issues. He ana lysed the chronic maladies in a new perspective and offered practical suggestions to deal with them. Alongwith demolition of the evils he emphasised on the positive, constructive aspects. The common people to whom he referred were not an abstract concept. He depicted a concrete, real picture of the downtrodden, exploited, deprived sections of the people whose uplift was his main objective. He scoffed and jeered at ridiculous and frivolous suggestions such as raising crops of foodgrain in earthen vessels and on terraces of residential premises. The official propaganda was a farcical show, he said.

Lohia's contention of per capital daily income of three annas of a vast majority of people created a sensation. In the course of his speech he hinted at a sweet dream of the ruling hierarchy. He remarked, "Our ministers had cherished a fond hope of joining the ranks of the uppermost strata of the society by venturing a long leap forward during the process of levelling down the people of the upper class and levelling up of those in the lower strata. The process resulted in a tragic distortion. Sixty per cent of the families have to maintain themselves on a monthly earning of twenty-five Rupees. It indicates that twenty-seven crore Indians manage to keep their body and soul together within three annas per day per capita. On the other hand three rupee per day have to be spent on the upkeep of the prime minister's pet dog".

Lohia further stated, "An agrarian labourer earns twelve annas each day, while the daily earning of a teacher amounts to Rs. Two. The amount spent each day on the Prime Minister's ostentatious living exceeds Rs. Twenty five thousand. Fifty lakh people comprising the affluent section have ruined the country".

Making a pointed reference to the ever-increasing non-productive expenditure on administration Lohia revealed, "The central government incurred annual expenditure of Rupees One thousand crore in 1948, whereas the amount has now risen to a high level; Five thousand five hundred crore Rupees. Fifteen years back the ratio of government servants to the population stood at one and a half per cent which has increased to three per cent. It needs to be specifically mentioned that these incumbents are pen-wielding white-collared employees contributing little to national production".

Corruption was getting more and more rampant due to the connection between business and politics. Two members of the same family had as though got themselves divided into two portions, one occupying the ministerial chair and the other taking to trade. Prime Minister Nehru himself had become the patron of the culture of casteism, nepotism and fascination for charming society women. His relatives and hundreds of persons belonging to his community were recruited in several departmental services of the Central Government. It has resulted into thunder in the form of heavy prices of commodities and corrupt practices. Focussing the reality vividly in an objective way Lohia demanded, "I would like to direct your attention to certain matters such as prohibition of liquor and narcotics, abolition of flesh trade consolidation of agricultural land holdings and restriction of trade in gold. In spite of coercive and outrageous methods adopted for the implementation of the regulations relating to these matters the desired outcome does not appear to be forthcoming. The evils which used to be practised unrestrained and overtly, have now gone underground. The motives of the government are frail and fragile, they have not been firmly imbedded deep into he popular mind. Like a child sitting in a swing, the government tends to oscillate to-and-fro. After a programme of prohibition of over a decade or so, all the restrictions on liquor are removed. The process is repeated without a long term view".

Expressing his anguish and indignation over the Chinese debate Lohia interpreted afresh the motion of contact revolution (revolution through touch) held by Nehru. A revivalist seeks to touch proletarian revolutionary force while masquerading as a revolutionary pseudonymously. The Chinese debacle was a fallout of the wrong policy that Nehru followed. Lohia had been consistently criticising and unveiling Nehru's policy towards China ever since 1948. Nehru had pleaded long back that every country that is the master of its land is entitled to secure its legitimate, rightful position in the United Nations, but he did not stick firmly to his stand. There are two countries who claim to the have the name China. Nehru embraced Communist China unceremo-niously discarding the claim of Taiwan or Formosa which is ruled by the Kuomintang Party led by Gen. Chang-Kai-Shek. Lohia led an assault on Nehru's wrong policy regarding China. Addressing the Lok Sabha he categorically reiterated that Communist China was an aggressor. Lohia stated, "China is a belligerent country that has invaded our motherland. It is disgraceful that India has been pleading the cause of China supporting its claim for membership of UN. If there is a son with soul do dead as to entertain the desire of getting his mother married to a rapist what would be our reaction?" A member commented that the simile of a son seeking to appease the rapist depicts bad taste. Lohia flung a furious repartee, "It may be so but the actions being taken are as utterly loathsome and abominable".

Prime Minister Nehru had roared like a lion on 12th October 1962, that the Chinese assailants would be thrown out of India's boundary line. After 37 days his wailful lament on 19th November, reminded the house of a piteous bleating of lamb. His throat was choked up with despair. Lohia scoffed at Nehru's disillusionment about the practice and profession of the so called friendly neighbour and exhorted him to take a lesson from the episode, Lohia said, "It is the Prime Minister's grievance that China played a treacherous game. His complaint is totally wrong. Two thousand five hundred years back the eminent political thinker and theoretician Chanakya had laid down a doctrine of state policy. If a ruler complains that he was betrayed by the enemy, a ruler deserves to be instantly deposed. He forfeits his right to rule. Chanakya's doctrine is fully relevant in the present context. The ruler must be full of restraint over his mind. He should not be ruffled by feelings of joy and sorrow".

Nehru's temperamental infirmity often prompted him to appease the tough and rude as also to harass and cause suffering to the humble and gentle. In Lohia's view the most civilised behaviour should be to be broad before the meek and frail whereas to torment the mighty and villainous. He who wields power or wealth should exercise control over his mind and speech. The corollary of swarfing a sceptre is to offer assurance of protection. Illustrating his stance, Lohia pertinently referred to the revolt of the tribal Nagas and the incursion of the alien foe, said Lohia;

"The Naga tribals in the north-east are India's rural children. Their habitat was ruthlessly scorched by aerial bombardment. The Portuguese civilians and army men fled after the police action in Goa. The planes of the air force pursued their ships and attempted to drop bombs, but when the Chinese infantry advanced across the border, the air force did not take any action to block their path. Does the Government have any valid explanation?" The Indian ambassador in USA was made to answer the question. He justified the inaction by arguing that the government felt afraid that the mighty well equipped air force of Chinese Communist regime would retaliate ferociously.

Lohia stirred a sensation by raising the controversial point of three annas per day income of a vast majority. The employees in government offices were directed to compile statistical data. On the basis of a note compiled by an economist, Nehru asserted in the Lok Sabha that Lohia's affirmation was baseless. He claimed that per capita daily income amounted to fifteen annas. Lohia challenged the verity of the Prime Minister's statement, and pleaded that between the two of them the one whose assumption would be found wrong, would have to vacate the legislature. Nehru commented that Lohia had a frivolous mind whereupon Lohia called the Prime Minister timid, filthy and mean; and perceived that he had scant knowledge about firm and factory, Nehru declined the challenge. Lohia succeeded in holding a two-and-half hour debate over the topic after a lot of correspondence.

During the course of the debate, planning minister Nanda stated that the daily per capita income of twenty seven crore people on the lower social strata was assessed to be seven annas and a half. Nehru's assurance was found to be wrong. Lohia exhorted the Prime Minister and Planning Minister to decide mutually as to who is right between the two. Lohia offered a suggestion to the planning commission that if it is eager to function earnestly and with serious motives it ought to divide the concept of national income in four categories 1. The Lowest 2. The Highest, 3. Medium & 4. Average.

The planning minister had based his statement on the findings of the National Sample Survey held by the Government. He made it clear that the daily per capita average income amounts annas seven and half. The National Sample Survey Organisation had not assessed separately the statistics of income and expenditure of sixty per cent of the population i.e. twenty-seven crore who constitute the lowest strata the bottom. The method followed was that of dividing the total national income over sixty per cent of the population. Obviously the planning ministers statement does not present a real authentic picture, said Lohia.

Lohia's persisting demand pressed the government to constitute an enquiry committee to assess per capita income. Lohia affirmed that Prof. Mahalnowis Committee which had gone into the question of national income and submitted its report amply proves his contention of three annas daily income of the poor. The government was hesitant in publication of the report though its summary had already been publicised by the Press. The committee had concluded in its study that Uttar Pradesh ranked among the poorest states. The appalling squalor and poverty of a vast majority of the people of Uttar Pradesh, Bihar, Rajasthan, Madhya Pradesh, Orissa, Andhra Pradesh was borne out by the findings of the committee. Both Nehru and Lohia were elected members of Lok Sabha from Uttar Pradesh. Lohia further said in his speech. "The poverty ridden Uttar Pradesh is unfortunate in having a worthless fellow like me and an ignorant person like the Prime Minister as its representatives in the National Parliament".

The Prime Minister had told the house on 22nd August 1960, that the national income had risen forty two per cent and per capita income had increased twenty per cent. Lohia wondered as to where the income rise had vanished. A committee was formed on 14th October 1960, to ascertain the reality. Lohia revealed relevant data to indicate that the situation in rural sector is ghastly unacceptable and unjust. He said, "There are in our country 34% families in the rural areas whose landholdings are smaller than one acre in size. On the other hand, barely 1% of the families own and occupy, 24% share of arable land. The figures are amply eloquent. I have received letters from some persons who cannot believe that vast multitudes of people are keeping their body and soul together in a paltry income of three annas a day. It may be proved to true by putting together the data in a different way. The land labour numbers about seven crore. According to a conservative estimate the number of peasants with landholdings smaller than an acre each comes to sixteen crore. The artisans who have neither adequate tools nor regular employment are about three, crore in number, about 25% of the urban residents who are mostly slum-dwellers or reside on the footpaths live at starvation level. The tribals, destitute widows, desolate mendicants and others portion add their numbers to the categories of the poor and deprived. Taken together nearly thirty crore people do not get more than three annas each per day for their basic necessaries. Eradication of poverty of our brethren living a life of penury and indigence should get the top most priority".

The Lok Sabha realised the harsh reality on account of Lohia's explosive exposures. Not only was the level of national income poor, but its distribution among various sections of the society was extremely uneven and unjust. A small minority of 5% of the population takes away as big a share as 30% of the national dividend while the remaining 70% is shared by a vast majority of 95%. Twenty-seven crore people sustain themselves on a daily earning of three annas each. Sixteen and a half crore can afford to spend only one rupee per day for their livelihood. Fifty lakh people are fortunate enough to be able to incur an expenditure of Rs. thirty-three per day for maintenance. A few among the affluent category can spend each a thousand rupees each day, and even more.

Commenting on Lohia's speech the english daily *Hindustan Times* belonging to Birla group of journals observed that an unfortunate lower section of the society might be living on a level of income even less than three annas a day. Analysing the reasons for the ever-rising misery and squalor of the masses Lohia expressed the view that, "Modernisation of consumption has taken place without paying due attention to modernisation of production. The foundation of the production process on which the superstructure of modern consumption has been erected, continues to be that of the medieval age. India has been attempting to imitate the west. The standard of living of political leaders, bureaucrats and businessmen has been ever on the rise, whereas the common man could not make any headway. Three lakh persons emerge on the administrative plane as bureaucrats every year. The British rule comprised three lakh civil servants whereas the present government has a heavy contingent of fifty lakh".

Lohia's comment on the daily cost of Rs. 25 thousand over the upkeep of the prime minister was made a target of vociferous attack. Nehru's lackeys and cohorts pleaded that the amount being spent was relatively insignificant, and that it would be worthwhile to spend even millions. In this context Lohia recalled an anecdote of Gandhiji's strong objection raised during 1916, by patriots of those days against the very heavy expenditure that was being incurred by the exchequer over the pompous style of living of the Viceroy and his paraphernalia. Supporting the patriots' plea for a substantial reduction of the expenses the Mahatma had argued, "India is a country of starving emaciated millions plunged in miserable condition. If it is so imperative to spend lavishly to keep the Viceroy alive, his end would be considered preferable".

Lohia's vehemence of speech and way of argument was devastating. His presence led to a metamorphosis of the Lok Sabha. It had assumed the form of a prison in the years past, on account of its obsolete conventions, rigid concepts of parliamentary etiquette, regulations for enforcement of counterfeit discipline, impact of age-old feudal system, worn out and stifling procedure, complex and intricate methodology. The customary practice of the usage of the alien English language served as an impediment in the way of free and frank debate. It had made the atmosphere of the house dreary, morbid and morose. Lohia stormed the prison and liberated the members of the opposition from the conceptional shackles. Breezes of free air started blowing in the temple of democracy. Articulating the essence and function of democracy Lohia told the house, "The democratic method of attaining power by defeating the minority element with the help of greater numerical strength benefits the victor if there is at least partial though not total influence of specific concepts and policies on both the victor and vanquished. The Indian National Congress has turned into a graveyard of policies and a cadaver of concepts. It has become imperative to develop democratic institutions outside the Parliament house, in farms, factories and roads. Democracy does not exist in its framework and formulation. Although both are equally necessary, democracy has no existence unless its soul is deeply entrenched with its grace and glory.

A parliament devoid of its soul was condemned by Lohia as "a seat of mockery, heresy and perfunctory formality where the rulers and members get together for rumination like beasts". From time to time Lohia raised a hue and cry on the floor of the house on matters of crucial importance such as democracy, parliament, parliamentary language, parliamentary conventions etc. with a view to make the Lok Sabha vibrant and vital mouthpiece of the popular voice. During the period of the Pakistani war, Lohia allowed that Parliament was highly potent weapon, fourteen times mightier than a battle tank or a fighter plane. He thus implicitly indicated that India proudly possesses a prestigious weapon which our hostile neighbour miserably lacks. "Democracy takes concrete shape in the form of elected parliament. The Lok Sabha, the principal wing of our national parliament implies debate and logic. Truism underlies debate. It is a crime to change pieces of weight in the scale while weighing an article. Similarly tricky and deceitful interpretation of one's argument and statement to suit the need of the hour should be deemed a crime. A discussion and debate sans truth and genuineness is no debate. It is futile to talk about democracy if there is no place for parliament".

Emphasising the imperativeneed of freedom of press for the development and growth of powerful democracy, Lohia revealed that about fifty to seventy per cent of news items published in Indian newspapers are those furnished by the Press Trust of India. He expressed his impression about PTI that probably there might not be any other news organisation in the world that excels it in damaging the freedom and truthfulness of the press. Free press is the soul of democracy while truth is the soul of the press. Proprietors of factories and big business are also the owners of most of the prominent newspaper organisations. They are closely related to PTI so are the influential cabinet minimisers. Its higher ranks are occupied mostly by aristocratic hierarchal elites. This triangular dominance has reduced PTI to a filthy unreliable agglomeration".

It was Lohia who had raised his voice in protest against the imposition of Presidential rule in Kerala in 1965. He asserted that according to democratic practice, the Kerala state legislative Assembly alone had the right to decide in the matter. In the situation of constitutional crises the only remedy in a democratic regime is to offer an opportunity to the democratically elected representatives to form a government. If the government thus constituted, goes astray the people would realise its worth and bundle it away.

The question of the propriety of participation of government servants in active politics was raised by Lohia in a different context. They are not allowed to enroll themselves as members of a political party and to take part in politics. To that extent they are deprived of their civil rights. Lohia took the view that if the government prohibits Its employees from participating in political activities, socialism would be tantamount to slavery, as under a socialist regime the number of employees of the government would continue to rise.

As regards uprooting of corruption Lohia believed that election reforms was not the total remedy. He however offered three important suggestions. 1. Restriction of plying of transport vehicles on days of voting; 2. Prohibition of distribution of voter slips by candidates; slips should be distributed to the voters by the government machinery; and 3. There should be proportional representation on the basis of number of votes polled, rather than choice of individual member from each constituency. It is the soul of democracy that really matters, and not the felt or hide that covers the body. Lohia aspired to make Indian democracy a vivid, vital lively organism restoring its soul which it seriously lacked. He earnestly desired that the parliament should take the form of a mirror in which the true image of the sorrows and grievances of the exploited and downtrodden would be vividly reflected. He used to see to it that every day one adjournment motion for half an hour debate would be moved thereby inviting attention of the house, and implicitly of the nation, to the untoward incidents occurring in some part or the other of the country. Lohia's bitter comment on the proceedings of the Question hour reflects his ire and disgust over the callous stance of the rulers. Remarked Lohia, "During the question hour the ministers rarely offer a full and satisfactory answer. Often times they do not know the answer themselves, On several occasions the ministers employ undesirable tactics of manoeuvers and manipulations to conceal the facts. Stringent action ought to be taken against such crafty ministers. Unfortunately however, every effort is taken to rescue them from the comments and criticism levelled by the opposition. It is serious violation and infringement of the letter and spirit of the constitution".

The proceedings of the Lok Sabha had all along been such a routine, dull affair that it could not make any impact on the public opinion. Due to the absolute domination of the Congress Party and its leader Nehru, the Lok Sabha spoke in one voice. The voice of the opposition was feeble and inert. Usually it used to be scared by the numerical superiority of the ruling party. Its voice was drowned away by the din and noise of the treasury benches and their supporters. The debates which were provoked by Lohia and his colleagues in the Samyukta Socialist Party invited the attention of sizeable section of the people towards the proceedings of the Lok Sabha. Nevertheless the common people took little interest therein. Lohia analysed the reason thus, "During the debate the whole matter includes a wordy duel between the ruling party and the opposition. Those who excel in the skill to vanquish get wide applause on the floor and outside. The provision of law rules and regulation are unceremoniously transgressed in the dexterity of vanquishing the rivals. For the healthy growth of democracy both obedience and disobedience are equally injurious. Today in our country obedience is on the rise where disobedience is necessary. On the other hand, disobedience is gaining ground in the domain of obedience".

It was impossible to raise the quality of the debates in the Lok Sabha to higher level unless the common people grow more conscious of their rights and duties as citizens of an independent democratic country. Lohia and his associates in the Samyukta Socialist Party (S.S.P.) struggled hard relentlessly to break the mire or labyrinth which was strangling the democratic structure. The group of members of the Socialist Party (SP) which was later designated Samyukta Socialist Party (S.S.P.) in the Lok Sabha was an enviable lot for other political parties in the house. The SP group comprised young parliamentarians of a very high order who with mutual cooperation and joint effort often succeeded in harassing the ministers on urgent issues of public interest. Plucking up their hearts they staged sit in strikes in the well of the house on several occasions. They staged walkouts from time to time to register their protests against the government. The speaker drove them out of the house as punishment for their belligerency many a times. The SP members under Lohia's leadership behaved valiantly and ingenuously on all occasions of crisis. Any member of the Congress, i.e. ruling party would call for the suspension of opposition members pointing mostly at the SP group, and the speaker would declare his decision. On one such occasion, B.P. Maurya, a member moved for suspension of the proceedings of the house. The speaker rejected his motion. As Maurya persisted for acceptance of his motion, the speaker suspended him from membership for fifteen days. When the marshal was summoned in the house to bundle out Maurya physically, Lohia intervened to ask the marshal to take his hands off the honourable members body. The speaker directed the marshal to withdraw. In an attempt to move backwards hurriedly the marshal's feet slipped and he fell down on the ground. Maurya voluntarily left the house. Raising his voice against the speaker's decision to summon the marshal, Lohia said with resent, "It is not proper and just. Maintenance of the glory of the house would be possible only if the glory of the nation is rescued. Clarifying that the glory of the country and its parliament was identical, Lohia further urged the speaker, "The expulsion should not be limited to apply only to the opposition ranks, those ministers who act in contravention of the provisions of Law, should be expelled too. Possibly such episodes might be deemed grotesque and ungracious but future historians might possibly observe that some members of parliament suffered hardships for safeguarding the honour and prestige of the country and its democratically elected parliaments".

The relations between the speaker and Lohia were very cordial, Lohia once remarked, "Mr. Speaker, in my life I have obeyed no one else to the extent to which I have obeyed you". The Speaker replied, "I would like to assure you that I have been thankful to very few persons to the extent to which I am full of thanks for you". In another context Lohia had urged the Speaker, "Sir, I always feel respectful apprehension for you. I would humbly expect you to be kind to me". The speaker expressing his regard had noted, "I hold Dr. Lohia in very high esteem. He says that he feels afraid of me. Perhaps I am much more frightful of him". During the debate on the unfortunate Bastar happenings the ruling party succeeded in getting the motion of expulsion of Ramsevak Yadav, Madhu Limaye and Kishen Patnayak passed by majority. The speaker summoned the marshal. Lohia roared taking exception to the move, "Are we bent coercive measures? We are in the house of Lok Sabha. It is not a market place". Consequently the speaker adjourned the house for the day rather than physically bundling out the three opposition members with the marshal's assistance. On several occasions the speaker had to side with the government. Lohia would often allow, "Sir, I would abide your order, but never that of the crowd. The crowd of the Congress members creates disturbance in the house and deprives the opposition its freedom of expression". Lohia spared no efforts for safeguarding the rights and privileges of the members. He solemnly affirmed in the house. "Even if one member disagrees, the ruling cannot be deemed to have emanated from the Lok Sabha. The legitimate presumption is that I am entitled to express my opinion even if I am deemed a lunatic and all others as sane or, in the alternative, I may be the only sensible person in a multitude of the insane, and can logically persist for the exercise of my legal and constitutional right".

Lohia never did deliberately disrespect the speaker, in his endeavour to prevent the Lok Sabha from its conversion into an ecclesiastical congregation. He earnestly sought to make it the nation's brain. If the speaker's ruling would unjustifiably support the government action, Lohia used to reiterate his view that, "The speaker or the chair person ought to be a non-party man. If he is a party member he ought to possess such free, unfettered and strong will that would enable him to issue direction and suggestions to the leader of the ruling party without any reservations. Mr. Speaker, you have been occupying a cool chair whereas I have taken hot seat. It is my mission to create new power in the country by kindling the flame of popular unrest. It is your obligation to maintain a balance between the two rival sides and thus expedite the business of the legislature. I would humbly prevail on you to widen the plain of the ramparts of our constitution rather than narrowing it in a constricted closet".

Expressing deep concern over the deteriorating health of Gopalan a communist member from the opposition rank, Lohia said, "The parliament is a living organisation. When any of its limits is afflicted the whole body feels grief and pain". Lohia made it a point to speak in Hindi, his mother tongue, during the entire proceeding of the Lok Sabha. He thus raised the honour and prestige of the people's languages. The alien English language had reigned supreme over the central legislature till then. The parliament represented the crores of Indians whereas English was the language in which handful of the elite upper class took perverted, hypocritical pride. Although the members had to communicate with the voters in their respective mother tongues for soliciting votes, they were the slaves of English. In this respect the opposition members in no way differed from the members of the ruling party. They felt that they could not make any impact on the house and secure due publicity in the print media unless they spoke in English. They were not totally wrong in this assumption, Prime Minister Nehru, his colleagues in the cabinet and party and the prominent national newspapers had by their method created an impression as if English, was their mother tongue. Lohia was the first national leader who strongly protested against the attitude of servility towards English although he had superb mastery over English. He unexceptionably persisted in speaking in Hindi, and as a sequel to his emphatic assistance on speaking in the people's language a sea change took place in the attitude of the members. Lohia was a senior, popular leader and an eminent thinker. Members who laboured under the misapprehension that it was undignified to speak in their own languages in the national parliament, ceased to feel any hesitation in expressing themselves in Hindi and the state languages. Lohia's Hindi speeches changed the environment. He restored tongue to the members who had been silent till them. The popular languages which used to be silent on account of the dominance of an alien language grew inhumanly vocal. Earlier the debate happened to be a pseudomorphous formality as English was practically the sole medium. The debate was more purposeful, lively and exciting as it got rid of the shackle of snobbish ostentation. Lohia introduced the colloquial, spoken language of the common people in the Lok Sabha. Nehru despisingly designated it as the market dialect. The use of a good many Hindi words was often made a target of attack having been styled as unparliamentary. If the phrase 'go to hell' is permissible, why not its Hindi paraphrase 'Jahannum main jaye' certain Hindi words such as Khopadi' (head), 'Aural' (woman) Jantu (worm) were deemed controversial. Lohia pleaded that these words were not unparliamentary: the distinction lies between words of alien and indigenous languages. Words originating in veiled forms gradually advance towards more conscious, explicit substitutes. Lohia believed that the parliament and judicial courts were the two places where a language refined and assumed an elegant form. What essentially matters is not parliamentary language but parliamentary ethos.

The process of demolition of the prison which English language constituted enraged the people who thrived by making English their mainstay. Their speeches in parliament were not significant for the points raised or suggestions presented, but for the decorative rhetoric of English languages. They were being deprived of their privilege. The battle for the defence of people's languages which Lohia initiated prompted a member representing Tanjore in Tamil Nadu to put forth his demands arguing that, the members should be granted the right to speak in regional languages. Necessary arrangements ought to be made to translate forthwith the speeches from regional languages into the Union Official Languages. It has not been statutorily laid down that only persons knowing Hindi and English are entitled to get elected to the parliament. Why then are we not allowed to speak in the house in our mother tongue?" He argued.

Lohia had to encounter successively three prime ministers in the parliament. They were Jawaharlal Nehru, Lal Bahadur Shastri and Indira Gandhi. He urged them to desist speaking in English in any of the two houses of parliament. On the basis of articles 343 to 351 of the constitution, he pleaded that all the Indian languages ought to be given their rightful, legitimate place in the functioning of the national parliament. He asserted, "The use of English must cease at any cost. I am not particular about the use of Hindi which has constitutionally been accepted as the Union Official language". Indulal Yagnik a veteran member commended Lohia's efforts for enhancing the honour of the regional languages and English, Lohia soon realised that members of the ruling party as well as the opposition hold practically similar views on the isstle of removal of English. Lohia proposed that a round table conference should be held to decide as to which languages would be suitable substitutes for English. Had Lohia not fought out the issue with perseverance and persistence English would have continued to dominate over the parliament.

The Director of the Indian School of International Studies in Sapru House rejected an application submitted by Vaidik, a research scholar, for scholarship and leave on the plea that it was written in Hindi instead of English. Some of the members including Madhu Limaye sought to invite the attention of the Education Minister to this matter. The minister expressed his inability to interfere in the matter as the institution concerned was an autonomous body. He further stated that the financial aid which the government grants to the said institution is not based on any consideration about language. Lohia claimed that under subclause 3 of article 343 of the constitution, English had no place in the domain of public education. The speaker directed him to take recourse to the judiciary for legally valid interpretation of the constitutional provisions.

Replying to a supplementary question, the Education Minister told the house that the academic council had taken a policy decision in the matter of language applicable for exceptional situation. The Board is entitled to grant permission to a student to submit the thesis of his research in a language other than English provided that the Board was convinced to its satisfaction that adequate research material was available in the language in which the student might be proficient and that at least guide and examiner would be available well versed in the language in which the thesis of research would be compiled. The Minister's answer enraged Lohia. Lohia restrainedly commented that the minister had failed to make any distinction between the language as medium of perception i.e. study, and that of expression i.e. writing the thesis. Thus he had made a mess of the application of the medium for various purposes. The minister further said that the programme and policy of the institute had laid it down that the thesis of research ought to be written only in English. He thereby provoked a member Bhagwat Jha Azad to question whether the institution was meant to serve the cause of barely two percent portion of the population well-versed in English. Another member Tyagi commented that if those who run the institution were ignorant of Indian languages, they deserved to be dismissed. Ultimately the institution had to obey the dictate of the Lok Sabha and amend its regulations so as to enable its research students to submit three articles and these in any Indian language. Prior to the amendment not a single thesis written in Indian languages was submitted to the Board. Lohia alongwith his colleagues belonging to the S.S.P. also fought against the convention prevalent till then regarding the English text of the President's address before the joint session of both the houses of parliament.

During the course of the debate Prime Minister Lal Bahadur Shastri once assured the house that, "Although I am speaking in English. Just now, in future I shall speak in Hindi". Press Trust of India the news agency as also the Press Information Bureau of the central government released the news item of Shastri's speech to the press adding the word also, thereby totally changing the affirmation of the Prime Minister. Next time when Shastri started speaking in English, Lohia addressed him a letter urging on him, "You ought to be courageous enough to declare that you do not have the will power to act upon your pledge and that the political parties to which you belong does not permit you to abide by it". Shastri retreating from his declared stand sent reply stating that,

'I never meant to say that I shall altogether abstain from speaking in English."

Participating in a debate on the motion regarding formation of a committee of members of the legislature to go into the working of the public sector enterprises, Lohia stated that enterprises both in the private and public sector were equally inequitable and both have equally adopted each other's views. Lohia commented bitterly, "The enterprises in the private sector have learnt the call of mismanagement from those in the public sector, whereas the units in the public sector have adopted the stance of exploitation and expropriation from the finns in the private sector. It has been commonly experienced all over the world that the private sector is superior in the matter of administration and management to public sector, while it is worse in respect of greed. The state enterprises manage the affairs badly but they are more conscious of their obligation to the society and state. Both the sectors really adopt each other's views. Little difference is found between the business units of Nehru i.e. the public sector, and Birla i.e. the private sector. The soul of private sector business pervades the body of public sector enterprise. Congress, the ruling party of is partly Swatantra Party and partly communist character. The futile debate to decide the superiority of either the public or private sector is often held as a same routine affair". Certain criteria for public sector units were proposed by Lohia which included inter alia 1. ethos of equality and justice 2. democratic relations between labour and management 3. equality in wages 4. promotion of public interest & 5. management efficiency.

Members of various political parties took pride in getting designated as socialists. They were enamoured of the concept of nationalisation of various sectors of economy. They gave little thought to the soul of economy. They gave little thought to the soul of socialism. Criticising such namesake socialists, Lohia sought to explode the concept of nationalisation as panacea for a variety of social maladies. In the Lok Sabha he said, "It is often argued that nationlisation of banks would lead to socialist order. And that nationalisation is the essence of socialism. Mere changing hands of management of institutions would not result in emergence of socialism. The communists are very much fascinated with the professions and practices of the State of Soviet Russia".

The hue and cry of various political parties about

nationalisation of certain sectors of economy was in Lohia's opinion, futile and frivolous. Taking into consideration the poverty and low purchasing power of the teeming millions he proposed that the state should supply the basic necessities of life to the people at a cheap price. He had suggested that fine grain should be distributed at the rate of eight annas i.e. fifty paise kilogram, while coarse food grain should be sold at six annas per kilo. The figures relate to the prices prevailing during early seventies. Lohia alleged that the business community and the administrative machinery are both equally hands in gloves in the matter of exploiting the common man. With the connivance of the state officials, grain merchants in Bengal were hoarding rice while the people had to starve. Lohia advocated nationalisation of the profession of auditing accounts. He agreed, "The big industrial enterprises ought to be nationalised forthwith. The various controls and restrictions imposed on small industries should be removed. The profession of chartered accountants needs to be nationalised as they play in the hands of the capitalist businessmen rather than presenting a true and correct picture of the business entrusted to them for auditing. The auditors are mainly responsible for the deceit, dishonesty and fraud in trade and industry".

In the course of his speech on the no confidence motion against Lal Bahadur Shastri regime, Lohia proposed a formula for regulating both the private and public sectors of the national economy. He believed that his programme was superior to nationalisation. He was eager to stipulate a ceiling on the amount of individual expenditure. He presented a motion in the Lok Sabha for formulation of a committee to study and report on the proposal to fix one thousand five hundred rupees per month as the ceiling for expenditure. Speaking on his motion on 4th August 1967 he observed, "The debate over three annas versus fifteen annas was the former portion of the backdrop of the motion. The latter portion laying down the ceiling is the symptomatic assumption. The fact of expenditure presumes some source of earning. Measures to curb expenses on luxurious way of life should be adopted. It is a matter pertaining to wealth. Karl Marx arrived at solution of the dilemma about the institution of wealth. The Sanskrit upanishadas which are the pinnacle of India's cultural heritage offered a solution to the various anathema of insatiable greed for wealth. The lure and desire of wealth, as also the desire and fulfillment of consumer needs both have to be reconciled judiciously. Expenses incurred from the public exchequer on officials comprise both salary and perquisites. India ranks first among the countries that provide for perks in the matter of scope and extent. If the quantum of expenses is statutorily restricted, the perks will be abolished".

In the course of the debate on third five year plan Lohia said on 9th December 1963, "The plan has been made by persons who are stupid though erudite and devoid of direction and patriotism. An attempt is being made to implement the plan, by persons vulnerable to corrupt practices and self-centered isolation. It is replete with meaningless formula verbose babble bewildering maze and fails to manifest any distinct path and direction. The Soviet and American economic systems have so confounded, our planners that they are bereft of nationalist feelings. Under the plan a stupendous amount of thirty to forty billion rupees is being wasted on imitation of the West, pompous display, vain ostentations, pageantry and indulgent gratification. Every five year plan led to the enhancement of level or standard of living of about twenty-five thousand people on the upper strata of the society rather than improving the lot of the poor and needy. Lohia laid down three main criteria of the success of a development plan. They were: 1. the quantum of progress and growth as compared with the past 2. the growth in comparison with neighbouring countries and other or; developing countries of the world and 3. hopes and aspirations of the people.

Criticising the approach of the plan Lohia commented, "The model of consumption has been borrowed for the purpose of our planning process from America and Soviet Russia, whereas the pattern of production continues to be age old indigenous type. Our peasants till the land with the type of plough which has been in vogue for the last fifteen centuries. Basically the most modern type of super structure has been constructed on the medieval foundation of production and manufacture. Several other countries of the world which brought about scientific development had fixed the order of priority as scientists, tools and structure, in our country the order had been precisely the reverse of this process". Revealing the nature of relationship of the mechanism set for the implementation of the plan with the administrative machinery Lohia strongly criticised the prevalent dichotomy. He remarked; "The council of ministers epitomising the state decides the policy and issues directives to act upon it. The bureaucracy which functions as the administrative mechanism is held responsible for implementation of the policy. Bureaucracy acts upon the state policy. Less than thirty per cent of the members of the council of ministers were participants of the revolutionary activities such as freedom movement. The bureaucratic officials who stand in the second row of the ruling hierarchy happen to be hereditary slaves. The way of exercising effective control over them is still unknown to the persons at the top. This has led the country to the tragic situation of stagnation. . . Revolution has been imprisoned".

Analysing the reasons that led to the dismal failure Lohia pointed his finger at the ostentatious slogan mongering for abstract socialism. He proposed his programme of concrete socialism to the Lok Sabha elaborating the items of foremost priority thus: 1. all the primary schools in the country should be of one and the same type 2. The rail carriages should have only one class for passengers 3. A ceiling of Rs. one thousand should be imposed for monthly expenditure 4. English language should be eliminated from official and public affairs. 5. Free irrigation facility should be provided for all arable land where it would be technically feasible.

The relationship between political power and business in the country has grown deceptive, fraudulent, corrupt and sour. With an allusion to this unhappy social environment Lohia piquantly remarked, "So long as the father goes on making a headway in his ministerial authority, the son advances rapidly with long strides in his. business affairs". Lohia made a suggestion to legally prohibit the minister's kith and kin extending to two generations, entry upto any field for which quota, permit or licence has been stipulated.

A section of professional Indian economists expressed the view that in the developing economy corruption is a concomitant of growth. Lohia vehemently refuted this contention. He pleaded that corruption had no place in a backward economy, corruption indicates not only lack of honesty but sheer want of perception and sensibility as well. Revealing the unfortunate reality, Lohia said, "Corruption has been rampant at Gangotri, the top most place, where the river Ganga originates. So it would be a futile effort to seek to cleanse the plains spread over the lower level. Delhi the national metropolitan country degenerated to the low level of a handsome adulteress. On one side crores of our countrymen are suffering pangs of starvation and squalor whereas about five million people of the privileged class are raising their standard of living to a higher level of the affluent society of Europe and America. The era of Mahatma Gandhi's leadership was remarkable for simple living and sublime sense of duty. In sharp contrast, the age of the Prime Minister of free India ushered in a regime of voluptuous luxuty and fashionable, upper class style. By way of illustration Lohia pointed to the difference in the common apparel of persons in public life, whereas dhoti & kurta were the garments of prestige during free independence years, coat and pants had taken their place thereafter. Criticising the undesirable change in attitude Lohia remarked, "The Government had concealed the mouth of truth with gold flask. The members of parliament who could not be allotted ministerial offices have been silenced with financial provision of two billion rupees under various pretexts. Independence of thinking is being strangled".

Some of the top ranking ministers their sons, sons-in-law and other kinds had made crores of rupees within a period shorter than two decades. They could accomplish this achievement not by resorting to trade and industry but by securing contracts or licenses for foreign trade. Lohia urged upon the legislators to ponder seriously over the burgeoning corruption and find out measures to root it out. He said, "During all these years about four hundred ministers in collaboration with government employees numbering approximately one crore had acted arbitrarily and with favouritism. If this is allowed to continue the entire state would be doomed".

In the course of his speech during debate on the President's address on 17th February 1964. Lohia forewarned about the impending disaster. He bitterly commented, "The rail of administration has been advancing rapidly without restraint. It faces the danger of either falling into a fathomless ditch or dashing against a rock. The motorman to whom the responsibility of driving it has been entrusted has ceased to operate it. The rail has been heading forward recklessly. The only thing that I can do in such a dangerous situation is to shout and cry halt!" Charactersing the introductory portion of his speech as the voice of his soul, Lohia put the question, "Is there any problem that you have solved?" When there was no reply from the treasury benches, Lohia remarked proceeding further, "The government of today is well-versed in creating problems whereas it is unable to solve them... I would like the Central vigilance commission to examine in depth the data relating to the Prime Minister's fund, trust, grant and disbursement. You cannot improve the situation just by catching the small fry and prosecuting the petty offenders. A few days back Prime Minister Nehru was weighed in gold in Punjab in order to allot the gold for public purpose. It was reported in the press that the gold was procured by public contribution. The affidavits affirmed by the Punjab. State government servants revealed later that gold from the government treasury was utilised for weighing. The funds were not raised from donations made by the people".

In the Lok Sabha, Lohia moved an alternate motion on food situation on 24th September 1964, wherein he made the following observations. 1. The triangle formulated by the Ministers, bureaucrats and businessmen has deteriorated the food situation 2. The prices have risen as the extravagant government spending has adversely affected the circulation of the currency as also the taxation system. 3. No ceiling has been imposed on expenditure 4. Foodgrains worth fifteen billion rupees had been imported during recent years from foreign countries which prevented growth of indigenous production of food. 5. The import-export policy is totally in doldrums 6. The policy relating to vital matters such as speculative trade and raising loan is wrong. The rate of current profit is excessively high. As a sequel to this situation, economic life is in ruins, especially availability of foodgrains in adequate quantity and at reasonable prices has become a mirage. 7. The dual price policy for food grains as cheap and open has resulted in starvation, corruption, profiteering being unbridled.

Various articles of food including pulses, sugar, mango, banana, were being exported thoughtlessly despite food shortage in the country. The poor were being deprived of a part of their food in order to earn foreign exchange. The foreign exchange thus earned was being spent to a large extent for the import of articles of luxury and extravagance. The wrongs of the government in both commission and omission provided ample ground to Lohia for criticism and ridicule. He ably presented his well thought out programme which included agriculture price policy, water policy, land army, food brigade and literacy brigade. The government plan totally ignored agricultural development. Lohia emphasised the imperative need of capital investment in the agricultural sector irrespective need of any consideration of immediate return. "Trade and industry yield high return on investment while agriculture yields substantial return only to those big landowners who have large expanses of over five hundred and upto a thousand acres. The government is guilty not only of its reluctance to catch the thief or rather its coalescence with the thief; it is guilty of wrong policy regarding the mutual relationship between industry and agriculture". In these words Lohia indicted the government of delinquency.

A world renowned expert had estimated in 1948 that not more than thirty percent of the arable land in India could be irrigated by construction of big dams and excavation of canals. Eighty percent of the arable land would have to depend on tanks and wells for the purpose of irrigation. Taking this into consideration Lohia made the suggestion that machines and tools required for excavation of tanks and wells should be imported from the advanced industrialised countries so as to increase the area of agricultural land under irrigation. If fertilisers are used for raising crops without adequate supply of water, production would decrease instead of rising to the desired level. Making a reference to the drought and food supply position in the country Lohia put the question, on 2nd December 1965, in the Lok Sabha, "Who is responsible for the drought and precarious position of food supply that leads to the starvation of forty-eight crores of people? The central government cannot shirk its constitutional obligation by pointing towards the state governments, Article 47 of the constitution has clearly laid down that the central government has to shoulder the burden of providing relief to the—people during periods of disaster such as famine drought, scarcity and starvation. The government usually seeks to escape from the allegation of failure by declaring that there had been no starvation deaths. The immediate cause of death might be some disease such as fever or diarrhoea but the malnutrition and starvation is the root cause of the disease. Irregular and scant supply of foodgrains leads to starvation deaths". Crores of people especially in the remote and backward rural areas get to eat a few morsels after several days of total starvation. They fall a prey to common diseases and die within a few months. It matters little whether the government liberalises the trade in foodgrains or takes it over. It ought to comply with its obligation to feed the people. The people should march to the residence of the minister and officer concerned and ask them to feed the hungry first and then to take their own meal. The people should refuse to die silently of starvations" The Food Minister of the Indian Union had, in fact, never been the food minister. He had been functioning as a food procurement minister. He was more active in procuring food from abroad than in India.

The term starvation death should be clearly defined, Lohia thought and sought to raise the issue on the floor a number of times. In the context of the precarious situation in West Bengal, S.M. Bannerjee moved a closure motion on 8th March 1966. Police squads from Uttar Pradesh were deployed in Bengal to suppress the people's voice of discontent and rage. Sometime back police squads from West Bengal had been deployed in Assam to put down ruthlessly the unrest of the people. Lohia put the question, "If the people throughout the country would start an anti-hunger movement, where would the government get the police companies for deployment? About one hundred fifty municipalities maintain statistical data about birth and death. Lohia sought to know whether it would be possible to ascertain from them the figures about starvation death from them. The minister did not offer a clear definition of the term, starvation death despite. Lohia's persistent plea. So Lohia offered his definition. If the deceased person did not get more than a hundred gram of food every day for two to four months prior to his death, it should be considered a starvation death. Lohia challenged the minister to offer his definition, if he did not accept this reasonable meaning of the term. The minister did not agree with Lohia pointing out that starvation was distinct from malnutrition.

Lohia stated that thirty crore poor people in our country consumed food per day each equivalent to about seven hundred calories. He asked the food minister to explain in terms of calories, the quantum of food available each day per capita below which the starvation level might be concluded. The minister told the house that people can sustain on twenty or thirty gram foodgrains per day, Lohia urged the minister to state whether thirty or twenty? The daily *Hindustan Times* had published an article written by Dr. Sukhatme of the World Food Organisation in September 1964. The internationally reputed statistician had pointed out that four out of ten people in the world live at starvation level and one out of the four hungry is an Indian. Sukhatme defined hunger as malnutrition. Lohia reckoned the figure of starving Indians as thirty crore with an allusion to Sukhatme's findings. He exhorted the minister to state distinctly the data relating to sixty percent of Indian population in the lowest social layer comprising the downtrodden deprived and extremely poor. This ill-fated section of the populace sustains on a daily per capita provision of about two hundred fifty to three hundred grams. The ministers were mis-representing the facts by stating the averages relating to fortyeight crore population.

Despite Lohia's earnest pleas and entreaties, the food minister adamantly persisted in his style of crude formality. He went on modifying his statements from time to time. Subramaniam, the Food Minister, Bhoothalingam the bureaucrat and Seth Jeetpal the businessman were all equally guilty. The triumvirate was looting the country. Lohia deplored the prevalent system of transferring and promoting or upgrading the guilty officials. He wanted the errant bureaucrats to be exemplarily punished with imprisonment and fine. With a view to better the economic life of the country the triangular clan would have to be smashed.

A sizeable number of issues were raked up by Lohia in his effort to present the abstract masses in concrete form. The poor people who pulled rickshaws with hands lived a dreary and pitiable life of rigorous labour, anguish and squalor. On Lohia's initiative the Lok Sabha held a half hour debate on the unfortunate lot of rickshaw pullers. Their plight was more of draught animals than human beings. During a period of barely eighteen years subsequent to the attainment of independence, the number of rickshaw pullers multiplied ten times. The hasty light of villagers to urban areas is one of the obvious reasons. The age-old caste system led to the degeneration of the rural society converting it practically into a prison. Disgusted of the crippling social barricades of the village life and attracted to the pompous enchanting display of urban social environment, the hungry exploited section of the village folk have been flying to the towns and cities in ever increasing numbers. Thus they seek to liberate themselves from the shackles that had tied them for centuries, even though it meant their partial conversion into beasts of burden.

The imperative need to pull the rickshaw by hands for physical sustenance of sizeable section of the people is a disgraceful blemish for a free, democratic, large country like India, Lohia felt and brought up the issue in the Lok Sabha Responding to Lohia's question the minister told that pulling a rickshaw does not adversely affect the puller's health. Lohia advised the minister to emulate the example of judges in the modern Western world, who reside with the prisoners for some time to observe the condition of the prison and realise how it affects the mental and physical make-up of the inmates. If the ministers concerned. Jagjivan Ram and Shah Nawaj Khan would pull a rickshaw for about a month they would come to know the reality about a rickshaw puller's life. An expert medical practitioner who was closely in touch with the rickshaw-pullers had told Lohia that if a young man below the age of nineteen years or a person of advanced age above forty pulls the rickshaw habitually, his lungs are so badly affected that he falls a prey to some incurable disease or the other and succumbs to death within years. Several members of the house got excited over the minister's statement that pulling a rickshaw does not cause any injurious effect on the puller's health.

The issue of other sections of the poor people including vagabonds arid tramps so called was also raked up by Lohia alongwith the one relating rickshaw pullers. Under section 109 of the Criminal Procedure Code such men are arrested and put in jail on trivial charges. They come to the cities in search of employment. As they have no kin in the city they roam aimlessly through the streets to pass time, till about midnight. The policemen harass them to for being vagabond. Lohia raised a hue and cry against section 109 pleading for its abolition. He argued, "So long as section 109 is not removed from the statute, weapons, everybody is susceptible to moral degeneration".

Under the auspices of the convention for eradication of caste system Lohia used to fight on the streets. He fired the cannon in the Lok Sabha roaring, "Our country has been suffering from the dreadful social disease of caste discrimination for over a millennium and half. Since the last fifteen years it has been assuming the face of an abominable pestilence virtually amounting to a form of leprosy. The clamour for equality of opportunity is unjust and iniquitous. We shall have to adopt in its stead, the tenet of preferential opportunity for the class deprived and downtrodden for centuries". As regards the remuneration and emoluments for scavengers Lohia held the view that the level of scale should be raised so high that people of higher castes would also be attracted to disgustible functions. Therein lies the hope of ironing out the rigid of caste discrimination. Lohia raised the issue of emoluments and working conditions of scavengers in the Lok Sabha on 13th July 1967.

During the debate on the report on development of the scheduled castes Lohia pointed out the condition of the downtrodden backward classes has been deteriorating more and more. The population of the scheduled castes and scheduled tribes exceeded ten crores. Adding to this figure the people belonging to other backward classes and religious minority communities, whose social and economic plight is little better, the aggregate depressed and backward population exceeded thirty-five crore in 1967. The aforesaid report indicated that out of the 8394 union government employees in the higher cadre, persons belonging to scheduled castes and scheduled tribes numbered only 91 and 16 respectively. Under the provisions of the constitution and regulations framed thereunder 11½% seats have been reserved for S.C. and S.T. candidates together. In this context Lohia said in a note of bitter comment, "I would like to propose that the provisions of reservations in union and State services should be totally dropped, and the government should candidly and honestly declare that it does not feel it necessary to provide preferential opportunities for the Harijans and aboriginal tribals. If on the other hand the government is intent on retention of the provisions about reservation, it should take all necessary steps to allot the seats to the depressed class candidates according to the predetermined percentage irrespective on away consideration about suitability and efficiency. This would be the only proper way to rectify a wrong. The five-year development plan had provided an amount of over Rs. nine lakhs as outlay for hostels meant for Harijans and tribal students. The actual expenditure incurred however come to Rs. seven a half lakh and several other items had to face shortage of funds. "We have not been fighting the battles on an adequate number of fronts to further the cause of emancipation of the out-castes", said Lohia. The judiciary too is unable to administer natural and legal justice as the judges are biased in favour of the hierarchical traditional caste system of social structure. Lohia made a reference to a recent verdict passed by a judge in Pune. An accused who was charged with an offence of murder was acquitted by the judge. The sister of the accused had fallen in love with a youth of lower caste. The judge in whose court the case was proceeded had observed in his judgement; "The accused had found out that his sister had been enticed by a villain-according to social custom his sister cannot marry a butcher". The murder was adjudged legally justifiable. Lohia deplored the reality that judges entertaining such biased and prejudiced views presided over the judicial & legal proceedings. Leading a ferocious assault on the prevalent caste system which practically incarcerated the constituents of society in a bondage akin to slavery, Lohia reiterated his view that, "so long as the venomous shackle of caste system which is a bane for the Indian society continues to prevail, the persons occupying high positions would give every encouragement to their caste and to forge ahead briskly. The distinction between the big and the small and the barriers between them, apply not only to language, approval, residence, menu of food, locality, but they extend to a wider field. There is a barrier between their thought and talk justice and injustice as also honesty and dishonesty so long as the barriers dividing the people as high and low, big and small superior and inferior are not demolished the society cannot be freed from the strangle hold on the octopus of caste system. Lohia observed; "The transformation of society takes place and revolution succeeds only when the popular will and law work together in unison. It is the present position that the law relating to annihilation of untouchability has been written in statute books but peoples will does not accompany the law. If the people do not have the will and the mettle to implement a law it becomes superfluous and not worth even the paper on which it might be printed. It is no use just to enact a legislation however beneficial it might be".

In the Lok Sabha, Lohia was the first member to ventilate the cause of the woman, the suffering smallest human being. He lost no opportunity to plead for equality between man and woman. He raked up a number problems facing the women such as the cruel beatings they had to suffer their starvation, shortage of water, absence of toilet facilities, the burning pain of the eyes caused by smoke in the kitchen etc. all in silence. He named Jinnah's sister as Mr. Fatima Jinnah to which the lady members took objection. Lohia made the suggestion that irrespective of a person's gender he or she should be mentioned as Shri or Mister. He sought to discontinue the practice of referring to the fair sex as madam, lady member, chairwoman and the like. In one line Lohia made a reference to two politicians as, "Two women the Delhiwali and the Lucknowwali" One was the Prime Minister and the other a state Chief Minister. Some members raised a hue and cry, dubbing Lohia with impropriety and lack of parliamentary courtesy. They wanted him to abstain from speaking the dialect of the market in the parliament house Lohia retorted, "One's mother sister, daughter are all women. In what way a is woman residing in palatial premises a different entity?" Renuka Ray a Congress member got so exasperated at Lohia's repartee that she exclaimed, "Who is Lohia to slight the top ranking ladies of our land? The Indian women are strong supporters of our lady Prime Minister (Gandhi)".

On a number of occasions Lohia vented resentment in the Lok Sabha against blind faith, absurd religious astrological forebodings, idolatry, amulet, rosary, oblation on the altar and innumerable, queer social traditions. The concept of divine incarnation is totally inconsistent with reason and democratic way of life. The hope that the heavenly lord would descend on the earth to rescue the human society from ruin is all humbug. The feudal belief that the legendary Jahangir bell would ring to administer justice is a deception, said Lohia exploding such myths.

Secularism is a basic tenet of Indian constitution. Defining the term Lohia explained that it connects our life on the earth. To be free from religious belief is an aspect of it. Lohia did not believe in god, regeneration, previous birth, heaven and health. He told the Lok Sabha, "There is some basic disorder in Hindu religion. Perhaps it is pseudo culture. During the days of Chinese incursion, appeals were addressed to the countrymen to have tears in their eyes. In reality it is necessary to construct a barrage to stop the tears if they start to roll down over faces?" Tracing the reasons leading to the absence of heat of opposition in Indian policies Lohia revealed his expectations that the leaders of the Harijans and tribals would rend the sky with full throated shouts of revolt and resentment. But silence reigns where loud sound is expected to ring. More than eighty per cent of the Harijan and tribal representatives in the Lok Sabha belong to Congress, the ruling party. Lohia revealed the bitter truth that out of the there hundred ambassadors and high commissioners deputed abroad during the last eighteen years, not a single person hailed from Harijans or Girijans (meaning people of the mountain, or tribals).

During the debate on foreign policy in 1963, Lohia quoted the great poet Ravindranath Tagore; "Where the head is raised high and find is free from fear" and said, "unless our national foreign policy is doubtless it cannot succeed in safeguarding and furthering the interest of the country". Nehru had laid down two criteria for foreign policy national interest and world order. As regards the first criterion, Lohia's comment was particularly piquant. He observed, "We have lost our territory stretched over an area of eighteen thousand square miles. If we add to it the Kailash mountain and Manas lake the area regularly and forcibly robbed by our neighbour this aggregates to about one lakh square miles. From the perspective of world order our foreign policy is obviously guided and directed by alien powers. India's foreign policy has no principle and direction and vision. The last fifteen years we have been witnessing a fallacious rhetoric of world peace and diplomacy of deceit. The main test of any foreign policy lies in relationship with neighbouring countries. None of our neighbours has more intimate relationship of affinity with India, rather with China". India Pakistan confederation, World Development Corporation, friendly relationship with the entire humanity on global level, were some of the ideas which Lohia presented before the Lok Sabha. Enumerating the five principal inequalities between the countries in the world viz. production, prices, armaments, technology and land, Lohia proposed that the coloured people of the world should invite to fight against them with the active collaboration of the liberals among the whites Lohia's analysis and observation of the intricacies of the world situation aimed at amelioration of the lot of the common man. In the context of the rivalry between two communist world powers Lohia commented, "Although Russia and China both claim to abide by the communist ideology, the gap of inequality between the two is astoundingly wide. China believed that Marxism was the panacea that would remove the divergence between the two and elevate China to a higher lever. But there has not been the slightest indication of the possibility of narrowing down the wide gap between two million coloured exploited suppressed people on the one side and one million mighty white people on the other. This painful reality has made China so desperate as to prefer going astray recklessly on the global level. China is irritated on account of its failure to attain equality with Russia. Regarding the question of granting recognition to the Communist government of mainland China, Lohia stated unequivocally, "If in a country the government would be firmly in saddle for a long period and would be strong and effective it should be accorded formal recognition and political and diplomatic relations should be established with it. Exception to this general rule might be made if—1. The Government would be acting against humanity. & 2. If it has made an aggression and annexed the territory of the neighbouring country.

Lohia felt that there had been total chaos in respect of defence policy, foreign policy and production policy of the union government. On 17th July 1967, he made a reference to the impending risk of foreign aggression and lack of will in the government to counter it. In his typical style of scoffing derisively at the tragic, anomalous situation he said", Indian foreign policy is a housewife whose husband is food supplies and son is the army but it has distorted to the position of a childless widow. If a man replaces a woman it may be said that has become analogous to a widower who is bereft of progeny. "It is advisable to introduce an element of resilience in our defence and foreign policy matters. We should never hesitate to seek assistance from any power for our defence as may be necessary and possible. It would not be proper to align with any particular power". Prime Minister Shastri attended a non-allied summit conference. Lohia had sought the Prime Minister's statement on his stand in the conference. Lohia firmly believed that attempts to change the international boundary between neighbouring countries forcibly by coercive measures are ways of imperialism and colonialism, He detested such tactics irrespective of the colour of the colonial master. Whether white, black, yellow or brown. He had expected the Indian Prime Minister to raise the vital issue in the conference. What should be India's stand point in the non-aligned countries summit conference? Lohia's answer to this question was as clear as sunlight. He told the Lok Sabha, "Hypocrites profess to be devotees of Ganga when they happen to visit river Ganga. When in proximity of Yamuna. They feel no hesitation in displaying devotion for Yamuna". A member commented, "The two join each other in a conference" Lohia proceeded further, "Political hypocrites profess to be pro-Soviet when in Moscow and loyal to America when in Washington. Those who believe that Ganga and Yamuna are ultimately one identity should accept the challenge of forging unity between Soviet Union and USA".

During the course of debate in Lok Sabha on 16th November

1965 about international affairs and policy of the government Lohia observed, "There has been lack of motivation and will in respect of our strategy. We have been adhering to fake ideals and ultra practicality. Our fake ideas resulted into our readiness to give political asylum to Dalai Lama who fled Tibet. But our sense of ultrapracticality disallowed us from taking due advantage of the opportunity his presence afforded. It is the universally accepted principle that the place where Lord Rama resides is Ayodhya. Obviously Tibet is Dalai Lama's territory. It has been his residence and demand under his rule. India ought to accord diplomatic recognition to the Lama's government". Referring to the controversies about Vietnam and East Germany Lohia argued, "Our Prime Minister was wrong in arresting a religious preacher in Vietnam. He should not have interfered in the affairs of Vietnam to the detriment of American interest and in favour of Soviet Union. It would be just and proper for India to accord diplomatic recognition to the government of East Germany irrespective of any consideration of America's possible irritation". India's foreign policy had been emphasing on peaceful co-existence between nations with divergent views. Lohia challenged its propriety and legitimacy. He said that the coexistence between the two world powers Russia and America had all alongwith full of rebuke and censure instead of being peaceful. Lohia vehemently pleaded that the stereo typed verbose rhapsodical foreign policy ought to be abolished.

After the Indo-Pakistan ceasefire agreement, Bhagwat Jha Azad moved a proposal seeking India's withdrawal from the Commonwealth. Participating in the debate Lohia urged Shri M.C. Chhagla, the then Foreign Minister, to play the role of a judge rather that of an advocate. The Foreign Minister in his speech addressed to the United Nations spoke for thirty-one minutes like an advocate pleading his client's cause and four minuted like a loyal soldier of his country. Lohia expressed his belief that if Chagala had spoken for thirty-one minutes like a soldier, rather than an advocate, India would have won its case. Lohia pointedly brought out the fact that the Security Council of the United Nations rarely addresses the issues of America's intervention in Vietnam or the Soviet Union's armed interference in Hungary, its satellite in East Europe. The council adopts resolutions merely in the affairs of those countries that are weak, helpless, backward, and militarily so feeble as to be unable to proceed on the way they might choose.

The Arab Israel armed conflict grew acute during May-June 1967. The Lok Sabha held a debate on 6th June 1967 about the explosive situation in West Asia. Lohia held the Soviet Union as guilty as the Western Imperial Powers for the formation of Israel as the motherland of Jews in the Arab territory. He told that Jordan, Saudi Arabia, Iraq were the products of international manouvering of Western Powers. Both America and Russia incite these countries of the coloured people to fight against each other. The two world powers derive major political and economic benefits thereby. Lohia analysed the Indian policy in the context of the situation in West Asia. He said, "Our policy relating to Arab-Israel controversy comprises four element viz. affinity for the Arab states, affection for the ethnic Arabs, fondness for the community of Jews and conceding the birth and existence of Israel as a State". Usually Lohia commented that "our union government belonged to America bodily and Russia mentally. When the body and mind are separated from each other, body acquires primary importance. He held the view that, "Indian government ought to formulate a foreign policy of self-respect, under which not merely Arabs and Israel, but the various territories on the map of the world which have been cut asunder by the imperial powers would be rejoined in love, trust and fraternity. There has been an implicit understanding between America and Russia under which a lute is being played, the melodious sound of which drowns the servants throughout the world in sound sleep. The two world powers have arrived at a consensus on the point of alluring a potentially mighty country like India to lie in a stupor, so that it might not attain strength. In fact both the world powers required the: emergence of a power which would counter the challenge flung by China".

On matters of foreign policy Lohia made his last speech in the Lok Sabha on 14th July 1967, during the course on debate over the Tibet issue. It was a very excited debate in which stalwarts such as Kriplani, and Nath Pai besides Lohia examined the concepts of sovereignty and suzerainty in various aspects. Communist party member Mukherji opposed the motion tabled by Socialist members. Mukherji was full of praise for the Chinese communist revolution, Lohia laid bare the fallacies of Mukherji's arguments. He told the house, "Human history has witnessed a number of revolutions in the past. The series of revolutions would have no end. It is wrongly claimed that the Bolshevik revolution of Russia was the first and

Chinese revolution under the leadership of Mao ze Dong was the last revolution". The main thrust of Lohia's speech was the need of the liberation of the people of Tibet from the domination of Chinese communist party government. Justifying the demand for the restoration of Tibet's independence, Lohia said, "I am not in favour of waging a war against China. At the same time would not make an agreement of peace with China so long as it does not! rectify its ways. We have to pass through a third round. In the affairs of Tibet we have to affirm that it had been an independent country in the past and would continue to be free in future. The relationship between China and Tibet is not analogous to that between India and Kashmir. It is akin to the relation between China and Sinkiang or between England and Malaga".

During those days Lohia was not keeping good health. Mentally, too, he was disturbed. A youth of about twenty-six approached him and asked whether there was any likelihood on the liberation of Tibet in near future. Lohia got nostalgic memories of the past when he was the same age as the visiting stranger overwhelmed him, when he was in his twenties he rolled in anguish over the slavery of his motherland. Being a resident of a country of thirty-five crores of people he was fully confident of a bright future for India. Lohia tried to give solace to the youth. To pacify his excitement he said, he felt that some day Tibet would be a free land, as the world had been advancing along the path of multilateral progress towards the ultimate ideal of freedom. Narrating to the Lok Sabha the report of his dialogue with the aforesaid youth Lohia proceeded further, "The leaders of China are mistaken in their belief that the distinct ethnic identify of the Tibetan race could be eliminated. Chinese families are being given every encouragement to inhabit Tibet. Such efforts would intimately prove futile. The new race that might emerge in Tibet would not be Chinese in nationality and character. It would retain its Tibetan ethos and identify. I feel it would rise in revolt united by against the Chinese expansionist aggressors and would attain its goal of national independence. The state of India was defined by poet laureate Rajeshwar of the Court of Kanauj, the last metropolis of ancient India. The poet had indicated that our paramount power had an expanse over the territory from Bindusar in the North to Kanyakumari in the South. Bindusar was a synonym for Mansarovar. When India would emerge as a mighty country among the community of nations in the world, the said age-old definition might well apply to it. The Himalayan lake Manas had constituted a portion of Indian territory for ages". The motion on the issue of Tibet tabled by some of the members of the opposition had little chance of being passed in the parliament. The majority of the Congress party in the central legislature was capable and nasty enough to uphold any proposal and defeat the best of the motions meant to further national interest. Nevertheless it would be noteworthy to observe that some of the Congressmen spoke favourably on the controversial issue and Hanumantaya a veteran southern Congressman, abstained from voting.

The Chinese officials used to humiliate the diplomats working in the Indian embassy in Peking. The issue came up for discussion in the Lok Sabha on 14th July 1967. Lohia held the view that "India should not adopt the attitude of retaliation. We shall have to formulate some coherent policy on Chinese affairs. On the one hand we dub China as an aggressor and expansionist power, on the other hand we have been strongly supporting its claim for admission to the UN as a full-fledged member. On one side India declares that it will not tolerate the retention of even an inch of Indian territory in China's possession, on the other, India has no hesitation in swearing by the Colombo proposals which are inconsistent with our solemn declaration. While we announce that we shall maintain our age-old relationship, in the same breath we state that the issue will have to be given fresh thought. The position of dangling between two distinct, mutually contradictory status points is disastrous. In fact the ministers do not lay down India's foreign policy. A fragment of our bureaucratic structure which holds the charge of foreign affairs is determined upon waging a stake hither and some other thither. I solemnly affirm that China's style of behaving with our diplomats has left no alternative for us except to sever diplomatic relations with it. Such a serious decision warrants the will and firmness to act. The crux of the matter is, how far it would be desirable and practical to attempt to improve the relationship between the disabled infirm flexible on one side and the crazy, infatuated bully on the other". Lohia knew fully well that the initiative would have to be taken by those in power in order to shun the arrogant neighbour. He humbly entreated the treasury benches, "I have very great regard for you and hold you in high esteem as you are mighty. Being weak and ineffective I detest myself. The term coexistence is repeated too often. Some people hold the view that good and evil both would prevail in the world side by side. I conceive that in the ensuing three or four decades, either good or evil will have to be eliminated permanently in view of the production and stocking of armaments of mass destruction such as atom bomb hydrogen bomb and long range missiles. The coexistence of good and evil is impossible. We had to relinquish Tibet, and even admitting that Tibet did not belong to India it is hard to know how it happened to belong to China. In recent years China had to undergo a phase of what is known as cultural revolution. I often feel that a little bit of the said cultural revolution would be welcome in India. I consider China to be a monster, but I would like to cite for emulation its example in the matter of will power and determination".

The attention of the Lok Sabha was drawn by Lohia to a very important matter on 14th May 1966. He proved on the basis of authentic evidence that the size of the territory of free India had reduced substantially. He cited the data provided by the UN and the Indian government in their reports. The data furnished by the UN indicates that a territory of 1,22,222 of square kilometres has disappeared. The statistics available with the Union government state that an area of 8,043 square miles is not traceable. Lohia remarked after presenting the data, "Every Indian would be enraged and struck with horror to know that India has be deprived of a large portion of its land since independence". Mother India comprises its people and land. The area of its land has been on the decrease. Is it that in our country land. The house on being pressed heard that the annual report of the UN for 1960 deducted from the total figure of Indian territory an area of 2,22,300 square miles which comprised the state of Jammu-Kashmir". Both the Prime Minister and Education Minister gave the clarification that the Congress party government at the Centre cannot be held accountable for the reduction of the figure of Indian territory. Lohia sought to call a motion of breach of privilege against the Education Minister on 22nd August 1966. He argued, "I want to point out that the Education Minister has not merely made a wrong statement; but he has purposefully concealed the fact and thus misled the house. The difference between the figures furnished by the UN and our government, amounts to two and a half lakh square miles of area". In fact, the area of Indian territory has increased after 1961 on account of the accession to India of the areas till then held by the French and Portuguese rulers. Goa, Diu, Daman, Nagar Haveli, Pondicherry, and Mahe were added to India's domain. Lohia commented, bitterly. "When a firm reaches the verge of insolvency its account books get such a bad shape that they lose credibility, similarly when the land area of a country is decreasing and is being robbed, the documents of the country are badly deteriorated". Lohia suspected that certain manoeuvering tactics were being considered at the official and the government levels to relinquish some more Indian territory. Expressing his suspicion, Lohia said in the Lok Sabha, "It was told on behalf of the government that Long Ju valley is just a mile or two area. Infact Lang Ju is a valley spread over an area of a few hundred square kilometres we have lost it. Is Bara Hati too being left out? We have to take into consideration the underlying facts. Till the year 1960, the UN used to accept without any reservations the data submitted to it by the government of India. But now the UN declared Jammu-Kashmir a disputed area. Lohia brought this factual position to the notice of Shri Chhagla, the foreign affairs minister. The minister explained, I can understand in good faith Lohia's allegation of wrong statement. However, strongly protect against his allegation levelled on me of having spoken a lie". The speaker ruled out the issue by declaring that the house had not been misled (by the minister concerned).

The controversy over loss of Indian territory to the benefit of alien powers had been so intensely irritating Lohia's mind that prior to his death he again raked up the issue of the area of Indian territory on 8th August 1967. The house had been pursuing the matter for about two years. But the minister concerned had all along been evasive. Chhagla's mistake ultimately came to light. The census was taken in 1960, and the area of Indian territory was being surveyed. It was an imperative obligation of the government to submit its report to the UN. The government forwarded its incomplete report alongwith a note of explanation stating that the survey had been still in progress. The Minister had conceded the reality. UN got an opportunity to point out the discrepancy. Lohia commented that the folly of the government afforded an opportunity for the secessionist forces to plead for separation on Jammu-Kashmir from the Union of India. The minister told the house that the government had clearly stated in its report that its report about area was merely provisional, and it should not be treated as full and final. The government had registered its protest with the UN against treating the obviously provisional data as final. But the notice of protest had not been taken up for hearing till then.

Kripalani, a member on the opposition side had remarked on the issue in his typical ironical style, "The disputants on the controversy regarding the data of area of Indian territory are fighting in vain. The great saint Ramakrishna Paramashansa's observation is relevant in this context. The saint had said that certain happenings in the universe make us ridicule the acts of God Almighty. When two claimants to the ownership of a piece of land differ with each other on the matter of their portion and the boundary line dividing the plots God decrees that both are wrong as the landowner is God. The government of India on the present day, incidentally, holds the view that all this land over which there is a dispute between India and China belongs to God".

Lohia raised a number of novel and queer issues in the Lok Sabha and made the government pay serious attention to them. Lohia's efforts proved each time that there had been some thing wrong. He initiated a half hour debate on the topic of criticism of Indian History. The debate resulted in giving proper direction to the traditional way of thought. This was the first opportunity afforded to the members to discuss certain aspects of social science. The UN had constituted an international commission to compile a comprehensive history of mankind. Lohia raised objection against the contents of the book on the subject published by UNESCO. Compilation of the book was the joint responsibility of UN, UNESCO and the Indian government. Lohia was eager to invite the attention of the parties concerned to certain fundamental elements expecting to change the direction thereby.

Elaborating on the essential purpose of history Lohia said, "History" indicates the lesson that mankind derives from the past events. It is the creator of the present which is supposed to apportion happiness and sorrow to all in just and equal ratio. If history is observed and written in the wrong way the present and future of the society would be moulded in wrong way... Leonard Woody the author of the book published by UNESCO is mistaken in assuming that structures such as the northern gate of the renowned Buddha stupa of Sanchi was the product of observation and adaptation of Chinese wooden architecture. No Indian historian came forward to disprove the assumption but a Russian Scholar Diecnov Arelin attempted to contradict it. Lohia after thus narrating the background told the Lok Sabha that the said book has mentioned the title of another book, Five thousand years of Pakistan. A member commented on this as foolish and absurd. Another member remarked that it was rascality not absurdity.

Lohia referred to the contents of UNESCO'S book and stated that it has mentioned ancient Chinese and Egyptian poetry. The writer holds the view that three thousand back there was nothing like poetry in India, so no comment could be made about ancient India poetry. M.S. Aney claimed that Tilak's treatise on Orion has produced evidence to prove that the hymns and verse that had been compiled in the Rigvedas were composed six thousand years back. Lohia told that, "The book is silent on verses in Rigvedas. Gowardhan Sharma who had undertaken a project on excavation in Kaushambi has arrived at the conclusion on the basis of radio carbon test that the utensils found there belonged to the period between 2035 B.C. to 640 AD. The writers on Indian history presume that if some renovation occurs in any field of social life it is the outcome of some foreign contact and influence. What type of rejuvenation it is, which occurs frequently? This type of stream of thought will have to be done away with. Coordination may be divided into two types slave and master. India never learnt the coordination of the master during the last thousand years. There has all along been a "slaves coordination". Lohia put the blame squarely on India historians too. He made no distinction between Indian and foreign historians. There has been the difference in perspective. In compilation of history India had ever been unfortunate. Expressing his concern over it, Lohia said, "India might be built or demolished on the basis of mathematics and history. The science of Indian history is suffering from the disease of dependence. Foreign writers of Indian history right from Farista to Vincent Smith consider every victory over India as inevitable and beneficial for India. Indian historians are parasitic in nature and follow the course of foreign historians.. The book published by the Indian government on the 1857 revolt is untrue and unscientific.

Minister Chhagla was angry at Lohia's criticism of the book written by Sen. But Ranga, Nath Pai, and a few others applauded

Lohia. He made it clear that it is wrong to recognise minor changes at the surface level as rejuvenation; surrender as assimilation and splitting as cultural varieties. After the debate in Lok Sabha historian Mujumdar too repudiated the Education Minister Chhagla saying that ". . . . the minister had told the house during the course of debate" that UNESCO had compiled a History of Mankind. My criticism of the volume on the prehistoric period was forwarded to the UNESCO beforehand which was later included in the book. "In fact no such criticism was forwarded. Obviously government of India is responsible for wrong interpretation of facts. Even the National Commission failed to express its protest after the drafts were distributed". That was Mujumdar's comment on Chhagla's explanation. Mujumdar was one of the three Indian members of the UNESCO Commission.

Lohia was going to the parliament house in a taxi some day in March 1966, Prime Minister Gandhi too was going in the same direction in her car. The police officers stopped Lohia's taxi from proceeding further. Communist member Ram Sevak Yadav sought the raise the issue of the privileges of members of parliament, on 16th March 1966. The Deputy Speaker refused to grant them permission. Lohia put forward three reasons publishing the demand for raising the issue in Lok Sabha. 1. Equal rules and regulations for all for traffic on roads. 2. No discrimination would be permissible between members of parliament in respect of uniformity of treatment. 3. Government servants inclusive of police officers should be made fully aware that they too compromise the government in their specific positions. They are the, symbol of the government and superior to ministers.

When Lohia raised the issue, Kripalani narrated his traffic experience. Several members, had similar experiences. Ranga, Laxmimal Singhvi, O.P. Duvedi, H.N. Mukherjee Hemkant Barua were also happy that the issue had been raked up. In the states the position was still worse. MPs and MLAs were mutely suffering the humiliation. Dr. Karni Singh appealed to the Prime Minister to put an end to this unwelcome undesirable practice; as all are equal. Prime Minister Gandhi pleaded that due consideration ought to be given to the specific position of Prime Minister. She said that it had been the current practice in most of the countries in the world.

Hemkant Barua said that it prevails in the backward

countries. Gandhi claimed that even in the advanced countries it did prevail. Barua emphatically contradicted her statement. Lohia intervened to say that if in Britain any Prime Minister dares to enforce such discriminatory treatment he would have to quit his office the next day. A member said that no such practice prevailed in Sweden. Prime Minister Gandhi said, "I have observed while I was accompanying the president in America that the practice prevailed there. Lohia exclaimed, "Oh, she argues to be President". Limaye said, "You are the Prime Minister. So you should compare your position with that of the British Prime Minister, not the President of America". Prime Minister Gandhi said, "Some special arrangement will have to be made for the transport of the Prime Minister. It has been made for the convenience of only the Prime Minister, not for other Ministers".

The Deputy Speaker gave the ruling that in India all roads freely open and all legislators are equal. However specific provision has to be made for the Prime Minister. Lohia did not agree. He said, "The Prime Minister has stated that she holds a 'special position.' I wish that the Lok Sabha should abolish her special position, if there be any, and throw away the person too who asks for it. This is the Lok Sabha all members are equal here". Lohia raked up the issue of Prime Minister's wrong statement again as a matter of order. Under the constitution, the President holds a special position, Prime Minister is the source of power and authority, while the President is the source of honour and respect. If power and honour both merge with each other, democracy will vanish. The Prime Minister's special position and honour must end. The speaker of the house ruled that the point of constitutional power should be got clarified by the judiciary. Lohia remarked; "Whenever the persons who function as speakers of legislative houses at central and state levels found if difficult or inconvenient to give a ruling they got rid of the trouble by advising the parties to knock the doors on the court of justice!"

With his entry into the Lok Sabha Lohia started attempting to expose the wrong or misleading statements of ministers. It was a war of nerves in which his courage, valour, sobriety, restraint were on test. Prior to his arrival on the scene, the Lok Sabha had acquired the habit of swallowing down mis-statements. Lohia himself told that even though the ministers' wrong statements were detected after incessant efforts lasting over number of weeks or months the ministers did not hesitate to present wrong information and place away from the house. It was widely presumed that the Ministers had the prerogative to tell a lie as their special privilege. Lohia had exposed Nehru's misstatement the cost of his own popularity.

The American president Kennedy was assassinated in November 1963. Lohia used to respect Kennedy as a rare diplomat and he expressed his grief over has inability to transfer the remaining part of his life to the departed leader. Lohia was of the opinion that after assuming office as the executive head of USA, Kennedy rose to a still higher level of eminence. His vigor and enthusiasm grew. In the controversy between whites and Negroes Kennedy displayed his courage and righteousness. It was Friday when he breathed his last. The burial took place on Monday. Prime Minister Nehru had ample time at his disposal to take flight from Delhi and participate in the funeral, but Nehru had lost his decisive power probably due to growing age. Russia deputed its deputy Prime Minister Khrushchev. The Russian leader went to the American embassy in Moscow and paid his tributes to Kennedy, Nehru waited in Delhi looking to Moscow. His sister and a state Governor, Vijayalaxmi Pandit represented India at the function in Washington. In the list of order of honours Shrimati Pandit ranked lower than two hundred. Though the President, and the Prime Minister were present in the American embassy at Delhi for paying tributes, the condolence message was read by a Cabinet Secretary. Lohia felt sorry that international protocol was not observed in this matter.

The Prime Minister told the Lok Sabha that it was not possible for him to leave India and reach Washington on time. This statement was wrong. Prime Minister of China flew over Indian skies in his journey to Washington. India granted him the permission on China's request. In the Lok Sabha Nehru replied to a question that the Chinese Premier could have flown by an alternative route, but it would be a longer round about way. Lohia pointed out that Nehru's statement that it was not possible for him to reach. Washington on time for the funeral was wrong. The decision to allow the Chinese Premier to fly over Indian territory was wrong and objectionable. The relations between China and India in those days were hostile. China had declared unilateral ceasefire. The speaker disallowed raising further questions in the matter of Chinese premier's flight over India.

Those were the days when to utter even a word against Nehru was regarded an offence. Lohia had made it clear that he had no personal animosity with Nehru. The controversy related to differing policies. Prime Minister Nehru abused and called Lohia names. He referred to Lohia as a mannerless bully & liar. Tyagi observed in this context that Nehru often mentions thus certain persons for whom he has affection, Lohia considered it necessary to explain his position. He said, "It is a fact that I too had affection (for Nehru). But now I have ceased to be affectionate towards him. I want to make this amply clear so that there should be no scope for misunderstanding".

Through George Fernandes, Lohia came to know that the Chinese the government might be willing to recognise Kailash Man Sarovar and the east-flowing Brahmaputra as the Indian border. Edgar Snow had told so to George. Lohia informed this to the Lok Sabha on 16th June 1966 and asked the Prime Minister and defence minister whether they would try to know the mind of Chinese leader. Defence Minister Chavan replied, "We have read Edgar Snow's statement on the subject, no political action can be taken relying on such statements". Lohia said that Edgar Snow was not an insignificant figure. Vijaylaxmi Pandit rose to support Chavan and said that Snow's statement was two years old. Pandit was wrong but the speaker disallowed Lohia to speak and point out the mistake. After working incessantly, Lohia at last succeeded in making a statement in the Parliament on the 3rd of March 1965. Having realised her mistake, Mrs. Vijayalaxmi Pandit confessed that the article which she had referred to was entirely different and the latest article by Edgar snow certainly exceeded the expectations stated in the Colombo proposal.

Despite incessant efforts, Lohia's attempt to expose the Defence Minister did not succeed. India had already sent her contingent to the Congo in order to serve on the UN operations there in 1965. Initially, the Indian soldiers received the same salaries as their counterparts from other countries. However, later on, they were discriminated against. For example the European soldiers would receive $ 600 per month, whereas the Indian soldiers would receive only $ 200. When this issue was raised in the Parliament, the Defence Minister did not answer the query correctly. Lohia wrote several letters to the military adviser to UN, Maj. Gen.

Rikke, in this connection. The replies from Rikke revealed the fact that in the beginning, the Indian soldiers used to get the same salary as others, but later on they were paid less. In this letter, Rikhe lamented the fact that the contingents working under the UN flag were receiving discriminating treatment. The Defence Minister, however, turned a deaf ear to this issue also.

The Defence Minister had also made a false statement regarding the death of the late Lal Bahadur Shastri, the then Prime Minister of India. The Minister had informed the House that the Prime Minister's suite was equipped with a Hotline telephone, which on being just lifted, alarmed the doctor or any other employee there. The Defence Minister made such a statement so as to create an impression that all the precautionary measures were taken to protect the life of the Prime Minister. Lohia, however, had substantial evidence to disprove the statement made by the Defence Minister. As per his information, no such telephone was located in the Prime Minister's suite and the Premier had to face death unattended. Lohia wanted to raise this issue or the House, but the speaker did not allow him to do so. Lohia had demanded a parliamentary or a judiciary probe into the matter. Thus, Lohia exposed false statements made by the Minister for Food, the Foreign Minister, the Defence Minister etc. and pointed out the inconsistencies and contradictions in their arguments and tried to awaken the people.

Anti-Congressism was the main plank over which Lohia contested the fourth Lok Sabha elections. As per his expectations, the opposition won 238 seats out of the total 521 in Lok Sabha. They had only 17 seats less to fulfill the requirement at two-thirds majority. Their influence in the House was tremendous. Lohia was quite upset regarding the defeat of Kishan Patnayak and some other colleagues in the election. He had already staked his election. First of all he could hardly spare any time to look after his own constituency, and secondly because he had raised some sensitive issues like the common Civil code.

The fourth Lok Sabha commenced on the 16th of March on the very first day, at the time of the election of the Speaker Lohia demanded for secret ballot for the election. He believed that this would enable the inner voices of the MPs to come out. Sanjeeva Reddy won the election. The President addressed the two Houses of the Parliament in English. The use of English was strongly protested. In fact, it was not impossible for the President to learn Hindi in his political career of 17 years, but he spoke in English in accordance with the Government Policy.

The first session of the fourth Lok Sabha began and Atal Bihari Vajpayee introduced the no-confidence motion on the floor of the House. Six states had non-Congress governments. The attitude of Congress towards these states was full of partiality. The problem of Rajasthan was especially critical. On the 7th of March, police firing had taken place, Curfew was imposed, and finally, internal emergency was proclaimed in the state. The despotic aspects of Indira Gandhi's rule were becoming clearer day by day and hence the opposition decided to introduce the no-confidence motion. Several opposition leaders spoke on this occasion Smt.Gayatridevi described the events in Rajasthan in details. Although Lohia was not feeling well, he was asked to speak.

He started his speech in this way; "The Congress bastion is creaking but no better house is taking shape as yet. During the last 20 years, Congress and Government have become alternative to each other. It is for the first time that there are number of non-Congress governments in various states. This is the reason why the no-confidence motion against the Congress government in the Centre is introduced". "Europeans used to experiment their wicked and evil inventions in Luxemburg first. Only after getting favourable results there, they used to introduce these to the whole of Europe. In the same way these gentlemen have started their despotic practice from Rajasthan by proclaiming President's rule in that state. Gradually this practice will spread to U.P. and if possible everywhere in the country. I wish to say, on my behalf and on the behalf of many people like me who are here, as I understand it, common man in the country is the with us and whatever be the number of people today enjoying special privileges like former kings, squires of the Indian feudal states, the Indian republic shall surely smash these privileges and these royal families shall have to be swallowed by the Indian Republic, so that they would be able to internalize the spirit of Democracy. Among those who have won the assembly elections this time, about 100 belonged to the old royal families and about 100 to the newly born royal families. Whether a person is competent or not, whether he has concern for the nation or not, if he happens to belong to a royal family, if he has a little bit of smartness, has an easy access to a post in India's foreign embassies All these people are, in fact, destroying the principles and practices of democracy. It will have to be accepted that common man will be the architect of the Indian Republic and therefore, a time will come soon when we shall have to do away with the concept of royal heredity and make the common man the vehicle of democracy. There is no place for heredity & family traditions in a democracy.

During the course of his speech, Lohia referred to Dharam Teja of the Jayanti Shipping Company. Dharam Teja was a criminal. He was free on bail and was spending time in France with his wife. The Prime Minister and the minister for transport had assured the house that Teja will be caught wherever he might be. The receipts of 'Mitsubishi', a Japanese company, had been found with him which had proved his offence regarding the theft and the violation of foreign exchange rules. Teja had travelled by a chartered aircraft for attending a marriage ceremony in a minister's family. Sanjeeva Reddy misled the House by harping on whether the marriage was of the son or the daughter of the Minister. The Minister admitted that the corruption amounted to Rs. 3 crores. Teja had kept Rs. 90 lakhs in the Bank of England. It was a joint plan to loot the Government and the Jayanti Shipping Company. Lohia demanded immediate arrest of Dharam Teja and said that the court would definitely put him behind bars for at least 200 years.

At that time, the black clouds of famine shadowed the country. Lohia appealed that all must determine to bring about a new era of self discipline fight out the tendency of work-shirking and do away with the practices of nepotism etc. "This is of course not possible for the present government" said Lohia and taunted, "It only requires 25 members from the treasury bench to come and join hands with the opposition to tackle this situation". In continuation of his argument Lohia said, "I have received many signals from the other side indicating that 30 members are ready to join us provided there should be no further defection from the opposition, and everyone of us will form the government through coalition. When I was listening to Atal Bihari Vajpayee yesterday, I felt that Vajpayeeji, Dangeji and Gopalanji could easily come together and run the government".

Pandit Jawaharlal Nehru had his account in the Lloyd's Bank of England. He should have closed his account as per the new foreign exchange rules after independence. But this account continued to exist even in the 1950s and the 1960s in one or the other illegal way. When one man started stating certain facts with photographs, Nehru asked the finance minister to settle the issue. Lohia raised the issue in the Lok Sabha and clarified. "I am always blamed or criticizing the Nehru family. But this is not so. When a group of people believe certain things or practices to be harmful, then it becomes a duty for them to attack the origin of that practice and expose the reality of its progenitor. I have not done anything more than that".

The Home Minister and the Finance Minister, however, refuted the allegations made by Lohia. The Home Minister stated that Panditji had a royalty account with his foreign publishers since 1936. The royalty Nehru received for his books published by foreign publishers used to be paid in this account. The Home Minister argued that, that account was in full conformity with the existing provisions of the Law and was not illegal. In 1947, Panditji had £ 3,86,401 in his account and all the additions to this amount was the money from India. Lohia and Limaye both demanded that the matter be referred to the Privilege Committee because the statements made by the two Ministers were contradictory. It was natural to expect no action on the matter. The same happened.

The Shah of Saudi Arabia had presented a diamond necklace to Shrimati Indira Gandhi during her visit to that country in Nov.-Dec. of 1955. When Lohia raised this issue in the Lok Sabha the answers given by the Prime Minister to the question were self contradictory. On the 18th of March 1967, she said in the Lok Sabha that keeping such valuable presents with oneself was not allowed at all. They were to be handed over to the immediately. But because the necklace was so valuable, it was given to the Reserve Bank of India. Lohia asked about the exact date of surrender, to which she replied that she did not know the exact date. She said that the necklace was not with her and hence she did not kriow who actually surrendered it and when. The same question was raised in the Rajya Sabha on the 3rd December 1966. Begum Anis Kidwai said, "When Pandit Nehru was the Prime Minister, everybody was free to go to his residence for a week and see such valuable gifts, whether it was golden necklace, a diamond necklace or any other type of jewellery. After a week, it would be surrendered to the treasury". The Prime Minister gave one more explanation in this regard, which further complicated the matter. She informed the House, The issue regarding the fate of the gift articles presented to me and my father by the Shah of Saudi Arabia was discussed at some length by the then finance minister, Krishnamachari and Prime Minister Nehru and something had already been decided about their disposal. In the meanwhile, Morarji Desai had taken over as the new finance minister. Prime Minister Nehru wrote to the new Finance Minister on the 2nd of April 1958 in which he referred to the discussion that had taken place between him and Krishnamachari regarding the disposal of the gift articles and accordingly, the articles were sent to the ministry of finance by the Prime Minister's secretariat the next day. After further discussions with the ministry of finance over the matter, it was decided that those gift articles be deposited with the Reserve Bank and the State Bank.

The different statements made by the Prime Minister revealed that she received the necklace in 1955 and it was surrendered to the Reserve Bank on the 3rd of April 1958. Lohia raised the question: Where was the necklace for three years?' One MP— 'Around a neck'. Lohia —"Around whose neck?.... The people of India would like to know what is the treasury after all. Why not make certain rules with respect to the treasury by which all its money can be taken out and utilized for irrigation purposes. Wherever a Government or a nation takes to the path of untruth and accumulation of wealth it can't solve the problems of hunger". During the course of the debate, Lohia registered his displeasure at the acceptance of valuable gifts at the official level and stated that the Prime Minister of a civilized country or his relatives accept only mementoes and not valuable presents! Lohia stated, "The last 20 years have been an era of covetousness, consumerism and accumulation for the rich and it was the poor classes which were adversely affected in the process".

During the same period, Stalin's daughter, Svetlana had come to India. She was the wife of Mr. Brajesh Singh, the then Foreign Minister. After the death of Brajesh Singh, Svetlana had come to India to disperse his ashes in the Ganga. She had love and respect for India and wanted to spend the rest of her life here at Kalakankar. At that time, she was staying at Dinesh Singh's residence, in Kalakankar. During the course of private discussion with Dinesh Singh, she expressed her desire to settle permanently in India.

Dinesh Singh pointed out the possibility of strong opposition of the Russian government. On the 16th of January, Svetlana met the Prime Minister. She also met some other Ministers. Dinesh Singh told Svetlana that it was only after discussing the issue with the Soviet Government and if its views were found favourable that her request would be considered. By constantly reminding Svetlana of the Indian heat and the effects it might have on her health and of her daughter, the government of India tried to persuade her to leave India. In fact, the real reason was that the government of India did not want to incur the Soviet's displeasure. The opinions expressed by Dinesh Singh were, from Svetlana's point of view, the opinions of the Government of India expressed informally. In the end, she was frustrated and went away to Switzerland.

Svetlana had already met Lohia. She had been denied the stay in India. Lohia felt so bad as if India had refused to welcome her daughter-in-law while responding to this issue on the floor of the House, Lohia said, "Every individual has his mother, a physical mother—who be gets him. Svetlana's mother is Russia! However, human beings also have another mother and that is the entire Earth! Svetlana suffered a lot from her physical mother' she felt shattered. She therefore embraced India as her spiritual mother. This is Svetlana's story, very plain and yet painfu!"

Lohia had invited Svetlana to stay at his house. He told her to fight, mere praying, petitioning would not help. Svetlana answered that life was not all that simple. The government was unnecessarily distinguishing between visa and refugee. The explanation given for this was that Svetlana was not a guest of the government of India; as such a request had not been made by her. It was election time. Lohia was so busy that he could hardly apply his full mind to help her. Had he known that Svetlana was so strong that she would fight, he would have compelled her to stay on in India. Lohia well remembered the way Margo Skinner was forced to leave India. "I am ashamed because I could not save a woman". Lohia made an appeal to the Government: "This problem is neither of Russia nor of America; plainly it is of India. India has always been an asylum for refugees. .. Till today citizenship has been defined only in terms of physical characters. However, it has a psychological dimension too". Because of the treatment meted out to her, Svetlana was disillusioned with politics. She even said to Lohia, "You have won the fight for freedom, buy it seems that you shall have to fight one more battle for freedom by which you shall free yourselves from Russia and America". After narrating this incident in the Lok Sabha, Lohia said, "I believe that it is not a small thing for Russia that Stalin's daughter left USSR; the harm was done. If Svetlana had been allowed to stay here, this could have been rectified a line. Because she was not able to stay in India, she went away to Switzerland. Please remember that this is a deep-seated injury which is unlikely to be cured. The press in America and the countries of Europe that enjoy great freedom will dig out her story. And then that will be a more severe blow to Russia. Had Svetlana stayed in India, it would have been good for Russia too". Lohia assured that if the government of India invites Svetlana respectfully, I am prepared to forget what happened in the past. I still feel that if Indo-USSR relations are to be improved, Svetlana should be brought over here. I just called Svetlana, a champa flower. A chameli is presently occupying, the seat of power. In such time if the poor champa has to go around for getting refuge it does not become to our country. I remember the last Mughal Emperor of India, the unfortunate after 1857 revolution who lamented. "I could not get even two yards of land in my country". The Government was not ready to accept its mistake over the Svetlana issue. Hence Lohia proposed that a Privilege Committee should probe into the issue because the statements made by the Prime Minister, the Commerce Minister and the Foreign Minister were contradictory to each other. Lohia took the Svetlana issue to such a height that everybody including the Congress members were moved by its humanitarian appeal. Laxmikantamma said that "the humanitarian aspect of the question is much more important than the political aspect. If hundreds of foreign women can stay in our ashrams and shrines, why can't Svetlana". During the course of the debate Nath Pai asked whether or not Svetlana had made a petition to the Prime Minister Chhagla answered negatively. The Prime Minister was sitting right in front of him. But she kept quiet. According to the constitutional process, keeping quiet in the face of some untruth is understood as being parting to that untruth. All the efforts taken by Lohia were vain because of the cold and apathetic attitude of the Government. The proposal to refer the Svetlana issue to the privilege Committee was rejected. Since the Minister had no courage to face the Privilege Committee, the fate of Truth was decided by a vote.

The issues and problems related to the police had come to the fore in the capital right since the middle of 1966. In Delhi, policemen right from the rank of the constable to the sub-inspector had formed their union, The Delhi Police Non-Gazetted Employees Union. From a total of about 15 to 16 thousand employees, about 12 thousand became members. But the moment the police department started agitating for their demands, the government decided not to entertain them. Lohia had already thought minutely about the relations between the police the people and the government. He reminded the House of what Lord Edenborough had written in 1858 after the uprising of 1857. 'The soldiers should be more afraid of their officer than of the enemy. Increase the differences between the Bengal Army, The Bombay Army and the Madras Army; intensify their petty rivalries and infightings, because these are beneficial to us. Make different platoons on the basis of district, caste, tribe colour, etc". 'Divide and Rule' was the old basis of the organisation of the army and the Police.

During the course of the police agitation, terrible atrocities were committed. The Border Security Force was brought into suppress the agitation. In several public meetings, Lohia asked the people to take an oath: "We, the common people and the police, take an oath that we shall not harm each other, shall prevent moral crimes, shall not accept bribes shall be ever vigilant and help in arresting wrong doers and help each other in leading a simple and decent life". On the floor of the Lok Sabha too, Lohia focussed the attention of the House on the 18 hour long duty of the police, their shabby quarters, the 57 times difference in the salaries of constables and officers and the sub-human life of the constables and other police employees. He further stated that if the police set up their association, then it will automatically improve the administration as the core of the system will radically change. Lohia appealed to the police to tell the government, "We shall no doubt abide ourselves by your just orders, however, we won't obey your unjust orders. Orders may be of two types; one right or just and another, wrong or unjust. I wish to tell the police that they should disobey that order which is wrong and illegitimate. Here we should be able to distinguish between loyalty and servitude".

The police issue at that time was a burning issue. In the air of the fourth general elections, the agitation seemed to subside. There was one more reason for this. The people felt that the police should not set up an association, leave aside the question of making an agitation for that matter! If indiscipline haunts the police, society will break apart. There was also a fear of large scale anarchy. The fourth Lok Sabha started on the 16th of March and continued till the 8th of April. On the 14th of April seven persons leading the police agitation were removed from office. Actually they could have been persuaded, remanded, or at the most suspended. But the dismissals amounted to fuelling the fire. The Police were disarmed. Police constables from the High Court, Ministers' residences, were immediately replaced by the Central Reserve Police Force personnel. Orders under the criminal procedure code 144 were proclaimed in Delhi. Many police employees were dismissed. When Lohia enquired about this to the Home Minister Chavan, he said that only duties' were being changed This was totally untrue. The Police employees started flooding first the Rashtrapati Bhavan and then the residence of the Home Minister in thousands agitating against these dismissals. They were shouting slogans of '*Police Sipahi Bhai-Bhai*'. As soon as they reached the residence of the Home Minister, without any warning, twenty shells of tear gas were opened on them. Though the Home Minister himself admitted later, "When I was addressing the demonstrators in front of my house, they were not only listening to me peacefully, but also displayed their faith and confidence in me". The Congress President Kamaraj advised the demonstrators to solve problems by peaceful negotiations and warned the government to pay immediate attention to the legitimate demands of the Police employees. But this was answered by arrests and beatings with bayonets of thousands. The Punjab armed police were given liquor so that having been intoxicated, they could beat their own brothers mercilessly. Almost all opposition parties called for a general strike on the 22nd April 1967. Lohia, Bhoopeshh Gupta, S.M. Bannerjee, Nirmalchandra Chatterjee and other leaders held public meetings in support of the strike. The Jan Sangh and the P.S.P. opposed the police agitation and well as the call for a strike, then, the Marxist Communists also turned away and the proposed strike had to be withdrawn. Lohia regretfully said, "One can understand if someone has to accept defeat for want of necessary strength, but it is simply incomprehensible that one accepts defeat even without fighting. And one should not make any effort to hide this weakness. It was a golden opportunity to break a century and half old wall of mutual suspicion existing between the Delhi police and the people. Nothing much happened. Only a brick here and there has been loosened. But the great work that could have been done, we couldn't do it. I am not able to understand what to say for the policemen who are perhaps being beaten up still. I can only say to them that in any war, the first battle is never the last battle". On the 24th of May, Lohia tabled an adjournment motion over the issue of the police agitation. It was almost an end to the rule of law. Many men and women were put behind the bars at Tihar jail without being tried in the court. It was also suspected that a few of them might have died in the jail. Actually the policemen should have been given the salaries with provident fund for the month of April. The amount had already been withdrawn from the treasury by the Inspector General, but was not given to the policemen. Lohia brought these facts to light and said, "Discipline is necessary and especially in the police and the army, it has to be there...But when there is injustice and exploitation in the government and mutual relations between the employees of the government are such as can't be understood by common people, then discipline suffers".

Lohia appealed to the Home Minister, Chavan, "I felt that when a Quit India rebel of Satara is a home minister, there would be an effort to recognise the police. But it seems that the position of ministers is such that whoever goes there falls from virtue instead of bringing about reconstruction and restructuring of the old. If ever power comes to my hands, mind well that my people will bring about this change even at the risk of their own lives. I have always tried my best that ministers stop accepting unnecessary salutations etc. Remove the police from their bungalows. This pomp and luxury is a professional habit of the ministers. I hope that our ministers shall work hard. How many men dare and follow an altogether different path? It is only lions and perhaps the brave that tread a different path". Lohia had always maintained that one organ of the government is the police and the other organ is the Border Security Force. The Government was using one to suppress another. "Look at the way the government talks. It is said that in a very novel, efficient manner, the whole, 'operation' was carried out in 20 minutes. The country in which the army is invited time and again to tackle the law and order situation, that army is likely to loose its morale and feel itself incapable in the face of external attack". At this time, many 'members through their speeches in the Lok Sabha, made people aware of the difficulties faced by the police. N.C. Chatterjee was a member of the Representative Committee. He made it clear that neither Lohia or Banerjee and Gupta have made any improper demands. The police were demonstrating peacefully. Why then were they treated in this way? The Home Minister while speaking on adjournment motion showed a copy of a newspaper which allegedly stated Lohia saying that, "the police agitation in Delhi was in fact a revolution. Had there been unity in the opposition parties Delhi would have been in his hands for fifty thousand people would have been killed in the process".

This news was totally incorrect & mischievous, and Chavan humiliated Lohia in every possible way during his speech. Lohia said, "I am not in the habit of saying such things. I do wish however, that Delhi be under the control of the whole of India which today is under the control of a very few". I consider myself to be useless in bringing about this revolution. This is the only difference between you & I. The day when you would also think yourself to be alike & join hands with me, really great things would start taking place in the country. In the whole of the civilized world, in almost all countries, the police have a right to form their trade union". The Home Minister did not answer Lohia's question about changes in the 'duties' of the police. His words spit venom on Lohia, but didn't provide answers to his questions. After contacting, some of the Delhi people, Delhi weekly. '*Dinamaan*' found the common people sympathetic towards the police employees. Had the Home Minister accepted the legitimate demands of the police, the movement would have achieved a new direction. Lohia was being accused of provoking the Police. Lohia said; "If anybody has at all provoked the police to do the wrong thing, It is the Home Minister. Lohia ended his speech by saying; "Allright, we have displayed our anger on each other. Now at least say that you will do something!" There was no question of the adjournment motion being accepted, and that is what happened. The police agitation was suppressed. But the police wrote a saga of self-suffering and sacrifice. The ghastly majority of the Congress in the Lok Sabha and the disunity among the opposition parties were among the reasons why the movement was not successful. Gradually 90% of the police employees returned to work and to continued suffering and without even a single problem solved.

Nath Pai introduced a Bill proposing the amendment of Article 268 of the Indian Constitution on the 9th of June 1967. This Bill, which was to take India's fate down to the dumps was a very important one, but the attendance of members receiving full pay and facilities was less than even one-fourths. The then Prime Minister, Indira Gandhi, wanted the power to make the Parliament sovereign and as fate should have had it, Nath Pai, an opposition member had given this weapon in her hands. It was possible to restrict the right to property even by a constitutional proposal. Parliament had no authority to curtail the fundamental rights, though it could increase them if it so wished". The third Lok Sabha also had discussed the relations between the parliament and the supreme court. While talking on that occasion, Lohia's balanced outlook was seen "Quarrels for selfish gains are harmful, but quarrels for the general good lead to benefits. In the modern civilisation, the more the distribution of authority, the more will be the decentralization of power. An English judge, Francis Bacon had said 400 years ago that judges are lions, but under the crown. Today, judges are sitting besides the crown. "Parliament and the Court are on an equivalent plane. When the making of a land is concerned, the parliament is supreme and when taking decisions on the land is concerned, the Judge is supreme". Actually the Indian constitution regards the parliament, the Judiciary and the executive to be autonomous in their respective fields. Kripalani too said that it is wrong to leave fundamental rights at the mercy of the Parliament, because its majority is deceptive. Lobo, Prabhu, Piloo Mody, Madhu Limaye, Vajpayee, etc. participated in the debate and vehemently opposed the Bill. Lohia spoke on the 21st of July. His speech was historical importance and was prophetic. "This question is not of the relationship between Supreme Court and the Parliament. The question is of the character of our nation. In the place of amendment of this constitution, it will soon be written, "amendment of any, article, anything of this constitution. When this Amendment Bill will be passed, there would be no talk of whether it is in relation with property, or rights of liberty or with respect to the centre state relationship". Showing a red signal,

Lohia sarcastically asked, "Does this mean that the Parliament also has the power to make amendments in the goals and objectives of the constitution?" The Proposer, Nath Pai answered affirmatively. He declared, "If fundamental rights are encroached upon, or curtailed, I will definitely oppose the attempt". The unseen destiny was revealed through Lohia who said, "Fine, you will condemn it and I will too, but our condition at that time will be the same as of the communists and the socialists in Germany. If this Bill is passed, it will be the most unfortunate thing for our country. I am telling this to you with great pains. It is quite possible that I be proved wrong with the help of this amendment. I am seeing the unseen future. You are giving such a powerful weapon in their hands with which they will destroy the whole character of our country. This has all happened in the history of mankind". Nath Pai said, "The Court will help the people" Lohia replied, "Forget about the Court. Till then a man like me would be finished. But Nath Paiji will also be kept in jail". Lohia reminded the House that by a similar law, Hitler's dictatorship was established. Lohia gave a complete analysis of political conditions in Germany of that time. According to him, if the bill becomes a law it would be capable of finishing the constitution too. "I don't know who is going to become what at that time, someone will be the head of the Army, someone will be the President, someone will be the Prime Minister". Then Lohia mentioned the incident when Hitler had issued an oath to obey him and said: "Only the Social Democratic Party voted against the Bill. In this context I wish to mention the name of that person, Otto Wells, here with respect. I may not live till a person like me may be able to do something, but perhaps you may become Otto Wells".

"I earnestly request Nath Paiji to withdraw the Bill and refrain from getting his hand stained", said Piloo Mody. "Don't even touch it. Let the Law Minister do it". History afterwards proved that this Bill, which was passed later didn't affect the private property rights, but it was used to constrict the fundamental rights and the seven freedoms by Indira Gandhi. But neither Lohia nor Nath Pai survived to see this.

In the Budget Session of the Fourth Lok Sabha, Lohia raised a new cultural issue on the 28th of July 1967 and astonished the House. He severely criticised the functioning of the Sahitya Academy and the Sangeet Natak Academy. After discussing such academies in foreign countries, he told the House that they were managed by experts. "Here, in India, Sahitya Academy consists of people like Trigun Sen, Chhagla, Deshmukh, Keskar, Shah, Indira Gandhi i.e. ministers. In the same way, there are people like KPS Menon, Narayan Menon, A.K. Chanda, B.L. Jha and Balraj Sahani in the Sangeet Natak Academy. Every job is governmental, every man is of the bureaucracy. There is such a great influence and control of the government and the bureaucracy on every walk of our life, that even culture, music and drama are not left out. The President of the Sahitya Academy is Radhakrishnan, Sangeet Natak Academy Chairperson is the Prime Minister. The people who are not even distantly related to culture and literature are dominating the field". The attitude, that these academies should be controlled by the government because they are being funded by the latter, was wrong. Lohia appealed to change this attitude and said, "About 150 years ago Beethoven was conducting his orchestra. The king whispered something to the person sitting next to him. Beethoven immediately stopped the orchestra and said just one thing—'When the king speaks, everyone keeps silent.' The king got the message that one should keep quiet when a musician like Beethoven is performing".

Lohia's efforts to free these academies from governmentalisation, groupism, restrictions and control, remained incomplete because of his death. On the 11th of August 1967, Lohia had raised the issue of their autonomy once again. He was told that the question was meaningless because the academies were already enjoying autonomy. Lohia said that when the president appoints the chairpersons of all the three academies and the latter have governmental elements in them, they just can't be autonomous. Lohia again demanded that a committee be set up to deal with the matter and said, "At least give me an assurance that you will give thought to my suggestions". This was Lohia's last but one speech in the Lok Sabha.

Lohia entered the Lok Sabha on the 13th of August 1964 and his speech on the 12th of August 1967 proved to be his last one on the floor of Lok Sabha. In this very short time, he asked hundreds of written and oral questions, tabled various adjournment motions. Lohia got only about three and a half years in the Lok Sabha. He had to face the first Prime Minister Nehru, then Lal Bahadur Shastri and then Indira Gandhi. In the third Lok Sabha,

Indira Gandhi usually kept quiet. The ministers faced the attacks of the opposition. It was for this reason that Lohia called her a deaf and dumb doll. But this deaf and dumb doll of the third Lok Sabha was quite aggressive in the Fourth Lok Sabha. She was aware of her inability to answer the questions by reason and intellect. So she fought her opposition using weapons like falsehood, manoeuvreing and goondaism. She well knew that Lohia, was the biggest obstacle in her path. So she had asked Randheer Singh, Shashibhushan and 10-12 other MPs to deal with Lohia in the same way as is said of King George III of England. He had managed to have a few such men in the then House of Commons who would protect the interests of the Crown and would uphold his position against criticism from Parliament. They were called the King's men. In the Fourth Lok Sabha, the 'Queen's men' would start shouting and creating obstacles as soon as Lohia stood up to speak. They used to start abusing him by calling him: son of a wretched money-lender. A thief of 10 lakhs, 'son of a pig' surviving on the mercy of the Nehrus' etc. Whenever 'Lohia presented any letter or document as evidence they would start shouting, this letter is fake one.' Once Sheelabhadraji charged Lohia for taking a bribe of Rs. 1 lakh for signing a petition. As the S.S.P. members in both the Houses took strong objection, Sheelabhadraji apologised: Lohia's terror in the Lok Sabha was such that even ministers used to get scared. Once, when the confidence motion against the Speaker of the Lok Sabha, Hukum Singh, Lohia suddenly stood up and refering to the documents in his hands he said, "Before I read this document, please have a good look at it. After seeing this, there would be no need to say anything". There was a great commotion in the House. The Prime Minister and the Speaker refused to accept the papers. Lohia smiled. The document was a photocopy of a letter written to a minister by Sardar Hukm Singh!

After the death of Lohia, Lok Sabha became lifeless and remained just a darbar of the sycophants of Indira Gandhi.

32. THE LAST STRUGGLE

On the lawns of the Willingdon Hospital, New Delhi, people had gathered in groups of hundreds. One of them muttered in sheer annoyance: "You neglected your body as if it belonged to you alone". He was referring to Lohia who had just died in that hospital. Lohia belonged not to himself alone, but to thousands of his colleagues and millions of his downtrodden, countrymen for whose welfare his services were still required. He wore himself out like sandalwood for spreading fragrance all over the world but that fragrance was not adequate enough to counteract the foul stink in the afflicted world. That muttering man who groaned as if his heart has been pierced by a spike, further said: "Your body belonged to us. What right did you have to squander the fortune of others?"

In fact Willingdon Hospital is a hospital for V.I.P.'s. But generally no V.I.P. dares to undergoes an operation there. Morarjibhai and Yashwantrao Chavan got themselves operated by Dr. Shantilal Mehta, the well-known surgeon, at Bombay. Even for Indira Gandhi's operation, Dr. Shantilal Mehta is reported to have carried with him to Delhi his entire surgical kit including gloves after getting it sterilized in Bombay. Moreover, like other government hospitals, Willingdon Hospital too carried ill-repute as a slaughter house. But being opposed to getting operated in a private hospital on account of its costlines, Lohia got himself admitted to Willingdon Hospital. Obviously this was quite in keeping with his attitude on many similar issues. He was guided by the principle of equality and that was evident in everything he did, whether it was in his opposition to separate schools for the children of the rich and of the poor, or his demand for the abolition of classes on railways, or his insistence on halting at government

Dak bungalows, or, in fact, his opposition to the reservation of anything whatsoever for the privileged classes. He believed that railway coaches would improve only if the rich travelled by the same class as the poor. He also felt that the schools and the educational system would improve only if the children of the rich and of the poor were educated together in the same schools. Could it be due to such ideas that he entered a public hospital for operation and eventually died there like a commoner? This looks natural for the noble soul that Lohia was. But this idea of his should have been opposed by others, for Lohia was a mine of gold, and it was agonising that adequate care could not be taken to save him. Although very few knew that he was to undergo an operation, surprisingly enough not even one of them insisted that it must be performed in a good hospital at Bombay, Madras or Calcutta. They all loved him no less, but such an idea did not strike any of them. Perhaps they could not comprehend what a terrible blow indeed, there was in store for all, for this lack of alertness.

It is true that Lohia had high blood pressure and his heart was somewhat weak. But during the last few years of his life, the blood pressure had remained steady and within limits. It had not gone beyond 180/110. Periodic medical checkups had indicated that the heart was sound. He had no diabetes either. Then how could a disorder arise after the operation?

In October 1966 urine trouble had appeared. Frequency of urination increased, especially at night. He was already having his periodical general checkups at the Willingdon Hospital. Accordingly he had had a checkup in November. Everything was normal except an enlarged prostate gland, for which doctors had advised him an immediate operation. But Lohia postponed it. Lohia became aware of the seriousness of his illness during the electioneering period in 1966. He also realised that the operation was unavoidable. The election campaign had been an extremely strenuous one for Lohia. Even his party colleagues troubled him in no small measure. Everyone desired Lohia to campaign in his constituency. The S.S.P. contested hundreds of seats of Vidhan Sabhas and Lok Sabha. How could Lohia campaign in all constituencies? He neglected his own constituency and toured as many constituencies as possible. He contested elections for the party on the principle of non-Congressism. In this election campaign Lohia had to undergo enormous physical hardships. He worked late through the night, till as late as about 3 a.m., travelled indiscriminately, and faced great irregularities of food. He himself never said even a word about his health. He already had complaints about ear, nose, eyes, and blood pressure. To them was added the strain of election. However he never uttered even a word about his own health unless he was pressed to do so by others.

Once the elections were over. Lohia had a medical checkup in April 1967. The VIP report showed enlargement of the prostate gland, all other; things being normal. Even then he was not mentally prepared for an operation. Delhi police were on strike, and Lohia addressed a meeting on the lawns of the Willingdon Hospital. The Budget session of the parliament was as important session. Lohia for a while attended it and laid before the house his policy of putting a ceiling on income and expenditure. To have a second opinion on his ailment, Lohia, at the end of March, consulted Dr. B.N. Roy, Professor of Surgery, All India Institute of Medical Sciences. Dr. Roy expressed his view that there was no urgency about the operation. He prescribed the course of six injections. The course was over by the end of June. Dr. Roy examined him again, advised that the operation was imperative otherwise there was a danger of a damage to his kidneys. Perhaps Lohia considered surgical treatment as contrary to the principle of non-violence. But there was no other go. He had many programmes coming up and it was essential to be fit for pursuing them. Thus he had no time to spare for illness. He had received an invitation from the Martin Luther University at Hale in East Germany for participating in the celebrations of the 450 the anniversary of Martin Luther's defiance of the order of the Catholic Church. He was glad to receive the invitation. It was suggested to him that during his visit to Germany he could as well get himself operated there. He turned down this suggestion.

In August-September he toured Bihar and Bengal but thereafter he himself felt the performance of operation 'imperative. Climbing a staircase or walking some distance became difficult for him. He had well established relations with Brigadier Lal of the Willingdon Hospital who assured him that the operation was a simple one, as simple as that of an appendix or tonsils and that he would be allright within 8 to 10 days. However, Lohia wanted to consult for Ayurvedic treatment an MP who was also a renowned Ayurved expert. But parliament being not in session, the MP was out of Delhi. So Lohia decided to get himself operated immediately. With some difficulty he got a room (No.17) in Willingdon Hospital. Lohia was admitted to the hospital on 28th September. All medical reports about his health were presented to the hospital. He was thoroughly examined by the doctors there. Doctors, nurses and other staff of the hospital became his close friends. They were all attracted towards Lohia. He started getting to know from the doctor the details about his operation. When asked about his blood group, the doctor was surprised about his ignorance about it. Lohia asked his friends not to have any discussion about the operation. He reminded them that in foreign countries it is customary not to discuss about the illness of their leader. In fact it was not in his nature to discuss with others about his own health.

On the morning of the day of his operation he was given 4 'Adelphane' tablets. To Lohia this appeared rather strange since administering such a strong dose of adelphane implied a sudden fall in blood pressure. Pre-operation tests had indicated that blood, urine, heart, blood-pressure etc. were all normal. It is said that the doctor, who was in charge of anesthesia, apprehended a rise in blood pressure. So at night Lohia was given certain tablets and sedatives. This made Lohia drowsy. Even then, he had a shave, got himself sponged, changed clothes and got ready for the operation. He signed the pre-operation declaration form. At 9 o'clock he was carried on the trolley to the operation theatre on the upper floor. A prostate gland operation normally takes 45 minutes or at the most 90 minutes. But in the present case it was over only at 12.30 p.m. Later on it was learnt that anesthesia had become effective after one hour and the operation actually commenced at 11.00 o'clock. Blood pressure had suddenly fallen during the operation and there was profuse bleeding. Doctors struggled, removed the enlarge prostate gland with great difficulty and sent it for biopsy. Generally 1 and a 1/2 bottles of blood are transfused during such an operation, but Lohia had to be given 5 1/2 bottles of blood. Glucose was administered by piercing a needle on one hand, blood through a needle on the other hand and saline through a needle at the ankle of the foot. Intermittently Lohia gained consciousness and complained about pain in the hand and the wound.

1st October: The operation being over, this was the second day. Lohia was restless yet mentally extraordinarily conscious.

Intellect was functioning with alertness. In the evening he bad shivering and passed the night under the effect of a heavy sedative.

2nd October: This was the third day. Complications began. Temperature rose. Blood pressure went up. Toxicity due to inadequate sterlisation began to spread. His friends in Delhi got frightened. Radio announced that his condition was vety critical. This news spread all over the county. Telegrams were sent to all the party branches. S.M. Joshi, the president of the party was informed that the chances of the Lohia's survival were only 25%. Generally a period of 48 hours alter an operation is considered to be critical. Every one was anxiously looking forward to see Lohia getting over this critical period.

3rd October: Fourth day dawned. Socialists from all over the country began to gather in large numbers, in the hospital compound. Everyone made dash to Delhi by whatever transport he could avail of. There was utter confusion all over. It was a gathering of the huge family of the celibate. Nobody was related to him by blood and yet everybody felt a relationship closer than the blood. All were overpowered with grief, and started moving near about Room No.17, to have a glimpse of Lohia. Who could control this situation? Nobody. Some of the prominent leaders maintained restraint and balance. Others thought that calling of ministers, the Prime Minister or the President might ensure better attention to Lohia. But Lohia was actually troubled by this hubbub.

Two specialists from Bombay, Dr. Colabawala and Dr. Dastur, who had arrived at Delhi on 3rd October, suspected that Dr. Lohia's wound had become septic and advised that the wound be opened, pus removed, culture prepared and examined. But Brigadier Dr. Lal disliked the coming of specialists from outside. He was afraid he would be exposed, when his mistakes would come to light. The Next two days i.e. 3rd and 4th October passed in anxiety with neither improvement nor impairment. From 4th onwards there was overall progressive impairment, the improvement during the day being more than offset by the impairment at night. It was an atmosphere of worry, anxiety, fear, and dreariness. Lohia was locked in a fierce struggle with death. Each day presented a new facet of struggle. At one moment he would appear to have pulled round. What a brave fight! A heart rending and hair-raising fight indeed.

4th October: At night, the condition became serious, Breathing became heavy. Doctors and close friends were summoned. People gathered in large numbers. Onlookers were astounded by the spectacle. The hospital compound was full of people, hundreds were waiting there without food or water or sleep, with deep anxiety in their mind and with his entire life concentrated in their eyes. A spectacle unique in the history of Willingdon Hospital.

5th October: The day marched on. The hearts of all began to beat faster and faster. What was the night in for? This night too unfolded a dreadful spectacle. Strong hiccups were recurrent. All the doctors came running. Saline was administered through a needle in one hand, glucose through a needle on the other on the other and oxygen through a tube in one nostril. Now the filth in the stomach was being aspirated through a tube inserted in the other nostril. Enema was also given. Lohia patiently bore all these sufferings. The dangers which were now regularly appearing every night made the hearts all heavy. Their faces became dark, and they appeared as if they had aged 10 years. With eyes full of tears they would look at each other, lower down their heads in agony and move hither and thither with blank faces.

6th October: The day passed off, without much trouble, but night presented a different spectacle. The temperature rose to 105 degrees. It was brought down artificially by placing cloth paddings soaked in ice on the head, round the neck, in the arm pits and practically all over the body. In the morning it was announced that blood pressure, temperature and pulse had become normal. At 10 a.m. Brig Lal examined him and was about to tell that the danger was over. Just then the telephone rang. It was a call from Dr. Riches, a specialist in England who cautioned on the phone, "You must be very patient with your patient. He expressed the possibility of a wound at the place of operation. Immediately the faces, which had just brightened up, darkened. The situation became unbearable. Patience was strained beyond limit. Everyone realised with horror that the improvement seen on the morning of the 7th was momentary and deceptive and not a lasting one.

8th October: It was Sunday, being a weekend no British specialist would be available at home. Perhaps the measure adopted during the day to bring down the temperature, i.e. use of ice, had rebounded. At night strong shivers started. They were stopped by means of hot-water bag, blankets etc. However the general condition continued to be critical.

9th October: As the day dawned, anxiety weighed heavily on everyone's mind. Lohia's condition became precarious. Breathing went on becoming feebler and feebler. All the doctors stood around his bed with heads bent down and hands locked in a fold. Brig Lal had perhaps started muttering prayers. People with sorrowful faces, glanced at doctors and nurses coming out of Lohia's room and gathered around them. But what could the doctors and the nurses say to the people? Lohia's life had all along been a life of miracles and so was it even now. If one moment he was collapsing, the next he would indicate sudden improvement. The barometer of his health showed continuous rise and fall. Breathing, which had been growing feebler and feebler had been revived by a series of quick injections. A telephone call was received from Dr. Benedov of England. He suggested that the would be opened.

At the instance of Morarjibhai, Dr. Shantilal Mehta, the well-known Bombay surgeon, arrived at Delhi. He opened the wound and drained of the pus. American Dr. Davis urged from Ludhiana the importance and necessity of Shantilal's action. Dr. Vig and Dr. Rao of Delhi Medical institute and Dr. Baldev Singh, a brain specialist were also on the way. Dr. Udappa of Banaras, Dr. Koshi of Madras, Dr. Dharkar of Madhya Pradesh and Doctors Dastur and Colabawala of Bombay held consultations and carried on the treatment. There is a well-known proverb: *Too many cooks spoil the broth*. However, in the present case things happened otherwise. Barring rare points of differences, they were generally unanimous. Due to the interest taken by Morarjibhai, nobody now cared for the displeasure of the Brig Lal. After the removal of the pus from the wound, the number of white blood cells came down from 150,000 to just 40,000 by the evening. The temperature also became normal. The presence of the dangerous germ *pyocyaneus* was detected. The rare medicine, which can act on it was brought. The presence of this germ clearly indicated how unclean was the atmosphere in the hospital. It was also said that no antibiotics had been administered before the operation as a preventive to the hospital infection. The socialists, having no faith in God had now bowed to Shantilal. They had faith in science and heaved a sigh of relief that the medical efforts were bearing fruits. Then Dr. Alken from Germany jointed the team and hopes were rekindled that everything would be allright. The toxins had been entirely eliminated from the blood. How then could Lohia, who has been dear to us beyond life, leave us in the middle?, thought Lohia's friends.

Even in such a hopeful atmosphere great anxiety prevailed. Night was approaching. Everyone hoped it would pass on smoothly. It was learnt that Lohia's kidney had ceased to function. The German doctor advised that Lohia should be left alone to nature. He expected that medicines already administered would act and perhaps the kidney would start functioning. Most of the people returned home highly depressed. The remaining few relaxed on the lawns of the hospital. And what a wonder: On the 10th morning the kidney was normal but the breathing became hard. This was set right by 'Bird's respiration'. Now everything was normal, thanks to the hard work of the three doctors, Dr. Shantilal, Dr. Davis and Dr. Alken. However, Dr. Davis considered it was miracle. The normalcy lasted for the day. At night suspicion of cancer was expressed. In fact there was no reason to worry about cancer since treatment of the same was available in the world. Thus the main problem was to maintain kidney, heart, blood circulation, blood condition, temperature, etc. normal. However, people got enraged with Dr. Lal and other doctors in the hospital, when the possibility of the cancer was expressed. They felt that Dr. Lal and his colleagues were playing a foul game to save themselves from a charge of negligence in case Lohia died. Afterwards it was announced that septicemia had developed. It was really a matter of shame for the medical world that septicemia should have developed when ultramodern scientific equipment and medicine were available. Had the A-I treatment, that was administered by the team of doctors on the 10th day of operation, been available on 3rd and 4th of October, things might have turned out entirely different. The German doctor Dr. Alken had said: "First rate treatment is being administered in a third rate hospital". Night advanced nearer. How could it be halted? It came as it was bound to. All had gone home with a heavy heart. It was an ominous night, then the end came. Telephone bells rang allover the country. Lohia had gone! Gone—forever. Just on the previous night Dr. Davis said: "So far there was only one ray of hope, but there are two now". Another doctor said: "On the 6th night death had almost snatched away Dr. Lohia. But we could manage to get him back". Again on 9th morning death had dragged him still nearer to itself but the trio of doctors—Dr. Shantilal Mehta, Dr.

Davis and Dr. Alken scored over death. However, that night death ultimately succeeded in approaching stealthily and laying its icy hand on Lohia.

The last 12 days of Lohia were the days of grim struggle between him and death. It was an ordeal indeed! Doctors were overwhelmed with his popularity among the people. Some doctors said: "We have been practising for 20 years and have seen thousands of patients but had not come across even one so tenacious and so strong willed as Dr. Lohia". The very talk of Lohia would make everyone speechless. On the night of 2nd October, even in unconsciousness Lohia had talked in a clear tone on remission of land revenue. Normally while in a state of unconsciousness a man lets out his troubled mind and suppressed emotions. But this great man was so deeply in love for the people and the politics, that nothing besides welfare of the people could flow out of his mouth.

Coming out of the effects of anesthesia, words flowed out of Lohia's mouth uninterruptedly in Hindi, Bengali, German, and occasionally in English too. He would enquire as to how the party was functioning. That kind hearted soul would ask why so much money was being spent on him for medical treatment when the poor in the country had to go without any treatment whatsoever. He didn't like that people should gather around him leaving aside their normal duty. He urged them to go back and carry out their assigned tasks with zeal. He would never fail to enquire whether everyone got food to eat. He would express his anxiety about the cultivators in U.P. and Bihar. Once he was out to issue a public statement about the remission of land revenue in U.P. However, as he was talking, he became unconscious. Off and on he would go on talking as if he was addressing the speaker of the Lok Sabha and enlightening him about truth and justice, freedom and honour. Socialist programme was being continuously presented by him. Once Lohia asked one of the doctors: "Will I be all right?" The doctor said: "Certainly". So Lohia humorously added, "Doctors also are ignorant like politicians. Both grope in the dark". Once after Morarji Desai had called on him somebody asked, "What did Morarji say?" Lohia replied humorously and smilingly, "Nothing new. As usual, he advised me to remain calm and peaceful here also as in the Lok Sabha. After removing the pus from Lohia's wound, Dr. Lal said to him, "Well, Doctorsaheb, you will now be allright". To this Lohia sharply replied: "Well! so far you had been telling me lies. However, now perhaps you might be speaking the truth. When someone else again said: "Doctorsaheb you will be allright now", Lohia said, "So you also have joined the tribe of liars is it?"

There is no doubt that Lohia had tremendous willpower. But he overstrained it and as a result would feel fatigued. On the precarious night of 6th October, he said: "It is all finished now. I am now due to go. I am going". But even if slight improvement due to the doctors' efforts became noticeable, Lohia would respond to those efforts in the state of extreme exhaustion. He would say "Experiments, experiments, all experiments and would give full cooperation to the doctors in order that their experiments should not be unsuccessful. Once he said: "I have been observing all of you, I am fully exhausted. So now please will you leave me alone". But the "doctors would say to him, "No doctorsaheb, you are getting better, improving". In turn Lohia also would respond afresh with all his will power. When Delhi's brain specialist asked Lohia his name he told it correctly and gave such clear answers to all his questions that the doctors were simply amazed. One of his questions was "What was taking place in Montreal?" Pat came the classical reply, "An industrial fair" Then Lohia said: "You, doctors have put so many questions to me, may I put one to you?" "Why I am not getting well?" In his unconscious state Lohia often said: "Razia was surpassed by Rani" What could this expression means? Razia was a popular queen of Delhi. She strove for the welfare of the people. Perhaps Lohia wanted to convey that the existing queen had killed the tradition of Razia. On the night of 10th Lohia thanked the German doctors in German. However, twenty-four hours later, this pauper King, whose death oscillated between consciousness and unconsciousness, insensibility and semiconsciousness had perhaps realised that it was a lost battle. Maybe he felt that medical science had failed in its struggle with death and had consequently opted for a permanent rest. Many people thronged into his room. He would sometimes look at them and show that he recognised them. By merely hearing a voice he would know who were around, However he never called out to anyone. All those who had gathered there were dear to him, but even then some were naturally closer. These people had a fond hope that Lohia would recover, they would be able to talk with him. However, these hopes were belied. On his own he never he called out to anybody except Prof. Rama Mitra, the joint editor of *Mankind*, who also stayed at Dr. Lohia's residence lat 7, Gurudwara Rakabganj Marg. By the time Rama Mitra came Lohia had become unconscious again. Since last two days Lohia was insisting upon Rama Mitra to take him back home.

The entire city, particularly the Delhi of the poor, was overpowered with anxiety. Rickshaw-pullers, taximen, sweepers, everyone asked; 'How is Lohia?' As soon as it was learnt that blood-transfusion was essential, nearly 150 persons-partymen and others —offered their blood. Ultimately blood was taken from 30 of them. Huge crowds gathered around the Willingdon Hospital. People in numbers with heavy heart thronged around the radio to listen to the news about Lohia's condition. The entire atmosphere was tense. Around the hospital people would listen about Lohia's health and quietly walk along. The entire masses of the poor all over the country had been most grieved with the anxiety as to who would now take up their cause and fight for their welfare.

As regards his party colleagues, their grief was unbounded. Lohia never liked anyone crying in the public. Even then tears were rolling down. Everyone was quietly wiping his face and trying to console others around. They felt they had lost such a great man, such a jewel as Lohia. They blamed themselves for their having failed to act when his condition took a turn for the worse on the 3rd and the 4th day after the operation due to the negligence of the doctors. Chandrashekar the Secretary of the Congress Parliamentary Party and Madhu Limaye demanded an enquiry into the circumstances that led to Lohia's death. The government rejected that demand but ordered a comprehensive enquiry into the working of all the hospitals in Delhi by appointing a commission. The report of the commission is revealing enough. Its findings were serious enough for anyone to conclude that Lohia was practically thrust into the jaws of death. Lohia all along fought with all his might with mismanagement of public affairs and ultimately himself became a victim of the same. Hundreds of poor people must be daily becoming victims of the mismanagement in public hospitals. Perhaps Lohia walked into the jaws of death for unraveling the agony of the poor in such hospitals.

Lohia died of heart failure at 1.05 a.m. on the 12th of October 1967. His body was removed to his residence at 7, Gurudwara Rakabganj Road. It was lying there in eternal rest and his lips were set at one end in a serene smile. A meeting of party workers was held in the back yard at which it was, decided that his body should be cremated at the electric crematorium in Delhi. He had expressed that his body should be given to the Medical College at Lucknow. However with the advent of electric crematorium in Delhi, he had expressed his desire to be cremated there. He was against religious rites after death, in fact, when his rather Hiralalji died, he didn't perform the religious rites. Lohia's colleagues respected his desire. They managed to arrange his final journey in this world in a very simple manner within about Rs.150 and didn't accept any money offered by his admirers. The expenses of the German doctor had also been duly paid. Lohia hadn't allowed excessive expenditure to be incurred on him by getting himself admitted to the public hospital. He stuck to his principle of doing only what was possible for a common man to do. There was widespread belief that the Govt. of India invited eminent doctors from outside and bore their expenses. This is totally wrong. Lohia's friends bore all expenses. Lohia was always critical of government expenses on V.I.P.s. His colleagues knew his views on religious rites after death. Lohia once wrote, "There is no limit to the money that is being squandered on ceremonies relating to birth, marriage and death and the pomp that is exhibited on such occasions. There is a temptation to follow custom and fashion. We must learn to overcome such temptations. Why should there be so much fuss about a dead body? What is there in a body without life? In fact a dead body should be disposed off in a swift, simple, clean and inexpensive way".

All old friends of Lohia came to see him during his illness. Jayprakash Narayan used to come twice in a day and sit by his side for hours. Aruna Asaf Ali, the Kripalanis, Kamaladevi Chattopadhya, Mridula Sarabhai, V.K. Krishna Menon, Kamaraj and others used to come regularly. Ganga Saran Babu, Prem Bhasin, H.V. Kamath, Shirubhai Limaye and other members of the P.S.P. called on him, President Zakir Hussain, Indira Gandhi, Morarjibhai Desai, Yeshwantrao Chavan, Jagjivan Ram, K.K. Shah, Dr. Trigun Sen, Dr. Chandrashekar, Baliram Bhagat, Pant, Dr. Sushila Nayyar, Ram Subhag Singh, Ashok Mehta, all members of the government called on him.

On the 12th since dawn people had lined up outside his residence. They included ministers, high officers, the rich and the poor, the old and the young, men and women. Everyone stood in a line, moved along and finally placed a wreath on his body, as a mark of their last respects. This went on till about 2 o'clock. A truck bedecked with party flags and garlands had been kept ready. People advanced to take his body out. A pathetic heart rending burst out Morarjibhai. Jaiprakash, Yeshwantrao, Kripalani shouldered his body and brought it out of the house. Cries of "Long Live Dr. Lohia" rose from all over. His body, wrapped in party flags and covered with garlands was placed on the truck. Nobody got on the truck. Some persons even walked barefooted. The funeral procession passed on in silence with no religious chants nor utterance of the name of Ram.

At the electric crematorium, wreaths were laid on his body by all parties and on behalf of various institutions. Then the body was placed in the burning chamber and the smiling face of Dr. Lohia disappeared for ever. The door of the burning chamber was closed. A condolence meeting began. Jayprakash Narayan was the first to speak. His voice was choked with emotion and face streaked with tears, he said "I am older then Rammanohar by 8 years. Really it should have been my turn to go and he should have been standing here in my place". Sanjeeva Reddy, the speaker of the Lok Sabha said; "The man who set the empire on fire is himself now burning in fire. We must keep alive his feelings about justice and his furor over injustice". While paying his homage Yashwantrao Chavan said: "The Lok Sabha was there much before Lohia entered it. However, on his entry it became lively and animated. No more shall we hear his voice. In a sense the Lok Sabha has now turned lifeless". Tarakeshwari Sinha was overwhelmed with emotions. She said: "Today all, around, there prevail gloom and depression. Tears roll down unceasingly. Never I have come across a noble soul like Lohia. He never went after collecting any material benefits. I used to fight with him in the Lok Sabha. Yet his humane affection for me never declined. Now that central hall—may be Lok Sabha itself has become lifeless. It is said that Lohia was a lone fighter and trod along a solitary path of his own. Such a path provides a beacon of light for people like us to follow". S.M. Joshi said: "It was Lohia who taught us that the interests of the party cannot be different from the interests of the nation. He was leader not of only of our party, but the leader of all the downtrodden people". Kripalani, Aruna Asaf Ali, Kamaraj, Hiren Mukherji, Brij Mohan

Toofan Hansraj Gupta, and Chandrashekar all paid homage to Lohia. A meeting of the party workers was held on the 13th. It declared its determination to bring into practise the ideology of Lohia. A vow was taken that Lohia's ideals, unlike Gandhiji's, will not be allowed to be compromised. It was decided to continue the publication of the periodicals, *'Jana'* and *'Mankind'*. The chairman of the party called for the collection of funds for the socialist school and fervently appealed to the party members to observe restraint.

Lohia left at a very inopportune moment. That produced a tremendous void. He consistently moved society with its new revolutionary ideas arising out of his creative imagination. His goblet of the nectar of his ideas never became empty. Had he lived for the few years more the fate of India would have been different. Why then did he leave at such a crucial time? The party workers felt, why did he go away leaving such a huge burden on our weak shoulders? Was it because we didn't allow him any rest throughout his life? But then does a mother ever get angry with her child? He should not have punished us for our lapses in such a dreadful manner!

"The Times of India" reports, 23rd January, 1968

EXPERTS DEPLORE CONDITIONS IN DELHI HOSPITAL

'*The Times of India*' News Service

NEW DELHI, January 23 : The special inquiry committee set up by the Union Government to go into the medical facilities in Government hospitals in the capital is believed to have described the sterilisation facilities and maintenance of the operation theatre in Willingdon Hospital as "deplorable" .

The committee, headed by Dr. K.N. Rao, director general of health services, was set up soon after the death of the socialist leader, Dr. Ram Manohar Lohia in Willingdon Hospital.

The committee's draft report is awaiting the approval of Dr. Rao, who is expected to return to New Delhi from Geneva on February 11.

PRE-OPERATION STEPS

The members of the committee are believed to have expressed the opinion that pre-operation precautions taken by the hospital authorities in the case of Dr. Lohia were 'far from satisfactory'.

The committee is reported to be of the view that if the sterilisation facilities had been up to the mark, the wound could not have become septic. Lack of proper laboratory facilities was given due weight by the committee in finalising its findings.

The members, however, are reported to have stated that the course of treatment after the operation could not have been improved upon.

Although investigation of the causes which led to the death of Dr. Lohia was not included in the terms of reference of the committee, it is believed to have become apparent in the course of the inquiry that proper care on the part of hospital authorities might have averted the tragedy.

UNUSUAL METHOD

It has been found that the senior surgeon, whose name had been mentioned earlier, had not himself performed the operation although he supervised it. The operation was performed by some junior surgeons.

It has also been established that the normal course of operation for prostrate gland would have been through the stomach. But in the case of Dr. Lohia the operation was performed in a method considered, 'very unusual' by the members of the committee.

It was only at a late stage that other specialists were invited to give their opinion. It was then too late, according to the members of the committee.

The members of the committee are: Dr. K.N. Rao, Chairman, Dr. Shantilal Mehta, Dr. B.K. Aikat, Dr. A. Venugopal, Dr. M.M. Sidhu, M.P., Dr. K.K. Menon, deputy director general of armed forces medical services, and Dr. P. Dinesh, deputy director-general of health services, who is also secretary of the committee.

INDEX